Russian Foreign Policy in the 21st Century

Russian Foreign Policy in the 21st Century

Edited by

Roger E. Kanet
Professor, Department of International Studies,
University of Miami, USA

palgrave
macmillan

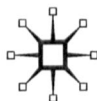

First published 2011 by
PALGRAVE MACMILLAN

Palgrave Macmillan in the UK is an imprint of Macmillan Publishers Limited,
registered in England, company number 785998, of Houndmills, Basingstoke,
Hampshire RG21 6XS.

Palgrave Macmillan in the US is a division of St Martin's Press LLC,
175 Fifth Avenue, New York, NY 10010.

Palgrave Macmillan is the global academic imprint of the above companies
and has companies and representatives throughout the world.

Palgrave® and Macmillan® are registered trademarks in the United States,
the United Kingdom, Europe and other countries.

ISBN: 978-0-230-27167-8 hardback

This book is printed on paper suitable for recycling and made from fully
managed and sustained forest sources. Logging, pulping and manufacturing
processes are expected to conform to the environmental regulations of the
country of origin.

A catalogue record for this book is available from the British Library.

Library of Congress Cataloging-in-Publication Data

Russian foreign policy in the 21st century / edited by Roger E. Kanet.
p. cm.
ISBN 978-0-230-27167-8 (hbk.)
1. Russia (Federation) – Foreign relations – 21st century. I. Kanet,
Roger E., 1936–

DK510.764.R865 2010
327.47—dc22   2010027591

10 9 8 7 6 5 4 3 2 1
20 19 18 17 16 15 14 13 12 11

Printed and bound in Great Britain by
CPI Antony Rowe, Chippenham and Eastbourne

Contents

Preface

The editor wishes to express his sincere appreciation to the authors of the chapters in this volume, both for the quality of their analyses and for their willingness to revise and update the original drafts of their papers in response to various editorial suggestions for clarification and for the strengthening of the arguments presented. The original idea for a volume focusing on the prospects for future relations between the Russian Federation and its near neighbors and with the West emerged from the planning for a set of interrelated panels that were organized for the Ninth International CISS Millennium Conference of the International Studies Association, held on June 13–15, 2009 in Potsdam, Germany. We wish to thank Dr Felicia Krishna Hensel and Dr Howard Hensel, the long-time organizers of these stimulating conferences, for granting us the opportunity to come together in what was for us, in effect, a small workshop within the context of the larger conference. All but two of the authors were able to present, share, and comment on the initial drafts of the papers at the conference and, therefore, to benefit from the intellectual stimulation that resulted from these personal interactions. The other two, who had not been able to join us in Potsdam, have been able to complete and contribute their chapters to the final publication.

The reader may be interested to know that over the past few years most of the authors involved in this project – authors from across Europe, Australia, and North America – have, along with several others, been engaged in a number of other joint efforts to examine Russian foreign and security policy. In most cases the projects have developed much as this one did, with a series of papers presented originally at a professional conference at which the authors were able to interact with one another and contribute to the perfection of one another's contributions. During this time and through these panel sessions we have evolved into something of an informal research group and have, no doubt, begun to influence one another's interpretations of the reality of Russian policy.[1] Just as important, we have begun to build together a series of analyses of Russian foreign and security policy.

On behalf of all the authors, the editor wishes to thank the many others who have made important contributions to the final draft, in particular anonymous readers for the publisher and the publisher's production staff. Their contributions have helped to ensure the clarity and readability of the final manuscript.

Note

1. The projects to which I refer include the following: Maria Raquel Freire and Roger E. Kanet (eds), *Key Players and Regional Dynamics in Eurasia: The Return of the "Great Game"*, Houndmills, UK: Palgrave Macmillan, 2010; Roger E. Kanet (ed.), *A Resurgent Russia and the West: The European Union, NATO and Beyond*, Dordrecht, The Netherlands: Republic of Letters Publishing, 2009; Roger E. Kanet (ed.), *Russia, Re-Emerging Great Power*, Houndmills, UK: Palgrave Macmillan, 2007; and Roger E. Kanet (ed.), *The New Security Environment. The Impact on Russia, Central and Eastern Europe*, Aldershot, UK/Burlington, VT: Ashgate Publishing, 2005.

Contributors

John Berryman teaches International Relations in the Department of Politics of Birkbeck College, University of London, and is Associate Professor in International Studies at the American Institute for Foreign Study, London. His research focuses on Russian foreign and security policy and he has held a British Council Award for research in Russia. His recent publications in the field of Eurasian security include "Russia and China in Eurasia: The Wary Partnership", in Maria Raquel Freire and Roger E. Kanet (eds), *Key Players and Regional Dynamics in Eurasia: The Return of the "Great Game"* (2010); "Russia, NATO Enlargement and the New 'Lands in Between'", in Roger E. Kanet (ed.), *A Resurgent Russia and the West: The European Union, NATO and Beyond* (2009); "Russia and China in the New Central Asia: The Security Agenda", in Roger E. Kanet (ed.), *Russia: Re-Emerging Great Power* (2007); and "Putin's International Security Priorities", in Roger E. Kanet (ed.), *The New Security Environment: The Impact on Russia, Central and Eastern Europe* (2005). He also has a research interest in sea power, and has been awarded the Julian Corbett Prize in Modern Naval History by the Institute of Historical Research, University of London. He is a member of the International Institute for Strategic Studies and the Royal Institute of International Affairs.

Joan DeBardeleben is Chancellor's Professor at the Institute of European, Russian, and Eurasian Studies, and Director of the Centre for European Studies (EU Centre of Excellence) at Carleton University in Ottawa, Canada. She has published extensively on Soviet/Russian and Central European political developments, with particular attention to public opinion, federalism, environmental issues, and privatization. Her recent edited publications include *Activating the Citizen: Dilemma of Citizen Participation in Europe and Canada* (with Jon H. Pammett, 2009); *The Boundaries of EU Enlargement* (2008); *Democratic Dilemmas of Multi-level Governance: Accountability and Legitimacy in the European Union* (with Achim Hurrelmann, 2007); and *Soft or Hard Borders: Managing the Divide in an Enlarged Europe* (2005).

Tuomas Forsberg is Professor of International Politics at the University of Tampere. He is also docent at the University of Helsinki and University of Lapland. He has previously worked at the University of Helsinki and at the George C. Marshall European Center for Security

Studies, Garmisch-Partenkirchen, Germany, and at the Finnish Institute of International Affairs. He gained his PhD at the University of Wales, Aberystwyth, in 1998. His research has dealt primarily with European security issues, focusing on the EU, Germany, Russia, and Northern Europe. His recent publications include a coauthored book entitled *Divided West: European Security and the Transatlantic Relationship* (2006), and the coedited *Europe in Context. Insights to the Foreign Policy of the EU* (2007), as well as articles in the major scholarly journals *Cooperation and Conflict, Europe-Asia Studies, International Politics, Review of International Studies*, and *European Security*.

Graeme P. Herd is Head of the International Security Programme at the Geneva Centre for Security Policy (GCSP), which he joined in 2005. He has published on a variety of international security issues in journals such as *Armed Forces & Society, Cooperation and Conflict, International Politics, Journal of Peace Research*, and *Security Dialogue*. Recent books include *Great Powers and Global Stability in the 21st Century* (2010); *Stuarts and Romanovs: The Rise and Fall of a Special Relationship* (2009); *The Ideological War on Terror: World Wide Strategies for Counter Terrorism* (2007); and *Divided West: European Security and the Transatlantic Relationship* (2006).

Roger E. Kanet is Professor in the Department of International Studies of the University of Miami, where he served as Dean of the School of International Studies, 1997–2000. Prior to 1997, he taught at the University of Illinois at Urbana-Champaign, where he was a member of the Department of Political Science and served as Head of that Department, 1984–7, and as Associate Vice Chancellor for Academic Affairs and Director of International Programs and Studies (1989–97). He has published more than 200 scholarly articles and edited more than twenty-five books. Recent publications include: coedited with Maria Raquel Freire, *Key Players and Regional Dynamics in Eurasia: The Return of the "Great Game"* (2010); *The United States and Europe in a Changing World* (2009); *A Resurgent Russia and the West: The European Union, NATO and Beyond* (2009); coedited with Edward A. Kolodziej, *From Superpower to Besieged Global Power: Restoring World Order after the Failure of the Bush Doctrine* (2008); *Russia, Re-Emerging Great Power* (2007); and *The New Security Environment: The Impact on Russia, Central and Eastern Europe* (2005). He is a member of the Council on Foreign Relations, New York.

Nikita Lomagin, Doctor of Sciences (History, St Petersburg State University), J.D. (St Petersburg State University), is Professor of World Economy and was Deputy Dean and Associate Professor at the Faculty of International Relations at St Petersburg State University, 1994–8. He is the author of *Introductions to IR Theory and foreign policy analysis* (2001) and of *International Organizations* (1999). He is also author of *In the Wrench of Hunger. The Blockade of Leningrad: An Account of German and NKVD Intelligence Documents* (St Petersburg, 2001); *The Unknown Blockade* (St Petersburg, 2002); *Blockade of Leningrad* (Moscow, 2005); *Soldiers at War: German Propaganda and Soviet Army Morale during the Battle of Leningrad, 1941–44* (Pittsburgh, 1998); and coauthor of the forthcoming *The Siege of Leningrad* (Yale University Press). He is author of chapters in volumes such as *Russia. Re-Emerging Great Power* (2005) and *Dimensions of Security under Putin* (2007). He has published articles and working papers on Russian Foreign Policy in *Journal of St Petersburg State University, Pro et Contra Journal, Journal of University of Michigan*, GSPIA, and the Finnish Institute of International Relations, and on the NATO web page. He has been a research fellow at the University of Michigan Law School (1995), GSPIA (1996), University of Limerick (1997), College of Europe (1998), George Washington University (1998), and the Finnish Institute of International Relations (2000), and a postdoctoral fellow at Harvard University, the Davis Center (2002), and the Kennan Institute (2005). He has been the recipient of research grants from the Soros Foundation, Moscow Public Science Foundation, University of Michigan Law School, the Pew Foundation, NATO, IREX, and Harvard University. He is a member of the International Institute for Strategic Studies. His research interests focus on contemporary Russian foreign policy, international organizations, and modern Russian history.

Susanne Nies holds a PhD in Political Sciences, Slavistics and Romanistics from Bonn University (Germany) as well as a diploma from the London School of Economics (Economics of the European Union). She completed the habilitation in international relations in Sciences Po, Paris, as well as at Free University, Berlin. She has held appointments at the Boell Foundation, Germany (1989–95), a Lectureship in Political Sciences from DAAD in Nice (1995–2000), a research position at Free University, Berlin (2000–2), and CERI (2002–4), as well as IRIS (2004–7). She teaches at Sciences Po, Paris. She has published extensively on Russian politics and, most recently, on European energy issues. Currently she heads the IFRI (Institut français des relations internationales) Brussels Office and is also a senior research fellow in the IFRI energy program.

Bertil Nygren is Associate Professor of political science at the Swedish National Defence College and at the Department of Political Science, Stockholm University. He has held various administrative positions at

Stockholm University, including Head of Department and Deputy Head of Department, 1994–2001. His most recent monograph is *The Rebuilding of Greater Russia: Putin's Foreign Policy Toward the CIS Countries* (2008). He has also published articles and chapters in various anthologies on Russian politics, especially foreign policy. These include an article in *Problems of Post-Communism*, vol. 55, no. 4, July/August 2008, and chapters in Roger E. Kanet (ed.), *Russia: Re-emerging Great Power* (2007); in Kjell Engelbrekt and Jan Hallenberg (eds), *The European Union and Strategy. An Emerging Actor* (2008); in Charlotte Wagnsson, James Sperling and Jan Hallenberg (eds), *The EU in a Multipolar World: Security Governance Meets Great Power Gambit* (2009); in Roger Kanet (ed.), *A Resurgent Russia and Europe*, Dordrecht, The Netherlands, 2009; in Kjell Engelbrekt and Bertil Nygren (eds), *Russia and Europe: Building Partnerships, Digging Trenches* (2010); Bertil Nygren, Bo Huldt, Patrik Ahlgren, Pekka Sivonen and Susanna Huldt (eds), *Russia on our Minds. Russian Security and Northern Europe, Strategic Yearbook 2008–2009* (2010).

Ingmar Oldberg is Associate Director of Research at the Swedish Defence Research Agency (FOI) and a member of a team writing biannual reports on Russian developments for the parliamentary Swedish Defence Commission. He has written and edited many books and reports on Russian foreign policy, specifically toward Western Europe and CIS neighbors, as well as on Russian regions, for instance Kaliningrad. His most recent publications include *Reluctant Rapprochement: Russia and the Baltic States in the Context of NATO and EU Enlargements* (2003), and *Membership and Partnership: The Relations of Russia and Its Neighbours with NATO and the EU in the Enlargement Context* (2004).

Vladimir Rukavishnikov is currently an independent expert–consultant. He was Professor at the Department of Global Politics and International Relations of the State University – Higher School of Economics in Moscow, Russia since 2003. Prior to 2003, he served as Head of Department of the Institute of Socio-Political Research of the Russian Academy of Sciences. Rukavishnikov has published (in Russian and other languages) more than 250 scholarly articles, essays and papers, and authored and edited over fifteen books. His recent books include *Cholodnaya Voina, Cholodnyi Mir* [Cold War, Cold Peace] (2005). He is listed in Marquis *Who's Who in the World*.

Antti Seppo is a PhD candidate in International Relations at the University of Helsinki. He has worked on the project "EU as an International Actor," funded by the Academy of Finland, since 2007 together with Tuomas Forsberg, whose focus is on EU–Russia power relations. He is currently working on his PhD, which deals with post-Cold War German foreign and security policy and the issues of war and peace in respect to German involvement in Afghanistan. He has recently coauthored an article with Tuomas Forsberg, entitled "Power without Influence? The EU and Trade Disputes with Russia", *Europe-Asia Studies*, vol. 61, no. 10, 2009, pp. 1805–23.

Peter Shearman taught for twenty years at the University of Melbourne, where he was Director of the MA in International Politics program. He is now a Principal Fellow in Political Science at Melbourne University, but currently resides in Thailand and is a Senior Fellow at the Institute for Security and International Studies at Chulalongkorn University in Bangkok and teaches in the Masters Program in International Relations at Webster University in Bangkok. Dr Shearman has published widely on Russian foreign policy and world politics. Recent publications include *Australian Security After 9/11 – New and Old Agendas* (2006) and *European Security After 9/11* (2004).

Mette Skak is Associate Professor of peace and conflict research in the Department of Political Science, University of Aarhus, Denmark. Her research focuses on Russian foreign and security policy, and she has recently edited and coauthored a Danish-language volume on the so-called BRIC Powers (Brazil, Russia, India, and China) – *Fremtidens stormagter. BRIK'erne i det globale spil: Brasilien, Rusland, Indien og Kina*, Aarhus University Press (2010). She is the author of *From Empire to Anarchy: Postcommunist Foreign Policy and International Relations* (1996); "Back in the U.S.S.R.? Russia as an Actor in World Politics", Copenhagen; *DUPI Working Paper* 2000/7 (29 pp.), "The Socialization of Democratic Norms in Russia: Is the Glass Half-empty or Half-full?", pp. 190–208 in Trine Flockhart (ed.), *Socializing Democratic Norms* (2005); "The logic of foreign and security policy change in Russia", pp. 81–106 in Hedenskog *et al.* (eds), *Russia as a Great Power* (2005).

Charles E. Ziegler is Professor and University Scholar in the Political Science Department at the University of Louisville. A specialist on Russia and Eurasia, Ziegler is coeditor (with Judith Thornton) of *The Russian Far East: A Region at Risk*, University of Washington Press (2002), and author of *The History of Russia*, 2nd edn, Greenwood Press (2009); *Foreign Policy and East Asia*, Cambridge University Press (1993); and *Environmental Policy in the USSR*, University of Massachusetts Press (1987). In addition, he has written over fifty book chapters and articles for such professional journals as *Comparative Politics, Political Science*

Quarterly, British Journal of Political Science, Problems of Post-Communism, Asian Survey, Asian Security, and *Demokratizatsiya.* Ziegler has held an International Research and Exchanges Board Advanced International Research Opportunity grant, a Senior Fulbright Fellowship to Korea, an International Affairs Fellowship of the Council on Foreign Relations, and the Hoover Institution National Fellowship. He has served as Executive Director of the Louisville Committee on Foreign Relations since 1990. He is also a 4th degree black belt in taekwondo. His current research focuses on energy in Russia and Central Asia.

Introduction: Russian Foreign Policy in the 21st Century

Roger E. Kanet

It is now almost twenty years since the dissolution of the Soviet Union and the emergence of the Russian Federation as its major successor state. During those two decades the Russian political system has undergone major restructuring, while its domestic and foreign policies have experienced significant changes. At the outset many – in both Russia and the West – hoped, even expected, that Russia would soon join the democratic and capitalist West. For reasons that will be discussed in the following chapters, this has not occurred. Western, especially US, triumphalism, the fragility of the economic and political legacy inherited by Russia, and the pull of the authoritarian political past have all contributed to a quite different trajectory – especially over the course of the past decade. The Russia that has emerged is a political and economic hybrid that combines aspects of electoral democracy with top-down management of both the political and the economic system. As Herd notes in his contribution to this volume, probably fewer than 20 per cent of the political elite in Russia support a policy that emphasizes what would be recognized as democracy in the West.

Although the contributors to this volume bring quite different perspectives to the analysis of the Russian Federation and of Russian foreign policy, and reach, at times, quite different conclusions, it is fair to say that the overall interpretation of Russian policy presented in the following pages and of those factors that have influenced the changes in that policy during the past two decades is a more nuanced understanding of Russian decision makers than the assessments that appear to dominate both the scholarly and, especially, the policy debate in the West. Questions about the nature of Russian policy in the second decade of the 21st century are of central importance in understanding Russia's place in Europe and the world, and assessing the prospects for dealing with some of the most important challenges to regional and global security.

Was the Russian military intervention in Georgia in summer 2008 an indication of Russia's inherent aggressiveness and imperial intent, or was it, rather, intended to demonstrate to the United States and NATO once and for all, after a decade of failure, that further incorporation of areas of special interest to Moscow into the Western security zone was totally unacceptable? Is President Medvedev's proposal for a Eurasia-wide security organization – in ways similar to Russian proposals at the beginning of the 1990s – meant to encourage serious discussion and negotiation, or is it meant to gain a few propaganda points in the current competition with the United States and the West? Is the Russian Federation a potentially reliable partner for Europe and the West – in the energy realm, in expanded security relations? Can Russia be expected in the foreseeable future to enter the security community[1] that has emerged in Europe over the course of the past half century? Alternatively, will relations between Russia and its Western neighbors, including the United States, remain largely characterized by conflict and possible confrontation?

Not all of these questions are posed explicitly in each of the chapters that follow. However, one or more of them lies close to the core of the analysis of each specific aspect of Russian foreign policy – whether the analysis emphasizes the internal debate in Russia concerning the appropriate model for the development of the economy and polity or the appropriate relationship between Moscow and its near neighbors in the coming years. The various authors provide quite different answers to some of the questions – such as those associated with the "facts" of the Russia–Georgia war. However, a more careful assessment of the analyses demonstrates that underlying explanations overlap to a substantial degree even in cases of apparent disagreement.

The chapters that follow are divided into three groups. The first four chapters examine the broad contours of Russian policy, including both the factors that influence policy and important instruments of policy implementation. The four chapters in Part II examine relations with near neighbors along Russia's borders – the former Soviet republics – with special emphasis on the war with Georgia and its impact on those relations. The final group of five chapters examines Russia's relations with the West, including Europe's two major multinational organizations, the European Union and NATO.

In the opening chapter, "History, Russia and the West, and Cold Wars," Peter Shearman addresses the question of whether, as some analysts assert, Russian relations with the West early in the 21st century in fact represent a new stage in, or a continuation of, the Cold War. Shearman dismisses the appropriateness of this claim, but notes the importance of such matters as psychological factors, conflicting interests, and ideological differences in the new competition that has emerged in recent years. However, the global bipolarity and the competition between two opposed socioeconomic systems that were central to the Cold War no longer exist. He concludes by noting the lessons learned from the Cold War and the broad range of overlapping interests of Russia and the West, which should contribute to cooperation in the future.

Chapter 2, "Aims and Means in Russian Foreign Policy" by Ingmar Oldberg, begins with an examination of the most recent version of Russia's national security concept, which focuses on external threats to Russia, rather than on internal challenges, as in earlier versions of the security concept. He then notes the importance for Russia of its membership in various formal and informal international organizations and groupings – from the United Nations and the G-8 to the CIS and the Shanghai Cooperation Organization – as it pursues the objectives associated with the security concept. Oldberg then tracks the role of minorities, the military, peacekeeping operations, and energy policy in the implementation of Russian policy.

In the next chapter, "Russian Modernization Pathways: Foreign Policy Implications," Graeme Herd examines the ongoing debate in Russia concerning the most appropriate model for modernization and economic development, and the impact of that model on Russia's commitment to reestablishing itself as a great power. Herd points out that the model favored by Prime Minister Putin, a conservative approach associated with the term "sovereign democracy," has far greater support across the Russian political elite than the more democratic approach associated with President Dimitri Medvedev. This fact has important implications for Russian relations with Europe, because the conservative model comes into direct normative conflict with the principles that undergird governance in the West.

The fourth and final chapter in the first section of the book, by Vladimir Rukavishnikov, concerns "Russia's 'Soft Power' in the Putin Epoch." The author begins with a discussion of the concept of soft power, including the problems involved in trying to "measure" it, and of the various views in the literature about the lack of – or revival of – soft power in the Russian Federation's foreign relations, especially with neighboring states. He then examines in some detail the impact of the Russian language and culture, as well as economic ties, on Russia's relations with neighboring states. He notes the rather dramatic decline of Russian-language schools and of access to Russian-language media in this region. When it comes to the Russian political model, Russia exercises relatively little influence in international affairs. Although Russia was fully justified in intervening in Georgia in August 2008, that intervention "severely damaged Russia's image," Rukavishnikov concludes.

The second section of the book deals explicitly with Russian relations with the neighboring states of "the near abroad" following the military confrontation between Russia and Georgia in 2008. In Chapter 5, entitled "Russia and Georgia – From Confrontation to War: What is Next?," Bertil Nygren tracks the factors, especially since 1991, that led to the military confrontation. The various secessionist movements in Georgia, Russia's conflicting roles as both interested party in these secessions and nominally disinterested peacekeeper, the Rose Revolution of 2003, and the reorientation of Georgia's politics toward the West, including expected NATO membership, are all part of this background. The focus of the remainder of the chapter is on the impact of military operations on the resolution of the secessions, Moscow's inability to generate support for its position among other CIS states, the erosive effect of the war on Russia's relations with the European Union and with the United States, and the broad implications for Russian policy toward other neighboring states.

In Chapter 6, "The Russo-Georgian War and EU Mediation," Tuomas Forsberg and Antti Seppo are concerned with the role of the European Union, represented especially by French President Nicolas Sarkozy, in mediating an end to the fighting. They note that, although EU officials viewed their role as successful and positive, others were more critical of the failure of the EU to prevent the fighting. After outlining the main tenets of mediation theory, the authors provide a detailed outline of efforts, both at the United Nations and within the European Union, that finally brought the fighting to a close. They note that the EU and its role in the negotiations closely reflected the model of the impartial mediator, as it "refrained from putting blame on either of the parties for the outbreak of the war." They conclude that a serious drawback for the EU as it attempts to mediate conflicts is its lack of hard power that it might employ as "sticks."

One of the most interesting recent developments in Russia's foreign policy has been the claim that Russia has a sphere of privileged interest along its borders with former Soviet republics, much as the United States has made similar claims for almost two centuries concerning the entire Western hemisphere. Mette Skak analyzes the development of this claim in Chapter 7, entitled "Russia's New 'Monroe Doctrine'." She notes that already in the early 1990s a member of the Presidential Council began to use the term to characterize Russia's interests in its near neighbors and relates the idea to Russia's strategic culture – a concept developed five decades ago by Nathan Leites and modified more recently by Jack Snyder and others. However, it was not until after the Russia–Georgia war of August 2008 that the usage was "codified" in President Medvedev's five principles of Russian foreign policy. The author concludes that US renunciation of the original Monroe Doctrine will likely be required for Russia to consider abandoning its parallel security concept.

In Chapter 8, "Russia, Central Asia, and the Caucasus after the Georgia Conflict," Charles E. Ziegler is primarily concerned about the likely impact of the military hostilities in Georgia on Russia's relations with the countries along its southern border. Ziegler notes the central importance of continued NATO expansion eastward in the Russian calculations to intervene in Georgia. The response of Russia's putative allies in the CIS and CSTO, however, was not encouraging from Moscow's perspective, since none of them was willing to provide real backing for Moscow's policy, although Russia's position in the Caucasus, in particular in competition for influence with the West, has been strengthened. He concludes by noting that the military confrontation was likely a unique event throughout the broad region, since, unlike Georgia, the other regional states have not pursued a policy that challenges Russia and its role throughout the area.

The third section of the book concerns the relations of the Russian Federation with the West, and includes five chapters on Russian foreign and security relations, NATO expansion, and the European Union.

In Chapter 9, "Medvedev's 'Fourteen Points': Russia's Proposal for a New European Security Architecture," Nikita Lomagin lays out in some detail the proposal of the Russian president for the creation of a new security organization that would incorporate both the current members of NATO and the members of the CIS and CSTO. Lomagin argues that the proposal is a serious one and that only the incorporation of all Eurasian states within a new comprehensive security system will meet the security concerns of all the states involved and, possibly, provide the mechanisms for the integration of China and other Asian states into such a system.

Chapter 10, "From the 'New World Order' to 'Resetting Relations': Two Decades of US–Russian Relations," by Roger E. Kanet, argues that the deterioration of relations between the United States and the Russian Federation stems, in part at least, from the US refusal to recognize Russia as an equal, especially for the first decade or so after the Soviet collapse, and the US insistence on pursuing its policy objectives – such as NATO expansion – despite the opposition of Moscow. Since his election as president, Vladimir Putin has strongly resisted and challenged the United States on a broad range of issues where the two countries' interests seemingly diverge. Whether the two countries will be able to "reset" their relations and focus on issues of common concern is not clear.

In Chapter 11, "Russia, NATO Enlargement, and 'Regions of Privileged Interests'," John Berryman revisits a number of issues considered by other contributors to this volume. Of special importance is the impact of the August 2008 war between Russia and Georgia on relationships within NATO and the EU, including especially the issue of the ability of NATO to fulfill security commitments made to its newest members, as well as Moscow's assertion that it will assure its interests in neighboring countries viewed as being of special concern to Russia.

In recent years the European Union has developed special relationships with neighboring countries and regions to both the south and the east. In Chapter 12, "Revising the EU's European Neighborhood Policy: The Eastern Partnership and Russia," Joan DeBardeleben is concerned with the recent friction in EU–Russian relations, as well as the place of Russia in the EU's overall policy toward neighboring states to the east. Her central argument is that Russia's initial refusal to be considered as simply part of a larger EU neighborhood has resulted in a two-track EU approach to relations with eastern neighbors that is likely, in the long term, to result in two quite different policy approaches, which may, in some areas at least, be contradictory.

In the final chapter, "The EU–Russia Energy Relationship: European, Russian, Common Interests?," Susanne Nies examines what is likely the most important issue in Russian relations with the European Union. She is especially concerned about the areas of mutual or complementary interest on which a long-term and stable relationship can be built. She concludes that, despite a variety of political and economic interests, both sides share the objective of stable supplies and markets and of the existence of reliable rules that will undergird the exchange.

Given the current volatility of the international financial, economic, and security systems, it is likely that much will have changed in the international environment within which Russia and its Western partners are operating by the time that this volume appears. However, the major elements of relations outlined here are likely to remain directly relevant – as they have been for the better part of the past decade.[2]

Notes

1. The author is using the term 'security community' in the sense originally developed by Karl Deutsch (1957) of a group of states for whom warfare has become virtually unthinkable.
2. The manuscript went to press before the elections in Ukraine in early 2010, as well as before the chaotic developments in kyrgyzstan.

References

Deutsch, Karl W., Sidney A. Burrell and Robert A. Kann (1957) *Political Community and the North Atlantic Area; International Organization in the Light of Historical Experience*, Princeton: Princeton University Press.
Kupchan, Charles A. (2010) "NATO's Final Frontier: Why Russia Should Join the Atlantic Alliance", *Foreign Affairs*, vol. 89, no. 3, pp. 100–13.

Part I

Foundations of Russian Foreign Policy

1
History, Russia and the West, and Cold Wars

Peter Shearman

Introduction: the need to remember

We forget history at our peril. This is not to suggest that history repeats itself, but rather that we need to know where we have come from to understand where we are today and how we arrived at this particular juncture, and thereby better to appreciate possible futures. "Lest We Forget:" these are iconic words in the English language, words that most people immediately understand as relating to the millions of young citizens who lost their lives fighting for their countries in the two World Wars of the 20th century. "Lest We Forget" is a term associated with war and the need not just to recall those who were sacrificed but also to remember the lessons of war, and to offer a reminder that we should remain vigilant to ensure that war does not occur again. Europe suffered greatly in the wars of 1914–18 and 1939–45, and there are numerous tombs to unknown soldiers across the length and breadth of the continent. In the United Kingdom alone there are over 100,000 war memorials, prominent in any town or village.[1] We also have Remembrance Days with parades and commemorations in which citizens are asked to pay their respects to the war dead and to contemplate the evils of warfare. The wars that inflicted so much pain and destruction during the first half of the 20th century had multiple complex determinants, but central to them was the power of nationalism and the idea of the national sovereign state and great power politics.

However, the long Cold War of the second half of the 20th century is largely a forgotten war. In a way, the celebrations that took place in November 2009, commemorating the twentieth anniversary of its ending with the demolition of the Berlin Wall in November 1989, were evidence of this fact. World leaders briefly took the stage, both those who were in power when the Berlin Wall was coming down and those in power twenty years later. This provided photo opportunities and media coverage and editorials about the Cold War and its ending; yet the celebrations did not engage or mobilize large numbers of veterans of the Cold War or the general publics in the principal countries. The celebrations had much of a temporary one-off feeling, which failed ultimately to galvanize the mass publics in any country of the former Cold War belligerents. It is remarkable that the Cold War is a forgotten war, for a number of reasons. First, it lasted so long and effectively defined the international politics of the second half of the 20th century. Second, it was during the Cold War that we came closest to nuclear Armageddon, in the Cuban missile crisis of October 1962. Third, the Cold War was multifaceted and complex, incorporating both power politics and competing ideologies and alternative socio-economic systems. During the Cold War capitalism faced its greatest challenge in the form of Soviet communism. Fourth, and perhaps most importantly for future lessons, is that the Cold War ended *peacefully*, without major interstate war leading to a blood-fueled international power transition.

The end of war always brings about major structural changes in the conduct of international politics, and the ending of the Cold War between the United States and the former Soviet Union was no exception, with the ramifications still being worked through today. At the time, however, it was considered that both sides in the Cold War conflict emerged as victors; unlike in other major (hot) wars, where victory for one side was considered by definition as a loss for the other. With the end of the Cold War Americans and Russians both saw themselves as sharing a victory over the death of Soviet communism. However, as will be argued, one of the major problems in the immediate post-Cold War era was that the United States and other Western countries very quickly came to see themselves as the victors, and the policies that emanated from this view eventually led post-Soviet Russia to develop a crisis of identity and a sense of humiliation in the face of what was viewed in Moscow as Western attempts to undermine Russian power and interests. This in turn led, in an action–reaction cycle, to increased tensions in Russia's relations with the United States and the West, as Moscow sought to rekindle its influence in international affairs through more assertive policies, which often conflicted with Washington's. This has led many, both academic specialists and foreign policy officials, to utilize once more the rhetoric of Cold War to describe relations between Russia and the West (Lucas, 2008; Furman, 2006; Gorodetsky, 2003; Sakwa, 2008; Simes, 2007). We have, as it were, gone back to the future.

My argument here is that, although there is much evidence to support the view of a "New Cold War" between Russia and the West, ultimately the term is not only a bad fit to analyze contemporary relations, but also a potentially dangerous one that could result in a kind of self-fulfilling prophecy. The historical analogy does not work; while we need to remember history, we have to get it right. Getting history wrong is dangerous. One should also acknowledge here that there are those, principally among sectors of the Russian political elite, although there are some too in the West, who hold the view that the Cold War between the US and Russia never actually ended. The argument is that post-Cold War political leaders carried with them the old Cold War mind-sets of rivalry and confrontation. Old thinking was difficult to eradicate after a century of hostility, and, although ostensibly President Bill Clinton's policies sought to assist post-Soviet Russia's transition to democracy and the capitalist market, in reality the Washington Consensus model ended up having the opposite effect, as Russia became mired in socioeconomic problems and degenerated into a potentially failing state. Despite a large number of pressing foreign policy concerns, Clinton gave priority to Russia from the beginning, spending during his first three months in office fully half of his time devoted to foreign policy on Russia, and as president he met with Russian leader Boris Yeltsin on eighteen separate occasions (Marsden, 2005, p. 50; see also Wedel, 2001). Clinton and Yeltsin met more often than any other American and Russian (or Soviet) presidents had, yet in the end bilateral relations deteriorated, as what may well have been good intentions on the part of Clinton resulted in widespread resentment in Russia as the economy spiralled into crisis. By the time that the first post-Cold War presidents in Washington and Moscow had given way to their predecessors, US–Russian relations, and Russia's relations with the West generally, were again in the throes of what many saw as another Cold War.

Defining Cold War

It is necessary to return briefly to the original Cold War in order to establish definitions and categories, before examining Russia's complicated relations with the West since the fall of the Berlin Wall. It will be demonstrated that Russia and the West cannot be engaged in a new Cold War if we are to retain a sensible, rigorous, and workable definition of what is meant by the term Cold War. This is not to say that the Cold War is only of historical interest. On the contrary, as indicated above, an understanding of the Cold War and its ending offers lessons for contemporary international relations. Also, given the emerging balance of power in the international system, and the potential for competition between the American and Chinese socioeconomic and political models, it might be appropriate to argue that a new Cold War is more likely to emerge between the US and China. The original Cold War had its origins in and was centered in Europe; any Cold War between the US and China would be centered in Asia. However, due to both structural and cultural factors, relations between the major powers in Asia are also unlikely to be transformed into a Cold War. Yet, again, there are still important lessons to be learned about the original Cold War, which would be useful for analysts and policy makers to consider regarding both Russia's relations with the West and the emergence of China as a major power challenging US influence in the Asia Pacific region.

Looking back to the end of the Cold War some twenty years ago, three things are worth recalling. First, political scientists did not predict it. This was true of both International Relations scholars and Soviet Studies specialists (Shearman, 2000). Kenneth Waltz, the leading realist scholar, for example, considered bipolarity stable and could not foresee its imminent or even long-term demise (Waltz, 1979); John Lewis Gaddis, the doyen of Cold War diplomatic historians, stated just three years before the Berlin Wall fell that "... short of war, which no one wants, change in international relations tends to be gradual and evolutionary. It does not happen overnight" (Gaddis, 1987, p. 219). Yet of course the Cold War did end short of a shooting war, and did end suddenly, and, with the breaching of the Berlin Wall, effectively overnight. Even on the day that the Berlin Wall was penetrated, up until that very moment no one anticipated it. On the day that the Soviet Union disintegrated, just two years later, in December 1991, no one had expected it, certainly not the leading academic specialists of the day. Soviet specialists, to a man or woman, with not a single exception (despite what some might have said later, in retrospect), did not even consider the possibility that the Soviet Union would disappear as it did just two years after the fall of the Wall.

Second, politicians did not expect it. Soviet leader Mikhail Gorbachev and German Chancellor Helmut Kohl held a press conference after a meeting in June 1989, and they were both asked if they could foresee the time when the Berlin Wall would ever come down. Gorbachev answered that it was a problem inherited from history, and that history would eventually resolve the matter, and it was much too early for contemporary leaders to make predictions about this. Pressed by journalists to say when they thought this might come to pass, the two leaders indicated that it would be long after their incumbent leaderships, sometime in the distant future of the next, the 21st, century (Gorbachev, 2009). It fell just four months later.

Third, it should be noted that many politicians were unenthusiastic about the ending of the Cold War. British Prime Minister at the time, Margaret Thatcher, and French President Francois Mitterrand both expressed concern about the reunification of Germany, fearing this could result in Bonn/Berlin once more becoming a great power that would threaten peace and stability in Europe. Thatcher relates in her memoirs how she and Mitterrand discussed how they might prevent German reunification, and at the same time ensure that not only NATO but also the Warsaw Pact continued to exist in order "... to create a background of stability" (Thatcher, 1993, p. 794). US president at that time, George H. W. Bush, recalls that Thatcher's objection, expressed to him on the matter of unification, was that in her view "...it had not been carefully thought out in a larger, strategic context" (Bush and Scowcroft, 1998, p. 235). Clearly this thinking was based upon a historical reading of German aggression in the first half of the 20th century and an assumption about how emerging great powers threaten the equilibrium of the international system and the balance of power. This was the kind of realist logic that assumes that great power transition cannot occur without war and conflict. Yet the Cold War and systemic change took place without war breaking out between the major powers, which offers, as will be shown, a lesson worth remembering for the foreign policies of the great powers in the contemporary era.

There has only been one model of a Cold War, based upon the relationship between the so-called "Superpowers" of the 20th century, the United States of America and the Union of Soviet Socialist Republics, linked to the wider East–West conflict. A Cold War is defined on the basis of a status of relations between core players on a spectrum ranging from alliance at one end to a hot war at the other, with entente, détente, and Cold War gradations in the middle. A Cold War is therefore based upon a level of tensions between actors in which, short of a hot shooting war, relations are tense and strained on all indicators of state power: military, cultural, economic, political, and diplomatic, in a zero-sum game in which one side's gain is seen automatically as the other side's loss. The Cold War pervaded all aspects of social and political life and was impossible to avoid. The Cold War not only shaped the security strategies of both sides, determining military alliances; it also shaped political and economic institutions, social relations, and cultural developments. It divided Europe and split Germany (and Vietnam and Korea).

Although there was no direct fighting between the main protagonists of the Cold War, there was fighting by both principals and third parties, as well as fighting between allies on both sides, in what came to be termed the "Third World," and these conflicts were tightly linked to the Cold War. One can only understand America's war in Vietnam (1960–75) or the Soviet Union's war in Afghanistan (1979–89) in the context of the Cold War. There were also numerous crises that brought the world to the brink of major conventional war (over Berlin, Cuba, and the Middle East) and, especially in the case of the Cuban Missile Crisis of 1962, to the brink of nuclear war.

The Cold War, then, had two essential logics: it was in part a contest in traditional Great Power balance of power terms; but it was also in part a global competition between two contesting socioeconomic and political systems, each seeking to remake the world in its own image. Another way of putting this is to say that the Cold War had an external, structurally determined component linked to power relativities, and an internal component reflecting ideological differences. It was both a great power conflict and a conflict over ideas. Even those third parties who wanted nothing to do with the Cold War, due to its structural dynamics, were forced to identify and define themselves in the context of the Cold War. Hence the Non-Aligned Movement grew out of a sense of grievance against the international system of bipolarity and the global superpower competition, yet its very purpose was to demonstrate its members' attempts to remain aligned against neither of the two Cold War protagonists. The Non-Aligned Movement's rationale, therefore, was closely tied to the bipolar conflict. The question of bipolarity is important, for the structure of a system with only two main poles is bound to attract and repel other state actors. We should turn now to outline the evidence offered in support of the idea that Russia and the West are engaged in a new Cold War, or an ongoing continuation of the original Cold War. This is done, in the following section, in relation to the two principal defining features of the Cold War: strategic great power conflict and ideological competition. First, however, brief mention should be made of the psychological dimension.

Russia and the West: a new Cold War?

The psychological dimension: continuation of negative stereotyping and mutual hostility

A number of arguments are made to support the view that the relationship between Russia and the West is best described as a Cold War. As noted above, for some there is the assumption that the Cold War never actually ended. The Cold War was in part fueled by political leaders and institutions that had been schooled in the mind-set of negative stereotypes of the other as the principal protagonist, breeding suspicion and undermining mutual trust. On both sides, foreign and security policies had for so long been based on mutual threat perceptions that a negative psychological image of the "other" had become so firmly established that it was difficult to escape from it. Although the Berlin Wall turned to rubble and communism collapsed, the psychological dynamics that bred hostility between Russia and the West, particularly between Russia and the US, were much more difficult to eradicate. Dmitry Furman referred to the new Cold War as a natural extension of the earlier one, except that this time the "struggle" between the two protagonists came to be centered on the former territories of the USSR, in what came to be called the "near abroad." Furman states, "Obviously, the struggle between Russia and the West for Ukraine and Belarus is a direct extension of the struggle between the Soviet Union and the West for Poland, Hungary, and Czechoslovakia..." (Furman, 2006). Lilia Shevtsova, in seeking an explanation for the cooling in relations between Russia and the West following Yeltsin's departure from the political scene, points to what she considers to be the inherent anti-Westernism that was fostered under Putin's leadership. Putin turned to the Cold War past in order to develop a strong sense of national identity and solidarity among Russia's post-Soviet elite, and seeing the world through the prism of Russia–US relations was a "...guarantor of [Russia's] status in the world." Shevtsova says of the Russian political leadership that it is "...desperate to preserve the attribute of its former superpower status [and] Russia continues to view the outside world through the prism of its relations with the United States" (Shevtsova, 2006a, p. 313). Another observer claims that "...the image of the West as an enemy has become the sole ideological justification for Putinism" (Piontovksy, 2006). Thus, by the turn of the 21st century, old anti-Western thinking had become once more dominant among both the Russian elite and the wider population, and this psychological dynamic helped to foster the new Cold War.

It is not so much that Russian elite circles resented the US for its economic and power status, but more that "Russian exceptionalists hate American exceptionalists" (Shevtsova, 2006b, p. 42). Shevtsova did not simply accord blame to Putin and the new Russian elite for fostering a new Cold War, lamenting that "...ageing Cold War hawks on both sides of the ocean still mutually reinforce each other's views" (Shevtsova, 2006b, p. 52). There is some evidence to support these claims. Russian

Foreign Minister Sergei Lavrov, reflecting on contemporary problems in US–Russian relations, stated in the summer of 2008: "Paradoxically, there was more mutual trust and respect between the two states during the Cold War" (Lavrov, 2008). Recent surveys show that Russians view the US as a more dangerous and threatening state than either Iran or China (cited in Kuchins, 2007). It is a remarkable fact that, after the murder of the Russian journalist Anna Politkovskaya in 2006, 19 per cent of Russians considered that it had been organized by overseas opponents of Putin seeking to undermine Russia's authority (*Gazeta.ru*, October 30, 2006). Politkovskaya was at that time the forty-second Russian journalist to be murdered since 1992, providing further evidence of the problems that the Russian Federation was experiencing in developing democracy and civil society. It seemed that events in each country reinforced old Cold War negative stereotypes of the other, and this gave way to a continuation and a reinforcement of tensions in bilateral Russia–US relations, and in Russia's wider relationship with the rest of the West. The fact that Putin in the late Soviet period was an officer in the KGB, and would later became head of the FSB, its Russian successor under Yeltsin, has added to the perceptions of a leader wedded to old Cold War thinking. Spy scandals have also helped to reinforce Cold War stereotypes about the nature of the Russian Federation.

Continuation of great power competition

Furman's argument about the new Cold War assumes that similar logics are at play in contemporary relations between Russia and the West as in the original Cold War, and in particular in relations with the US. Tensions are driven by a competition for influence over key actors in the post-Soviet space motivated by great power politics, while also being exacerbated by diverging political and social systems (Furman, 2006). Despite promises by the West not to expand NATO when Gorbachev agreed to the unification of Germany, the Western alliance not only continued to grow, taking in former Warsaw Pact members and then former Soviet Republics, but was also employed against Serbia, a fellow Slav nation and ally of Russia, in defense of Kosovar Albanians in 1999. The fact that Russia was left on the outside of an expanding West in the form of NATO, and an enlarging Europe in the form of the European Union, inevitably impacted on Russian elite sensibilities and sense of identity. The West also sought to gain inroads and influence in the former Soviet territories in Eurasia, with the US after 9/11 setting up military bases in Central Asia. Lavrov uses the Cold War term of "containment" to describe US foreign policies towards the Russian Federation and its nearest neighbors (Lavrov, 2008). In his annual address in 2006 Putin referred to the arms race and promised that Russia would not fall behind, but would keep pace with the United States in nuclear weaponry. For Boris Nemtsov, a leader of the Union of Right Forces, Putin's address reminded him of the old Cold War Soviet leader Leonid Brezhnev. He argued that Putin's political discourse "... dates back to the 25th Party Congress of the CPSU" (Nemtsov, 2006). Nemtsov was referring to Brezhnev's insistence on ensuring parity with the US in nuclear forces, hence maintaining strategic bipolarity. Further evidence cited by many to support continued strategic great power competition between the two former Cold War protagonists include the following: US and Western support for the "colour revolutions" in former Soviet territories, and criticism of Russia during its short war against Georgia in August 2008; competition for influence in the Caspian Sea and Southwest Asia; Russia's employment of energy as an instrument for maintaining influence in Ukraine; Russia's arms sales to, and good relations with, states critical of the US, such as Venezuela; Russia's reluctance to challenge Iran over its nuclear policies; Russia's attempts to build closer military ties to China and other neighbors through the Shanghai Cooperation Organization (SCO); and President Medvedev's proposals for creating a new security architecture in Europe, which Western critics see as an attempt to undermine the cohesion of NATO and to split the West. Mark Smith argues that Russia is seeking to play a key role as a "... citadel of anti-NATO forces, thus echoing the bipolar competition of the Cold War" (Smith, 2007a). Russia has emphasized the importance of the SCO for maintaining security in Eurasia and as a counterbalance to NATO, while the organization also has the potential to become the progenitor of a gas cartel similar to the oil cartel OPEC, with Iran, an associate SCO member, deepening its cooperation with Russia in energy projects. Iranian President Mahmoud Ahmadinejad has openly suggested that Russia and Iran cooperate in "... pricing gas and forming the main gas routes [to] prevent the threats of domineering powers and their aggressive interference in global affairs" (*Moscow Times*, 22 June, 2006). Other issues that have led to disputes include US plans for a national missile defense, and American criticisms of Russia's democratic reversals, which Russia views as attempts at interference in its domestic affairs to foster US political and economic interests.

One current example of an issue that has reflected tensions in relations concerns disagreements about how to handle the nuclear problem with Iran. Russia has at times demonstrated ambivalence about the prospect of a nuclear-armed Iran, and, although it has stated opposition to proliferation, it is suggested that Moscow also sees the benefit of undermining US domination of the international system. In addition, Russia has been reluctant to support tough economic sanctions due to its own stake in Iran, which is large and continues to grow. Hence, some see Russia as having a vested interest in maintaining tensions between the West and Iran, for this could increase Russian influence as a potential partner for Iran, help to keep the price of oil high, and bring gains for Russia in the image stakes, since US standing in the wider Islamic world could be further undermined if Washington were to undertake strong sanctions or perhaps even military action against Tehran (Smith, 2007b). In this reading of Russia's relationship with the West, and in particular the US, each side structures its security policies based upon the potential threat that the other side poses.

Continuation of ideological competition

The end of the original Cold War was also, for Francis Fukuyama, the "end of history;" that is, the end of ideological conflict and the final victory of liberal democracy (Fukuyama, 1992). However, some twenty years later Fukuyama states that "The question for international politics is whether the Russian path represents a stable model of development that in future years will attract other imitators..." (Fukuyama, 2007). According to Freedom House, Russia under Yeltsin in the five years from 1991 was the only country to have moved from democracy to authoritarianism. From "partly free" in 1991, by 1995 Russia had become "not free" (Freedom House, 2005). The fall of the Berlin Wall, then, did not denote the end of history for Russia and the natural progression to democracy. Rather, it became apparent that it was possible to successfully develop and integrate into the global capitalist economy without following the democratic path followed by Western countries. Perhaps, therefore, a new Cold War ideological conflict had arisen; this time pitting what the Russian elite came to refer to as a "sovereign democracy" versus western "liberal democracy."

According to Edward Lucas, the new Cold War's ideological conflict is between "...lawless Russian nationalism and law-governed Western multilateralism" (Lucas, 2008, p. 18). This argument lacks substance and should not detain us further, for clearly Russian nationalism does not pose an ideological threat to the West, nor does the West engage in multilateralism with no consideration of its own individual national interests. A more powerful argument is that of Azar Gat, who posits that Russia's neo-authoritarian state-led economic model poses a real challenge to the dominance of the liberal capitalist market model of the US and the West for other developing countries (Gat, 2007). Once again, as in the 20th-century Cold War, Russia is seen as offering an alternative developmental path for other countries to follow, particularly those in the Third World. With the failure of the Washington Consensus model in Russia under Boris Yeltsin's leadership, his successor, Vladimir Putin, instigated a centralized, state-driven economic model that saw impressive economic gains in a relatively short time span. It is not so much nationalism, then, that challenges the West, or an absence of legal regulations, but rather the state-driven nature of economic development. Furman maintains that "The Russia-West struggle in the CIS is a struggle between two irreconcilable systems, as was the one between the world of capitalism and communism [and] the Cold War...will only stop when Russia moves from managed democracy to democracy proper" (Furman, 2006, pp. 72, 74). The basic argument here is that the Russian elite views the world in bipolar terms in the ideological sphere, with the US as the evil other with whom Moscow is in competition on a global scale, with both sides seeking to fulfill their respective historical missions by exporting their own favored systems.

Russian specialists make counterclaims about the ideological basis of American foreign policy, seeing it not only as designed to compete strategically with the Russian Federation, but also as driven by a "democratic messianism" that seeks to gain control over Russia by an ideological encroachment into domestic politics (Karaganov, 2006). It is worth recalling that it was under Clinton that "democracy promotion" was first pushed as a key component of US foreign policy. Clinton's Secretary of State, Warren Christopher, stated during his confirmation hearings that of all foreign policy issues "...none is more important than helping Russia demilitarize, privatize, invigorate its economy, and develop representative political institutions" (quoted in Marsden, 2005, p. 50). Warren went on to say that in his view "...helping the Russian people to build a free society...is the greatest strategic challenge of our time" (Marsden, p. 47). Russians considered this to be evidence of the US seeking to foster democracy not for the good of their country, but rather for American national interests, as it was essentially exporting its own political values and in the process undermining Russia's own indigenous political culture. In what has come to be referred to as "soft power," US attempts to impose its own ideology and values on the rest of the world were viewed as an instrument for gaining influence in the domestic affairs of other states. Understandably, Russian leaders considered that the US under Clinton was trying to take advantage of a weakened Russia in order to enhance its own political, economic, and security interests. As Dmitri Simes put it, "Washington's crucial error lay in its propensity to treat post-Soviet Russia as a defeated enemy" (Simes, 2007, p. 36). In so doing, it helped rekindle antagonism, creating a situation in which each side ended up viewing the other through the prism of the old Cold War.

Some twenty years after the fall of the Berlin Wall and the end of the Cold War, there was an apparent consensus in influential circles on both sides of the former Iron Curtain that Russia–West relations were in a period of a new Cold War. This was based, as demonstrated above, first of all on a psychosocial dynamic in which old negative stereotypical images persisted. Second, at the strategic level, both sides have continued to compete in the security realm, this time the central theatre being in Eurasia, particularly among the former republics of the Soviet Union. And, third, with the failure of liberal democracy to take hold, Russia has developed a new statist ideology that challenges the West's dominance in soft power terms. Therefore, in psychosocial terms, structural/systemic terms, and ideational terms Russia and the West are in the throes of a new Cold War.

Problems and dangers of the Cold War thesis

Some of the above arguments supporting the idea of a new Cold War between Russia and the West may sound convincing, but they are fundamentally flawed. Returning to the two defining features that are necessary for a Cold War, strategic bipolarity and competing ideologies, the argument does not hold up. We no longer have bipolarity in the international system, and, despite what Gat and others might argue, Russia does not offer an attractive and realistic alternative socioeconomic and political model for other states to follow. Russia does not threaten, wish, or claim to remake the world in its own ideological image. In the original Cold War Soviet Russia did indeed pose an existential ideological threat to the West. An important element of the original Cold War was a global contest between capitalism and communism. It was only after World War II, with the relative growth of Soviet military and political power, that this ideological contest came to dominate international relations. Communism spread to East and Central Europe, largely imposed by Soviet tanks, and communist parties were strong in the immediate postwar period in Italy and France, with Greece engaged in a civil war which communists at one stage looked set to win. The competition between the two socioeconomic systems took on a global dimension, with communism spreading to parts of Africa, Asia, and the Caribbean. The very legitimacy of the Soviet regime was founded on its status and identity as the leader in what was termed the "world revolutionary process." The USSR was in a very real sense obligated to further the Marxist goal of encouraging, financing, and where necessary supporting through military means, the spread of communism. Although under Putin's leadership Russia moved away from the liberal democratic model of development, leaders in Moscow care very little about how other countries establish their domestic arrangements. It is their foreign policy behavior that counts, not the nature of their political systems. The idea that Russia was seeking to expand its influence by exporting its model of "sovereign democracy" to other countries has no concrete evidence whatsoever to support it. Insofar as there is a real alternative model for developing countries, it is perhaps offered by China, not Russia. Russia's growth has been based on a one-dimensional reliance on energy exports. Very few states are blessed with such rich endowments of natural resources. China has maintained communist political control to direct state capitalism and to integrate into the global capitalist system by producing cheap manufactured goods for export, and this could offer a more attractive model for others to follow. However, despite the financial and economic crisis that hit the US in 2008, it is not conceivable that China could pose an ideological challenge that would threaten the basis of Western democracy in the 21st century in the same way as Soviet communism did during the long Cold War in the 20th century. Perhaps a more potent challenge to Western democracy is the rise of radical Islamic fundamentalism. However, this is an ideological challenge that threatens Russia as much as, if not more than, the West. Even before 9/11 Putin was calling for cooperation with the US and other western countries in countering what he saw as the dangers posed by Al Qaeda and other Islamists. China, too, shares the same worries. Both China and Russia have their own Muslim ethnic minorities that threaten to undermine the integrity and territorial sovereignty of their countries. Neither Russia nor China wishes to challenge or undermine the fundamentals of the US or the global economy because they both are tightly integrated and dependent and reliant on their workings. The bottom line is that Russia and the West cannot be in a new Cold War, because whatever ideological differences they may have do not translate into a wider challenge in international relations.

In terms of military security and military power, in 1945 only two major powers emerged that could reasonably pose a major threat to each other; hence, we refer to strategic bipolarity. From the perspective of power politics and based on previous structural shifts in the global balance of power, bipolarity was bound to lead to antagonism between the two central poles, the USSR and the US. Hence, the structure of the international system, along with the internal dynamics of two opposing socioeconomic systems, resulted in the unique feature of Cold War. Neither of these elements pertains today.

The end of the Cold War was brought about by an end to strategic bipolarity and by the collapse of Soviet communism. Hence we witnessed an end to the superpower balance of military power and to the ideological conflict between capitalism and communism. In terms of both hard power and ideology, the West can be said to have "won" the Cold War. Although Gorbachev and then Yeltsin at first argued that both sides were victors, it quickly became evident that in both Washington and Moscow most considered that, on the contrary, the end of the Cold War marked a victory for the West and a defeat for Russia. The Cold War was a zero-sum game, and the final denouement was bound to see one side winning, and the other losing.

Learning from the Cold War

Finally, we can identify a number of lessons from the ending of the Cold War in the 20th century. The first lesson is that, although the conflict was in part linked to the balance of military power, academics and political leaders overdetermined the role it played. Too much attention was placed on counting tanks and missiles and developing Grand Strategies to counter a possible military strike from the other side. As the originator of the "containment" strategy himself noted, the US gave far too much emphasis to the military dimension, hence helping to turn the conflict into a global military competition (Kennan, 1987).

The second lesson is that not enough attention was paid to the power of national identity, which was always remarkable, given that the Soviet Union was essentially the last of the great European empires. Polarity was an important feature of the Cold War, but at the end of the day it was not the movement of poles in the structure of the international system that brought about an end to the Cold War, but the actions of Poles in the Gdansk shipyards and the Solidarity movement, which challenged communist power. It was not Great Power nationalism that brought about an end to the Cold War, but the national forces of those imprisoned in the Soviet bloc who wished to break away from Moscow's control. Academics and politicians tended to ignore the power of nationalism and the claims for sovereignty, which in the end were responsible for the unraveling of the Russian/Soviet Empire. Czechs and Slovaks, Poles, Hungarians and (East) Germans wanted freedom from both communism and Soviet imperial control. The Baltic peoples wanted a return of their sovereignty, taken away from them in the Nazi–Soviet Pact of 1939. It is most unlikely that Russia's neighbors would once more accede to having their domestic affairs determined by Moscow, assuming even that Moscow would wish for it.

The third lesson relates to the peaceful end of the Cold War, marking the first time that the world had witnessed power transition in the international system without major power war. There is controversy over the ending of the Cold War, but one essential feature is the role played by nuclear weapons and the fear of mutually assured destruction. Both sides were acutely aware that any crisis in relations could spin out of control and result in a nuclear exchange. Both sides shared one important common interest during the Cold War, and that was survival, and each shared a stake in the survival of the other, for if one side was destroyed then the other would go down with it. Hence, the one arena in which the former antagonists of the Cold War developed close coordination was in arms control. Although often difficult and tense, arms control talks led to agreements that effectively managed the arms race in such a way that it would not end in heaps of radioactive rubble. The lesson here is the need for adversaries to negotiate on issues relating to security and weapons of mass destruction. Another important feature of the Cold War worth noting is the fact that it was between two states that were not geographically proximate and did not have any disputes over territory, thereby providing less likelihood of armed conflict. It has been empirically and scientifically demonstrated that disputes over territory between geographically contiguous states are most often the triggers for war (Senese and Vasquez, 2008). There was, therefore, always less likelihood of war between the superpowers. Another feature here is that the Cold War antagonists were *not* interdependent economically. On the contrary, they represented radically alternative systems, in what Fred Halliday termed an "inter-systemic conflict" (Halliday, 1995). The contrast here with US relations with China is clear: although not neighbors, the two states do have a potential territorial dispute over the status of Taiwan. Also, in an emerging multipolar Great Power system in Asia, there are multiple territorial claims between, for example, India and China, China and Russia, and in all three countries there are ethnic minorities seeking independence. Furthermore, China *is* tightly integrated into the global economy; whereas the value of the ruble in the Cold War was of no consequence to Washington, the value of the Chinese currency is a sensitive issue. Whereas the Soviet Union had the military capacity to annihilate the United States, it never had the economic power to stop Americans shopping. The US and China are mutually interdependent, in what is perhaps the most imbalanced bilateral economic relationship in history. Wars have also often been fought between states that are more mutually dependent in the economic realm.

A fourth lesson is that even superpowers cannot determine events in the Third World through military means. The US experience in Vietnam and the Soviet experience in Afghanistan are testimonies to this. It is necessary to see regional conflicts for what they are, identifying their local, indigenous roots, and to avoid simplistically fitting them into a Cold War framework. Leaders should be wary of the dangers of misperceptions and to steer clear of inappropriate historical analogies.

A final lesson, perhaps, is that we should be wary of academic consensus, and should always be willing to challenge conventional wisdom.

Conclusion

Lest we forget: we all remember where we were on 9/11/2001, when the twin towers fell in that spectacular and grotesque act of catastrophic terrorism; but how many of us know where we were on 11/9/1989, the day that the Berlin Wall fell after demarcating the division between East and West for more than a quarter of a century? The point I wish to end with is this: 11/9 was the day the world changed, not 9/11, and we would do well to remember this. The world after 9/11 looked much the same as the world before 9/11, and the same issues that confronted the world then are still with us today: nuclear proliferation and the problems here relating to Iran and North Korea and the potential for terrorists getting the bomb; problems relating to globalization; a rising China; potential for conflict over Taiwan; conflicts in the Middle East and post-Soviet states; Kashmir; terrorism and the rise of radical Islam; anarchy and violence in parts of Africa; issues of equity between North and South; AIDs and pandemics; energy and environmental security; global warming; and the problems of nation and state building in different theatres of the world. Issues in today's news media are the same as before 9/11. Although Russia and the US have different views on some of these issues, they share common concerns over most of them. Where there are differences, they are not determined by any overarching global competition, structurally determined by a global balance of power, or by ideological competition. The danger would be in a Cold War discourse giving rise to such perceptions, which could end up fitting the template of Russia–West relations to issues that are not related to them. It is not a Cold War mind-set that is required, but a reset in relations to move beyond old stereotypes. This appears to be on the way to being realized during the first year of President Obama's tenure in the White House. Even in the arena of arms control, where both the US and Russia still account for the bulk of the world's nuclear missiles, the two sides recognize that, in order to avoid proliferation of WMD to other states and even terrorist groups, a wider multilateral forum is necessary. Obama's nuclear summit in Washington DC in April 2010 was evidence of this. We are not going back to the past in Russia's relations with the West, but forward to an uncertain future; but we should remember the past for the lessons it provides as we move forward.

Note

1. A United Kingdom charity, the National Inventory of War Memorials, estimated this figure. The organization was set up to establish an inventory of all war memorials in the UK and to monitor their condition. It does so with the support of the Imperial War Museum. For information on this organization visit its website: www.ukniwm.org.uk. In Australia, another part of the "West" as understood politically, strategically, and ideologically during the Cold War, there are some 7,000 war memorials across the country, despite the fact that the bulk of the population live in only five urban areas along the coastal rim (Inglis, 1999). None of these memorials explicitly commemorate those who served in the Cold War. In Arlington Cemetery in Washington DC, both the Korean War and the Vietnam War are represented in the Tomb of the Unknowns section. The Memorial Wall in Washington also honors US armed forces who lost their lives in Vietnam. Yet both of these wars in Asia during the second half of the 20th century were tightly linked to the Cold War East–West confrontation between the two superpowers, and can only be fully understood within this context.

References

Bush, George and Scowcroft, Brent (1998) *A World Transformed*, New York: Vintage Books.

Freedom House (2005) "Freedom in the World Comparative Rankings: 1975–2005", at http://www.freedomhouse.org/template.cfm?page=15&year=2005 (accessed June 23, 2010).

Fukuyama, Francis (1992) *The End of History and the Last Man*, New York: Free Press.

Fukuyama, Francis (2007) "The Russian Model", *The American Interest*, online blog at http://blogs.the-american-interest.com/contd/?p=626 (accessed June 23, 2010).

Furman, Dmitry (2006) "A Silent Cold War", *Russia in Global Affairs*, vol. 4, no. 2, pp. 68–74.

Gaddis, John Lewis (1987) "The Long Peace: Elements of Stability in the Postwar International System", in John Lewis Gaddis, *The Long Peace: Inquiries Into the History of the Cold War*, NY: Oxford University Press, pp. 215–245.

Gat, Azar (2007) "The Return of Authoritarian Great Powers", *Foreign Affairs*, vol. 86, no. 4, pp. 59–60.

Gazeta.ru (2006), October 30. http://www.gazeta.ru/intnews.shtml (accessed June 22, 2010).

Gorbachev, Mikhail (2009), an interview with Gorbachev, *The Nation*, October 28.

Gorodetsky, Gabriel, ed. (2003) *Russia Between East and West: Russian Foreign Policy on the Threshold of the Twenty-First Century*, London: Frank Cass.

Halliday, Fred (1995) "The End of the Cold War and International Relations: Some Analytic and Theoretical Conclusions", in Ken Booth and Steve Smith (eds), *International Relations Theory Today*, Cambridge: Polity, pp. 38–61.

Inglis, Kenneth S. (1999) *Sacred Places: War Memorials in the Australian Landscape*, Melbourne: Melbourne University Publishing.

Karaganov, Sergei (2006) "Dangerous Relapses", *Russia in Global Affairs*, vol. 4, no. 2, pp. 76–84.

Kennan, George (1987) "Reflections on Containment", in Terry L. Diebell and John Lewis Gaddis (eds), *Containing the Soviet Union*, New York: Pergamon-Brasseys, pp. 15–19.

Kuchins, Andrew (2007) "Review of Dangerous Relations", *The National Interest*, no. 91, September–October, pp. 92–96.

Lavrov, Sergei (2008) "Russia and the World in the 21st Century", *Russia in Global Affairs*, no. 3, July–September. Online at http://eng.globalaffairs.ru/numbers/24/1210.html (accessed June 22, 2010).

Lucas, Edward (2008) *The New Cold War: How the Kremlin Menaces Both Russia and the West*, London: Bloomsbury.

Marsden, Lee (2005) *Lessons From Russia: Clinton and U.S. Democracy Promotion*, Aldershot: Ashgate.

Moscow Times (2006), June 22. http://www.themoscowtimes.com/related/politics/ (accessed June 22, 2010).

National Inventory of War Memorials, www.ukniwm.org.uk (accessed April 10, 2010).

Nemtsov, Boris (2006) *Izvestiia*, May 26. http://www.izvestia.ru/archive/26-05-06/?3 (accessed June 22, 2010).

Piontovsky, Andrei A. (2006) "The Third Road to Serfdom and its Foreign Policy Implications", Hudson Institute website, May 1. http://www.hudson.org/index.cfm?fuseaction=publication_details&id=5563 (accessed June 21, 2010).

Sakwa, Richard (2008) " 'New Cold War' or 'Twenty Years' Crisis'? Russia and International Politics", *International Affairs*, vol. 84, no. 2, pp. 241–267.

Senese, Paul and Vasquez, John (2008) *The Steps to War: An Empirical Study*, Princeton: Princeton University Press.

Shearman, Peter (2000) "Nationalism, the State, and the Collapse of Communism", in Sarah Owen Vandersluis (ed.), *The State and Identity Construction in International Relations*, New York: St Martin's Press.

Shevtsova, Lilia (2006a) "Russia's Ersatz Democracy", *Current History*, vol. 105, no. 693, pp. 315–320.

Shevtsova, Lilia (2006b) "Double Vision", *The American Interest*, vol. 1, no. 4, pp. 49–53.

Simes, Dmitry (2007) "Losing Russia: The Costs of Renewed Confrontation", *Foreign Affairs,* vol. 86, no. 6, pp. 36–52.

Smith, Mark (2007a) "A Review of Russian Foreign Policy", Conflict Studies Research Centre, Russian Series, Defence Academy of the United Kingdom.

Smith, Mark (2007b) "Russian Perceptions of the Iranian Nuclear Issue", Advanced Research and Assessment Group, Middle East Series, no. 07.33, October.

Thatcher, Margaret (1993) *The Downing Street Years*, London: HarperCollins.

Waltz, Kenneth (1979) *Theory of International Politics*, New York: Random House.

Wedel, Janine R. (2001) *The Strange Case of Western Aid to Eastern Europe*, New York: Palgrave.

2
Aims and Means in Russian Foreign Policy

Ingmar Oldberg

Russia is generally considered one of the great powers in the world, and is as such of key importance to European security. After Vladimir Putin became president in 2000, Russia's foreign policy became more ambitious and assertive thanks to its growing economic power and concentration of political power, at the same time as changes in the world offered opportunities that Russia could exploit. Dmitrii Medvedev, president since 2008, continues this policy in close cooperation with Putin as prime minister.

This chapter will explore Russian foreign policy strategy under Putin and Medvedev by analyzing its aims and principles as proclaimed in official documents and statements and comparing them with the political, military and economic means that are used in policy practice. The analysis will thus investigate the degree of consistency of goals and means, and in which ways the actual policy has been successful in the face of external resistance.

The chapter first presents and examines the proclaimed general aims. It then addresses the political means to reach these aims by looking into Russian policy regarding international organizations, border issues, separatism, and Russian minorities abroad. In the military dimension the uses of bases, peacekeepers, and military activities are singled out for scrutiny. In the economic dimension, finally, Russia's use of trade and transport, especially in the energy field, to further its aims is examined before the findings are summarized.

One conclusion is that Russian foreign policy is quite contradictory, or, to put it in a more complimentary way, *pragmatic*, but consistently aims to increase Russia's standing as a great power. There remains a gap between ambitions and results.

Overriding aims

Since Soviet times, if not before, Russian leaders have been keen on outlining long-term plans and doctrines, in which the aims and means of their policy are explained to the people and the surrounding world. Just like Putin in 2000, President Medvedev after his accession to power launched a new Foreign Policy Concept and a new National Security Strategy (*Kontseptsiia vneshnei politiki Rossiiskoi Federatsii 2008, Strategiia natsionalnoi bezopasnosti Rossiiskoi Federatsii do 2020 goda*). Among the basic objectives, Medvedev's Concept mentioned the following:

- Safeguarding the security of the country, strengthening its sovereignty and territorial integrity as well as its position as "one of the influential centers in the world;"
- Creating good conditions for Russia's modernization, raising living standards, consolidating society and securing the competiveness of the country;
- Promoting a "just and democratic world order" based on collective principles and the supremacy of international law;
- Creating good relations with Russia's neighbors and eliminating hotbeds of conflict in the adjoining regions and other parts of the world;
- Seeking consensus with other states and international organizations;
- Defending the "rights and interests of Russian citizens and compatriots abroad" and promoting the Russian language and the cultures of Russia abroad;
- Creating "an objective perception of Russia in the world as a democratic state" with an independent foreign policy.

The Concept is primarily concerned with Russia's state interests and its position in the world. The calls for a "democratic" world order or "multipolarity" are clearly directed against the dominating position of the United States. External security is placed before economic development, which is largely seen as a means to an end. There is a clear risk of conflict between promoting the primary goal of strengthening Russia as one of the strong centers in the world and defending the Russians abroad on the one hand, and territorial integrity and the seeking of consensus with other states on the other. Not surprisingly, there is little concern for democracy and human rights in the Western sense. Russia is claimed to be a "sovereign democracy," which must be respected abroad; an alternative value centre, as it were, as opposed to Western democratic "Messianism" (Monaghan, 2008, p. 728 ff).

The Concept further describes Russian foreign policy as balanced and "multi-vector" because of Russia being a vast Eurasian country. It claims that Russia bears a responsibility for upholding security on both a global and a regional level, and is ready for common action. Throughout, priority is given to the adjoining region of post-Soviet states (excluding the Baltics). Further NATO enlargement to this region is seen as a serious threat to Russian security (*Kontseptsiia*, 2008, pp. 4–14).

The above goals are repeated in the National Security Strategy, though internal security was given more attention, in proposals for a new European security system (see below) and in many other subsequent statements. After the war with Georgia in 2008, Medvedev formulated five short leading principles, at one and the same time proclaiming the primacy of international law, advocating a multipolar world, expressing interest in friendly relations with all states, giving priority to protecting Russians everywhere, and talking of regions of "privileged interests" (Medvedev, August 31, 2008; September 2, 2008). In the following analysis a distinction will be made between Russian policy outside and inside the post-Soviet space.

The political uses of international organizations

Turning now to the issue of which means are proclaimed and which are used in practice in order to reach the different aims, we first look at Russian policy in the most important international organizations. Since Soviet times the United Nations has been seen as the main custodian of international law and an aim in itself. However, the UN is also an important tool for promoting Russia's status as a great power and the aim of a multipolar world. Russian officials highly value its role as one of the five permanent members of the Security Council (SC) with a veto power. Russia strongly defends the principle that the member states' military actions must be sanctioned by the SC, and participates in some peacekeeping operations. Following this principle, Russia (along with China) opposed the NATO attack on Yugoslavia in 1999 and prevented the US-led invasion of Iraq from getting a UN mandate, unlike the invasion of Afghanistan. In recent years Russia has helped to preclude, for instance, harsh sanctions against President Mugabe's dictatorship in Zimbabwe, the genocide in Darfur, North Korea's nuclear blasts, and Iran's nuclear programme (*Der Spiegel*, 2008, p. 27; Felgenhauer, May 28, 2009).

Russia also appreciates its membership in the G-8 forum of the world's leading industrial states since 1997, allegedly as a means to exercise collective leadership in the world (*Kontseptsiia*, 2008, p. 5). In 2006 Russia was entrusted to hold the presidency, and made energy a priority issue. It has recommended including China, India, and Brazil, which are seen as allies against the United States, in the forum. However, membership in the G-8 forum is mainly a matter of prestige, since the forum cannot take binding decisions, and Russia does not fully qualify to participate in economic discussions. Furthermore, Russia can easily be excluded or circumvented, such as when the foreign ministers of the other states condemned the Russian war in Georgia in August 2008 (McKeeby, 27 August, 2008). When the United States, in late 2008, took the initiative to convene the leaders of the twenty most important economies (G-20) to discuss the deepening global financial crisis, and the G-20 then became institutionalized, Russia virtually had to go along with this, and even suggested intensified interaction with more countries than the twenty. On the other hand, Russia wanted to keep the G8, and praised a proposal of having G-8 summits during the G20 summits (Medvedev, September 26, 2009). Russia also took the opportunity to blame the crisis on the "unipolar economic model" and proposed, together with China, the creation of a new global financial system with a new supernational reserve currency based on a basket of currencies, obviously including the ruble, which would weaken the position of the US dollar (Medvedev, March 29, 2009; Sergeev, March 17, 2009). However, this idea gained little response, partly because many states have large reserves in dollars.

Russia also values its membership in regional organizations. Most important among these is OSCE, which includes the European states, the USA, Canada and all post-Soviet states, and which works on a consensus principle. In the 1990s Russia wanted this organization to replace NATO, though without success, and in the 2000s Russia has been irritated by OSCE's criticism of the war in Chechnya, calls for withdrawing Russian troops from Georgia and Moldova, and promotion of democratic reforms in ex-Soviet republics. Russia has used its veto to hamper OSCE operations, for instance after the 2008 war in Georgia, when it prevented OSCE from monitoring in South Ossetia. Instead, Russia has demanded that OSCE should focus on security issues such as fighting terrorism. In 2007 Russia also suspended its adherence to the treaty on limiting conventional weapons in Europe (CFE), which was one of the main achievements of OSCE's precursor, the Conference on Security and Cooperation in Europe (CSCE).

During a visit to Berlin in June 2008 Medvedev launched the idea of a new pan-European security pact, which then became a centerpiece in Russian foreign policy, and in November 2009 a draft treaty was proposed, outlining conflict-solving mechanisms (Medvedev, June 5, 2008; November 29, 2009). The pact was to be elaborated by all the states and organizations from "Vancouver to Vladivostok," reaffirm the basic principles of the UN, and have a legally binding character. A key principle would be that no party to the treaty should increase its security at the expense of any other, and references were made to the enlargement of alliances, more specifically eastern expansion by NATO. The planned US missile system in Poland and the Czech Republic was also mentioned as a relevant issue. Further, arms control mechanisms and reasonable thresholds should be determined (*Kontseptsiia*, p. 10; Medvedev, October 8, 2008). Nothing was said about democracy or human rights. The intention was evidently to replace OSCE and the Helsinki Accord of 1975, which included these principles, as well as the CFE. The obvious overall aim of the proposal was to boost Russian influence in Europe at the expense of NATO. Some European states, such as France and Germany, were willing to discuss the Russian proposal, but did not want to replace existing structures such as OSCE, and several states pointed out that Russia itself had recently violated the proposed principles in its war against Georgia (Klein, 2009, pp. 6 ff.).

Russia, furthermore, is the only state to have a joint council with NATO (NRC). This council, in which both sides are equal, was created in 2002 to promote cooperation in the war on terrorism, concerning the spread of weapons of mass destruction, crisis management, and arms control. Along these lines Russia and NATO hold regular meetings, common exercises, and so forth. NATO strongly condemned the Russian intrusion into Georgia, and cancelled meetings with Russia, but in late 2009 the council started work again. Russia's proposal for a new European security treaty and its participation (with arms transit) in efforts to stabilize Afghanistan were discussed at a summit (NATO–Russia Council, December 17, 2009). Still, Russia continues to view NATO as the main military threat and as being dominated by the United States, and the Council has proved irrelevant to Russia's main concern, namely, NATO enlargement to include more post-Soviet states (see below).

As a counterweight to NATO, Russia cultivates its relations with the European Union, which is mainly viewed as an economic organization with whose members Russia conducts most of its foreign trade. There has been a partnership agreement (PCA) with the EU since 1997, a joint council (PCC), cooperation in four fields ("common spaces") with roadmaps and action plans, and regular meetings on many levels. The problem is that Russia wants to be treated as an equal partner and does not want to adapt to EU standards. Decision making in the Union is also slow and complicated. Russia is, further, suspicious of EU support for democracy in the former Soviet area and its ambition to solve "frozen conflicts" there (see below). Russian leaders have criticized the new EU Eastern Partnership program with six former Soviet republics as an intrusion into Russia's sphere of influence, and expressed the fear that anti-Russian countries could turn it into a partnership against Russia (Medvedev, May 22, 2009, p. 6). Another problem for Russia is that the EU overlaps with NATO and includes several ex-Communist states, which are highly suspicious of Russian ambitions. They have contributed to stalling negotiations on renewing the PCA, which lapsed in 2007. To overcome this resistance, Russia has relied on cooperation with the great EU powers Germany, France, and Italy, which are on better terms with Russia.

Furthermore, since 1996 Russia has been an active member of the Council of Europe (CoE), which embraces all European states except Belarus. Russian leaders often stress that Russia belongs to European civilization and culture. True, the organization, as a special champion of democracy and human rights in Europe, has criticized Russia on many occasions. But Russia remains in the organization, and even held the presidency in 2006. The best explanation for this is probably that Russia views the CoE as a useful means to advance issues like minority rights (against Estonia and Latvia) and free movement across borders. The CoE can also be used as a counterweight to EU ambitions to create its own legal space without Russia – and the United States is not member ("Towards a united Europe", p. 104 ff.).

Besides these all-European organizations, Russia is a member in more limited organizations with adjacent states, such as the Council of Baltic States, the Arctic Council, and not least the Black Sea Economic Cooperation (BSEC). Russia appreciates these organizations as means to solve regional issues, but it has no more influence in them than much smaller states, some of which are NATO members, and the prestige value is limited.

As counterweights to Western organizations, Russia, as the biggest country in Asia, is furthermore actively involved in the Asian-Pacific Economic Cooperation (APEC), and it is an observer in ASEAN (Association of Southeast Asian Nations) and – on the strength of its Muslim minorities – the Organization of the Islamic Conference. Russia also values its participation in less institutionalized groupings, such as the six-party negotiations concerning Korea, the Quartet of states trying to solve the Israeli–Palestinian conflict, and the 5+1 states engaged in negotiations with Iran on nuclear issues. Participation in all these forums contributes to Russia's status as a great power with interests all over the world. However, the first mentioned Asian organizations have little concern with security issues, and in the latter groupings Russia plays a minor role in the shadow of the United States.

Apparently as a response to this, Russia is trying to develop a strategic triangle with its old friend India and with China, two great powers that have the biggest populations in the world and have developed very fast in recent years. Extension of this triangle includes the Shanghai Cooperation Organization (see next section), and the BRIC, including Brazil. At a meeting in 2005 Russian Foreign Minister Lavrov stressed that Russia, China, and India have similar views on international law and multipolarity, separatism and terrorism (Blagov, June 3, 2005). The problem here is that China and India have been enemies in the past, neither wants to be led by Russia, and both are economically oriented more towards the United States and the West than towards Russia. China is, in fact, emerging as a second superpower along with the United States (G-2), thus taking over the position that the Soviet Union once held.

It may be concluded that Russia, through its active engagement in international organizations and groupings since the 1990s, has gained prestige and recognition and maintained its position as a great power, thus in practice contributing to a multipolar system. Russia has influence, especially in the UN Security Council on the strength of its veto power, even if this has repeatedly been circumvented. In other cases Russia is only one of many equal members, the field of activities is limited ,or no binding decisions can be taken. Russia's proposals to create a new security system in Europe or a new global financial system have little chance of success.

By engaging in so many different international organizations in many parts of the world, Russia is able to balance them off against one another. However, since this has not been very successful, Russia also exploits differences among the members inside the organizations in the classic game of divide-and-rule. In practice, bilateral relations continue to play a key role. When the new President Barak Obama spoke in favor of resetting relations after the Bush period, Russia was positive. Before their first summit in April 2009, Medvedev therefore emphasized the need for equality and mutual benefit, and that the states had a "special responsibility in world affairs" concerning strategic stability and nuclear security. He also proposed that Russia and the United States could help lead the effort to establish universal rules and discipline in creating a new global financial system (Medvedev, March 31, 2009). In April 2010 a new strategic arms reduction treaty was signed (Medvedev, April 8, 2010). Such cooperation with the United States as an equal thus serves to elevate Russia above the other great powers.

Organizations in the post-Soviet space

As mentioned, Russia gives priority to integration with the former Soviet republics (except the Baltic states), which are still very dependent on Russia in different respects and degrees. This is probably also its most important means of underpinning its great power status in the world. Replacing the Soviet Union in 1991, Russia thus created the Commonwealth of Independent States (CIS), which has a plethora of organs; hundreds of meetings have been held and thousands of declarations issued. Medvedev's Foreign Policy Concept stressed the value of safeguarding the common heritage and the common security against threats such as international terrorism, extremism, drug trade, transnational crime, and illegal immigration, and the principles of international law were proclaimed (*Kontseptsiia* 2008, pp. 4 ff.).

Under the impact of the Rose Revolution in Georgia in 2003 and the Orange Revolution in Ukraine in 2004, the fight against Western-type democracy became a prominent task of the CIS, where most states are authoritarian or dictatorial. As a counterweight to Western election monitoring agencies, the CIS formed its own agency, which has regularly approved all elections among the members as free and fair (Hedenskog and Larsson, 2007, pp. 19–27).

However, the CIS has proved to be a highly bureaucratic institution, where the implementation of decisions has been minimal. It is marred by conflicts, between several members and Russia, and among the members themselves. Turkmenistan declared itself as neutral at the outset, the key state Ukraine has not signed the Charter, and Georgia left the CIS after the war in 2008. Membership in the organization did not hinder the more democratic Georgia, Ukraine, Azerbaijan, and Moldova from forming their own pro-Western organization (GUAM) in 1997 and striving to join NATO and the EU ever since.

Faced with these problems, Russia has focused on cooperation with the most willing partners in certain fields, especially in the Collective Security Treaty Organization (CSTO), nowadays encompassing Russia, Belarus, Armenia, Uzbekistan, Kazakhstan, Kyrgyzstan, and

Tajikistan. The organization is based on common defense if a member is under attack, but also aims at cooperation against terrorism, separatism, organized crime, and so forth. It has a joint secretariat, a joint staff and a collective security council, and many joint exercises have been held (Möller, 2007, pp. 3 ff.). In 2009 a collective operational reaction force (CORF) with a joint command was formed, which, according to Medvedev, would be on a par with NATO. Russia dominates the command, contributes most of the troops and the costs, and provides weapons at favorable prices. The CSTO has faithfully toed the Russian line on NATO enlargement and democracy, and in September 2008 it backed the Russian war against Georgia (Medvedev, September 5, 2008). However, joint reaction forces had already been created in 2001, although – as Medvedev admitted in 2009 – this had remained a paper product. In 2009 the member states could only agree on contributing a battalion-size unit each, which were to remain under national control and on national territory, at the insistence of Belarus and Uzbekistan (Felgenhauer, February 5, 2009; McDermott, January 26, 2010).

Besides the CSTO, Russia uses the Shanghai Cooperation Organization (SCO), which includes four Central Asian states and China, while India, Pakistan, Iran, and Mongolia became observers in 2004–5. Originally designed to solve border problems and build confidence after the breakup of the Soviet Union, the SCO's agenda includes fighting the "three evils" of terrorism, separatism, and extremism. It has some permanent organs; regular top-level meetings are held, as well as military exercises, which most often have a counterterrorist facade. In addition, the SCO opposes Western-type democracy and NATO enlargement and serves as a counterpoise to Western organizations. In 2005 it called on the US to give a deadline for withdrawing its military bases, even though these had been established to fight terrorism in Afghanistan. In this way China is involved in keeping NATO out of the region, while Russia can maintain its old ties with the Central Asian states through the CSTO and the EEC Eurasian Economic Community (EurAsEc). On the other side, the SCO legitimizes greater Chinese presence in the region, and the Central Asian states can use it to play the big neighbors against each other, even if they are more afraid of China (Oldberg, 2007, pp. 13 ff.) In the economic field, Russia mainly relies on the Eurasian Economic Community, which has the same members as the CSTO, but with Ukraine, Moldova, and Armenia as observers. Here Russia has 40 per cent of the votes and bears a corresponding share of the costs. Within this community only Russia, Belarus, and Kazakhstan have been able to form a customs union in 2010, but the others are invited to join (Medvedev, November 27, 2009). A serious problem with the EurAsEc is that it is challenged by the integration efforts of the EU.

Russia has its closest ties with Belarus, which, despite being a member of the above organizations, entered into a "union state" with Russia in 1999. Military integration in particular has progressed, with a common air defense, many exercises, and integrated military industries. President Aleksandr Lukashenko fully supports the Russian view of NATO enlargement and Western democracy, and in 2008 he praised the Russian war against Georgia (Medvedev, August 19, 2008). However, while Putin wanted Belarus to become a part of Russia, Lukashenko retained his dictatorial control of his country and insisted on equal terms in the union. Plans for a common constitution and a common currency have failed. In 2009 Belarus started to take part in the EU Eastern Partnership, at the same time as it joined the Customs Union (Marples, May 18, 2009; August 7, 2009).

One may conclude from the above that, while Russia is the undisputed leader in the CIS area due to its size and the common heritage, the multilateral organizations have been of limited use in bolstering Russia's position as a great power. Most useful are the military CSTO and the SCO with China, whereas the CIS mainly serves as a meeting forum. The EurAsEc has boiled down to a few states, and even the union with Belarus has remained a paper product. All the organizations are largely inefficient bureaucratic formations of undemocratic countries. In order to reach its goals of control and integration in this region, Russia also has to rely on bilateral relations with the other countries, and on political, military, and economic tools other than organizations.

The flexible use of borders and territorial integrity

As a means of reinforcing international law, Medvedev's foreign policy concept mentions the importance of legalizing Russian land and maritime borders. Russia has reached border agreements with China, with which it has good relations, and even ceded some contested islands in the Amur River. However, with regard to Japan, which is allied with the United States, Russia has refused to return four Kuril Islands conquered during World War II. With regard to the NATO member Norway, since 1977 Russia has not accepted its claim to an economic zone based on the median line principle in the Barents Sea and around Svalbard, and a few incidents of illegal fishing occurred in the 2000s. However, the countries managed jointly to administer a fishing regime in a gray zone in the Barents Sea, and in early 2010 they finally agreed on dividing the disputed area into two equal parts (Hönneland, 2009, p. 35 ff; Medvedev, April 27, 2010).

This issue is connected with Russia's claims to a big chunk of the Arctic Sea up to the North Pole on the basis of the extension of the Siberian continental shelf. The claim has been underpinned by more or less scientific expeditions and increased military presence. However, economic interests are clearly also at work. Medvedev has stressed that the Arctic Sea is estimated to contain one-fourth of the world's assets of oil and gas, and that the exploitation of this is a guarantee of Russia's energy security. The Russian Security Council has issued an Arctic doctrine (Medvedev, September 17, 2008; Sovet Bezopasnosti, March 27, 2009).

When Estonia and Latvia reconstituted their interwar republics in 1991 and questioned the border changes that Stalin had carried through during the war, Russia defended the present borders. However, when Estonia and Latvia abandoned their revision claims and wanted to sign a border treaty in order to qualify for NATO and EU membership, Russia refused for this very reason. In 2005 Russia finally signed border treaties with Latvia and Estonia, but the latter was abrogated because the ratification act of the Estonian parliament referred to the interwar border (Oldberg, 2007b, pp. 59 ff.).

Within the CIS, Russia signed a border treaty with Belarus in 1994, but Ukraine, which strove for NATO and EU membership, had to wait until 2003. However, this agreement has not resulted in the demarcation of the border. Conflict erupted concerning the sea border in the Sea of Azov, where Russia tried to take control of an island in the Kerch Strait. Finally, the parties agreed to share control over this gulf, which means that NATO ships could be barred from entry (Hedenskog, 2004, pp. 20 ff.).

Border issues are inevitably connected with the problem of territorial integrity and separatism. Medvedev's Concept repeatedly professed the principles of international law, including nonviolence, state sovereignty and territorial integrity, but also endorsed people's right to self-determination, which contradicts the integrity principle. When the Soviet Union fell apart, Russia recognized the sovereignty and territorial integrity of the other ex-Soviet states, and fought two wars against separatists and terrorists in Chechnya to keep Russia together. These principles also became fundamental to the CIS and other organizations.

Russia, furthermore, became an ardent champion of the integrity principle in the international arena. In 2008 Russia strongly resisted international recognition of Kosovo, referring to the risks it posed to Spain, Great Britain, and so on (Kvitsinsky and Shtodina, 2007, p. 32). Another reason for the Russian view of Kosovo, however, was that Russia saw Serbia as a brother Slavic country, which was under attack from NATO. In the 1990s, Russia opposed UN sanctions against Serb separatists in Croatia and Bosnia-Herzegovina, which were supported by Belgrade. Only after the Western powers had forced the Serbs to give up did Russia also accept these new states.

Furthermore, despite its condemnation of separatism in Chechnya and Kosovo, Russia has de facto backed it up in some CIS states. As noted, Russia is closely allied with Armenia, which in the early 1990s "liberated" the Armenian enclave Nagorno-Karabakh in Azerbaijan; and since then Russia has served as a mediator in this "frozen" conflict (Larsson, 2006a, pp. 61 ff.). From the early 1990s onwards, Russia also helped the secessionists in South Ossetia and Abkhazia (until 2004 also Ajaria) in Georgia and the Transnistrian region in Moldova – incidentally states leaning towards the West – in many substantial ways. In the cases of Nagorno-Karabakh and Abkhazia, Russia condoned the fact that hundreds of thousands of Azeris and Georgians fled or were expelled and were not permitted to return.

When the war in South Ossetia erupted in August 2008, President Medvedev declared that Russia still recognized Georgia's sovereignty, but that territorial integrity was a complicated issue, which partly depended on the people's will. Georgia was said to have started the war and committed genocide on Russian citizens and Ossetians, and similarities with Kosovo were again pointed out (Medvedev, August 12, 2008).

After the war Russia soon recognized both South Ossetia and Abkhazia as independent states and concluded military alliances with them. However, the problem was that very few countries recognized these "states," not even Russia's closest allies in the CSTO and SCO. Apparently aware of the problem, Prime Minister Putin once conceded that Russia could "swallow" Kosovo's independence if the West were to recognize Abkhazia and South Ossetia (Putin, August 29, 2008). Theoretically, both sides could return to the principle of territorial integrity after making these exceptions, but the West is not likely to enter into such a bargain.

More ominously still, Russia has at times also questioned the integrity of Ukraine. When NATO discussed its application for membership in April 2008, outgoing President Putin explained to US President Bush that Ukraine was not a real nation. If Ukraine joined NATO, the Crimea and the eastern parts would secede, he said (Larsson, ed., 2008, p. 78).

Territorial integrity is thus an oft-repeated principle in Russian foreign policy, which is given priority over humanitarian concerns, as in Chechnya and Kosovo. Russia has at the same time undermined this principle in practice by supporting separatists in CIS countries that crave NATO membership, thus turning the principle into a means to other ends. Humanitarian concerns were remembered only when Russians and their friends were at stake. This issue deserves a separate analysis.

The use of Russian minorities

According to President Medvedev's Foreign Policy Concept, the defense of Russian citizens and compatriots abroad was one of the most important aims. In relation to Western states, this is no security problem. The several million Russians who have emigrated since the 1980s, for example to Germany, the US, and Israel, are seen as connecting links, and Russia's main ambition is to help them keep their culture and use them in trade relations.

In ex-Soviet states, however, Russian minorities have become a problem to varying extents. When the Soviet Union collapsed, 23.5 million ethnic Russians ended up outside Russia. Putin referred to this in his address to the Federal Assembly in 2005, when he shocked the world by calling the collapse the worst geopolitical disaster of the 20th century (Putin, April 25, 2005, p. 1). Even if the numbers have shrunk due to emigration or reidentification, the Russian minorities are still sizeable, especially in Kazakhstan (29.9 per cent), Latvia (29.2 per cent), Estonia (25.6 per cent), and Ukraine (17.3 per cent) (Hedenskog and Larsson, 2007, pp. 30 ff.).

After Putin came to power and the Russian economy started to grow, the Foreign Ministry was asked to support the Russians abroad, using political parties and NGOs. Even though such support may be legitimate and meet the wishes of the minorities, Russia has often used the ethnic issue as a tool for political ends. Since the 1990s Estonia and Latvia have been accused in international forums of violating the human rights of the minorities in their legislation on citizenship, language, and schools. The Russian consulates distributed passports to former Soviet citizens, so that more Russians adopted Russian citizenship, rather than Estonian and Latvian, in the 1990s, and were therefore involved in the elections in Russia. In the spring of 2007 hundreds of young Russians rampaged through downtown Tallinn because the government had ordered the removal of a statue that symbolized the Soviet "liberation" of Estonia from fascism in 1944. The protests were backed by Moscow, economic sanctions were imposed, and the Estonian government fell victim to massive cyber-attacks (Ashmore, 2009, pp. 4–40). However, Russia's support for its compatriots in Estonia and Latvia backfired in the sense that the governments sought and obtained more support than ever from NATO and the EU, and the situation of the Russian minorities became more difficult.

In Georgia, Russia supported the South Ossetian and Abkhazian separatists when the central government tried to subdue them in the early 1990s. As many Georgians fled, some Russians moved in, and South Ossetians and Abkhazians, who went to Russia for jobs, were increasingly allotted Russian passports. As mentioned earlier, Russia excused its intrusion into Georgia in 2008 by alleging that Georgia had committed genocide on Russian citizens – or had at least intended to do so, which is a big difference (Putin, August 29, 2008). In fact, only a few hundred Ossetians died, while many more Georgians were killed or expelled in reprisal.

Russians also play an important role in the separatist region of Transnistria. Even though they make up only a third of the population, they dominate the leadership, and many hold Russian passports. Russia apparently wants the region to be autonomous, with strong influence on the central government, and a right to secession, if Moldova abandons its neutrality, whereas even the Communists, who were in power from 2001 to 2009, wished to incorporate Transnistria (Larsson, ed., 2008, pp. 80 f.). Now that a rightist, EU-leaning government is in power, the situation seems deadlocked.

Concerning Ukraine, which Russians view as the most important Slavic brother country, Russia has preferred to support pro-Russian Ukrainian parties, which can keep the whole country away from NATO, rather than openly to foment separatism. However, when President Yushchenko called for membership and NATO in 2008 took up the issue, Russian involvement increased in Crimea, the only region where the Russians are in a majority (Hedenskog and Larsson, 2007, pp. 37 ff.). As noted, Putin talked about secession of some regions, and a deputy prime minister cautioned that 92 per cent of the population of the naval base Sevastopol (about 100,000 people) were "our compatriots." Here, also, Russian passports have been distributed (Hedenskog, 2008, pp. 15 ff.; Interfax, June 14, 2008). However, when the pro-Russian Viktor Yanukovich was elected president of Ukraine in early 2010, he rejected the aim of NATO membership and signed an agreement to permit Russia to keep its naval base in Sevastopol for another twenty-five years. Russia had little reason to use the minority card any longer.

In sum, Russia is able to support its citizens and compatriots within the CIS in many ways. This is amplified by the fact that Russia retains great cultural influence though Russian mass media, which are available everywhere, the Russian language which remains a *lingua franca*, and old family ties across the borders. The distribution of passports, and thereby citizenship, serves to undermine loyalty to the host country, so most states do not allow double citizenship. However, this Russian policy has often backfired against the minorities and pushed the governments to seek support in the West. Finally, it should be observed that support for Russian minorities abroad has mainly been directed at the most West-oriented and democratic ex-Soviet states. Russia has not used the large Russian minorities in Kazakhstan and Belarus against their governments, and has largely refrained from accusing the Central Asian regimes of discrimination (Hedenskog and Larsson, 2007, pp. 4–46). Thus, Russian support for its diaspora is not a principle but a political means against perceived enemies.

Military means: bases for support or pressure

Medvedev's Foreign Policy Concept repeatedly stresses the importance of dialog and peaceful solutions as means for Russia to reach its goals. Violence, it says, must only be used in self-defense or if sanctioned by the UN. After the war in Georgia, Medvedev gave assurance that Russians are peace-loving and that neither the Soviet Union nor Russia had ever started a war (Putin, August 29, 2008; RIA Novosti, August 18, 2008). Yet, as shown above, Russia used its military power on a number of occasions.

During its economic crisis and rapprochement with the West in the 1990s, Russia dismantled its military bases in former Warsaw Pact countries in Europe and beyond, for instance in Cuba and Vietnam. However, when the United States backed up Georgia in 2008 and signed a deal with Poland on basing US antiballistic missiles there, Russia saw this as a growing threat. In response it strengthened its ties with Cuba, Venezuela and Libya, all hostile to the US, and there was talk about basing rights. Russia also obtained wider access to a port in Syria (Felgenhauer, September 11, 2008). In the CIS area the situation is very different. Although Russia withdrew its strategic nuclear forces and let the other successor states (except the Baltic countries) take over the military forces and installations on their territory in the 1990s, Russia kept, and still to varying extents maintains, bases for its air force, army and naval units in all these states except Uzbekistan and Turkmenistan. In the CSTO member states these bases serve the dual function of supporting the respective governments and demonstrating Russian presence to the United States and NATO. In Armenia the Russian bases support the country in its conflict with Azerbaijan and against NATO ally Turkey. In Kyrgyzstan Russia established a new air base in 2001, when the United States was permitted to establish an air base for the war in Afghanistan. Since then Russia has pressed for the removal of the US base, and in 2009 it nearly succeeded by using economic incentives (McDermott, April 28, 2009).

More intriguing, perhaps, is the use of bases in states with which Russia has conflicts. The 14th Soviet army group in Transnistria supported the formation of a separatist republic there in 1991. Part of the force was transferred to Transnistrian control and the rest was reduced to about 1,200 men in 2008. Moldova called for Russian troop withdrawal, and in 1999 Russia promised OSCE that it would withdraw, but since then it has dragged its feet, demanding that the process should be synchronized with resolving the status of Transnistria and the accession of the Baltic states to the CFE. In negotiations with Moldova, Russia has insisted on retaining its base in Transnistria as a "peace force" for at least twenty years (Larsson *et al.*, 2008, pp. 80 f).

Concerning Georgia, after 1991 Russia maintained four military bases there, which allegedly were to "protect" the country against NATO but in reality helped to support separatist regions. True, in 1999 Russia promised the OSCE to scrap the bases, but hardly had the last one, the naval base in Batumi, been evacuated in 2008 than the war between Russia and Georgia erupted. Because of this, Russia did not only declare Abkhazia and South Ossetia to be independent states and conclude military alliances with them, but also decided to deploy 3700 troops in each and build a new naval base in Abkhazia. Besides supporting the new "states," these bases are now a greater threat to Georgia than the former "peacekeepers," and complicate its striving for NATO/EU membership.

Most important for Russia has been the retention of its old naval base in Sevastopol with the headquarters of the Black Sea Fleet. According to an agreement of 1997, Russia was allowed to rent part of the port and some other objects on the peninsula for twenty years, with a possible five years' prolongation. Plans were made to move the base to Novorossiisk, but increasingly logistical and economic problems were pointed out. An obvious reason for this was the fact that retaining the Russian base was a way to stop Ukrainian President Yushchenko's efforts at NATO membership. When NATO discussed Ukrainian membership in April 2008, the

Russian population in Sevastopol, especially the naval personnel, rose in protest, with active support from Russia (Hedenskog, 2008, pp. 15 ff.). However, the tension was relaxed when Yanukovich came to power in 2010 and signed a new base agreement, prolonging the Russian lease by twenty-five years in exchange for a ten-year discount on the price of natural gas supplied to Ukraine. Thus, Russian military bases have often been used as a potent means of pressure against weak CIS states. They often serve as a basis for military activities, which is the next topic.

Military means: peacekeeping and military activities

Beyond the ex-Soviet borders Russian military activities have been greatly reduced since Soviet times, not least for economic reasons. Still, Russia has contributed peacekeeping forces and observers to several UN missions. However, during the war in 1999 Russian peacekeeping troops in Bosnia also surprised the world by a quick march into Kosovo, evidently in the hope of Russia getting its own zone of peacekeeping, but that did not succeed and Russia instead chose to contribute to NATO's peace force for a few years.

Furthermore, Russian forces have taken part in exercises with NATO and Western neighbor states, in which they have demonstrated the will to cooperate and exchange experience as well as to show the flag. True, Russia interrupted such exercises in 1999 as a protest against NATO's war over Kosovo and staged its biggest ever military maneuver with Belarus, training the use of nuclear weapons. But cooperation with NATO was soon resumed, mainly in the common interest of fighting terrorism. Russia joined NATO's Active Endeavor activities in the Mediterranean, but opposed extending them to the Black Sea.

As relations with NATO soured, in 2007 Russia resumed the Soviet practice of patrols with strategic bombers over the Atlantic, the Pacific, and the Arctic Sea. The Northern fleet started exercises as far away as the Mediterranean, which also became an area of operation for the Black Sea fleet. After the US and NATO sent warships with humanitarian assistance to Georgia in the aftermath of its war with Russia, Russia sent some of its best warships and aircraft to the Caribbean Sea for exercises, which should mainly be seen as a warning to the US to stay out of Russia's perceived zone of influence in the Black Sea region.

Russia has also increasingly used its navy to further its interests in northern waters. In connection with the Nordstream project to build a gas pipeline across the Baltic to Germany, Russian leaders talked about new tasks for the Baltic Fleet, and in response to the planned US missile base in Poland Medvedev in 2008 threatened to base short-range Iskander missiles in Kaliningrad (Medvedev, November 5, 2008).

Turning now to Russia's military activity in the CIS region, most of it takes place under the banner of "peace-creation" (*mirotvorchestvo*), which does not comply with the Western view of peacekeeping. Heavy weapons and forcible measures are applied and the principle of impartiality is infringed (Jonson and Archer, 1996, pp. 3 ff.).

Thus in the 1990s a Russian army division, formally acting as a CIS "peacekeeping" force, helped the government in Tajikistan win a bloody civil war against Islamists and supported resistance against the Taliban regime in northern Afghanistan. In 2004 the troops in Tajikistan became a permanent Russian military base by treaty.

Georgia is clearly the country most exposed to Russian military activities. During the Chechen wars Russia accused Georgia of harboring terrorists in the Pankisi Valley. It threatened to take unilateral military measures, and unidentified air bombings and incursions took place (Oldberg, 2006, pp. 7 ff.).

After Georgia tried to reconquer Abkhazia and South Ossetia in the early 1990s, Russian "peacekeeping" forces were stationed there, formally as a CIS force with UN observers and under an OSCE mandate, respectively. However, they consisted only of Russian forces, or were dominated by them, and Russia rejected demands to broaden their composition. Like the military bases, the forces supported the separatist regimes, engaged in intermittent fighting with Georgian forces and in illicit arms trade. When Georgian NATO membership became topical in 2008, the number of military incidents on both sides increased. Russia fortified its forces in both Abkhazia and South Ossetia and staged a big maneuver in North Caucasus in the summer. When Georgia attacked Tskhinvali, the capital of South Ossetia, in August, Russia very quickly struck back with superior units from the north, intruded into Georgia proper and destroyed vital infrastructure there. At the same time Russian troops invaded from Abkhazia, and the Black Sea Fleet from Sevastopol attacked and blockaded the coast, apparently to prevent foreign interference, and sank most of the small Georgian navy. The Russian air force bombed adjacent towns, and the government was subjected to cyber-attacks. Russia accused the United States of supporting the Georgian attack, and clearly set forth the task of crushing Georgia's military power and unseating the NATO-oriented President Saakashvili (Larsson *et al.*, 2008, pp. 18 ff.). After the EU, under French leadership, intervened to stop the war, Russia agreed to a ceasefire and withdrew in October from Georgia proper, though not to the original positions as agreed. EU/OSCE observers arrived, but they were refused entry into South Ossetia and Abkhazia unless these were recognized as sovereign states.

As a result of the war, Russia transformed its "peacekeeping" forces into permanent military bases and took over the border controls. Putin explained that Russia "only" wished to guarantee security in the region and preclude a new clandestine concentration of arms in Georgia (Putin, August 29, 2008). Russia has since then been very suspicious of Western aid to Georgia, and protested strongly against a NATO exercise in Georgia in May 2009.

In August 2009 Medvedev further called for (and got) a constitutional amendment, authorizing him to send troops into action abroad, for example to protect Russian citizens, thus admitting that the Russian invasion of Georgia had not been legal. Russia's territorial integrity was not under threat, there was no treaty obligation to assist South Ossetia, and the Federation Council had not given its sanction (Felgenhauer, December 10, 2009; Kvelashvili, August 14, 2009).

Even if Russia had, for the first time since the Soviet era, intruded into another country without invitation, won a short victorious war against a weak adversary, and improved its military positions, the war also had negative effects. Russia did not manage to topple Saakashvili, who only became more resolved to seek American assistance and to join NATO. Azerbaijan and the CSTO ally Armenia were afflicted by the destruction of Georgian transport routes to the Black Sea. As noted, the cohesion of the CSTO and the SCO was shaken, as no member state wanted to recognize the separatist republics. Russia further lost credibility as a champion of peace and compromise in the West, and its relations with NATO, the EU, and other international organizations were at their worst since 1991, as shown above. The war hastened the US missile agreement with Poland, and several Western neighbors started to talk about strengthening their defenses. However, in 2009 these negative effects started to subside.

In contrast, it should be noted that Russia did not sent any military forces to quell ethnic violence that erupted in southern Kyrgyzstan in June 2010, even though the interim government requested them (Felgenhauer, June 17, 2010). It remains to be seen whether this signifies a less interventionist policy in the CIS.

Economic means

Turning now from the military to the economic dimension, it is true that Russia's economy and foreign trade have developed enormously since the 1990s. However, Russia was hard hit by the global financial crisis in 2008, and most of its export still consists of raw materials, especially energy products but also gold, nickel, aluminium, and timber (Leijonhielm and Larsson, 2004). At the same time, Russian imports of industrial products and advanced technology from the West have increased. Russia nowadays imports even trucks and cars from China, rather than the other way round. A constant ambition, therefore, is to persuade other states to import more Russian manufactured goods.

However, Russia has become prominent, indeed number two in the world after the United States, in one type of industrial products, namely military weapons. Since the 1990s Russia has stopped distributing arms to its socialist allies around the world for free or on credit, and is instead selling all kinds of (non-nuclear) weapons to all countries that are able to pay. Russia's best customers are its old ally India and its new-old friend China. Russia has often taken advantage of Western political embargoes imposed on arms exports, for example to China (since 1989), Iran (since 1979), Sudan, and North Korea. In all cases Russia strives to make profits and generate goodwill, and in some cases it also supports anti-Western and anti-US states. Russia thus used arms deals to persuade Nicaragua and Venezuela to recognize South Ossetia and Abkhazia as states (Felgenhauer, September 17, 2009). However, Russian arms exports as a tool to win or keep allies may lose their competitiveness. China has reduced arms imports and started to export weapons on its own. Inside the CIS, Russian weapons are sold at preferential prices.

As for the CIS states, Russia has on many occasions exploited the fact that they are more economically dependent on Russia than vice versa due to centuries of integration. For instance, after Georgia arrested four Russians for espionage in September 2006, Russia staged a total blockade of communications and froze money transfers and trade. In 2009 Russia stopped the import of Belarusian dairy products, to which Lukashenko responded by not attending a CSTO summit (Marples, August 7, 2009). Occasionally EU states have also been hit by Russian trade embargoes, for example Denmark in 2002 on account of a Chechen conference in Copenhagen (Roth, 2009, pp. 8 ff.). Thus, in trade embargoes and pricing policies political motives are mixed with economic motives, such as favoring Russian companies.

Energy as a political lever

Thanks to rising demand and world market prices, energy has become the mainstay of the Russian economy and the most potent tool in its foreign policy. At the G-8 summit in 2005 President Putin boasted that Russia is the world leader on the energy market, with the biggest potential in oil, gas, and nuclear power taken together (Putin, July 8, 2005). Russia has indeed become the world's leading producer and exporter of oil and natural gas, and it has the largest reserves of gas and uranium.

The official energy strategy of 2003 explicitly mentioned these great resources as a political instrument, and so do the new foreign policy concept and the 2009 security doctrine. Since energy and energy exports are crucial to the Russian economy, the state has taken firm control of the sector by legislation, ownership, representation on boards, intelligence, and so on, at the same time circumscribing the activities of foreign companies. Transneft, which is totally state-owned, has a monopoly on oil pipelines. Gazprom, which dominates the gas market and de facto has an export monopoly in Russia, has expanded into other sectors. A key goal is to take control of oil and gas pipelines and gain control over the European gas market and its companies (Lucas, 2008, pp. 211 ff.). However, in the meantime Russian companies have neglected to make investments in exploration of new reserves and modernizing pipelines at home. In order to satisfy the rising demand in Europe, Russia therefore depends on importing energy from Turkmenistan, Kazakhstan, and Uzbekistan, which is then resold to Europe at higher prices. But these states also want to diversify their export markets. Thus Turkmenistan has recently inaugurated one gas pipeline to China across Uzbekistan and Kazakhstan and one to Iran (Socor, December 18, 2009; January 7, 2010).

Russian energy exports to Europe have grown since the 1990s, so that EU states receive about 30 per cent of their oil from Russia, with seven states exceeding 90 per cent. Moreover, Europe imports about half of its natural gas from Russia: for example, Germany 40 per cent, Greece 84 per cent, Austria 78 per cent, and the Baltic states and Finland 100 per cent in 2006 (Lucas, 2008, p. 212). On the other hand, Russia is even more dependent on EU states as a market, since 80 per cent of its oil exports and 60 per cent of its gas go to the EU (Larsson, 2006, pp. 178 ff.; cf. Meister, 2009).

It should be noted that Russia (USSR) has not stopped gas and oil deliveries to the old EU states except when transit is involved (see below), but its pricing policy may have political effects. Even if the dependency is mutual, the democratic Western states are more susceptible to embargoes and price hikes than Russia, since they have a free press and the governments are exposed to free elections.

Russia has used its energy power most often against the CIS states, which have remained accustomed to low prices since Soviet times, while their industries are mostly very energy-consuming. According to one Swedish study, Russia used energy (oil and gas) as a lever against CIS states on fifty-five occasions in 1991–2006, most of them being supply cuts. In most cases, political motives were involved, such as to influence elections and to punish bad behavior. Ukraine has been hit on many occasions. In 2007 the Russian ambassador to Kiev openly stated that the gas price would depend on which government was elected (Hedenskog and Larsson, 2007, pp. 46 ff.; Larsson, 2006b, pp. 201–226). The "gas war" with Ukraine in early 2009 strongly affected eighteen European states further downstream. However, before the presidential election in January 2010, Russia did not use the gas weapon, which may have to do with the fact that the two main contenders wanted to improve relations with Russia. When the new president Yanukovich agreed to prolong the lease of the Sevastopol, Russia agreed to grant a 30 per cent discount on Russian exports for ten years, and several deals were concluded. Russia also proposed to merge the states' main gas companies and that Ukraine should join the Customs Union, but Ukraine said no (Korduban, April 28, 2010; Medvedev, May 17, 2010). Russia has also often used its energy power against its closest ally Belarus, primarily as a means of taking over state-owned Belarusian infrastructure (Hedenskog and Larsson, 2007, pp. 73 ff.). In January 2010 Russia drastically raised its export duty on oil to Belarusian refineries, which have made good profits by exporting most of their production to the West. This can, however, also be seen as a reaction to the growing Belarusian interest in the EU Eastern Partnership mentioned above. As a counterargument Belarus claimed that the export duty violated the rules of CIS Customs Union, but it did not ratify it. In June Russia also reduced gas supplies, since Belarus did not accept a new price hike, while transit through Ukraine was increased instead, whereupon Belarus threatened to stop transit to Lithuania and Poland (Barry, June 22, 2010; Socor, January 5, 2010; Swirtz, June 23, 2010). The energy weapon has frequently been used against the Baltic EU states for partly political reasons. After Russia failed to gain control of the Latvian oil terminal in Ventspils in 2002, Russia closed the oil pipeline. In 2006 Russia closed its oil pipeline to Lithuania after the Mazeikiu refinery was sold to a Polish company, using technical problems as a pretext. After the statue incident with Estonia in 2007, Russian coal and oil deliveries were stopped (Roth, 2009, pp. 12 ff.).

A key goal in Russian energy policy is to get control over transport routes and escape dependence on transit countries, which can exercise counterpressure by raising fees, and tap from the pipelines if they themselves are under pressure. In order to escape such dependency, Russia has since the 1990s expanded or built new ports in the Gulf of Finland for its export of oil and coal directly to the West instead of relying on transit through Baltic states. In 2005 Russia and Germany agreed to lay a gas pipeline across the Baltic Sea, and a consortium was formed called Nord Stream, in which Gazprom holds 51 per cent. In 2009 Sweden and Denmark, after long investigations into the environmental risks of laying the pipeline across their economic zones, approved the project. Poland and the Baltic states opposed it, in part because they would lose transit income and they feared that they would become more exposed to Russian pressure (Lucas, 2008, pp. 215 ff.). For the sake of diversification, Russia has also built a gas pipeline across the Black Sea to Turkey (Blue Stream) and is now planning a South Stream to Bulgaria through the Black Sea, circumventing Ukraine and Turkey and forestalling the EU Nabucco pipeline project, which is planned to bring gas to Europe through Turkey, bypassing Russia. To this effect, Russia has signed deals, for example, with Bulgaria and Serbia, deals that include major Russian shares in their energy companies. The deal with Serbia was probably facilitated by common views concerning Kosovo.

Furthermore, in 1999 Russia signed an agreement on an oil pipeline across Bulgaria and Greece, in which it would have had a majority stake, in order to avoid Turkish restrictions on passage through the Bosporus (Lucas, 2008, pp. 227 ff.; Socor, May 28, 2009). However, this deal may be overtaken by a new agreement between Russia and Turkey, whereby Turkey would allow a Russian gas pipeline through its economic sea zone, and Russia would supply oil for a pipeline to be built across Anatolia to the Mediterranean (Socor, October 23, 2009). There is also a political element to the Russian project of building an oil pipeline in East Siberia to the Pacific coast. After long playing Japan off against China as recipients and participants, Russia arrived at the compromise of building it along the long border, but with a spur halfway to Daqing in China. The question is whether the resources will suffice for both markets (Larsson, 2006b, pp. 245 ff.).

Returning to Europe, however, Russian energy policy meets resistance from several EU states, which want to diversify imports and forms of energy, improve efficiency, and liberalize the energy market. The EU insists that Russia should ratify the EU Energy Charter, which would decouple energy producers from pipelines. In March 2009 the EU signed an agreement with Ukraine on renovating and expanding its gas pipeline system and integrating it with the European system. Russia reacted strongly, and instead proposed an agreement between producers and consumers ensuring that transit routes would be maintained and reno-vated (Meister, 2009, pp. 1 f.). At the EU–Russia summit in May 2009, Commission President José Manuel Barroso invited Russia to partici-pate in the project (Kupchinsky, April 28, 2009; Medvedev, May 22, 2009). The new Ukrainian president Yanukovich later supported this idea, presumably as a way to dissuade Russia from the South Stream project.

However, a still greater threat to Russian gas power is the fact that the United States has started to exploit its vast resources of so-called unconventional gas and in 2009 became the world's leading gas pro-ducer and potentially a net exporter through LNG. This has already led to sinking gas prices in Europe and threatens to make the construc-tion of Nordstream's planned second pipeline unprofitable. This may be the reason why the vast Shtokman exploration project (together with Norwegian and French firms), which should feed that pipeline, was postponed in early 2010 (Socor, February 9, 2010).

Turning finally to nuclear energy, many former Soviet and Warsaw Pact states (such as Ukraine, Lithuania, and Bulgaria), plus Finland, which had Russian reactors, depended on Russian nuclear fuel and services. Under Putin, Russia decided on a new large-scale nuclear power expansion at home and abroad. Agreements on building new reactors have been signed with Belarus (even though it was particularly badly hit by the Chernobyl accident) on Russian credits, Kazakhstan, Bulgaria, and Turkey. Outside that region Russia has built reactors in China, India, and Iran, especially in the latter case profiting from Western embargoes, and more reactors are on contract. Russia further covers one-third of European uranium needs, and sells ex-military ura-nium for civil use through the United States, satisfying 15 per cent of global needs. Russia claims to be able to undercut world prices for nuclear fuel and services by some 30 per cent, but concerning nuclear technology it faces tough competition from Western states (*Nuclear power in Russia*, January 20, 2010, pp. 26–8; Sariibrahimoglu, August 13, 2009).

Like many other countries, Russia thus makes frequent use of its eco-nomic means, especially in the energy sphere where it stands strong, to promote its economic interests. These are permeated with political concerns, handled as they are by top politicians. However, in general Russia is more dependent on the West than the latter is on Russia, and only with regard to the weaker CIS states has Russian economic power been fairly effective.

General conclusions

The policy doctrines cited in this chapter are primarily intended to guide Russian foreign policy, but they leave room for a very flexible implementation. The priorities are unclear, goals and means are mixed, and there are several contradictions, for instance between furthering Russian power abroad and good relations with neighbors. Support for Russians abroad is both a goal in itself and a powerful means to project Russian influence. The furthering of this aim in the post-Soviet space often collides with the principle of territorial integrity, evoking strong counterreactions and backfiring on the minorities.

Behind the often lofty principles, there is one common denominator in Russian foreign policy, namely, the proclaimed aim of increasing its international influence. Most important for Russia is to control the CIS region and keep NATO out of it. International recognition of Russia as a great power and the support for Russians abroad also serve the purpose of gaining domestic support for the political leadership in the Kremlin.

However, many of the CIS states and other neighbors see Russia as a *big* power, threatening their security and sovereignty, rather than as a benevolent great power. The Russian leaders seemingly find this very hard to understand.

In practice, the Russian political leadership conducts a pragmatic foreign policy, using its resources and upcoming opportunities ad hoc to the utmost. In international politics Russia continues to play a balancing game, exploiting splits among its partners. Instead of multilateral cooperation, it primarily relies on bilateral relations, in which it can prevail over weaker partners.

Russia has primarily used political means to achieve its goals, though it reserves the option to use military means, especially in the CIS, where its military power is overwhelming. It won an easy military victory against Georgia, though the political costs vis-à-vis the West were high, at least temporarily. In the early 2000s the main motive for using military means was to fight terrorism and separatism; after the Georgian war the protection of Russians abroad took the upper hand. Lacking attractive carrots in its foreign policy, Russia most often relies on sticks, but generally these have not been very effective.

Growing economic strength in the 2000s resulted in a more active and aggressive use of economic levers, especially in the energy field, where many EU and CIS neighbors depend on Russia. The control of pipelines is a powerful Russian lever, but this has also been met with countermeasures. In addition, Russia has been severely affected by the global economic crisis since 2008, and President Medvedev's growing stress on the need for modernization seems to push Russia to seek support mainly from the West. However, the fact that many CIS neighbors remain dependent on Russia and have been hit harder by the crisis invites continued Russian use of economic levers against them to win political and economic power.

References

Ashmore, William C. (2009) "Impact of alleged Russian Cyber Attacks", *Baltic Security and Defence Review*, vol. 11, pp. 4–40.

Barry, Ellen (June 22, 2010, "Russia trims gas over Belarus debts," *International Herald Tribune (IHT)*.

Blagov, Sergei (June 3, 2005) "Lavrov meets Chinese, Indian Counterparts", *Eurasia Daily Monitor (EDM)*, vol. 2, no. 108; www.jamestown.org

Felgenhauer, Pavel (September 11, 2008) "Moscow extends confrontation with the West to the Caribbean", *Eurasia Daily Monitor (EDM)*, vol. 5, no. 174.

Felgenhauer, Pavel (February 5, 2009) "A CSTO rapid-reaction force created as a NATO counterweight", *EDM*, vol. 6, no. 24.

Felgenhauer, Pavel (May 28, 2009) "Russia Skeptical on Imposing Sanctions Against North Korea", *EDM*, vol. 6, no. 102.

Felgenhauer, Pavel (September 17, 2009) "Venezuela's multibillion dollar Abkhazia and South Ossetia recognition fee", *EDM*, vol. 9, no. 170.

Felgenhauer, Pavel (December 10, 2009) "Russia removes constitutional constraints on military interventions abroad", *EDM*, vol. 6, no. 227.

Felgenhauer, Pavel (June 17, 2010) "Moscow caught unprepared by the carnage in the Ferghana valley", *EDM*, vol. 7, no. 117.

Hedenskog, Jakob (2004) *The Ukrainian Dilemma*, FOI-R-1199 – SE, Stockholm: Swedish Defence Research Agency (FOI).

Hedenskog, Jakob (2008) "Crimea after the Georgian Crisis", FOI-R 2587—SE.

Hedenskog, Jakob and Larsson, Robert L. (2007) *Russian Leverage on the CIS and the Baltic States*, FOI-R – 2280 – SE.

Hönneland, Geir (2009) "Cross-border cooperation in the North: the Case of Northwest Russia", in Elana Wilson Rowe, *Russia and the North*, Ottawa: University of Ottawa Press.

Interfax, June 14, 2008.

Jonson, Lena and Clive Archer, eds (1996) *Peacekeeping and the Role of Russia in Eurasia*, Boulder: Westview Press.

Klein, Margarete (2009) "Russia's Plan for a New Pan-European Security Regime", *Russian Analytical Digest*, no. 55, February 18, www.res.ethz.ch

Kontseptsiia vneshnei politiki Rossiiskoi Federatsii, Prezident Rossii. Offitsialnyi sait, July 12, 2008, www.kremlin.ru/text/docs/2008/07/204108.shtml (accessed August 11, 2008).

Korduban, Pavel (April 28, 2010) "Gas in exchange for naval base: a boon for Ukraine's weak economy", *EDM*, vol. 7, no. 82.

Kupchinsky, Roman (April 28, 2009) "Medvedev proposes a new 'energy balance' in Europe", *EDM*, vol. 9, no. 81.

Kvelashvili, Georgi (August 14, 2009) "Medvedev proposes legal mechanisms", *EDM*, no. 157.

Kvitsinsky, I. Shtodina (2007) "Today Kosovo, Tomorrow the World?", *International Affairs* (Moscow), no. 4.

Larsson, Robert L. (2006a) *Konfliktlösning i Kaukasien*, FOI-R – 2108 – SE, Stockholm: Swedish Defence Research Agency (FOI).

Larsson, Robert L. (2006b) *Russia's Energy Policy: Security Dimensions and Russia's Reliability as an Energy Supplier*, FOI-R – 1934 – SE.

Larsson, Robert L., ed. (2008) *Det kaukasiska lackmustestet*, FOI-R – 2563 – SE.

Leijonhielm, J. and Robert Larsson (2004) *Russia's Strategic Commodities: Energy and Metals as Security Levers*, Oslo: Swedish Defence Research Agency, FOI.

Lucas, Edward (2008) *The New Cold War*, London: Bloomsbury.

McDermott, Roger (April 28, 2009) "Manas scheduled to resume civilian status", *EDM*, vol. 6, no. 81.

McDermott, Roger (January 26, 2010) "Moscow boosts CSTO military dimension", *EDM*, vol. 7, no. 17.

McKeeby (August 28, 2008) "Russia's G8 partners condemn its role in Georgia Crisis", America.gov, www.america.gov/st/peacesec-english (accessed June 22, 2010).

Marples, David (August 7, 2009) "Lukashenko's gambit in relations with Moscow", *Eurasia Daily Monitor*, vol. 6, no. 152.

Marples, David (May 18, 2009) "Belarus participates in Eastern Partnership Inauguration", *EDM*, vol. 6, no. 95.

Medvedev, Dmitrii (June 5, 2008) "Speech at Meeting with German Political, Parliamentary and Civil Leaders", President of Russia website, www.president.kremlin.ru (accessed August 13, 2008).

Medvedev, Dmitrii (August 12, 2008) "Press statement following negotiations with French President Nicolas Sarkozy", ibid. (accessed August 13, 2008).

Medvedev, Dmitrii (August 19, 2008) "Nachalo vstrechi s Prezidentom Belorussii Aleksandrom Lukashenko", ibid. (accessed August 25, 2008).

Medvedev, Dmitrii (August 31, 2008) "Interview given by Dmitry Medvedev to Television Channels", ibid. (accessed September 4, 2008).

Medvedev, Dmitrii (September 2, 2008) "Interview with Television Channel Euronews", ibid. (accessed September 4, 2008).

Medvedev, Dmitrii (September 5, 2008) "A summit of the CSTO", "Press conference following the CSTO summit", ibid. (accessed September 8, 2008).

Medvedev, Dmitrii (October 8, 2008) "Speech at World Policy Conference", ibid. (accessed November 5, 2008).

Medvedev, Dmitrii (November 5, 2008) "Poslanie Federalnomu Sobraniiu Rossiiskoi Federatsii", ibid. (accessed November 5, 2008).

Medvedev, Dmitrii (March 29, 2009) "Interview with BBC", ibid. (accessed April 21, 2009).

Medvedev, Dmitrii (March 31, 2009) "Building Russian-U.S. bonds", ibid. (accessed April 21, 2009).

Medvedev, Dmitrii (May 22, 2009) "News conference following Russia-EU Summit", ibid. (accessed June 4, 2009).

Medvedev, Dmitrii (September 26, 2009) "News Conference following G20 Summit", ibid. (accessed October 5, 2009).

Medvedev, Dmitrii (November 27, 2009) "Answers to questions from Russian journalists", ibid. (accessed December 8, 2009).

Medvedev, Dmitrii (November 29, 2009) "European Security Treaty", President of Russia website, www.president.kremlin.ru (accessed December 8, 2009).

Medvedev, Dmitrii (April 8, 2010) "Joint news conference with US President Barack Obama", ibid. (accessed May 5, 2010).

Medvedev, Dmitrii (April 27, 2010) "Joint press conference with Prime Minister of Norway Jens Stoltenberg", ibid. (accessed May 5, 2010).

Medvedev, Dmitrii (May 17, 2010) "News conference following Russian-Ukrainian talks", ibid. (accessed May 25, 2010).

Meister, Stefan (2009) *Nach dem Gasstreit zwischen Russland und der Ukraine*, Berlin: Deutsche Gesellschaft für auswärtige Politik, no. 2.

Monaghan, Andrew (2008) "'An enemy at the gates' or 'from victory to victory' in Russian foreign policy", *International Affairs* (London), vol. 84, no. 4.

Möller, Karsten J. (2007) *CSTO, Collective Security Treaty Organisation*, Copenhagen: Danish Institute for International Studies.

Moscow News (2008) no. 34, p. 2.

NATO–Russia Council (December 17, 2009) "NATO Secretary General holds talks with Russian leaders", www.nato-russia-council.info/htm/EN/news_49. shtml (accessed December 22, 2009).

Nuclear power in Russia (2010) World Nuclear Association, www.world-nuclear. org (accessed January 20, 2010).

Oldberg, Ingmar (2006) *The War on Terrorism in Russian Foreign Policy*, FOI-R – 2155 – SE.

Oldberg, Ingmar (2007a) *The Shanghai Cooperation Organisation – Powerhouse or Paper Tiger?* FOI-R – 2301 – SE, June.

Oldberg, Ingmar (2007b) "Rysk-baltiska gränskonflikter och historiens betydelse", in Johan Dietsch *et al.*(eds), *Historia mot strömmen. Kultur och konflikt i det moderna Europa*, Stockholm: Carlssons.

Oldberg, Ingmar (2009) "The changing military importance of the Kaliningrad region", *Journal of Slavic Military Studies*, vol. 22, no. 3.

"Osnovy gosudarstvennoi politiki Rossiiskoi Federatsii v Arktike", Sovet Bezopasnosti Rossiiskoi Federatsii, www.scrf.gov.ru/documents/99.html (accessed June 1, 2009).

Putin, Vladimir (April 25, 2005) "Poslanie Federalnomu sobraniju Rossiiskoi Federatsii", Prezident Rossii website, www.president.kremlin.ru (accessed May 2, 2005).

Putin, Vladimir (July 8, 2005) "Meeting with Russian and foreign media following the G-8 summit", ibid. (accessed August 30, 2005).

Putin, Vladimir (August 29, 2008) "Interviu Predsedatelia Pravitelstva RF V.V. Putina", Internet-Portal Pravitelstva Rossiiskoi Federatsii, www. government.ru (accessed September 2, 2008).

RIA Novosti, August 18, 2008.

Roth, Mathias (2009) *Bilateral Disputes between EU Member States and Russia*, Brussels: CEPS Working Document, no. 319.

Sariibrahimoglu, Lale (August 13, 2009) "Turkey and Russia renew bilateral confidence", *EDM*, no. 156.

Sergeev, Mikhail (2009) "Kremlevskii arshin dlia 'Bolshoi dvatsatki'", *Nezavisimaia gazeta*, March 17.

Socor, Vladimir (May 28, 2009) "Sochi agreements and aftermath deflate South Stream hype", *EDM*, vol. 6, no. 102.

Socor, Vladimir (October 23, 2009) "Samsun – Ceyhan pipeline project designed to divert Kasakhstani oil", ibid., vol. 6, no. 195.

Socor, Vladimir (December 18 and 19, 2009) "Strategic implications of the Central Asia-China gas pipeline", *EDM*, nos. 230 and 231.

Socor, Vladimir (January 5, 2010) "Moscow using oil export duty to pressure Belarus", *EDM*, vol. 7, no. 2.

Socor, Vladimir (January 7, 2010) "Iran and Turkmenistan inaugurate gas pipeline", *EDM*, vol. 7, no. 4.

Socor, Vladimir (February 9, 2010) "Stokman gas project postponed: Implications for Russia, Europe and the US", *EDM*, vol. 7, no 27.

Der Spiegel (2008) no. 36.

Strategiia natsionalnoi bezopasnosti Rossiiskoi Federatsii do 2020 goda, Sovet Bezopasnosti Rossiiskoi Federatsii, www.scrf.gov.ru/documents/99.html, accessed May 14, 2009.

Swirtz, Michael (June 23, 2010) "Tensions rise as Belarus and Russia feud over gas", *IHT*.

"Towards a United Europe without Divides" (2007) *International Affairs* (Moscow) no. 2.

3
Russian Modernization Pathways: Foreign Policy Implications

Graeme P. Herd

Introduction

The term "sovereign democracy," which entered Russia's political lexicon in mid-2005, had by late 2007 become the unifying ideology of the ruling United Russia party – now headed by Prime Minister Putin himself. Its advocates within the presidential administration argued that a sovereign democratic state in the international system was politically and economically ("financial sovereignty") independent thanks to both a strong military and state control over key strategic economic assets. Throughout the two terms of the Putin presidential administration, a dominant progressive narrative held that Russia had reemerged from the chaos and disorder of the 1990s as one of a handful of centers of global power and influence. This reflected both larger global processes and strong leadership within the state.

The redistribution of power and resources within the international system created a "democratic multipolar" world. Analysts of international order have argued that the transition from a bipolar world in the Cold War to a unipolar moment post-Cold War has been crowned by an era of nonpolarity, where power is diffuse – "a world dominated not by one or two or even several states but rather by dozens of actors possessing and exercising various kinds of power" (Haass, 2008). Highlighting the emergence of an "interpolar" world – defined as "multipolarity in an age of interdependence" – managing existential interdependence in an unstable multipolar world is the key (Grevi, 2009). Under such conditions, the previous durable, tolerable hegemony exercised by a single state – the US – is understood to be "decreasingly sustainable" (Clark, 2009). Russia is understood, as a reemerging center of global power, to constitute one of the independent poles. As such it promotes multilateralism and a value-free (or "nonideological") foreign policy based on pragmatic interest, tacit realpolitik quid pro quos and the logic of market transactions (Herd, 2009).

In 2008 the stresses, strains, and outright contradictions between the rhetoric of this foreign policy narrative and the reality of Russian practice were already apparent, not least in terms of a "globalist–isolationist dichotomy" (*Gazeta.ru*, 2008). Russia is presented both as an independent center of global influence, evidenced by its nuclear United Nations Security Council Permanent Five status, and as having a preeminent managerial and order-producing role within Eurasian and post-Soviet space. This is an open, self-confident, and globalist narrative, underpinned by a notion of Russia as a strong and natural regional hegemon and center of global influence. At the same time, Russia also presents itself towards its own public as an embattled state, surrounded by external enemies bent on undermining its sovereignty and territorial integrity, whether through color revolutions, NATO expansion to post-Soviet space, Ballistic Missile Defence sites, or military bases in Central Asia. This is an inward, self-fulfilling and isolationist narrative strain. The Georgia crisis itself highlighted the contradiction between Russia's promotion of "sovereign democracy" as an ideal standard to be emulated by states that wished to be considered subjects rather than objects ("satellite" or "cloned" states with no independent control over their foreign and security policy processes) in international affairs, and its insistence on and enforcement of object status for states in its near neighborhood (the application of a doctrine of limited sovereignty).

The tensions and contradictions inherent in the application of sovereign democracy ideology in the domestic sphere found full voice during the recent financial crisis. Given that this crisis highlighted underlying domestic institutional, structural, and systemic tensions within the Russian Federation, its impact on the internal coherence of a sovereign democracy ideology was much more destabilizing and profound than the impact of the Georgia crisis itself on the foreign policy and international dimension. This crisis focused attention on Russia's dependence on a raw-material export-based economy, the pervasive effect of corruption (particularly on inward investment), and, most importantly, the claim by the self-enclosed status quo elite that performance matters more than procedural legitimacy. The social contract so characteristic of Russia's "sovereign democracy" – in essence an unspoken quid quo pro by which citizens support the current regime and its manipulation of the political system in return for increased prosperity – was brought into question. Public trust in the government's ability to manage the fallout of the financial crisis withered, as popular dissatisfaction and social unrest increased in response to rising food price increases and growing unemployment. Could the Russian government continue to deliver its part of the bargain, or was political change necessary?

The use of state funds by the Kremlin (presidential administration) and the White House (prime minister's office) to reward favoured oligarchs and allies, and to punish others by withholding funds, was complicated by two competing responses to the crisis, which could be characterised as "globalized Russia" and "besieged fortress." The first, led by Finance Minister Kudrin and apparently supported by President Medvedev, looked to macroeconomic stability, improving the investment climate by increasing business confidence and structural reform, and further integration into the global economy as the touchstone of economic recovery. Allowing free-market principles to determine winners and losers of the crisis would in effect promote political pluralism and extend, rather than further enclose, Russia's elite – a "reshuffling of the same deck of cards" to use President Medvedev's analogy – as "new blood" infused the political system. In opposition are statist "patriotic" military-security clans led by Igor Sechin, an influential deputy prime minister with a security service background, whose overriding impulse appears to be to consolidate a resurgent state at home through the purchase of distressed assets from the last vestiges of independent oligarchs, and where possible (for example, in Cuba, Nicaragua, Kyrgyzstan, and Venezuela) to buy strategic loyalty abroad. Making government loans available to specific oligarchs with terms and conditions that tie the oligarch closer to the state through the creation of monopolistic state conglomerates, and a consolidation of the banking sector by allowing some banks to fail and acquiring others, help to expand official state political and operational control over Russia's economy. De facto renationalization creates a more powerful institutionalized core state, albeit one that is inflexible and unresponsive and so, ultimately, unsustainable.

This debate over the best policy response to the financial crisis was transformed through 2009 and into 2010 by a wider and more fundamental questioning of the nature of Russian identity and future existence, by the preferred nature of Russia's modernization paradigm – whether to adopt democratic or conservative modernization. This debate has been shaped by two competing policy pathways, each questioned by a central dilemma inherent within its framing. Conservative modernization promises political stability and economic development in the short term, but might this lead to institutional and systemic paralysis and stagnation over the longer term? Democratic modernization promises economic development via political renewal over the longer term, but would the short-term political upheaval and disruption weaken the Russian state and derail this project?

This chapter first outlines the key contentions of the status quo conservative modernization pathway, before turning to identifying and analyzing the alternative democratic modernization possibility. Second, it identifies the challenges, obstacles, and dilemmas that opponents of each pathway suggest cannot be overcome or bridged and would thus lead to stagnation or collapse. Third, it concludes by identifying the lack of internal push factors for democratic modernization, as well as the presence of pull factors, not least the EU and Europeanization tendencies, and the lack of viable alternative pathways. It argues that growing dissonance between Russian foreign policy "democratic world order" rhetoric and the reality of its own internal governance is set to increase, as Russian elites accept the status quo – conservative modernization is here to stay.

Democratic or conservative modernization?

By late 2009, a series of speeches by President Medvedev reformulated the debate over necessary policy responses to the financial crisis into something much more profound and philosophical – the sustainability of Russia's current governance model and its preferred longer-term modernization paradigm. On September 10, 2009 President Medvedev published a remarkably frank article entitled "Russia, Forward!" This article noted that Russia's governance model appeared to be failing, proving vulnerable in the face of the global financial crisis. President Medvedev himself criticized Russia's "humiliating" dependence on raw materials, as well as its "inefficient economy, a semi-Soviet social sphere, an immature democracy, negative demographic trends, unstable Caucasus" (Medvedev, 2009a). In his November 12, 2009 Message to the Federal Assembly, President Medvedev went on to elaborate this theme further, noting that Russia could either modernize or deteriorate, and argued that modernization would provide a touchstone for "how we can overcome our chronic backwardness, dependence on raw materials exports, and corruption" (Medvedev, 2009b).

On November 24, 2009 Sergey Guriyev, rector of the Russian Economic School and Morgan Stanley professor, and Oleg Tsyvinskiy, a professor at Yale University and the Russian Economic School, wrote a scathing assessment of the utility of performance legitimacy following the death of the lawyer Sergey Magnitskiy in prison after being refused medical treatment – "What difference does it make if the RTS [Russian Trading System] rises or falls, or what happens to interest rates or the exchange rate, if our lives are worth nothing? Is it worth talking about the professional elite that might support modernization? Is it worth talking about fulfilling contracts, if the opposite party takes lawyers hostage? Is it worth discussing to what extent ownership rights are protected, if the owner has no right to life?" (Guriyev and Tsyvinskiy, 2009). On February 3, 2010, the *Institute for Contemporary Development* (INSOR) published a report that received widespread coverage, entitled *21st Century Russia: The Image of Tomorrow We Want*. As President Medvedev had created INSOR in 2008 to give him independent advice on economic and foreign policy, and Medvedev was a trustee on the board of the Institute, this report received widespread publicity. Such publicity was magnified as the report touched just about every exposed nerve by advocating that Russia should join NATO, end censorship, abolish the state security service, and adopt a Western-style democracy, entailing the separation of the courts from the state, of the legislative branch from the executive, and horizontal modernization (characterized as the de-bureaucratization of the vertical top-down corrupt, overregulated, and bureaucratic economic process) (Goltz *et al.*, 2010). Without change, Russia faced a strategic cul de sac that would lead to slow and steady strategic marginalization: "In a few years, when it turns out that Russia has nothing to boast about except export supplies of raw materials at prices that are dictated to us, we will be exporting people. And, not only the cleverest like now, but any workers, who are in demand in Europe, as is happening today in Latvia, for example. I frankly do not know what Russia should do in this situation. This problem will be one of the main ones for the president who is elected in 2012" (Kulikov, 2010).

In the wake of the "Forward Russia" article back in September 2009, a debate over the nature of Russian modernization occurred at the elite level between "democratic" and "conservative" modernizers. Before examining each proposition in turn, it is worth noting two areas of common agreement. First, "forced" or "authoritarian" modernization was not to be countenanced as a viable option, whether in its Tsarist or Soviet variant. As President Dmitry Medvedev stated: "I think all enforced modernizations are in the past" (RIA Novosti, 2009). Boris Gryzlov, chairman of the United Russia Party Supreme Council and chairman of the State Duma, agreed: "For us, the appeals to repeat modernization of the 'Stalinist type' – with mass repressions and numerous casualties, the modernization that took place in the USSR and certain other states – are unacceptable" (Gryzlov, 2009; Makarkin, 2010). Andrey Isayev, first deputy secretary of the United Russia general council presidium, reinforced this understanding: "Today, in assessing the varied experience in modernization, we can say that radical modernization is always accompanied by revolutionary explosions and broken human lives" (cited in Bilevskaya, 2009). Second, both sides of the debate agreed that the economic aspect of modernization should focus on technological innovation: "Unless we take measures to switch to a modern high-tech economy, we will never be able to cope with outdated technology or drastically change our economy, and then we will depend more on the cyclicality of the global economy" (RIA Novosti, 2009). Yevgeniy Gontmakher, a well-known economist and member of the INSOR management board, argued that: "The key lies in unshackling private initiative and freedom of enterprise. That is because innovations, their development, implementation, proliferation and, especially, export – if Russia really wants to be a strong country in that respect – are not a problem the state has to occupy itself with. The state should not be doing much more than just watching all of this very discreetly" (Centre TV, 2009).

However, there were also clear differences in approach – will modernization be led by a "Russian Erhard," a "Russian Deng Xiaoping," or a "Russian Lee Kuan Yew"? The advocates of "democratic modernization" argue that the sine qua non of sustainable modernization in Russia is political liberalization. Political liberalization is needed to overcome a status quo bureaucracy by introducing accountability and transparency to the decision-making process. As the mechanism for distributing public benefits is political, serious political change must occur before the economy can be modernized. The political economy is the key, as former Prime Minister Yevegeny Primakov noted: "The success of economic modernization in Russia depends to a large extent on the creation of the kind of political party system that would help the authorities to avoid erroneous decisions. A characteristic feature of such a system is party pluralism. Its normal development in Russia is being obstructed by two factors: The ruthless control from above directing the processes of party organizational development and the administrative clout that the strongest of the parties, United Russia, enjoys to an incomparably greater extent than other parties…; the creation of a mono-centric party and state system, even if there are many parties in the political arena, blocks the democratic process" (Primakov, 2010). This sentiment was echoed by the presidium of the opposition Russian People's Democratic Union, led by former Prime Minister Mikhail Kasyanov, who agreed that social and economic modernization in Russia would be impossible without changes in society and the political system: "Any actions to modernize the country must primarily envisage removing censorship and opening up the information space and all kinds of media, abolishing restrictions in order to ensure independent political activities, including freedom to establish and register political parties, to immediately establish the institution of free and honest elections as a fundamental institution for the power of the people" (Interfax, 2009b). The head of "A Just Russia Party," Sergei Mironov, noted that social conflict could be avoided by real political competition, as this acts as a safety valve, and the leader of the Yabloko Party, Sergei Mitrokhin, stated that modernization must begin with free media, which entailed ending the government monopoly of national media and its ability to censor content (Fedynsky, 2010; *Nezavisimaya Gazeta*, 2010). Although its proponents recognize that democratization efforts would be destabilizing in the short term, they argue that, without political liberalization and competition to replace clan consensus, not only will the institution of the presidency fail to function, but also real conflict will erupt in the longer term (Busygina and Filippov, 2010; Gontmakher, 2009; Shusharin, 2009).

The ruling United Russia party has been the leading advocate for the ideology of "sovereign democracy," and on the occasion of its eleventh Congress, held at the Lenekspo exhibition centre in St Petersburg in December 2010, the party embraced Russian conservatism and "conservative modernization." "Conservative modernization," according to Andrey Isayev, first deputy secretary of the United Russia general council presidium, represents a new stage in the eight-year ideological evolution of the United Russia party. Andrey Vorobyev, head of the party machine, noted that "Russian conservatism has become the logical continuation of the idea of sovereign democracy" (Bilevskaya, 2009). Boris Gryzlov argues that Russia's development must adopt a balanced and conservative approach to modernization – in essence, stability should be the watchword and "preserve and multiply" the slogan. He suggested that the framework of conservatism is more consistent, reliable, and effective in addressing the tasks of modernization than "other ideologies that are represented in our political spectrum" which "lack attention to the national interests of Russia, to the traditions of Russia" (Grzylov, 2009).[1]

Gryzlov characterizes conservatism as "the ideology of stability and development, the constant creative renewal of society without stagnation or revolutions" (Makarkin, 2009). Mikhail Remizov, director of the National Strategy Institute, argued that the main principle of Russian conservatism should be: "Create the new, while preserving the main thing, while preserving what makes us what we are" (Bilevskaya, 2009). Boris Makarenko, chairman of the Political Technologies Centre Management Board, argues that political analysts close to United Russia define "conservative modernization" as "conservative in terms of its content, nonviolent in terms of its methods, and democratic from the viewpoint of reliance on long-established national democratic institutions" (Orlov, Badovskiy and Vinogradov, 2010). "Conservative modernization" is thus presented as a gradualist and organic development, which, in the words of the Chief Editor of Ekspert magazine, V. Fadeyev (2009–10), represents "the very kind of conservative modernization that does not destroy the fundamental structures of the life of society." Vladislav Surkov, instigator of the concept of "sovereign democracy," now elaborated his vision of modernization in terms of "consolidated modernization," as antidote to "spontaneous" modernization, which opened the way to chaos and confusion: "Some people call this authoritarian modernization. It is all the same to me what they call it" (cited in Skobov, 2010).

First Vice Premier Igor Shuvalov reinforced this analysis when he stated: "We need the kind of modernization that must not exceed the threshold of normal losses. Otherwise all of this will mean for all of us a factor of high social instability that will cause this entire venture to culminate in a new wave [of instability]" (cited in *Vedomosti,* 2010). Accordingly, "conservative modernization" avoids the dangers of unmanaged democratization that led to chaos in the "wild '90s," characterized by "shock therapy privatization," delays in wage and pension payments, as well as the default of 1998: "the clever globalist interpretation of modernization – which calls for forgetting our own history and opening up the economy to global corporations, and in fact to place it under the control of other states – is unacceptable" (Grzylov, 2009).

However, "conservative modernization" is not without its detractors, not least those advocating "democratic modernization" as a viable alternative, who argue "Russia has fallen into a historical trap" and therefore "needs to make another modernising leap forward, but it faces doing so in conditions where too much is disposed towards inertia and decay" (Goltz *et al.*, 2010). On the twenty-fifth anniversary of perestroika, former Soviet President Mikhail Gorbachev remarked: "Russia will only advance with confidence if it follows a democratic path. Recently, there have been a number of setbacks in this regard. The democratic process has lost momentum; in more ways than one, it has been rolled back. All major decisions are taken by the executive branch; parliament just gives formal approval. The independence of the courts has been thrown into question. We do not have a party system that would enable a real majority to win while also taking the minority opinion into account and allowing an active opposition. There is a growing feeling that the government is afraid of civil society and would like to control everything" (Gorbachev, 2010; Samarina and Tsvetkova, 2010). Yevgeny Primakov identifies a key challenge to modernization as "the inertial thinking of extremely influential circles that insist that the main oil importers are gradually emerging from the recession and oil prices are stabilizing at a pretty high-level. In their opinion, continuing the course of preferentially supporting the major raw-material companies will recreate the favourable pre-crisis situation that contributed to the growth of GDP and the prosperity of the population in Russia" (Badovskiy, 2009a; Latynina, 2009; Primakov, 2010). In other words, the current rent-extraction model allows both the state bureaucracy and state oligarchs to use the mantra of political stability to preserve a status quo that enables them to enrich themselves through the control of resource distribution.[2] Elites will therefore not embrace anything but a conservative modernization paradigm. The political analyst Stanislav Belkovskiy is explicit on this point, arguing that for the Russian political elite democratic modernization "is definitely not needed for calm and quiet embezzlement of state billions, because in case of democratization the society can ask the ruling elite: where has the money gone, and where are the results of modernization?" Rather, the political elite "intends to use the term exclusively for its own opportunistic purposes connected to business. For the ruling elite of contemporary Russia modernization is a way to withdraw from the budget and budgetary funds a certain amount of billions of dollars for various projects of different degrees of adventurism and to embezzle these billions" (Ekho Moskvy, 2010). This view is shared by Avtandil Tsuladze: "Everyone knows that the corrupt bureaucracy is the main obstacle impeding the actual modernization of the country. This bureaucracy in its present form is Putin's main support beam, however. He offered the bureaucracy a programme of simulated modernization with completely tangible financial prospects and the promise of personnel stability" (Tsuladze, 2009a).[3] Anton Orekh, a prominent commentator on Ekho Moskvy radio, concludes that, due to the strength of such entrenched interests, "real modernization will only begin on the day when the last drop of oil is extracted from swampy Siberia" and major gas deposits run out in Russia. Under these circumstances, "modernization will have to be effected quickly and it will have to be forced" (Ekho Moskvy, 2009a).

Interestingly, both supporters and detractors of conservative modernization look to China to validate their positions. Supporters of conservative modernization argue that China has managed a large-scale economic modernization process with a single party system and while maintaining strict political control and internal stability. Advocates of democratic modernization, particularly INSOR Director Igor Jurgens, have been vocal in arguing that the debate about whether the USSR could follow the Chinese variant, or whether the Russian Federation could follow the Chinese variant, is pointless. Jurgens notes that the Soviet economy surged before economic development ran into the bottleneck of making large-scale political and national decisions. This is still to come for China, as is the challenge of maintaining stability, while around 700 million Chinese in Western China live without social security, pension provision, and central medical services. Moreover, even if China were to prove successful over the longer term and avoid the Soviet fate after seventy years (in 2019), China, unlike the multinational and multi-confessional Russian Federation, is a more mono-ethnic state (Han Chinese constitute 92% of the population, with 8% represented by 55 minority groups), with its own historical traditions and political culture. A Chinese model of conservative modernization is not a viable option.[4]

Conclusions

As Russia looks forward, potential non-European strategic partnerships to balance US power appear limited. Brazil, Russia, India, and China (the BRIC states) represented fast-growing developing countries, which were predicted in 2003 to form a powerful economic grouping that would surpass the share of global GDP of rich democratic states (the US and EU) by 2050, if not sooner (Goldman Sachs, 2003). With the financial crisis, it was argued that this prediction had been validated: the standing of the US and Europe as a credible model has been weakened; creditor autocracies now enjoy greater influence over and independence from debtor democracies and are less constrained in their behavior; protectionism, resource nationalism, and the weakening of core alliances all testify to the reassertion of state control over economies and societies. However, the notion that the BRIC states are unified and have the ability, as potential global powers, to balance the US is questionable. While BRICs are large, and may have shared the experience of high economic growth and relative economic backwardness, they have distinctive cultural and historical trajectories, as well as domestic political systems, economic development and structure, location, and interests (Cookson, 2010; Foot, 2009–10; Hurrel, 2007). These states may share uncertainty over US hegemony, but in practice they band together to improve their negotiating position with the US rather than balancing it. Thus, despite the foreign and security policy rhetoric coming out of Beijing, Brasilia, New Delhi, and Moscow, in reality multilateral global governance is only supported practically when it is in their interests – strategic mistrust and rivalry predominate. Will China, for example, ever support India's efforts to become a UN Security Council permanent member? When analysing Great Power involvement in the G8, G20 and UNSC, the status of their membership appears to be more important than their active participation leading to constructive outcomes. These emergent centers of global power privilege regional organizations (where they have a voice and a veto) above global bodies.

It is clear, therefore, that the modernization debate in Russia is here to stay, kindled by performance legitimacy questioning and elite continuity pressures. United Russia Party representatives have tried to bridge the gap between President Medvedev's rhetoric (democratic modernization) and stated intent and the current reality and the stated ideological preferences on which it is based (conservative modernization), with an uneasy hybrid formula "for stability and for development" and the "constant creative renewal of society without stagnation or revolution" (Badovskiy, 2009b).

Some analysts have argued that this debate about modernization paradigms cloaks a deep-seated, fundamental, and strategic division over Russia's future pathway at the very top of Russia's governance structure, with President Medvedev championing democratic modernization, while Prime Minister Putin upholds the conservative variant (Whitmore, 2010). While the fat years spawned the "Putin consensus" and golden stagnation, "the thin years are necessitating the abandonment of the mythology of 'nationwide unity', reawakening the late-perestroika struggle between 'progressive reformers' and the 'reactionary majority'" (Ikhlov, 2010).

Others argue, rather, that this debate reflects a more sophisticated and coordinated division of labor at work within the tandem that hitherto was identified as: "Mr. Medvedev is the good cop who talks up modernization, meets human-rights groups and negotiates nuclear-arms treaties with America's Barack Obama. Mr. Putin, the bad cop, runs Russia and distributes the money, as he made clear in the recent conference of his United Russia party" (*Economist,* 2009; Tsuladze, 2009b).

Mikhail Afanasyev, the Strategies and Analysis Director of the Nikkolo M Political Consulting Centre, notes two interpretations of INSOR. Is it a strategic laboratory under the President or "a sort of PR-agency for positioning the president as the transformer of Russia in the eyes of the West and of our progressive community?" (Afanasyev, 2010; Lipman, 2010). Andrey Illarionov, a well-known economist and former advisor to Putin, takes an even more questioning stance: "In recent months, the following story has become quote popular: There are two camps in the Russian leadership, Putin's and Medvedev's; the question is, which camp Medvedev belongs to. In actual fact, the mystery of the year is a slightly different question: is Mr. Medvedev part of the state leadership at all?" (Ekho Moskvy, 2009b). Still another interpretation looks to President Medvedev's limitations, if not sincerity: "One of Medvedev's chief shortcomings lies in one of his merits: He is a lawyer, and unlike Putin, a real one. And, lawyers are normativists, after all; they work with the environment that already exists. They are least of all inclined to change something seriously. Only the fifth sub-clause of Article Six of Paragraph Eight of the subordinate legislation of the agency for the oversight of the watermelon-casting industry [sic]" (Kolesnikov, 2010).

Russia's trajectory is shaped by the inertia of the past coupled with "stagnation" elites and risk-averse oligarchies with a vested interest in maintaining the current distribution and exercise of power, privilege, and wealth. In the final analysis, however, status quo continuity is underpinned by the strength of the Putin majority relative to the weakness of the Medvedev minority is viewed as critical to the adoption of conservative rather than democratic modernization. The "Medvedev minority" "is a minority of under 20 per cent" that "includes the classical middle class, which has shrunk to 7 per cent of the population. These are people with all of its indicators: They have something to protect; they put away money in banks; they care about their health and the health of their children; they think about a better education for their children; they must continue to work and save for this; and they are not indifferent to what will happen tomorrow, the day after tomorrow, and so forth. Small business is joining in this – perhaps not in a politically articulated manner, but instinctively" (Piontkovskiy, 2009). In other words, an internal bottom-up push generated through indigenous popular support for the adoption of a democratic modernization pathway is lacking. At the same time, external dynamic factors – not least the Europeanizing pressures emanating from the European Union, Russia's largest trading partner – pull in the opposite direction. The idea of "Europe" encapsulates three overlapping notions – territory, a set of particular norms and values, and a postmodern political construct. Russia is by geography part of a Europe that stretches from the Atlantic to the Urals. EU states, elites, and societies have acculturated democratic liberal norms and values, and this process has been driven by EU enlargement. The European Commission has prepared and presented to Moscow its project entitled "Partnership for modernization:" "If we proceed from the classic definition of modernization – that is, building a modern society in a certain country – then, naturally, it presupposes Europeanisation of Russia, and Europeanisation certainly presupposes democratization" (Ekho Moskvy, 2010). In response, Medvedev welcomed and extolled the virtues of the free exchanges of goods, services, and people, but not political liberalization. We share interests more than values, seems to be the message. Thus, Russia acknowledges its European cultural heritage and its affinity with the Westphalian model of a Europe of nation-states, but not the value-normative dimension. While Russia relates to an imagined Europe of the past, the EU relates to Russia as a prospective but dependent partner in the future. We can postulate that the more quickly Russia recovers from the financial crisis, the more marginal the pressures for structural reform, the greater the prospects for conservative modernization, the less democratic, and hence European, its strategic outlook will be. The tension generated between these competing internal and external pressures will only grow, and it will become more likely that Russia's foreign policy coherence, particularly with regards to its European Security Treaty, is undermined.

Notes

1. Gryzlov (2009) continues: "Modernization of Russia must be based on conservative values. These are patriotism, family values, historical memory, respect for traditions, a healthy and growing nation, guarantees of private property, and a respect for the law. It is accord between people of different nationalities and different religious beliefs. It is a sense of responsibility for one's own fate, one's own family, a sense of responsibility for the future of one's own country. And already such a sense of responsibility demands consistent, carefully thought out decisions. It demands planning of development. If we do not plan, that means others will plan for us."
2. "As Russia's political and economic models are inextricably intertwined, changes to power distribution in one destabilises the other and obstacles to change in one are rooted in the other. This means that the system of power is inflexible and carries in its design built-in resistance to change. It appears zero-sum – political loss translates into economic loss and vice versa – and this dynamic must add powerfully to status quo forces and conservatism in

Russia" (Herd, 2009, p. 20). "With all the intellectual squalor of the theo-reticians of 'sovereign democracy,' 'conservative modernization,' and other oxymorons, their consistency of thought and action cannot be denied them. This consistency is, of course, of a purely instinctive, reflex nature, but at the end of the day that is how any primitive organism striving to exist in the most favourable conditions of survival for itself behaves. It is, for example, like that tadpole which you can in no way extract from the bog and which at the genetic level has an interest in preserving the bog" (Tumanov, 2010; *Vedomosti*, 2009).

3. Avtandil Tsuladze, "United Russia in its own juices", Yezhednevnyy Zhurnal website, Moscow (in Russian), November 23, 2009. http://www.ej.ru/?a=archive&date=2009–11-23 [accessed June 21, 2010].

4. Extracts from interview with Igor Yurgens, director of the Russian Institute of Contemporary Development, by Andrey Barabanov and Vladimir Vorsobin are available on radio Komsomolskaya Pravda website, Moscow (in Russian), February 16, 2010. http://www.kp.ru/daily/24442/ [accessed June 21, 2010].

References

Afanasyev, Mikhail (2010) "Strategy is not ordered", *Gazeta.ru* website, Moscow (in Russian), February 15. http://gazeta.ru/archive.shtml?article=1&page=2&start=15.02.2010n (accessed June 22, 2010).

Badovskiy, Dmitriy (2009a) "The Modernization of Russia: Again at a Crossroads", *Russia in Global Affairs*, Vol. 7, No. 3, May–June, p. 30.

Badovskiy, Dmitriy (2009b) "Medvedev's orbit", *Gazeta.ru* website, Moscow (in Russian), November 24. http://www.gazeta.ru/archive.shtml?start=24.11.2009&article=1 (accessed June 22, 2010).

Bilevskaya, Elina (2009) "World standards of conservatism", *Nezavisimaya Gazeta* website, Moscow (in Russian), December 2. http://www.ng.ru/gazeta/2009-12-02/ (accessed 22 June 2010).

Busygina, Irina and Mikhail, Filippov (2010) "Democratization Is Not Cost-Free", *Vedomosti*, February 10. http://www.vedomosti.ru/newspaper/2010/02/10 (accessed June 22, 2010).

Centre TV (2009) Centre TV, Moscow (in Russian), November 25. "Senior member of Medvedev's think tank says free enterprise key to modernization." BBC Monitoring Former Soviet Union – Political: Supplied by BBC Worldwide Monitoring.

Clark, Ian (2009) "Bringing Hegemony Back in: The United States and International Order", *International Affairs*, vol. 85, no. 1, January, pp. 23–36.

Cookson, Clive (2010) "Bric nations see big shifts in scientific landscape", *Financial Times*, January 26, p. 3.

The Economist (2009) "Dmitry Medvedev's Building Project: Russian Modernization", *The Economist* (US Edition), November 28.

Ekho Moskvy radio (2009a) Moscow (in Russian), December 24. "Russian independent radio questions Medvedev's message of modernization". BBC Monitoring Former Soviet Union – Political: Supplied by BBC Worldwide Monitoring.

Ekho Moskvy radio (2009b) Moscow (in Russian), December 29. "Putin's ex-adviser says Russian modernization equals Stalinism". BBC Monitoring Former Soviet Union – Political: Supplied by BBC Worldwide Monitoring.

Ekho Moskvy radio (2010) Moscow (in Russian), February 11. "Russian elite intends to use 'modernization' to embezzle funds – pundit". BBC Monitoring Former Soviet Union – Political: Supplied by BBC Worldwide Monitoring.

Fadeyev, V. (2009–10) "Becoming a Nation That Is Worth Something", *Ekspert* No. 1 (687), December 28 – January 10.

Fedynsky, Peter (2010) "Kremlin Says Modernization Requires Political Competition", *Voice of America News*, January 22. http://www1.voanews.com/english/news/europe/Kremlin-Says-Modernization-Requires-Political-Competition-82399647.html (accessed June 22, 2010).

Foot, Rosemary (2009–10) "China and the United States: Between Cold War and Cold Peace", *Survival*, Vol. 51, No. 6, December–January, pp. 123–46.

Gazeta.ru (2008) Editorial, "Russia foreign policy seen suffering from globalist-isolationist dichotomy", *Gazeta.ru* website, January 9. http://www.gazeta.ru/archive.shtml?stripe=comments&start=09.01.2008&article=1 (accessed June 22, 2010).

Goldman Sachs (2003) "Dreaming with BRICs: The Path to 2050", *Global Economics Paper*, no. 99. http://www2.goldmansachs.com/ideas/brics/book/99-dreaming.pdf (accessed June 22, 2010).

Goltz, Alexander Yevgeny, Gontmakher, Leonid Grigoriev, Sergey Kulik, Boris Makarenko, Nikita Maslennikov, Sergey Plaksin, Alexander Rubtsov, Elena Shatalova and Igor Yurgens (2010) "Russia in the 21st Century: Vision for the Future", Abridged Report, Institute of Contemporary Development, January, pp. 1–22. http://www.insor-russia.ru/files/INSOR%20Russia%20in%20the%2021st%20century_ENG.pdf (accessed June 22, 2010).

Gontmakher, Yevgeniy (2009) "Political economy: Task for boss", *Vedomosti* website, Moscow (in Russian), November 20. http://www.izvestia.ru/archive/20–11-09/?2 (accessed June 22, 2010).

Gorbachev, Mikhail (2010) "Perestroika, 25 years later", *The International Herald Tribune*, March 13, p. 6.

Grevi, Giovanni (2009) *The interpolar world: a new scenario*, EU-ISS Occasional Paper No. 79. http://www.iss.europa.eu/nc/actualites/actualite/browse/6/article/the-interpolar-world-a-new-scenario/ (accessed June 22, 2010).

Gryzlov, Boris (2009) "To preserve and multiply: conservatism and moderniza-tion", *Izvestiya* website, Moscow (in Russian), December 1. http://www.izvestia.ru/archive/01–12-09/ (accessed June 22, 2010).

Guriyev, Sergey and Oleg Tsyvinskiy (2009) "Ratio economica: Modernization '37", *Vedomosti* website, Moscow (in Russian), November 24. http://www.vedomosti.ru/newspaper/2009/11/24 (accessed June 22, 2010).

Haass, Richard N. (2008) "The Age of Nonpolarity: What will Follow US Dominance?", *Foreign Affairs* 87, no. 3, pp. 44–56.

Herd, Graeme P. (2009) "Russia's Sovereign Democracy: Interests, Identity and Instrumentalisation?", in Roger E. Kanet (ed.), *A Resurgent Russia and the West: The European Union, NATO and Beyond*. Dordrecht, The Netherlands: Republic of Letters Press, pp. 3–28.

Hurrel, Andrew (2007) "One World? Many Worlds? The Place of Regions in the Study of International Relations", *International Affairs*, Vol. 83, No. 1, pp. 127–46.

Ikhlov, Yevgeniy (2010) "Conspiracy of non-equals", *Yezhednevnyy Zhurnal* website, Moscow (in Russian), January 30. http://www.ej.ru/?a=archive&date=2010-1-30 (accessed June 22, 2010).

Interfax news agency (2009b) Moscow (in Russian), November 23. "Russian opposition movement questions modernization targets". BBC Monitoring Former Soviet Union – Political: Supplied by BBC Worldwide Monitoring.

Kolesnikov, Andrey (2010) "From a thaw to slush", *Gazeta.ru* website, Moscow (in Russian), March 2. http://www.gazeta.ru/archive.shtml?start=02.03.2010&article=1 (accessed June 22, 2010).

Kulikov, Sergey (2010) "President's INSOR predicts profound new crisis – Russia with its fuel will not be needed by the world in future years and will lose its influence in the CIS", *Nezavisimaya Gazeta* website, Moscow (in Russian), March 5, p. 4. http://www.ng.ru/gazeta/2010–03-05/ (accessed June 22, 2010).

Latynina, Yuliya (2009) "A president cast in liquid S –", *Yezhednevnyy Zhurnal* website, Moscow (in Russian), December 29. http://www.ej.ru/?a=archive&date=2009–12-29 (accessed June 22, 2010).

Lipman, Masha (2010) "The new freedom of speech", *Yezhednevnyy Zhurnal* website, Moscow (in Russian), February 12. http://www.ej.ru/?a=archive&date=2010-2-12 (accessed June 22, 2010).

Makarkin, Aleksey (2009) "United Russia congress and problems of diarchy", *Politkom.ru* website, Moscow (in Russian), November 23. http://www.politcom.ru/9169.html (accessed June 22, 2010).

Makarkin, Aleksey (2010) "The fashion for modernization", *Yezhednevnyy Zhurnal* website, Moscow (in Russian), February 19. http://www.ej.ru/?a=archive&date=2010-2-19 (accessed June 22, 2010).

Medvedev, Dmitry (2009a) President Dmitry Medvedev, "Forward, Russia!", *Gazeta*, September 10, http://www.gazeta.ru/comments/2009/09/10 a_3258568.shtml and http://www.gazeta.ru/archive.shtml?start=10.09.2009 &article=1 (accessed June 22, 2010).

Medvedev, Dmitry (2009b) "Presidential Address to the Federal Assembly of the Russian Federation", The Kremlin, Moscow, November 12: http://www.youtube.com/watch?v=Gd9IeEdwcAg and http://archive.kremlin.ru/eng/speeches/2009/11/12/1321_type70029type82912_222702.shtml (accessed June 22 2010).

Nezavisimaya Gazeta (2010) "Editorial: Tandem modernization", *Nezavisimaya Gazeta* website, Moscow (in Russian), February 11. http://www.ng.ru/gazeta/2010–02-11/ (accessed June 22, 2010).

Orlov, D., D. Badovskiy and M. Vinogradov (2010) "Conservative Modernization-2010: The Configuration of Power and a New Political Agenda", cited by Boris Makarenko, "Modernization with Adjectives", *Politkom.ru* website, Moscow (in Russian), January 19. http://www.politcom.ru/arc/2010/17.html (accessed June 22, 2010).

Piontkovskiy, Andrey (2009) *Grani.ru* website, Moscow (in Russian), December 29 "Blind Alleys of 'Modernization'". BBC Monitoring Former Soviet Union – Political: Supplied by BBC Worldwide Monitoring.

Primakov, Ye. M. (2010) "The Choice Facing Russia", *Rossiyskaya Gazeta*, January 14. BBC Monitoring Former Soviet Union – Political: Supplied by BBC Worldwide Monitoring.

RIA Novosti (2009) "Medvedev predicts 'own way' to Russian modernization", RIA Novosti, December 24. http://en.rian.ru/russia/20091224/157343084. html (accessed June 23, 2010).

Samarina, Aleksandra and Roza Tsvetkova (2010) "NG Politics: Not yet perestroyka. But...", *Nezavisimaya Gazeta* website, Moscow (in Russian), February 16, pp. 8, 10. BBC Monitoring Former Soviet Union – Political: Supplied by BBC Worldwide Monitoring.

Shusharin, Dmitriy (2009) "Nonstateness", *Grani.ru* website, Moscow (in Russian), November 19. BBC Monitoring Former Soviet Union – Political: Supplied by BBC Worldwide Monitoring.

Skobov, Aleksandr (2010) "By his own hand", *Grani.ru* website, Moscow (in Russian), February 16. BBC Monitoring Former Soviet Union – Political: Supplied by BBC Worldwide Monitoring.

Tsuladze, Avtandil (2009a) "United Russia in its own juices", *Yezhednevnyy Zhurnal* website, Moscow (in Russian), November 23. http://www.ej.ru/?a=archive&date=2009–11-23 (accessed June 22, 2010).

Tsuladze, Avtandil (2009b) "In the Kremlin: The Reset of Russia. Part 2", *Yezhednevnyy Zhurnal* website, Moscow (in Russian), December 10. http://www.ej.ru/?a=archive&date=2009–12-10 (accessed June 22, 2010).

Tumanov, Boris (2010) "Instilling Unquestioning Military Discipline", *Gazeta.ru* website, Moscow (in Russian), March 2. http://www.gazeta.ru/archive.shtml?stripe=politics&start=02.03.2010&article=1 (accessed June 22, 2010).

Vedomosti (2009) "Editorial, Old canned goods", *Vedomosti* website, Moscow (in Russian), November 23. http://www.vedomosti.ru/newspaper/2009/11/23 (accessed June 22, 2010).

Vedomosti (2010) "Editorial: The choice has been made", *Vedomosti* website, Moscow (in Russian), February 15, pp. 1, 4. http://www.gazeta.ru/archive.sh tml?start=15.02.2010&article=1 (accessed June 22, 2010).

Whitemore, Brian (2010) "The Modernizing Tandem And Its Discontents", *RFE/ RL*, June 10. http://www.rferl.org/articleprintview/2067952.html (accessed June 23, 2010).

4
Russia's "Soft Power" in the Putin Epoch

Vladimir Rukavishnikov

Introduction

At the beginning of the 21st century experts realize that national security cannot be based on a nation's hard power alone. We live in a time when various kinds of power have become important. Hard power in international politics remains a crucial factor, economics too, but the influence of *soft power* cannot be ruled out as a negligible factor. The concept of *soft power* was introduced by Harvard Professor Joseph Nye in the late 1980s to describe the ability of a political body, that is, a subject of international law such as a state, to influence indirectly the behaviour of other political bodies (states) through non-military and non-economic means in order to achieve national interest (Nye, 2004). The idea was developed to improve American foreign policy in a rapidly globalizing world. However, in our opinion, this concept is also applicable to the foreign policy of the Russian Federation under Vladimir Putin.

There are conflicting viewpoints towards this issue which should be mentioned at the very beginning of this discussion. We have divided them into four groups. The first contains views pleasing for Russians but alarming for Westerners; the second includes views that are disappointing for Russians; the third group includes opinions that are both explanatory and shaming; and the fourth focuses on views that are basically anti-American in nature, and regard the entire notion as unacceptable. The following are examples of typical viewpoints of each group.

Group 1. In 2004 the Brookings Institution's Dr Fiona Hill presented her analysis of Russia's soft power. She came to the remarkable conclusion that, while Russia may not be able to rival the United States in the nature and global extent of its soft power, "Russia is well on its way to recovering the degree of soft power the USSR once enjoyed in its immediate sphere of influence" (Hill, 2004). She noted further that "...Russia has the potential to achieve the economic and cultural predominance in Eurasia that the United States has in the Americas" (Hill, 2004). We agree that Russia, like the former USSR, has a huge potential to dominate in Eurasia, although the real question is how that domination is used. Since Vladimir Putin came into office in 2000, Russia has indeed had the intention of increasing soft power *ambitions*; and we believe that, under President Dmitri Medvedev, the Russian Federation follows this line. However, ambitions are just dreams. In 2006 Romanian Nicu Popescu argued that Russia's soft power instruments are not simply the result of a Soviet-type propaganda machine and that Russia's "soft power ambitions" must be taken seriously by the West (Popescu, 2006). In addition, it is still open to question whether post-Soviet Russia is actually regaining the "soft power" and influence that the former USSR had.

Group 2. A year after Popescu's article, the Lithuanian scholar Nerijus Maliukevicius was very skeptical concerning the prospects of Russia's real influence on her neighbors: for him, Russia would find it even more difficult to improve her image abroad in future, because this country "started to lose the soft power resources it had" (Maliukevicius, 2007). He insisted that the flood of words about increasing Russia's soft power was nothing more than the eloquent rhetoric of the Kremlin, because informational geopolitics was more popular among the Russian authorities than the concept of soft power (Maliukevich, 2007).

Group 3. After the Georgian–Russian incident in August 2008 the Western media started to write about "Russia's decision to jettison 'soft power' in favour of brute military force." It is accepted as an undisputable fact in the West that the Georgian–Russian five-day war caused considerable damage to Russia's image.[1] However, in our opinion, the aftermath of the war in the Caucasus has shown that this was a premature diagnosis; the debates in the Russian parliament serve as evidence supporting our opinion.

Group 4. At the beginning of 2009 Sergei Chelemendik, a journalist from Slovakia, argued that the concept of soft power could not be used for an analysis of Russian foreign policy as a matter of principle, that it was initially developed to cover US interventions into the internal affairs of other nations (Chelemendik, 2009).

We understand that the theme we have selected for this chapter is broad and complex, and cannot be analyzed in all its details. Following an academic tradition, we begin this paper with a brief general discussion of the problem of the measurement of soft power, and then we turn to a description of the ingredients of Russia's soft power and their translation into political influence. Finally, we take a very brief look at the consequences of the Georgian–Russian military conflict and the State Duma hearings concerning this issue.

The Problem of Measurement of Soft Power. The assessment of a state's soft power is an important, but also a difficult, issue. It is important because today national soft power is one of the elementary aspects of geopolitics of any great state. It is difficult because various kinds of power are essentially linked, if not contested; moreover, the concepts are quite hard to measure, particularly in current complex and changing global political and economic circumstances.

There are several reasons why a researcher may wish to assess Russia's soft power. The first reason concerns the division of political influence[2] among participants in a decision-making body, such as the Security Council of the United Nations Organization. The scholar, of course, may try to infer the geopolitical influence of the given state from its hard power, considering the first as a direct or indirect consequence of the latter. But he or she is sure to meet significant difficulties by ignoring the impact of soft power. The assessment of soft power may provide an efficient feedback mechanism for those who want to realize how ideas and goals go through the networks of friends and foes (numerous pre-voting consultations in the UN Security Council could be taken as an example). And this is a second reason for examining soft power.

According to the definition, this concept is multidimensional. It emanates from the attractiveness of a country's culture, political ideals, and policies. Each of these components is hard to measure. And it is even more difficult, if not impossible, to construct an index aggregating measures of all the ingredients.

Scholars sometimes contrast a state's soft power with its hard power, which may be successfully measured by the Composite Index of National Capabilities (CINC).[3] This index of relative national power was developed within the framework of the Correlates of War project for the purpose of historical comparison. Its limitations are well known. Generally speaking, the CINC is just one measure of hard power, based on quantitative metrics such as a country's population size, concrete military assets, gross domestic product (GDP). To contrast soft power with hard power is counterproductive, since in our view these two concepts are twins, which help to describe national power more accurately. Moreover, it seems that today a nation's soft power depends more on the country's global economic competitiveness than merely the material ingredients of the natural capability of the state and its military might as a hard core of national power.

In short, soft power is not easily quantifiable; the concept does not allow quantitative measurement, either because of its fuzzy definition or by its very nature, but it does fit rather well into descriptive qualitative comparative studies.[4] In other words, we think that it is impossible today to estimate the influence of a nation's soft power *objectively*. Perhaps at some time in the future the social sciences will have more advanced measurement instruments. Today, foreign policy analysts can compare Russia's soft power with that of the former Soviet Union, the present-day USA, the European Union or China, so that they can "measure" Russia's soft power *indirectly* and *subjectively*.

Cultural–informational ingredients of Russia's soft power

According to Joseph Nye, soft power has three main components: 1) a state's *culture* (for some it means popular culture, for others language, classical music and literature, science and education, technical achievements, etc.); 2) its *political values* (here we view the impact of domestic politics on a country's image abroad); and 3) its *foreign policies*, in places where they are seen as legitimate and having moral authority (here we meet with the emotional impact of the media's assessments of actions performed abroad).

Let us start our analysis with Russia's culture. Is it still attractive to others? This is not a rhetorical question with a predictable affirmative answer. Although there are many discrepancies, if one compares the current situation with that of the Soviet period, there are also impressive similarities. Given the many differences between post-Soviet states, it is rather difficult to give a general answer to the question posed above.

Culture has many dimensions. Because we cannot explore all of them, we focus on the most important points relevant to our inquiry. These are described briefly below. Language is the core of culture. After and because of the breakup of the USSR, the Russian language lost the chance to become the third world language, but it is still the single available means of interpersonal communication for over 100 non-Russian-speaking communities and ethnic groups living in the territory of the former USSR. Knowledge of the Russian language helps millions of workers from the "near abroad" to find jobs in Russia,[5] businessmen to do business in Russia, politicians to come to a better mutual understanding with their Russian counterparts, and so on. We are sure that the Russian language will remain the main *regional* means of communication in Eurasia in the 21st century. Nonetheless, the decline of overall knowledge, and the radical change of status, of the Russian language in the "near abroad" are undisputable facts.[6]

A rapid reduction in the number of so-called "Russian schools" in the "near abroad" (mainly in Ukraine and Latvia) is the most painful and clear evidence of anti-Russian language action in recent years. This is the result of conscious policies of the authorities of neighboring states, who are hurriedly constructing their own new post-Soviet national identity. The list of examples of such nationalistic politics could be extended. Irrational Russophobia is behind many cases of anti-Russian action in the "near abroad." Such open Russophobia may be explained, of course, as a postponed emotional reaction to former humiliations experienced during the Soviet period at a personal level. Although these actions may sometimes be the product of historical memory, more often they look like the result of conscious geopolitical calculations, so that they are, at least in part, rational actions. Certainly, there may be plenty of complementary motives for the behavior of Russophobes. (Further exploration of this topic would take us too far from the main theme.)

Many foreign tourists come to Russia because of its marvelous *cultural heritage*. The attractiveness of prerevolutionary Russian and Soviet Russian cultural heritage to the rest of the world remains rather high. There is much evidence of this, and we need not go into much detail in supporting this point. If one considers the Russian Orthodox Church as a part of the Russian cultural heritage, then one has to take into account the religious renaissance that emerged in post-Soviet Russia in the 1990s and early 2000s because of a radical change of relations between church and state. The recent restoration of Russian Orthodox Church unity – an improvement in relations between church authorities on the mainland and leaders of its foreign (overseas) branches – should also be mentioned in this context.[7] The growing role of the Russian Orthodox Church in post-Soviet Russia may be viewed ambivalently, but improved church–state relations have certainly had a practical effect on the positive image of the Russian state among ethnic Russians living abroad.

Russia is a multi-confessional country. Signs of strengthening influence of non-Christian religions on politics have also been reported. Alas, the situation in Northern Caucasus is making a controversial impact on Russia's image in the Muslim world.[8]

The other point to be stressed here concerns the fact that the number of talented young people who come to Russia from the "near abroad" is much greater than the number of those who go in the opposite direction.[9] Russian universities are still attracting numerous foreign students, despite rumors about the low quality of Russian higher education.[10] This is an important form of cultural exchange that must not be underestimated. Russia's investment in the education of foreign students might be considered as an investment in soft power. Sadly, state expenditure of this kind is not high.

So-called "big sport" is undergoing a revival in the Russian Federation after a decade of decline. There is no need to review the recent achievements of Russian athletes at the international arena. They are well known. Overall, athletic victories help to raise the world's interest in Russia, and a sense of national pride at home. Russia's image abroad is created by tourists, to a certain extent, as well as by art exhibitions, song contests, cinema and theatre festivals, and other cultural events.

The influence of Russia's *modern popular culture* in the world is low to moderate – even in the "near abroad," in our view – and cannot be compared with that of American, Western European, or broader Western pop culture. In Russia's immediate neighborhood this has occurred for many reasons: official policies of time limitations for broadcasting programs and movies in Russian at local TV and radio stations,[11] the spread of the Internet, and so on – and, of course, because the Russian-speaking audience is gradually diminishing.

One may say that this means *'the American cultural imperialism'*, as French sociologists have termed it, is alive, and is not just a part of the cultural globalization of Eurasia in the 20th century.[12] Nobody talks about *Russian cultural neo-imperialism*, because, in our view, such a phenomenon does not exist!

The Kremlin started to reinforce its informational resources in the early 2000s. The state-controlled media bodies are supposed to disseminate ideological and political information favorable to the Russian authorities. Media targeted towards foreign audiences are considered by the Kremlin officials as channels of propaganda, as traditional instruments of information geopolitics, and as information warfare in cases of international crisis. Traditionally they are strongly criticized for inefficiency by experts at home and abroad.[13]

Investments in information, tourism, art, and sports ultimately work to increase Russia's soft power. So far, for understandable reasons, they are not large, but they should be noted in our brief review. One may also recall the assistance of the Russian governmental bodies to various NGOs and think tanks involved in so-called "people diplomacy," and to societies of teachers of the Russian language, and could add to the list scholarships to students from neighbouring countries, and so on. Nonetheless, so far we do not see a real counteroffensive of the Russian government in the cultural–informational area.

To recap, the total scale of cultural–informational exchanges in all forms between Russia under Putin and the rest of the world is less than it was in the Soviet period. Russia's foreign propaganda is basically old-fashioned and ineffective, and needs to be modernized. Russia's attractiveness in terms of culture and language is gradually diminishing, despite efforts by the Russian government to halt this process. But there is no way to improve Russia's soft power without increasing the attraction of Russia as a world cultural center.

The economics of Russia's influence

Russia's influence and soft power are also cultivated through trade, economic assistance, and military cooperation.[14] There is no cheap loyalty or attraction in the modern world; attraction and long-term loyalty are the result of permanent help and protection, even in the case of commonly shared or adopted goals.

Resurgent Russia at the beginning of the 21st century, from the economic viewpoint, appears among her neighbors like a mythical giant among his closest entourage. Russia is the most important trade partner for many neighboring states. Consumer goods from Russia are rather popular in the republics of Central Asia and Kazakhstan, basically because of their cost/quality ratio compared with Chinese goods, which are almost always cheaper than their Russian equivalents. Russian beer brands are a good example of this factor.

Russia gives generous loans to governments, provides credits to large development projects, and takes part in constructing hydroelectric stations, mines, pipelines, and so on. The country is an "energy superpower," providing electric energy and supplying gas and crude oil to its closest neighbors, as well as to Europe. Millions of *Gastarbeiter* working in Russia send billions of rubles to their families and, thus, indirectly help to raise local economies. All in all, the network of trade and economic ties with neighboring nations works positively to improve Russia's image and influence abroad, Russia's foreign policy officials say. Their opponents argue that the chemistry between neighbors is always more complex and complicated.

It seems that the second assessment is likely to be closer to the truth. Asymmetry of bilateral trade–economic relations always indicates economic and political dependency of the recipient country on the donor state.[15] Neither a flood of consumer goods nor numerous loans can automatically establish the attractiveness of the Russian Federation or increase Moscow's political influence.

One may question whether the energy, weaponry, economic blockades, and trade embargoes really help Moscow, or whether the growth of Russian economic might scares Russia's neighbors. This is a vital question in the context of our discussion. Russian business activity abroad sometimes meets an openly hostile, or at least ambivalent, reaction of governments, the public, and the media. For instance, according to a recent press report, "Russian investors are being driven from Eastern Europe because of political antagonism in countries such as Poland and Lithuania" (Cienski and Hoyos, 2009). The situation looks absurd in the current times of global economic recession, because Russian investments create new jobs, or at least safeguard existing jobs. Nonetheless, a wide expansion of Russian capital into foreign countries has been postponed "till better times."

The depicted reaction of local politicians and media indicates that Russian economic assistance and business interests are not supported *ideologically* and *diplomatically* to the required extent. We agree with this verdict.[16] Simply advertising is not enough. The Russians are not persuading others to adopt common strategic goals or to agree on the mutual benefit of the presence of Russian business in local economies. The Kremlin authorities and Russia's embassies consistently fail to convince nationalistically oriented political circles of the recipient states that close economic ties with Russia are not harmful to their national interest. Therefore, the low level of Russia's political influence in the immediate neighborhood is basically due to Moscow itself. The Kremlin should not blame competitors in vain for its own failures, but should counteract any efforts to push Russia out from neighboring states.

The Kremlin was not happy to watch the "colored revolutions" in Russia's "near abroad" (in Georgia, Ukraine, and Kyrgyzstan), but could do nothing to prevent them. Currently Moscow tries to use both the stick and the carrot in its relations with countries where "revolutionary" leaders governed. Moscow regards the area of the former Soviet Union and Eastern Europe as a "zone of Russian responsibility and interests." On September 1, 2008, President Dmitri Medvedev of Russia said, "Russia, like other countries in the world, has regions where it has privileged interests. These are regions where countries with which we have friendly relations are located" (cited in Kramer, 2008). And it was quite clear to which neighboring areas he was referring as a "privileged sphere of Russia's influence."[17]

Frankly speaking, there was no novelty in Medvedev's statement for those who believe that national geopolitical interests tend to be quite stable over time. Although this opinion has been criticized on different grounds, many Russian foreign policy experts share this point of view when talking about Russia's policy in the "near abroad."[18] These analysts justify Russia's intention to claim "the privileged spheres of influence" by referring to historic and cultural ties between Russia and neighboring nations with a certain feeling of nostalgia about the "good old days." Perhaps they dream of gaining some benefit from the reintegration of this formerly united territory.

Does Vladimir Putin, the real architect of Russia's policy and currently the prime minister of the Russian Federation share this viewpoint? According to some observers, "he made clear references to the glorious past of his country, seeking a reconnection with this time-honoured tradition of Russia's historical responsibility for Eurasian security."[19] Putin's motivations may be primarily political, but also mixed with other motives.

We refer to Medvedev's speech of September 2008, first of all, because the Russian president spoke plainly about safeguarding Russia's interests in the regions where Russia has traditionally held strong positions basically because of its "soft power," despite the fact that the term "soft power" was not explicitly used in his speech.[20] The international reaction to Medvedev's speech was foreseeable.[21] As for the former Soviet republics, they always react negatively to what they regard as Russia's reclaiming of complete military/economic dominance in the Eurasian region. They enjoy the benefits of cooperation with Russia, but, nonetheless, some of them passionately want to distance themselves from Russia.

Why? As noted earlier, Russian economic activity in the "near abroad" is threatening those politicians who hate "senior brother" and are scared of him. Post-Soviet Russia ("senior brother") for them is responsible for real or imagined crimes committed against their nation during the days of the Soviet Union and/or the glorious Russian Empire.[22] And they do not want to be dependent on "ex-senior brother," economically, militarily, or politically, as in the "good old days." The national ideal for the leaderships of Ukraine, Georgia, and some other post-Soviet states is national statehood built on their independence from Russia.

Various anti-Russian activities are justified by a strong desire to protect sovereignty and to create a new post-Soviet national identity. For this reason some national leaders and bureaucrats are making provocative statements, closing Russian-language schools, rewriting history books, supporting ex-Nazi soldiers, and doing many other things that raise the indignation of the Russians. But not everybody among the political elites in the immediate neighborhood has chosen openly anti-Russian behavior. Others, basically leaders of pro-Russian states, are paying for their recently obtained sovereignty by years of collaboration with Russia and an open demonstration of loyalty to Putin's regime, partly forced, partly conscious and voluntary. For them, "the goal justifies the means." Do they believe that their chosen behavior is legitimate, or has their faith in Russia been shaken? Their loyalty is driven by the economic might of a resurgent Russia. But, as has already been noted, generous economic aid does not always guarantee absolute loyalty of recipients. Without doubt, perceptions of Russia's politics and goals for the near future play a significant role in this "shaken faith."

This is the first brief answer to "why." The second answer derives from Russia's internal and external politics – that is, from the afore-mentioned second and third components of Nye's definition of soft power, which are strongly correlated in the case of this country. We will continue to discuss this point in the next section.

The third reason for the behavior of neighboring states can be found in the declining attraction of Russia in terms of its culture. To over-come this negative process is the main task of Russian society and state. To confront any anti-Russian actions and declarations is to strengthen Russia's image. Otherwise improving Russia's soft power will be an unachievable goal. The reader may identify other complementary expla-nations for the weakness of Russian soft power, since the list presented here is not complete.

Russia's values and policy validation

Ethnic Russians share the same basic values as other humans.[23] Not everyone who laughs at funny anecdotes about ethnic Russians and/or dislikes Russian politics can be labelled a Russophobe! These facts do not contradict the theory of "cultural stereotypes." Yes, stereotypes no doubt shape popular attitudes towards the Russians as a nation and to the Russian Federation as a state, but share their influence with the media and other factors.[24] There is no reason to consider anecdotes about Russians to be a principal indicator of Russophobia (leaving aside here the issue of a complex and permanent impact of media and propaganda on popular attitudes).

On the issue of political values and mass political behavior, a group of researchers found certain small discrepancies between Westerners and the Russians a decade ago (Ester *et al.*, 1997).[25] These discrepancies are still valid today, but, in our opinion, may well be explained through historical differences.[26] They are not fundamental, but temporal.

Perhaps in the future the discrepancy between values shared in the West and those in the East will finally be eliminated, and then scholars will no longer debate the value foundations of the foreign policy of Russia, the USA, or Iran. The role of political values in foreign policy is, doubtless, very important. But, in our view, too many Western scholars (American and British) overemphasize the role of values as the foundation of US foreign policy, as well as the differences between political values shared by Western and non-Western nations.[27] In fact, US foreign policy, as well as former Soviet or current Russian foreign policy, is a sophisticated version of *realpolitik*. The great powers like to speak about protecting democratic values or following certain principles in order to camouflage their genuine goals of intervention. Analysts in the West find it extraordinarily difficult to begin talking about the positive impact of domestic politics and foreign policy on Russia's *soft power*. There are at least two obvious explanations for this situation. One suggests that the difficulty is with the analysts. "They are not very good," some Russian colleagues argue. "The Westerners are not ready to understand resurgent Russia," others always say. That explanation is facile, but it strikes me as a bit too convenient.

Another obvious explanation is that analysts have problems getting started, because the general conclusion, of which they can find many examples, is that Russian political life is static and almost totally controlled by the Kremlin. Indeed, there is no serious political challenge to the governmental (say, Putin's or Medvedev's) domestic politics at home. The constructive–critical ideas of communists and the novel ideas of democrats are quickly co-opted by the mainstream liberals and conservatives, that is, "the United Russia," the power party. There is no strong political opposition in the parliament, because even the Communist Party fraction is too weak. The tiny non-parliamentary extremist parties and interest groups from both the left and the right extremes of the political spectrum have no popular support. The pro-Western parties tend to disappear, or drastically change what they advocate.[28] That would be unlikely in a Western-style democracy.

Overall, the political reality in the West is so different from that in the Russian Federation, in so many dimensions, that it is fair to say that, overall, political Russia does not meet a Western standard of democracy. There is a new and unique form of political regime (*tandemocracy*), which came in after Yeltsin's anocracy in the 1990s and Putin's quasi-democratic authoritarianism of the early 2000s (Rukavishnikov, 2009a). Anyone who looks at the matter closely will agree that this discrepancy is not helping Russia to win many friends in Western Europe or the USA.

International polls carried out soon after the Georgian–Russian war demonstrated the significantly negative impact of the conflict on Russia's reputation among the Western nations. This may be a temporary effect, but it must be noted. It should also be remembered that Russia's image in the West was already unfavorable before the war. This means that there are stable patterns of mainly unfavorable attitudes in the West towards Russia's domestic and foreign policy and towards the leadership of this great country. Such attitudes have been partly formed by numerous media reports focused on violations of human and civil rights during Putin's reign.[29]

Now we have to say a few words about non-Western public opinion polls. Of course, it matters greatly whether the Russian Federation is seen as a friend, an ally, or a foe by the government of the country where the poll has been conducted, and it also depends on media and other relevant circumstances. Simple respondents in most developing nations have a very vague understanding, if any, about Russia's domestic politics. The Russian Federation is still perceived there as a main foe of the US, as was the USSR in the past. In addition, it seems, the five-day war did not shift the stable balance of attitudes existing there.

The picture of popular attitudes towards Russia in former Soviet republics is complex and heterogeneous. The balance of attitudes varies from state to state (one may compare, for example, Estonia and Kyrgyzstan, Poland and Bulgaria) and/or even from region to region within a given state (for instance, in Western and Eastern parts of Ukraine). The general balance of favorable and unfavorable attitudes towards Russia in the post-Soviet space has not been reversed since the five-day war in the Southern Caucasus. And, perhaps, the very lack of radical change in the balance of opinions was frustrating for those who expected Russia's adherents in the "near abroad" to blame the Russian government for tough action against the Georgian aggression towards South Ossetia; this expectation was not realized.[30]

In our view, Russia's supporters in most developing nations, including the post-Soviet states, admire Putin's Russia for the resurgence of its economy and for reestablishing its great power status.[31] They favor Russia because they are comparing the Russian standard of living with their own lower level. Most of them are not interested in politics, with the possible exception of issues related to xenophobia or labor conditions for migrants.[32] Traditionally such people prefer a "strong hand" ruler as a guarantor of political stability of the state, associated with economic prosperity and military might.[33] Therefore Putin's authoritarianism escaped their attention, because for them Russia's "defective, or decorative, democracy" is no worse than the political regimes in their own states, which are either nondemocratic or unstably quasi-democratic in nature.[34] Most of Russia's admirers have strong anti-American attitudes inherited from the past. They favor power politics. For them, the five-day war was simply the Russians showing Georgians and "bloody Americans" "who is the master at home" (i.e. the real master in the Caucasus – Caspian Sea – Black Sea region).

Russia's soft power and the South Caucasus episode

The short war between Georgia and Russia in August 2008, which coincided with the Olympic Games in China, was predictable and expected, because tension between the neighbors had been escalating from year to year.[35] An influential Russian newspaper wrote that the August incident was *"a local war with global consequences."*[36] Happily, these gloomy geopolitical consequences have so far not materialized. The disposition of rival forces in the area of conflict has not drastically changed after Russia's victory, the consequent recognition of the rebellious Georgian provinces of South Ossetia and Abkhazia as independent states, and the stationing of Russian troops there on a regular basis. In fact, the victor simply confirmed the pre-war status quo.[37] There were voices in Russia that concluded that the frozen conflicts in South Caucasus had been ultimately solved by the war. This viewpoint seems to us unrealistic; it is just wishful thinking. In our view, the ultimate resolution of the frozen conflicts has only been postponed to some future year.

Official Russian propaganda termed the tough reaction to the Georgian aggression against South Ossetia the *peace-enforcing operation.*[38] For the Russians it was a just war, and they did not feel guilty about the size of their military intervention.[39] The public perceived the operation as retaliation for the attack on and killing of Russian peacekeepers by Georgians. No voices of dissent were heard in Russia.

To Russia's critics abroad, the picture could not be clearer: Russia's intervention in Georgia was considered a wildly disproportional response to the Georgian attempt to restore its national integrity and to punish South Ossetia separatists. In addition, they demanded on these grounds that the Russian military action should be immediately condemned by the international community. The friction between the West and Russia concerning the resolution of the crisis in the South Caucasus was compared by the Russian media with the previous controversy between Russia and the West over Kosovo – the dispute in which Russia lost face.[40] In contrast to the case of Kosovo, the Southern Caucasus incident renewed Russian self-esteem.

The short war in the South Caucasus had frightened politicians and the public at large in Russia's neighborhood and in Europe and the USA. Cold War fears returned! Some months later the Russian public was told that the Americans and Europeans had finally agreed that Georgia had unleashed the war and that Russia had been within its rights to respond, but many did not believe this "news." Not until the beginning of spring 2009 did the damage caused to diplomatic relations between Russia and the West by the five-day war begin to mend.[41]

Popular attitudes often do not match official state positions. Here we must refer to the point that cannot be avoided in our discussion; none of the CIS countries followed Russia's diplomatic action of recognition of South Ossetia and Abkhazia as independent states immediately after the five-day war. This might be considered an indicator of the actual political influence of Russia in the Organization of Collective Defence and Security and other main post-Soviet political bodies created by the Kremlin during the post-Soviet years.

The Russian Federation lost the information war that accompanied the aforementioned conflict. The analysis of "why" is outside the scope of this chapter. This fact was recognized by the Russian leadership, and was widely discussed by media abroad. There were sharp debates in the Russian parliament concerning the ways to make the Russian external propaganda machine more effective (Rodin, 2009). Konstantin Kosachev, chairman of the foreign affairs committee of the State Duma, even used the term "soft power" in his speech at the parliament hearings.[42] For him, "Russia is alone in a hostile world," because "we practically have no partners, who favorably talk about us." He offered the idea of creating a special body to coordinate the activities of different PR institutions working with foreign audiences, despite the opposition of the government to this proposal (Rodin, 2009). The Duma hearings demonstrated a lack of consensus about what to do and how to increase Russia's soft power at the top of the so-called "power vertical" in Russia. No doubt improving Russia's information policy is an important task, but, in our opinion, Russian politicians and foreign policy experts were reviving old phobias, talking about enemy propaganda, an unfriendly encircling of Russia, information wars launched against Russia, and so on. They were missing the essential point at issue (whether consciously or not is another question).

In fact, neighbors will only talk positively about a friendly, democratic, rich, and powerful country, which can protect and help them. Any real increase in Russia's ability to attract friends and allies will depend on how quickly Russia emerges from the current economic recession, and also on the standard of living of the Russian people, how happy and free they are at home. And, of course, Russia cannot enjoy the respect of other countries until it establishes the rule of law at home.

Concluding remarks

During the first eight or nine years of the 21st century Russia has recovered economically, but deteriorated politically – at least according to the mainstream Western and global media. Polls showed that Russia's image in much of the world rose and fell during this period. However, in most neighboring CIS states the favorable attitudes shared by the masses outweighed negative views of Russia. The picture of the political elite's attitudes is vague and varies from state to state.

The August 2008 Georgian–Russian conflict severely damaged Russia's image in the so-called "far abroad." The victorious outcome of the five-day war against Georgia definitely showed the resurgence of hard power, but it also raised questions about repairing Russia's political influence in the world as a whole, in Europe, and particularly in the "near abroad."[43] It is not clear at the time of writing, however, whether or not this clash has helped pro-Russian political forces in the world. The level of political influence of a given state depends basically on the state's image among the elites, not the masses. A cynic, skeptic, or both might say about the present status of Russia's soft power: "Injured soft power? – Who cares! – It is Russia's fate. This country is neither completely democratic, nor purely European. It has never depended upon soft power in pursuing its foreign policy."

This is true enough. In the recent past the Kremlin has paid too little heed to soft power. And nobody in the ruling circles today understands how soft power could be used to change the current situation. Once again: who cares? The impact of the economic and financial crisis will long outlast that of possible mistakes made during this period. In 2004 Dr Fiona Hill wrote:

> The current U.S. failure to capitalize on its own undisputed soft power and growing global anti-Americanism demonstrate the risks

involved, and the limits of soft power if a state is not seen to live up to its own values abroad or its foreign policy motivations are questioned overseas. It is by no means assured that Russia's increasing soft power will be used to positive effect. But the prospect is clearly there, and should encourage Russia's current leadership to chart a new regional policy for itself in Eurasia (Hill, 2004).

As for Russia, after the August 2008 war against Georgia, the creation of a new regional policy in Eurasia became even more important than it had been in 2004. Moscow should embrace a more flexible and multilateral approach in a new foreign and security policy to improve Russia's soft power and political influence in the world as a whole.

Notes

The views expressed here are those of the author alone. An earlier version of this study appeared as "The August 2008 Georgian-Russian incident and Russia's Soft Power", *The Review of International Affairs,* vol. LX, no. 1133–4, January–June 2009, pp. 9–24, and appears here with the permission of the editors of that journal.

1. Or, as Edward Luttwak put it in the *Daily Telegraph*, "Tanks once again decide what happens. *'Soft power', on which so many hopes had been pinned, has just been exposed as irrelevant* [our italics]. The Russians clearly do not care. Their tanks have rolled in, and nothing except a bigger, more powerful force can stop them" (Luttwak, 2008).
2. Some scholars think that the construction of measures of political influence is possible (Arts and Verschuren, 1999). However, we feel that the existing means of measurement of political influence are not particularly helpful in real diplomatic practice.
3. It is commonly assumed by international scholars that the Correlates of War project's Composite Index of National Capabilities (CINC) is the best measure of relative national power for comparative and cross-national studies. The basic indicators of CINC's economic component – a country's ratio in the global energy consumption and the relative size of iron and steel production – were chosen for the purpose of historical comparison. The same could be said about indicators of other CINC components (Rukavishnikov, 2007, 2009a).
4. We believe that soft power for foreign policy analysts may be somewhat like pornography for former US Supreme Court Justice Potter Stewart, who once said, more or less, "I cannot measure pornography, but I know it when I see it, and I think it ought to be decreased." We can say, "We don't know today how to measure soft power through quantitative metrics. But we feel when it ought to be increased."
5. The Russians call them "*Gastarbeiter,*" using the German wording.
6. In a few new independent states the Russian language is one of two *official* languages, while most of the former Soviet republics have lowered its former high status.

7. This fact may be interpreted also as an attempt to restore Moscow's control over Russian emigrant communities dispersed across the globe. Yet we agree that the political rhetoric hailing this event is colored in neo-imperialist tones. The rhetoric is a product of the pragmatic attitude of Putin's team towards this issue.

8. The military victory over separatist resistance in Chechnya is presented by official propaganda as the Kremlin's greatest success. However, the non-stop search for militants underground in Northern Caucasus continues from day to day, despite the recent (April 2009) announcement of the official end of the counter-terrorist regime in the Chechen Republic.

9. We have no official data about a flow of Russian brains to the CIS countries. Probably its size is statistically very low.

10. Unfortunately, according to the press, the general quality of higher education in Russia has declined compared with that in the Soviet period and, therefore, the international prestige of Russian higher education diplomas has diminished. There are voices calling for the introduction of European degree standards in Russia's system of higher education, which would be a radical break with tradition; this idea meets with skepticism among university professors.

11. Political decisions will have the effect of reducing Russia's cultural presence. The number of Russian movies is diminishing, creating a free niche which is being filled by American movies. Ukrainian subtitles have become obligatory elements in all Russian movies shown in the Ukraine, and so on.

12. "Globalization," some say, "is Americanization of the way of life across the world." This expression, in our view, captures an important characteristic of the cultural globalization process.

13. Due to lack of space we cannot take a closer look at the programs and the types of people who are invited to speak.

14. Here we disagree with Professor Nye, who wrote: "Soft power is the ability to get what you want by attracting and persuading others to adopt your goals. It differs from hard power, the ability to use the carrots and sticks of economic and military might to make others follow your will. Both hard and soft power are important in the war on terrorism, but attraction is much cheaper than coercion, and an asset that needs to be nourished" (Nye, 2003, cited from the web edition). For us, common goals are important for creating mutual understanding, friendship, and partnership relations, but they are not sufficient to establish a stable area of soft power influence.

15. The character of relationships between members in such international organizations as the Collective Security Treaty Organization (CSTO) may serve as an illustration. Of the seven countries that are members of CSTO in 2009, six are recipients of Russian aid. It is hardly necessary to say that this anti-NATO organization is totally controlled by Russia.

16. Too many authors expressed this idea in the Russian and foreign press to be cited (see, for instance, Popescu, 2006, p. 1).

17. Clearly, the western CIS countries – Moldova, Ukraine, and Belarus – as well as the South Caucasus and Central Asia constitute the core of what Russia sees as its strategic sphere of influence.

18. In this chapter we are not reviewing the mountain of literature with various viewpoints on this topic because of limited space. For that reason, as well,

the extremely important issue of stability/erosion of the Russian national interest is not discussed in this chapter.

19. Here is the continuation of the quote: "...Some observers think Putin feels duty bound to protect the interests of the estimated 25 million Russians living in former Soviet satellites, who feel vulnerable in newly independent and nationalistic states. Others point to European Union and NATO expansion, which, with the inclusion of the Baltic and four other East European countries, has brought western might to Russia's doorstep. The U.S. military build-up in Central Asia following Sept. 11 has added to those sensitivities [...]But the most likely explanation is the most obvious one: Putin is trying to preserve a vestige of the hemispheric might his country once wielded" ("Russia's Influence on Regional Politics", 2004).

20. "Russia would defend Russian citizens and business interests abroad," Medvedev said. "And it would claim a sphere of influence in the world" (cited in Kramer, 2008).

21. The evidence can be found in President Dmitry Medvedev's words: "We are not afraid of anything, including the prospect of a Cold War" (Ian Traynor, "Russia: we are ready for a new cold war", *The Guardian*, Wednesday, August 27, 2008, web-edition: guardian.co.uk). This statement surprised those in the West, who believed that Russia would seek to protect its war gains and advance its national interests by slowing opening up diplomacy, but not the Russian experts.

22. The myopic policy of ignoring the alarming tendency to falsification of history harms Russian national interest in the long run, and, as we can see at the time of writing, the Russian presidential administration has finally understood this.

23. This conclusion comes from a study of Russian psychological "uniqueness" conducted by Estonian scholars ("Sotsial'nye psikhologi", 2008). Other relevant sources make the same point.

24. Many older Lithuanians, for instance, like to watch the Russian TV channels and have expressed nostalgia about the Soviet time; at the same time, most Lithuanians dislike Putin's politics (Maliukevicius, 2007).

25. We are talking about traditional Western political values, such as those concerning classical capitalism, private property, liberal ideology, democracy, and so on.

26. We do not share the viewpoint that Russia has developed the "specific variant of democracy (so called 'sovereign democracy')" because of peculiarities of political values and political history. High-ranking Kremlin officials (Vladislav Surkov and his associates) developed the false idea of so-called "sovereign democracy" to justify Putin's regime, and presented this viewpoint in 2006. This viewpoint refers to the old principle of the superiority of state over the individual and society, which is considered to be at the core of the political values of Russians. We agree that this false idea served as an ideological basis for official propaganda of the Soviet era, but this principle is not valid today.

27. The creator of the term *soft power* likes to talk about values when speaking as a Harvard professor, but in the 1990s, as a high-ranking Pentagon official, Joseph Nye took an active part in implementing *power politics* because "it was not a suitable time for talking values" (the reader should remember that

the so-called "Americanization of peacekeeping" occurred in the Balkans at that time, for example).

28. We are talking here about the new right-wing democratic political party that has replaced the former *Union of Right Forces*.

29. This comes from the discrepancy in political values together with a negative assessment of Putin's domestic politics, and, at least in part, from the complex feeling of frustration that Russia's failed "transition towards democracy" had aroused in the West by the end of Putin's presidency.

30. The Georgian troops attacked Tskhinvali, South Ossetia's capital, first, at night, as Hitler's troops did in the invasion of the Soviet Union in 1941. Georgians killed Russian peacekeepers, thereby violating international law. It is quite clear to any unbiased observer who was the aggressor in this case. During the peace-enforcing operation Russian troops used offensive combat tactics, because it was a real war; the Russian troops were stopped at the threshold of Tbilisi for political reasons. In fact, the Russians acted in that *peace-enforcing* operation much as the Americans did in the Balkans in the 1990s and in the Desert Storm operation against Iraq in 1990.

31. It is evident that, although Russia's economy is not as diversified and modernized as it should be at the beginning of the 21st century, the huge oil revenues of the 2000s gave the economy a chance to start its recovery. And this recovery definitely affected Russia's image abroad.

32. One may add to this list such items as poor living conditions and access to health care for migrants; a lack of effective measures to ensure gender equality; unacceptable overcrowding and inhumane detention conditions in prisons (detention of migrants is frequently unjustified and "questionable"); a poor legal definition of anti-terrorism measures and special investigation techniques, and so on.

33. Certainly, domestic policy cannot be reduced to (macro)economic achievements or failures, but we wish to emphasize the core of Russia's admirers' perception of reality.

34. Public rejection in the West of Putin's way of ruling could reflect an opinion about the way in which his vision of democracy had been implemented, which is evident in the contrast between Russia's stated policies and its actual policies. As for the bulk of respondents in non-Western nations, they are politically uneducated and not used to living in democracies.

35. Given space limitations in this chapter, we cannot consider a chronicle of mutual provocations or military considerations.

36. A Russian commentator in an article in *Nezavisimaya Gazeta* in December 2008 linked the Georgian–Russian war with the poor status of US–Russia relations and the decline of American influence in the world. We do not agree with such an argument. We also have to leave aside the lessons that the Russian military has drawn from this asymmetric war. We agree that the confrontation between Georgia and the Russian Federation is a part of a geostrategic game. Therefore, the entire conflict can be viewed as a clash of the geostrategic interests of the actors involved. These actors included not only Georgia and Russia, but also Armenia and Azerbaijan with their "frozen conflicts" in Nagorno-Karabakh, which is potentially the most dangerous protracted conflict in the area of the Caucasus. Additionally, the regional powers, such as the EU, Turkey, and Iran, and global powers, such

as the United States and China, were part of the power configuration in the region, as well as the international organizations – OSCE, NATO, and so on. The geostrategic importance of the South Caucasus plus the Caspian basin is only partly based on the presence of energy resources. It is a corridor from Europe to Central Asia and farther to the East. The importance of the region for the transport of Caspian and Central Asian (Kazakhstan and Turkmenistan) energy supplies has grown as a result of the energy policies of consumer states in the EU that want to decrease their dependence on resources from Russia and the Middle East in light of the vulnerability of Persian Gulf supplies and growing pressure by the US on Iran. These issues are discussed, in part, in Chapter 13 of the present volume. A Western presence in the area is viewed as a vital requirement for the uninterrupted transport of oil and gas, because the Caucasus does not have a large share of global oil and gas reserves (just 3–4 per cent of the total). That is why the US, with its allies, is making efforts to end Russia's near-monopoly on the transport of energy supplies to Europe by creating alternative pipeline routes through Georgia and Azerbaijan. The United States is clearly defending its interests in the entire area, rearming and retraining Georgian troops, and assisting in the renovation of Azerbaijan's forces – all of which contributes to Russia's concern about the existing power balance in the region.

37. National leaders, the media, and the public at large perceive the relationship between Georgia and Russia in the past, the present, and the future in remarkably different ways. All agree, however, that high politics is a very personal issue. The Russian rulers dislike President Micheil Saakashvilli of Georgia, who repays them in the same coin. Saakashvilli, as a national leader personally responsible for a defeat, may quit in the near future, but his anti-Russian political heritage will determine the foreign policy of the next Georgian administration. An improved bilateral relationship may not be possible for Georgia and the Russian Federation, as the two countries have mismatched interests and bear a grudge against one another. The next generation of Georgian leaders will have to tolerate the consequences of humiliation, having no other opportunity but to reconstruct good relations with a powerful Russia.

38. We must also leave aside the discussion of lessons that the Russian military have drawn from this asymmetric war.

39. For the bulk of Russians, the clash between Georgia and Russia in August 2008 was only a symptom of the broader strategic positioning of the West and the Russian Federation in and around the South Caucasus. The mediator mission of the French president on behalf of the EU was considered at that time to be a proof of this diagnosis.

40. The Russian government was criticized at home (mainly by Moscow's nationalist-oriented press) for not recognizing the self-proclaimed republics of South Ossetia, Abkhazia, Transdnestria, and Nagorno-Karabakh in an immediate response to the recognition of independence of the rebellious Serbian province of Kosovo by the USA and its European allies. There were those who argued that formal recognition of the independence of these breakaway territories would have prevented the five-day war in South Caucasus, and that Russia's solidarity with Serbia in the case of Kosovan independence provided no benefits to either the Serbians or the Russians.

41. We are not reviewing here the various viewpoints on the question hotly debated in the Russian media of that time: "Was the US standing behind Georgia in the conflict with Russia?" It appeared true that the Georgians might have been hearing what they wanted to hear – or possibly thinking that the Russians were hearing something similar – but Washington's support of NATO membership for Georgia was clear enough: "We love you guys." The American love could achieve nothing in that particular case of the five-day war. The South Caucasus crisis, which practically coincided with the climax of presidential elections in the USA, has certainly damaged American positions in post-Soviet space. No doubt Washington will do all in its power to reenforce its influence and to maintain pressure on NATO allies, expressing numerous warnings about the farther enlargement of the sphere of Russia's influence and appealing for counteractions "to contain Russia's neo-imperial ambitions."

42. Here I must emphasize that, although we Russians have the word "influence" in our vocabulary, we do not have a precise equivalent to the English term "soft power." Generally speaking, the usage of the term in Russia is very similar to that in the West. It is now used – and often incorrectly – by political leaders, editorial writers, and academics. However, the entire concept has not had much of a hearing – perhaps, in part at least, because of difficulties in translation.

43. And, if we are not just talking about the rhetoric, we must agree that the future of Russia greatly depends on the answers to two highly important foreign policy questions. First (seen as the practicable question): how should Russia react to the unfriendly policy of some neighboring states, backed by NATO and Europe's authorities, keeping in mind the natural gas supply dispute, the possibility of an escalation of internal tension in Crimea, frozen conflicts in Caucasus, and so on – is it better to demonstrate toughness again with hawkish gestures, or to improve dialogue without losing face? Second (more generally): how can Russia increase its influence in the world, simultaneously confronting the USA and the EU, and promoting national interest in China, India, Latin America, Africa and our immediate neighbourhood?

References

Chelemendik, Sergei (2009) "Soft Power – miagkaia sila 'made in USA'". InoSMI, February 10 (http://www.inosmi.ru/translation/247352.html) (accessed July 4, 2010).

Cienski, Jan and Carola Hoyos (2009) "Russian investors face 'antagonism'", *The Financial Times* (web-edition), April 9. http://journalisted.com/article?id=1379240 (accessed July 4, 2010).

Ester, Peter, Halman Look and Vladimir Rukavishnikov (1997) *From Cold War to Cold Peace? A comparative Empirical Study of Russian and Western Political Cultures*, Tilburg, The Netherlands: Tilburg University Press.

Hill, Fiona (2004) "Russia's Newly Found 'Soft Power'", *The Globalist*, August 26 (http://www.theglobalist.com/StoryId.aspx?StoryId=4139) (accessed July 4, 2010).

Kramer, Andrew E. (2008) "Russia claims its sphere of influence in the world", *The International Herald Tribune*, September 1, 2008. http://www.iht.com/articles/2008/09/01/europe/01russia.php (accessed July 4, 2010).

Luttwak, Edward (2008) "Georgia conflict: Moscow has blown away soft power", *The Daily Telegraph*, August 17 (cited from http://www.telegraph.co.uk/news/worldnews/europe/georgia/2571274/Georgia-conflict-Moscow-has-blown-away-soft-power.html (accessed July 4, 2010).

Maliukevicius, Nerijus (2007) "Russia's information policy in Lithuania: the spread of soft power or information geopolitics?", *Baltic Security & Defence Review*, vol. 9, pp. 150–70. http://www.bdcol.ee/fileadmin/docs/bdrev13/7._Nerijus_Maliukevicius-Russian_information_policy_in_Lithuania.pdf (accessed July 4, 2010).

Nezavisimaya Gazeta (2008) "Pokal'naia voina s global'nymi posledstviiami", December 12. http://www.ng.-ru/itog/2008–1230/1_osetia.html (accessed July 4, 2010).

Nye, Joseph S. (2003) "Propaganda Isn't the Way: Soft Power", *The International Herald Tribune*, January 10 (web-edition). http://www.nytimes.com/2003/01/10/opinion/10iht-ednye_ed3_.html (accessed July 4, 2010).

Nye, Joseph S., Jr (2004) *Soft Power: The Means to Success in World Politics*. New York: Public Affairs.

Popescu, Nicu (2006) *Russia's Soft Power Ambitions*. Centre for European Policy Studies, Policy brief, no. 115, October. www.ceps.eu/ceps/download/1227 (accessed July 4, 2010).

Rodin, Igor (2009) "Duma v poiskax krepkogo kulaka (The State Duma is searching for a strong fist)", *Nezavisimaya Gazeta*, April 15. http://www.ng.ru/gazeta/2009–04-15/ (accessed July 4, 2010).

Rukavishnikov, Vladimir (2007) "Russia's Power and Competitiveness", *International Problems* (Serbia), no. 4, pp. 487–512.

Rukavishnikov, Vladimir (2009a) "Russia's Power and Competitiveness in the Past and the Present", ch. 2 in Roger E. Kanet (ed.), *A Resurgent Russia and the West: the European Union, NATO and beyond*, Dordrecht, The Netherlands: Republic of Letters Publishing, 2009, pp. 29–54.

Rukavishnikov, Vladimir (2009b) "The August 2008 Georgian-Russian incident and Russia's Soft Power", *The Review of International Affairs,* vol. LX, no. 1133–4, January–June 2009, pp. 9–24.

"Russia's Influence on Regional Politics" (2004). http://www.thecanadianencyclopedia.com/PrinterFriendly.cfm?Params=M1ARTM0012691 (accessed July 4, 2010).

"Sotsial'nye psikhologi: S 'russkogo kharaktera' net", *BBC Russian.com*, July 18, 2008. http://news.bbc.co.uk/go/pr/fr/-/hi/russian/russia/newsid_7513000/7513237.stm (accessed July 4, 2010).

Part II

Russia and the "Near Abroad" after the War with Georgia

5
Russia and Georgia – From Confrontation to War: What is Next?

Bertil Nygren

The South Caucasus is the most unstable CIS region and Georgia is the most unstable 'weak state' of that region, today as well as historically; traditionally it was a buffer against Turkey and Persia in the early 19th century (Trenin, 2002, pp. 47, 169 and 179–80). Georgia was united in the 12th century, before the Muscovy Russian state (but after the Kievan state), but, like Kievan Russia, was conquered by the Mongols in the 13th century. From the 15th century Georgia was dominated by Turkey and Persia, and sought Russian protection. Russia conquered Georgia in the first half of the 19th century. With the Russian revolution and the ensuing civil war, Georgian self-determination was regained in 1918, but lasted only until 1921, when the Red Army invasion forced Georgia into joining Armenia and Azerbaijan in the Transcaucasus Republic of the USSR (in 1922). Georgia became a Soviet Socialist Republic in 1936 and regained some of its cultural autonomy, but, as happened with the treatment of other borders in the Caucasus, Georgian borders also included non-Georgian peoples and cultures (such as Abkhazians and Ossetians). Today Georgia borders on violence-ridden parts of southern Russia – Chechnya, North Ossetia, and Dagestan. Georgia's post-Soviet history has been stormy, worth telling because of its many connections with the Russian–Georgian relationship itself. The pivotal part is Abkhazia (located at the eastern shores of the Black Sea), where armed clashes took place between Georgians and Abkhazians as early as 1989, also involving Soviet troops stationed in Abkhazia. In 1990 Abkhazia opted for independence from Georgia and chose its own president. In December 1991, armed clashes broke out in the Georgian capital, and Soviet forces were engaged.

The next year, in 1992, Abkhazian secessionists brought about a civil war that lasted for two years and resulted in several hundred thousand ethnic Georgians being expelled, together with the Georgian regular army. By late 1993 casualties amounted to some 10,000. The Russian forces stationed in Abkhazia often sided with the Abkhazian forces, but in the end Shevardnadze had to ask Russia to establish a demilitarized zone. Russia never formally supported Abkhazian independence, but nonetheless the Abkhazians put it to a referendum, resulting in a large majority vote (of those remaining in Abkhazia). During the Yeltsin years Abkhazia remained unstable and outside Tbilisi's control. Russian peacekeepers brought some stability, but clashes between Abkhazian and Georgian troops and paramilitaries never ceased.

The other breakaway republic, South Ossetia, also suffered a short war after it proclaimed its independence from Tbilisi. In 1992 a referendum confirmed that South Ossetians wanted to join North Ossetia and the Russian Federation. As with Abkhazia, Georgian attempts to establish control did not succeed, and Georgian paramilitary groups fought South Ossetian (and Russian) troops. Casualties amounted to some 1,500, but in general the situation was much more stable than in Abkhazia during the Yeltsin era. The two ethnic conflicts remained "frozen" and Georgia remained in an abnormal, unstable state. Russia and Georgia signed a Friendship Treaty in 1994 that guaranteed Georgia's territorial integrity; locally, however, Russian forces overtly supported the leaders of the breakaway republics.

Developments in Russia also contributed to the difficulties for Georgia. The reassertion of a self-confident Russian foreign policy under President Putin was particularly evident with respect to the CIS countries, and Russia's relations with Georgia have been the most sour of all Russia's bilateral relations with the CIS countries (the only other contender being Ukraine since fall 2004). The tense relationship all through the 1990s seemed to change in the last months of Yeltsin's rule, with his promise (at the 1999 Istanbul OSCE meeting) to withdraw Russian soldiers and military material and close four military bases in Georgia after almost a decade of repeated Georgian requests. But by then the second Chechnya war had begun, and the new Russian president had second thoughts. In addition, Chechen rebels often sought refuge from Russian forces in the Pankisi Valley in Georgia, which soon developed into a contentious issue. Georgia was also showing an open interest in seeking Western assistance, and the negative spiral was further reinforced after September 11, when Russia argued for its right to pursue Chechen rebels on Georgian territory: had it not been for overt warnings from the United States, Russian military intervention on Georgian territory might very well have occurred.[1]

Issues in Russian–Georgian relations

The three central issues – Russian military bases in Georgia, Chechens in the Pankisi Valley, and the separatist republics of Abkhazia and South Ossetia – will be treated separately below. The base issue was solved before the August 2008 war and need not concern us here.[2] Russia signaled that two new military bases on the Russian side of the Caucasus would be established close to Georgia. The second issue, the Chechens in the Pankisi Valley, has also receded in the last five years and need only to be treated superficially here. Chechnya played an important role in relations between Russia and Georgia, as it had earlier (in 1993), when Gamsakhurdia (after he was ousted in 1992 and Shevardnadze was sworn in as president) had used Chechnya to launch an attempt to regain power in Georgia. Furthermore, the Chechen field commander Shamil Basaev had already sided with Abkhazian forces against the Georgian military forces during the Georgian civil war, and during the first Chechnya war, in 1994–6, Georgia came out on the Russian side against the Chechen warriors. But when Aslan Maskhadov, the Chechen President, went to Tbilisi in 1997 and met Shevardnadze, Russia was dismayed. From the beginning of the second Chechen war in 1999, Georgia was accused of harbouring some 1,500 Arab mercenaries and 200 Taliban in the Pankisi Valley, as well as Chechen warriors. Russian combat helicopters had entered Georgia both in fall 1999 and again in early 2000. After September 11 Georgia feared direct Russian military action, especially since Putin openly linked developments in Chechnya with international terrorism and obviously believed that the United States would support Russian antiterrorism measures.[3] New air intrusions followed in fall 2001 and in early 2002. The Russian military regularly denied responsibility.[4] In spring 2002, Russian uncertainty about the US position on how to treat the Chechen warriors most likely helped to defuse the crisis for some time, despite Russian renewed air incursions. The May 2002 summit between presidents Bush and Putin also brought about the (futile) idea of joint Russian–Georgian military operations in the Pankisi Valley.

In August 2002, Russian troops, together with aircraft and combat helicopters, struck a blow against Chechen warriors. The Russian Foreign Ministry accused Georgia of "reluctance to take practical steps against terrorism" and advocated "targeted retaliatory operations" by Russian military forces (which Georgia described as "a call for war") (*RFE/RL Newsline*, August 1 and 2, 2002). Several warnings of Russian unilateral action followed in the next several months, and new air intrusions took place in the Pankisi Valley. This time, to Putin's surprise, the United States offered "strong support" for Georgia's independence, and tension between Russia and the United States increased. Also in August 2002, Georgian troops entered the Pankisi Valley for the first time, but the situation grew even worse. The Georgian parliament appealed to the UN, OSCE, the European Union, the Council of Europe and NATO for protection from anticipated "Russian military aggression" (*RFE/RL Newsline*, September 9, 12 and 13, 2002). The United States now came out in strong support of Georgia, opposing "any unilateral military action by Russia inside Georgia," and Bush urged Putin to give Georgia time to clear the Pankisi Valley (*RFE/RL Newsline*, September 12, 2002). In these verbal encounters it is evident that Russia gave in to US pressure to leave Georgia alone.

In April 2003, Georgia and the United States signed a bilateral security pact, which enraged Russia (Blagov, 2003). In October of the same year a new Russian military doctrine suggested the right to launch preemptive military strikes within the CIS, which caused further worries in Georgia (*RFE/RL Newsline*, October 10, 2003). With the Georgian "rose revolution" in late 2003, the issue of Chechen warriors in Pankisi Valley was overshadowed by new worries, although the issue reappeared in 2007, 2008, and 2009 (*RFERL Newsline*, March 14, 2007 and February 8, 2008, *RFERL Georgia*, October 28, 2009).

The third conflict issue, the status of the two separatist regions Abkhazia and South Ossetia, has been the most cumbersome for both Georgia and Russia to handle. The Abkhazian situation has been more difficult than the South Ossetian one. One very basic reason for the problems in both regions has undoubtedly been the fact that there are many actors involved with different interests; another is the very fact that the Abkhazian civil war relocated large numbers of ethnic Georgians who have been unable to move back to Abkhazia. When Putin came to power, the Russian peacekeeping forces in Abkhazia were needed even more, because of the resumed fighting between Georgian paramilitaries and Abkhazian forces. The fact that Chechen warriors took part on the side of these Georgian paramilitaries against the Abkhazian forces in the Abkhazian Kodori Mountains (close to Russia) did not alleviate the situation. Georgian regular forces entered the Kodori Mountains in the fall of 2001 and, after Russian protests, they were exchanged for Georgian border guards in early 2002. Georgian paramilitaries and

Abkhazian forces have clashed fairly regularly, but the situation worsened after the "rose revolution," when President Saakashvili decided to restore Georgia's territorial integrity and take control of Abkhazia and South Ossetia.

The first attempt to restore territorial integrity involved the district of Ajaria along the Turkish border in spring 2004, a crisis that threatened to develop into an armed confrontation between Ajarian paramilitaries and Georgian regular forces. In this conflict, Russia came to Saakashvili's assistance and the Ajarian leader decided to leave Ajaria (Arnold, 2004; Blagov, 2004; Gendzhekhadze, 2004; Medetsky, 2004). The conflicts in Abkhazia and South Ossetia, on the other hand, were soon to worsen, and as a result tensions between Georgia and Russia grew by fall 2004. One of the reasons for the increased tension was the Russian involvement in (illegal) presidential elections in Abkhazia in fall 2004. Another reason concerned the stalled negotiations over the future status of Abkhazia and South Ossetia within Georgia, and the fact that repatriation attempts were impaired by frequent assaults by both Abkhazian troops and Georgian paramilitaries. Several attempts to introduce plans for the future status of Abkhazia within Georgia by various parties in 2005 and 2006 failed. In addition, Russia was issuing Russian passports to Abkhazians, which hinted at the permanence of the constitutional rift.

In 2006 and 2007, some other issues in the Russian–Georgian relationship took over the front pages, especially the NATO membership issue and the trade war. These events also emphasized developments in Abkhazia. Both Abkhazian attacks on Georgian police forces on the internal border of Georgia and Abkhazia and atrocities in the Gali region and in the Kodori Valley helped make things even worse. In February 2007 there were new attempts at restarting the dialogue between Georgia and Abkhazia; but in March Russian air intrusions were reintroduced into the conflict, when two Russian helicopters fired on villages in Kodori Valley. In April, the UN discussed the Abkhazian situation and Georgia announced a new peace plan for Abkhazia, which was rejected by the latter. The situation was stalemated for several months. In July the UN managed to accompany the two sides to the negotiation table to solve some immediate issues. In August two Russian Su-24s attacked a Georgian village some 60 kilometers outside Tbilisi with missiles. Both the UN Security Council and OSCE failed to condemn the incident, since Russia blocked the issue. There were also Georgian air intrusions into Abkhazia and armed clashes in the Kodori Valley that poisoned the situation.

The independence of Kosovo worsened the situation further still. In early 2008 Russia threatened the "Cyprus model" for Abkhazia, and in February 2008 Abkhazian and South Ossetian leaders openly discussed the Kosovo model in Moscow, claiming the Kosovo decision as a precedent also for the two unrecognized republics within Georgia (*RFERL Newsline*, February 15, 2008; Whitmore, 2008). In March, Russia suddenly announced that it did not consider itself bound by the decision in 1996 to impose restrictions on trade and other links with Abkhazia and South Ossetia. In April Abkhazia again rejected a Georgian peace proposal. An incident in which either Abkhazian forces or a Russian airplane shot down an unmanned Georgian spy plane in the Gali region caused a diplomatic frenzy. The UN blamed both Russia and Georgia for sending a spy plane into Abkhazia. In June Georgia asked OSCE for help when Russia sent reinforcements of peacekeepers into Abkhazia, some 400 men, to repair a railway in Abkhazia (finished just before the war). While Medvedev, the new Russian president, tried to "talk down" the conflict, Saakashvili used war talk to get support from the West (Lobjakas, 2008). Abkhazia shot down another two unmanned Georgian spy planes, and Georgian rhetoric reached the highest level since the civil war. The West was concerned, but hesitated to blame either side for the escalating developments.

The summer of 2008 got hot in Abkhazia. In July, a series of bombs went off along the border of Abkhazia and Georgia proper, as well as in Sukhumi, and shootings took place at several places. The "blame game" went into full operation. The Georgian Ambassador to Moscow was withdrawn in response, and the German foreign minister visited Tbilisi and Moscow to mediate and to present a peace plan for Abkhazia drawn up by the members of the Friends of the UN Secretary-General for Georgia. Abkhazia rejected the plan, while Russia called it "extremely helpful" (Fuller, 2008a; *RFERL Georgia*, July 18, 2008). In late July the UN Security Council met again on the Abkhazian situation at Georgia's request.

In South Ossetia, where the situation had been fairly stable for several years, Saakashvili's attempt to take control (in 2004) also developed negatively. Negotiations on the status of South Ossetia followed basically the same pattern as those in Abkhazia – the various parties presented plans that were immediately rejected by other parties to the conflict. Here, as well as in Abkhazia, local South Ossetian military troops, together with Georgian paramilitaries, were active parties to the destabilization. Russian peacekeepers were not necessarily neutral in this conflict either, and the agenda for some Georgian paramilitaries was not always in Georgia's interest. Armed clashes were frequent in 2004 and 2005 and, as in Abkhazia, Russia had been issuing Russian passports to the South Ossetians. Peace plans were presented by the Georgian government in 2004 and 2005, arguing for a demilitarization of South Ossetia, but were countered by a South Ossetian peace plan in December 2005. As a further turn in the negative spiral of the conflict, when Russia closed the Verkhny Lars border crossing in summer 2006 and when Kokoity was reelected president in South Ossetia in November 2006, the Georgia-controlled part of South Ossetia elected its own president. In early 2007 the situation in South Ossetia deteriorated; several Georgian police officers were killed in separate acts, and in May and June there were several incidents of artillery shelling in South Ossetia. Shootings continued in August along the South Ossetian–Georgian line of demarcation; in September a bomb went off in Tskhinvali, and new shelling continued into the fall. New bomb blasts in February and March, and again in July 2008, were blamed on Georgian forces. When four Russian aircraft entered South Ossetia, Russia immediately conceded that they indeed were Russian aircraft looking for Georgian preparations to attack South Ossetia (*RFERL Georgia*, July 10, 2008).

In addition to these long-term conflict issues in the Russian–Georgian relationship, there were other issues that developed after the "rose revolution" and increased tension still further. In 2006 there was a virtual trade and cultural war between Russia and Georgia, when Russia stopped issuing visas to Georgians (Torbakov, 2006). Later in the spring a Russian "wine ban" and a ban on Georgian mineral waters were inaugurated (see Corso, 2006). In fall 2006, when four Russian military officers were arrested and accused of spying, Russia implemented an air transport and mail blockade. Furthermore, within Russia, Georgians were harassed, Russian visa requirements increased, and Russian sanctions on Georgian business in Russia became more severe (Lukyanov, 2006).[5] Georgia used the Russian WTO membership application as an instrument to cancel the Russian trade restrictions. Other trade issues involved the abolition of customs posts along the borders of Abkhazia and Georgia proper and between South Ossetia and Georgia proper. In early 2008, Georgia and Russia decided to maintain joint customs posts on these borders. Because of deteriorating relations with Russia, Georgia suspended further talks in 2008, although flights between Georgia and Russia were resumed.

Another conflict issue was the Georgian determination to achieve NATO membership. Georgia had already opted for NATO assistance in 1992 and had been a major beneficiary of NATO military assistance (some \$20 million worth of equipment each year since 1998). At the November 2002 NATO summit in Prague, Georgia made an official bid for membership, and in March 2003 Georgia was accepted as a NATO aspirant. After the "Rose revolution" in December 2003, Georgia's ambitions rose, and in April 2004 the new Georgian president handed over Georgia's Individual Partnership Action Plan (IPAP) to NATO. At the Istanbul NATO summit in June 2004, Georgia (and Azerbaijan and Uzbekistan) were invited to develop IPAPs with NATO, and in November the Georgian IPAP was approved. Further development stagnated for several years, and there were no promises of a NATO Membership Action Plan (the final stage before accession) in 2007. At the April 2008 Bucharest NATO summit, German and French hesitation prevented a membership offer being made.

The August war

The Russia–Georgia war in August 2008 drastically changed any possible future solutions to the separatist problems. Before looking at these changes in the Russian–Georgian relationship, let us briefly consider the war itself. First, although there had been warning signs also in South Ossetia since spring 2008, the most likely region for a war between Russia and Georgia had been Abkhazia. The most ominous sign of approaching hostilities was the Russian military exercises along the Russian–Georgian border from mid-July to the beginning of August, involving some 8,000 soldiers. During the first week of August, Russia accused Georgia of escalating the South Ossetian conflict, while Georgia accused Russia of assembling its troops (Lomsadze, 2008). The war began on August 7, 2008 after several days of artillery shelling from Georgian and South Ossetian troops. On August 7, after a short cease-fire, Georgia resumed its shelling, since South Ossetian artillery fire on Georgian villages close to Tskhinvali had resumed. Russian troops advanced through the Roki Tunnel during the night into August 8, and Georgian troops, therefore, shelled the area. Russian air strikes against Georgian military bases followed. Russia claimed that Georgia was conducting ethnic cleansing in South Ossetia, killing civilians by the thousands. By August 9, Russia had total control of Georgian airspace, and Russian troops advanced, to take control within a few days of Gori and the east–west highway through Georgia. On August 10 and 11, Abkhazia joined the war by taking control of seaside Poti and some neighboring areas. On August 12, French President Nicolas Sarkozy negotiated a cease-fire, in which the biggest mistake was the continued acceptance of Russian troops in neighboring areas of South Ossetia, in Poti and on the highway between western and eastern Georgia. Russia remained in these areas for two weeks.

The flow of events on August 7–8 is not yet fully understood, nor is the timetable of Russian armed involvement. The main question remains whether or not Russian regular troops (with or without the consent of the Russian political leadership), together with South Ossetian militias, had planned and staged the war situation, and Russian troops had entered the Roki tunnel before August 8, or whether the Russian reaction was a more "spontaneous" outbreak after a Georgian military miscalculation. Estimates vary.[6] These and similar questions will not be addressed here. Instead, we will focus on an analysis of what has happened in the relationship since the cease-fire and the Russian retreat from Georgia proper to the territories of South Ossetia and Abkhazia. In any event, it is obvious that the war constituted a turning point in Russian foreign policy that will haunt Russia and its neighbors for many years to come.

Postwar developments

One rather expected, and fully understandable, immediate act of Georgian revenge for the war was to announce Georgia's withdrawal from the CIS, which occurred formally a year later, in August 2009. Ukraine protested by requiring Russian air and naval forces to announce their movements 72 hours in advance. The Russian recognition of the two Georgian breakaway republics constituted a revenge act for the recognition by Western countries of the independence of Kosovo.[7] The most noteworthy effect of the war in the CIS region was the muted tone in which Russia and Georgia were criticized, and even more noteworthy was the response of the CIS countries to the Russian recognition of the independence of Abkhazia and South Ossetia that followed by the end of August – they basically kept quiet on the subject of recognition.

Other international consequences were evident. First of all, while Putin personally required that the CIS states take a stand on the war and on the recognition of South Ossetia and Abkhazia, Ukraine and Azerbaijan in effect supported Georgia, and Moldova also took a cautious stand for Georgia. Kazakhstan was very wary, as was Kyrgyzstan. Armenia refused to take a stand, as did Belarus. This disobedience by silence of CIS members was a high price for Moscow to pay for its own recognition of Abkhazia and South Ossetia. Furthermore, when the Shanghai Cooperation Organization (SCO) assembled in late August

2008, it offered only lukewarm support for Russia's initial operations in Georgia, but completely failed to follow Russia in the recognition of the two breakaway republics (Abdullaev, 2008). In other words, Russia did not even get support for its handling of the war and its recognition of the two breakaway republics from its closest allies.[8] This in itself points to the fact that CIS countries today understand that the proud declarations of the CIS on equality do not concern Russia itself – Russia is exempted from the rules it has set for others (Goble, 2008). Further silent protest by CIS members occurred in October 2009, when a CIS summit in Moldova failed to draw the leaders of Uzbekistan, Tajikistan, and Turkmenistan (Pannier, 2009).

Secondly, neither of the two breakaway republics, especially not South Ossetia, has any chance of sustained statehood. In addition, although most Abkhazians and South Ossetians already have Russian passports, the Abkhazian president Bagapsh has promised his citizens independence, not *Anschluss* to Russia (Fuller, 2008b). It remains to be seen for how long the present state of affairs – independence – will remain. Economic and other life support from Russia remains necessary, and Russia is effectively in control of both the economic and military spheres in Abkhazia and South Ossetia (Coalson, 2009). This situation has been reinforced by Georgia's initiation of an economic blockade on Abkhazia and South Ossetia in August 2009.

Third, the possible international repercussions are many. For example, the consequences for other frozen conflicts in Transdniestria and Nagorno-Karabakh are not clear (Bigg, 2008; Zurabishvili, 2008). Russia has also had to pay in its relations with the larger international community, where Russia, much to its own great surprise, lost both prestige and confidence (Lukyanov, 2008). Indeed, in fall 2009 Russia almost lost its place in the Parliamentary Assembly of the Council of Europe (PACE) (von Twickel, 2009).

Fourth, the Russian invasion of Georgia was bound to be reflected in more or less official Russian doctrines. In early September 2008 Medvedev gave an interview in which he outlined a new five-point doctrine, the second and third points of which described a multipolar world where Russia would have good relations with Europe and the United States, but would defend its citizens and its business community from any aggressive acts abroad, and would retain privileged interests in the CIS region (Medvedev, 2008b). This notion of defending Russians abroad targeted many of the CIS members, and also Estonia and Latvia. This was a major reason why so many CIS countries chose not to comment on the Russian invasion: obviously, they saw themselves as possible future victims. Medvedev's statements and talks with Sarkozy just after the war also gave some hints of the elements of the new doctrine as early as summer 2008 (Medvedev 2008a; 2008c).[9]

There were also other consequences for Russia. If the Russian invasion had been a clear punishment for Georgia's ambitions to join NATO (Felgenhauer, 2009, p. 177; Interview with Kakabadze, 2008) one might have expected an enforced membership plan for Georgia, but the invasion, in fact, did not speed up Georgian membership chances at all.[10] This was evident at the December 2008 NATO summit, which offered no clear membership prospects; informal NATO discussions in Poland in February 2009 also did not result in any conclusive stand. The new US presidential administration suggested that the prospects for Georgian (and Ukrainian) NATO membership had actually changed for the worse (Sindelar, 2008). The new US president Barack Obama's "reset" of relations with Russia further diminished Georgia's chances of NATO membership.[11] Generally speaking, the Russian–NATO relationship, frozen after the invasion, was fairly soon normalized, and in March 2009 the first signs of an improvement were visible (Fuller, 2009b; Lobjakas, 2009c; 2009d). Relations again temporarily deteriorated in April, when the long-planned joint military exercises of the US and Georgia were due to take place.[12] Russia regarded them as provocations, and just "by coincidence" the Russian Black Sea fleet ships based in the Ukrainian port of Sevastopol were preparing for large-scale naval exercises at the same time. Russia also refrained from taking part in the scheduled meetings with NATO. Russian military exercises also directly influenced the Russia–Georgia relationship. For example, Russian troops held military exercises in North Caucasus in June 2009, and in August there were military exercises in Abkhazia. Neither did mutual expulsions on spy charges alleviate the situation ("Russia's Lavrov…", 2009). An alleged Georgian spy was arrested in Russia in April 2009 and sentenced in August; another was arrested in August and sentenced in October. A Georgian charge against a Georgian citizen spying for Russia developed in spring 2010, as did another Russian spy charge against two Russian officers accused of having informed Georgia of the August war preparations.

Relations between Russia and Georgia, on the one hand, and the EU, on the other, were also affected by the war: for example, the EU attempt to speed up the development of the process of the European Neighborhood Policy (Lobjakas, 2009a; 2009b). Russian relations with the UN were not normalized until February 2009, when the UN mission in Abkhazia was finally extended (Krastev, 2009a). The UN mission never went into action, however, and it was hoped that the EU would pick up the tasks (Krastev, 2009b; Lomsadze, 2009a; Peuch, 2009). Discussions included the possible additional inclusion of US troops (Corso, 2009c). OSCE monitors were also vetoed by Russia and the existing OSCE monitors had to leave the breakaway enclaves.

Events in Abkhazia and South Ossetia also created difficulties in the Russian–Georgian relationship. Initially most important were the EU monitoring missions in Georgia, by which the EU put pressure on Russia to keep to the agreement concluded by Medvedev and Sarkozy in September 2008 (Ferrero-Waldner, 2009). Of the six points in the initial August agreement, one stipulated the convening of negotiations on security and humanitarian issues in Abkhazia and South Ossetia jointly mediated by the UN, the European Union, and OSCE, with the United States, Russia, Georgia, and South Ossetia and Abkhazia also present. The first three meetings in October, November, and December did not result in any agreements, but the fourth negotiation round, in February 2009, resulted in agreement on limited measures to preclude incidents of violence. Talks continued in May and July. Another issue developed when Russia signaled its intention to build a naval base in Abkhazia. Also in the spring Russia announced that it intended to take responsibility for the borders between the two breakaway republics and Georgia proper and to set up military bases on their territory (Coalson, 2009; Corso, 2009b). Both the United States and the EU expressed serious concern. The Abkhazian presidential election in December could not but create irritation in the West. In spring 2010 further plans to set up two additional Russian bases (one land and one naval) were presented.

In addition to these more serious consequences of the war and its aftermath for the Russian–Georgian relationship, there were other signs of deterioration, in themselves seemingly harmless, but indicative of developments. The Georgian contribution to the Eurovision song contest caused a stir in January 2009, and by April Georgia decided to abstain from participation. Another irritating issue in the bilateral relationship developed when a Russian soldier sought asylum in Georgia in January and received it in summer 2009 despite Russian demands for his extradition. A second asylum seeker appeared in July, and Georgia granted him asylum as well.[13] Two railway explosions occurred in June in Georgia, both blamed on Russia, and bomb and artillery explosions were heard also in South Ossetia. A Soviet-era memorial in Tbilisi was demolished to provide space for a new building, causing an uproar of discontent in Russia.

Tension rose in both enclaves as the anniversary of the war approached (Lomsadze, 2009b). To no one's surprise, in summer 2009 rumors were rife of a new Russian invasion of Georgia (Aptsiauri, 2009; Feifer, 2009; Fuller, 2009b; Lobjakas, 2009e; Whitmore, 2009). In August and September 2009 there were incidents of civilian ships destined for Abkhazia being detained by the Georgian navy, and in November Georgian fishermen were detained by Russian soldiers. Abkhazia responded by threatening Georgian ships, and Russia reciprocated by detaining Georgian ships off the coast and by deploying coast guards off Abkhazia. Furthermore, Georgia was also trying to find support for a boycott of the Sochi Olympic winter games. Later, a delegation of Russian scientists was refused entry into Georgia. In South Ossetia, Georgian books were burned on bonfires (Mikulova, 2009), and Georgia was astounded by reports that Abkhazia was to get Russian, rather than Georgian, phone area codes.

Despite all the negative trends, some practical cooperation between Russia and Georgia has actually taken place. In January 2009 there was a Georgia–Russia agreement on a hydropower plant, and Georgia has agreed to resume gas supplies to South Ossetia (cut off since August 2008). In September 2009 Russia and Georgia agreed to begin talks on how to reduce the risk of future use of violence in the relationship, and negotiations were to start by the end of the year. In early 2010 air transportation was resumed and the border crossing Verkhny Lars was reopened, both on Medvedev's initiative.

Conclusion

In conclusion, what is to be expected of relations in the years to come? Is a new war possible, or likely? After all, Georgia was not crushed and Tbilisi was not taken.[14] The most interesting issue by far is the very question of what will happen to South Ossetia and Abkhazia, since they are both totally dependent on Russia for their political, military, and economic survival. It would seem "natural" that Russia made use of this dependency and simply accepted an application from the two breakaway republics to become the ninetieth and ninety-first federation subjects of the Russian Federation. On the other hand, Russia might still reap some benefits from an uncertain situation, especially with respect to Georgia's future NATO membership: prospects for Georgian NATO membership would not benefit from a situation in which the very status and territory of Georgia as a state is unresolved.

Secondly, Russia is definitely back on the regional scene as a military power capable of taking care of security and defense issues in its immediate neighborhood, with or without the consent of the other CIS members. Russia will definitely continue to keep up the pressure to prevent NATO membership of its CIS neighbors. In spring 2010 it appears that Ukraine itself is defusing the issue, while it may have been reintroduced in the case of Moldova.

Thirdly, the international reaction that favored Georgia in the short run seems to favor Russia in the longer run. Russia is simply too important to Europe and the United States for punishments or bans to be implemented. Western threats of treating Russia as an unruly teenager unable to live by the rules of its parents will not have the intended effect on Russia. Therefore, what remains to be done is for the West to keep up moral pressure for change in Russia, but with a much more realistic time perspective (the long run) for its implementation. The problem for Georgia is, of course, whether or not it will survive very long while waiting for such changes.

Notes

1. The terrorist threat, especially the house bombings in Moscow in August 1999 and the many Chechnya-related terror attacks (e.g., on the Dubrovka Theatre in October 2002 and the Muzorka military hospital in July 2003) was very evident in Russia, and was legally recognized in the Law on Terrorism adopted in late 1998.
2. By summer 2001, two bases were abandoned, but with no agreement on the remaining two bases, which Russia wanted to keep for another fifteen years. The haggling over the remaining bases continued for another five years, until, unexpectedly, in spring 2005, Russia finally decided to give up the remaining two bases (which were actually due to be left by the end of 2007 and 2008 respectively). Russia handed over the Akhalkalaki military base in southern Georgia in July 2007, as promised in spring 2006. The second base in Batumi was to be handed over by the end of 2008. Military equipment from Batumi was transported to Russia in August 2007, and in November 2007 the Batumi base was emptied. The one remaining base, in Gudauta in Abkhazia, was not entirely emptied because of uncertainties surrounding its evacuation, and a few hundred Russian soldiers remained there to watch over the installations (Martirosyan and Ismail, 2005; Parsons, 2005).
3. The events in Chechnya "cannot be considered outside of the context of the struggle with international terrorism," Putin claimed (*RFE/RL Newsline*, 25 September 2001). Russian Defense Minister Sergei Ivanov argued that Afghanistan and Chechnya were "two branches of one tree...the roots of [which] are in Afghanistan" (*RFE/RL Newsline*, 4 October 2001). Even the US Ambassador to Russia, Alexander Vershbow, said that "Chechen separatists receive enormous help from abroad" and that several field commanders were

"foreigners" (see *Argumenty i fakty*, 2001, p.3). Foreign Minister Igor Ivanov claimed that the Pankisi valley had become a "stronghold of...international terrorists" and Defense Minister Sergei Ivanov suggested that Georgia was unable to control the Pankisi Valley on its own (*RFE/RL Newsline*, 20 February 2002).

4. Six helicopters bombed villages in the Kodori Valley and several Su-25 aircraft flew over the valley. Shevardnadze believed that the decision had been taken at a lower level (see *RFE/RL Newsline*, 29 and 30 November 2001).

5. In fall 2006, Russia deported some 4,600 Georgians by air to Georgia, as a response to the arrest of Russian spies in Georgia (Bigg, 2007).

6. Estimates vary also in one and the same volume on the war released less than a year after the war. See, for example, Felgenhauer, 2009; Illarionov, 2009; Popjanevski, 2009. The "blame game" started at an early stage (see Mukhanov, 2008; Pankin, 2008; von Twickel, 2008). The EU report on the war in September 2009 divides the blame between Georgia (for the attack on Tskinvali) and Russia (for the war on Georgia proper) (EU report, 2009).

7. For an analysis of similarities and differences between Kosovan and South Ossetian independence, see Oliker (2008).

8. The international community refused almost unanimously to grant statehood to the two Georgian regions. Only Nicaragua recognized the two breakout regions (in early September 2008). A year later, in September 2009, Venezuela joined in, and in December the micro island state of Nauru.

9. For Medvedev's official foreign policy doctrine, see Foreign Policy Concept, July 12, 2009.

10. Western discussions on Georgian membership became somewhat more cautious, especially in Germany and France (see Corso, 2008; Kucera, 2008).

11. Despite this, US support for Georgia was clearly manifest. In January 2009, the United States and Georgia officially became "strategic partners," the meaning of which was fairly unclear, except symbolically. In December 2008, Ukraine and the US signed a similar partnership (Corso, 2009a; Tully, 2009). Talks on the issue continued in June.

12. For the exercises, see Synovitz (2009).

13. A Georgian deserter was also found in Russia.

14. See Felgenhauer (2009), p. 180.

References

Abdullaev, Nabi (2008) "Medvedev Disappointed in Dushanbe", *Moscow Times*, August 29.

Aptsiauri, Goga (2009) "Russian Troops Try To Shift South Ossetia Border Markers", *RFERL Georgia*, August 3. http://www.rferl.org/content/Russian_Troops_Try_To_Shift_South_Ossetia_Border_Markers/1791641.html

Argumenty i fakty, 40(1093), September 2001.

Arnold, Chloe (2004) "In Georgia, Ivanov's the angel of political death", *Moscow Times*, May 11, p. 9.

Benita Ferrero-Waldner interview (2009) "EU's Ferrero-Waldner Discusses Georgian War's Aftermath, Integration Prospects", *RFERL Georgia*, January 22.

http://www.rferl.org/content/EUs_External_Relations_Chief_Discusses_ Wars_Aftermath_Integration_Prospects/1373498.html (accessed June 24, 2010).

Bigg, Claire (2007) "Georgia takes Russia to Human Rights Court", *RFERL Newsline*, April 4.

Bigg, Claire (2008) "Georgia Woes Could Send Ripple Through Other Frozen Conflicts", *RFERL war report*, August 27. http://www.rferl.org/content/ Georgia_Woes_Ripple_Other_Frozen_Conflicts/1194375.html (accessed June 24, 2010).

Blagov, Sergei (2003) "US-Georgian security cooperation agreement provokes outcry in Russia", *Eurasia Insight*, April 16. http://www.eurasianet.org/ departments/insight/articles/eav041603a.shtml

Blagov, Sergei (2004) "Amid celebration in Batumi, Georgian authorities move to reassert authority in Ajaria", *Eurasia Insight*, May 6. http://www. eurasianet.org/departments/insight/articles/eav050604.shtml (accessed June 24, 2010).

Coalson, Robert (2009) "Russia Steps Up Cooperation With Breakaway Georgian Regions", *RFERL Georgia*, April 30. http://www.rferl.org/content/Russia_ Steps_Up_Cooperation_With_Breakaway_Georgian_Regions/1619281.html (accessed June 24, 2010).

Cornell, Svante and Starr, S. Frederick (eds) (2009) *The Guns of August 2008. Russia's War in Georgia*, Armonk, NY, London: M.E. Sharpe.

Corso, Molly (2006) "Georgia pursues campaign against espionage", *Eurasia Insight*, March 31. http://www.eurasianet.org/departments/insight/articles/ eav033106.shtml (accessed June 24, 2010).

Corso, Molly (2008) "Moving On Toward NATO Without a Map", *Eurasia Insight*, December 3. http://www.eurasianet.org/departments/insightb/articles/ eav120308.shtml (accessed June 24, 2010).

Corso, Molly (2009a) "Washington and Tbilisi Signs Strategic Pact Sure to Irk the Kremlin", *Eurasia Insight*, January 9. http://www.eurasianet.org/departments/ insightb/articles/eav010909b.shtml (accessed June 24, 2010).

Corso, Molly (2009b) "Russian Border Guards in Abkhazia, South Ossetia Pose New Challenge for Tbilisi", *Eurasia Insight*, May 12. http://www.eurasianet. org/departments/insightb/articles/eav051209c.shtml (accessed June 24, 2010).

Corso, Molly (2009c) "European monitors in Georgia: a case of great expec- tations?" *Eurasia Insight*, July 6. http://www.eurasianet.org/departments/ insightb/articles/eav070609a.shtml (accessed June 24, 2010).

EU Report (2009). Independent International Fact-Finding Mission on the Conflict in Georgia. September 2009. http://www.ceiig.ch/Report.html (accessed June 24, 2010).

Feifer, Gregory (2009) "Friction Feeds Fears Of New Russia-Georgia Conflict", *RFERL Georgia*, June 29. http://www.rferl.org/content/Fears_Grow_Of_New_ RussiaGeorgia_Conflict/1765258.html (accessed June 24, 2010).

Felgenhauer, Pavel (2009) "The Escalation of the Russia-Georgia War", in Svente Cornell and S. Frederick Starr (eds) (2009) *The Guns of August 2008. Russia's War in Georgia*, Armonk, NY, London: M.E. Sharpe, pp. 162–80.

Foreign Policy Concept of the Russian Federation (2008), July 12. http://eng. kremlin.ru/text/docs/2008/07/204750.shtml

Fuller, Liz (2008a) "German Plan Offers Chance on Abkhaz Conflict", *RFERL Georgia*, July 19. http://www.rferl.org/content/German_Plan_Offers_Chance_Abkhaz_Conflict/1184866.html (accessed June 24, 2010).

Fuller, Liz (2008b) "What's Next For South Ossetia And Abkhazia?", *RFERL Georgia*, August 26. http://www.rferl.org/content/What_Next_South_Ossetia_Abkhazia/1194045.html (accessed June 24, 2010).

Fuller, Liz (2009a) "Does U.S. Charter Protect Georgia Against Renewed Conflict With Russia?", *RFERL Georgia*, March 11. http://www.rferl.org/content/Does_US_Charter_Protect_Georgia_Against_Renewed_Conflict_With_Russia/1508110.html (accessed June 24, 2010).

Fuller, Liz (2009b) "Does Russia Even Need To Invade Georgia?", *RFERL Georgia*, May 26. http://www.rferl.org/content/Does_Russia_Even_Need_To_Invade_Georgia/1739947.html (accessed June 24, 2010).

Gendzekhadze, Tamazi (2004) "Tbilisi offers Abashidze safe passage", *Moscow Times*, May 6, p. 1.

Goble, Paul (2008) "After Ossetia, Some Things Change And Some Remain The Same", *RFERL Georgia war special report*, August 15. http://www.rferl.org/content/After_Ossetia_Some_Things_Change_And_Some_Remain_The_Same/1191331.html (accessed June 24, 2010).

Illarionov, Andrei (2009) "The Russian Leadership's Preparation for War, 1999–2008", in Cornell, Svante and Starr, S. Frederick (eds) (2009) *The Guns of August 2008. Russia's War in Georgia*, Armonk, NY, London: M.E. Sharpe, pp. 49–84.

"Interview with David Kakabadze", (2008) in *RFERL Georgia war special*, August 10. http://www.rferl.org/content/Russia_Punishing_Georgia_For_NATO_Aspirations/1189974.html (accessed June 24, 2010).

Krastev, Nikola (2009a) "UN Security Council Extends Mission in Abkhazia", *RFERL Georgia*, February 14. http://www.rferl.org/content/UN_Security_Council_Extends_Mission_In_Abkhazia/1493041.html (accessed June 24, 2010).

Krastev, Nikola (2009b) "Georgia Slams Russia For Shutting Down UN Mission", *RFERL Georgia*, June 16. http://www.rferl.org/content/Russia_Vetoes_Western_Plan_For_UN_In_Georgia/1755138.html (accessed June 24, 2010).

Kucera, Joshua (2008) "No Discussion of Map for Tbilisi during NATO Meeting", *Eurasia Insight*, December 4. http://www.eurasianet.org/departments/insightb/articles/eav120408c.shtml (accessed June 24, 2010).

Lobjakas, Ahto (2008) "Georgia: Minister, Seeking EU support, Warns War with Russia 'Very Close' ", *RFERL Georgia*, May 6. http://www.rferl.org/content/article/1117418.html (accessed June 24, 2010).

Lobjakas, Ahto (2009a) "Citing Russian 'Aggression', EU Steps Up Neighborhood Plans", *RFERL Georgia*, January 21. http://www.rferl.org/content/Citing_Russian_Aggression_EU_Steps_Up_Neighborhood_Plans/1372874.html (accessed June 24, 2010).

Lobjakas, Ahto (2009b) "EU Foreign Ministers Discuss Eastern Partnership", *RFERL Georgia*, February 23. http://www.rferl.org/content/EU_Foreign_Ministers_Discuss_Eastern_Partnership/1497826.html (accessed June 24,2010).

Lobjakas, Ahto (2009c) "NATO Set To Normalize Relations With Russia", *RFERL Georgia*, March 4. http://www.rferl.org/content/NATO_Russia_To_Return_To_Business_As_Usual/1504000.html (accessed June 24, 2010).

Lobjakas, Ahto (2009d) "NATO's U-Turn On Russia Bound To Be Seen As An Embarrassment", *RFERL Georgia*, March 9. http://www.rferl.org/content/NATOs_UTurn_On_Russia_Bound_To_Be_Seen_As_An_Embarrassment/1506674.html?spec=2#relatedInfoContainer

Lobjakas, Ahto (2009e) "Russia Set For A Long 'Continuation War' With Georgia", *RFERL Georgia*, June 17. http://www.rferl.org/content/Russia_Set_For_A_Long_Continuation_War_With_Georgia/1756431.html (accessed June 24, 2010).

Lomsadze, Giorgi (2008) "Tensions Flare over Breakaway South Ossetia", *Eurasia Insight*, August 4. http://www.eurasianet.org/departments/insight/articles/eav080408.shtml (accessed June 24, 2010).

Lomsadze, Giorgi (2009a) "United Nations to leave Abkhazia", *Eurasia Insight*, June 16. http://www.eurasianet.org/departments/insightb/articles/eav061609c.shtml (accessed June 24, 2010).

Lomsadze, Giorgi (2009b) "Tension between Tbilisi and Moscow mounts as war anniversary nears", *Eurasia Insight*, August 4. http://www.eurasianet.org/departments/insightb/articles/eav080409c.shtml (accessed June 24, 2010).

Luklyanov, Fyodor (2006) "Saakashvili is playing a high-stakes game", *Moscow Times*, October 4, p. 12.

Lukyanov, Fyodor (2008) "Seven Theses Prompted By Russia-Georgia Conflict", *RFERL Georgia*, August 26. http://www.rferl.org/content/Seven_Theses_Prompted_Russia_Georgia_Conflict/1193933.html (accessed June 24, 2010).

Martirosyan, Samvel and Ismail, Alman Mir (2005) "News of progress on Karabakh talks gets cautious reception in Armenia and Azerbaijan" *Eurasia Insight*, May 20. http://www.eurasianet.org/departments/insight/articles/eav052005a.shtml (accessed June 24, 2010).

Medetsky, Anatoly (2004) "Tbilisi takes back Adzharia", *Moscow Times*, May 7, p. 1.

Medvedev, Dimitri (2008a) "Press Statement following Negotiations with French President Nicolas Sarkozy", August 12. http://president.kremlin.ru/eng/speeches/2008/08/12/2100_type82912type82914type82915_205208.shtml

Medvedev, Dimitri (2008b) "Interview with television channel Euronews", September 2. http://www.kremlin.ru/eng/speeches/2008/09/02/2331_type82916_206105.shtml

Medvedev, Dimitri (2008c) "Press Conference following Talks with President of France Nicolas Sarkozy", September 8. http://president.kremlin.ru/eng/speeches/2008/09/08/2208_type82912type82914type82915_206283.shtml

Mikulova, Kristina (2009) "S.Ossetia Purportedly Burns Scores of Books", *Moscow Times*, September 17.

Mukhanov, Vadim (2008) "Georgia Caused This War", *Moscow Times*, August 13.

Oliker, Olga (2008) "Kosovo and South Ossetia More Different Than Similar", *RFERL Georgia*, August 25. http://www.rferl.org/content/Kosovo_And_South_Ossetia_More_Different_Than_Similar/1193663.html (accessed June 24, 2010).

Pankin, Alexei (2008) "Finding Out Who's to Blame for This War", *Moscow Times*, August 12.

Pannier, Bruce (2009) "Russia Facing Resistance With Allies on CIS's Southern Flank", *RFERL Georgia*, October 9. http://www.rferl.org/content/

Russia_Facing_Resistance_With_Allies_On_CISs_Southern_Flank/1847880. html (accessed June 24, 2010).

Parsons, Robert (2005) "Russia agrees to pull troops from Georgia by 2008", *Eurasia Insight*, May 30. http://www.eurasianet.org/departments/civilsociety/ articles/pp053005.shtml (accessed June 24, 2010).

Peuch, Jean-Christophe (2009) "Is the bell tolling for UN, OSCE Missions?", *Eurasia Insight*, June 11. http://www.eurasianet.org/departments/insightb/ articles/eav061109a.shtml (accessed June 24, 2010).

Popjanevski, Johanna (2009) "From Sukhumi to Tskhinvali. The Path to War in Georgia", in Cornell, Svante and Starr, S. Frederick (eds) (2009) *The Guns of August 2008. Russia's War in Georgia*, Armonk, NY, London: M.E. Sharpe, pp. 143–61.

RFERL Georgia and *RFERL Newsline* are found on http://www.rferl.org

RFERL Georgia, July 10, 2008.

RFERL Georgia, July 18, 2008.

RFERL Georgia, October 28, 2009.

RFE/RL Newsline, September 25, 2001.

RFE/RL Newsline, October 4, 2001.

RFE/RL Newsline, November 29, 2001.

RFE/RL Newsline, November 30, 2001.

RFE/RL Newsline, February 20, 2002.

RFE/RL Newsline, August 1, 2002.

RFE/RL Newsline, August 2, 2002.

RFE/RL Newsline, September 9, 2002.

RFE/RL Newsline, September 12, 2002.

RFE/RL Newsline, September 13, 2002.

RFE/RL Newsline, October 10, 2003.

RFE/RL Newsline, March 14, 2007.

RFE/RL Newsline, February 8, 2008.

RFE/RL Newsline, February 15, 2008.

"Russia's Lavrov Drops NATO Talks Over Expulsions", (2009) RFERL Georgia, May 5. http://www.rferl.org/content/Russias_Lavrov_Drops_NATO_Talks_ Over_Expulsions/1621848.html (accessed June 24, 2010).

Sindelar, Daisy (2008) "With Obama win, NATO prospects for Ukraine, Georgia appear to shift", *Eurasia Insight*, October 10.

Synovitz, Ron (2009) "Russia and NATO At Odds Over Planned Military Exercise In Georgia", *RFERL Georgia*, April 23. http://www.rferl.org/content/Russia_ and_NATO_At_Odds_Over_Planned_Military_Exercise_In_Georgia/1614496. html (accessed June 24, 2010).

Torbakov, I. (2006) "Communications breakdown: Russia and Georgia engage in war of words", *Eurasia Insight*, February 23. http://www.eurasianet.org/ departments/insight/articles/eav022306.shtml (accessed June 24, 2010).

Trenin, Dmitri (2002) *The End of Eurasia: Russia on the Border between Geopolitics and Globalization*, Washington, DC, and Moscow: Carnegie Endowment for International Peace.

Tully, Andrew F. (2009) "Georgian Foreign Minister Hopeful About Accord With U.S.", *RFERL Georgia*, January 10. http://www.rferl.org/content/ Georgian_Foreign_Minister_Hopeful_About_Accord_With_US_/1368524. html (accessed June 24, 2010).

von Twickel, Nikolaus (2008) "Theories Swirl About War's Beginning", *Moscow Times*, August 28.

von Twickel, Nikolaus (2009) "Georgia Feuds Erupts in Council of Europe", *Moscow Times*, September 30.

Whitmore, Brian (2008) "In post-Soviet breakaway regions, eyes look longingly to Kosovo", *RFERL Newsline*, End note, February 19.

Whitmore, Brian (2009) "Is A Russia-Georgia War Off The Table?", *RFERL Georgia*, July 15. http://www.rferl.org/content/Is_War_Off_The_Table_In_Georgia/1776909.html (accessed June 24, 2010).

Zurabishvili, Salome (2008) "Moscow's Possible Motives In Recognizing Abkhazia, South Ossetia", *RFERL Georgia*, September 24. http://www.rferl.org/content/Moscows_Possible_Motives_In_Recognizing_Abkhazia_South_Ossetia/1291181.html, (accessed June 24, 2010).

6
The Russo-Georgian War and EU Mediation

Tuomas Forsberg and Antti Seppo

> I believe we can say with a straight face that the EU rose to the occasion. We have acted in unity, with determination and we have achieved clear results.
>
> Javier Solana, 2008

When the EU, under the French Presidency, acted as a peace mediator during the Russo-Georgian war in August 2008, it was widely seen as a sign of the EU's growing role in issues of war and peace in world politics. The EU acted swiftly and in a seemingly united manner in a difficult situation, and managed to broker a cease-fire between the conflicting parties. The EU also decided to establish a monitoring mission to Georgia and to launch an international fact-finding mission to investigate the origins and the course of the conflict. Together with the UN and the Organization for Security and Cooperation in Europe (OSCE), the EU is also hosting the peace talks between Russia and Georgia in Geneva. Jean-Pierre Jouyet (2009, p. 88), the French Minister for European Affairs, argued that the Georgian crisis was as important for European diplomacy as the Euro was for European economic politics. The EU Council report on the implementation of the European Security Strategy also highlighted the Georgian experience by declaring: "Our Georgia mission has demonstrated what can be achieved when we act collectively with the necessary political will" (European Council, 2008).

The achievements of the EU, particularly as far as the cease-fire was concerned, were often contrasted with the failure of the EU to deal with the Balkan crisis during the 1990s (Whitman and Wolff, 2010). Famously, the EU failed to act as a peace mediator in the Balkans during the 1990s. At that time "the hour of Europe" turned out to be an empty slogan. The cease-fire in the Bosnian war was achieved through NATO intervention and the peace through US-led negotiations at Dayton.

Despite the fact that the EU's role in the Russo-Georgian war was seen as a success by Solana and many other EU representatives and commentators, there were skeptical interpretations too. First of all, the EU was not able to prevent the war. Second, the EU did not receive all the merit points when mediating the cease-fire, since the conditions remained vague and not thoroughly implemented. Third, the EU has not so far been able to bring the parties toward a more lasting peace. Fourth, the role of the EU in the peace negotiations could not stand the test of the principles that the EU wanted to uphold. Finally, it was unclear to what extent the success could have been attributed to France rather than the EU.

In this chapter we will try to do two things. First, we will critically evaluate the conflicting claims about the merits of the EU's mediation effort in the Russo-Georgian war. While realizing that it is probably still too soon to present the whole story, we will construct an empirical narrative that helps to conceptualize the role of the EU with regard to the Russo-Georgian war and its peace negotiations. Second, and even more importantly, we will also try to take a closer look at the sources of the EU's influence in the crisis, based on a theoretical sketch that combines a theory of mediation with theories of the nature of EU power. If the EU was not successful in mediating conflicts in the 1990s but was successful in the 2000s, how can we explain the growing impact of the EU? Based on this analysis, we will draw some conclusions about the diplomatic role and influence of the EU on third parties, particularly with regard to international conflicts.

The concept of "success" is, of course, very slippery and is difficult to pin down in policy analyses (Baldwin, 2000). However, it is imperative at some point to try to evaluate the impact of the EU's policies, in order to be able to make sense of the EU as an international actor. Jørgensen (1998) suggests that the yardstick of success can be external, internal, or a combination of the two. External criteria mean that we have formed a baseline against which we measure success, whereas internal criteria mean that we take the stated goals and aims of the EU at face value for a yardstick of success. Jørgensen recommends a mixed approach, but how such a mix is best formed varies from case to case. Very seldom does a particular policy constitute full success or a complete failure. Moreover, to state that the EU was a successful mediator in the crisis is not the same as arriving at a conclusion that the EU's policies in respect to the Caucasus and Georgia have been successful on the whole. What is more, the EU's policy towards the Caucasus is, in any case, just beginning to take some shape, particularly in the form of the new Eastern Partnership Initiative of the EU. These remarks notwithstanding, we believe that, by analyzing the EU's policies and its impact in such a narrow area of policy as mediation, we are able to draw attention to some important aspects affecting the EU's policymaking capabilities and its influence on policy outcomes.

Mediation theory and the role of the EU

There are two principal types of successful mediation and three basic views of the sources and nature of the power of the EU in international affairs. In order to sketch a theory of EU mediation in general and its role in the Russo-Georgian war in particular, we combine these two typological theories into one. We will distinguish between the possible roles of the EU as an interested party playing a power political role, an interested normative power, and a neutral facilitator that is interested in achieving peace but not primarily in maximizing the national interests of the EU member states or promoting certain predetermined values.

Perhaps the best-known theory of conflict mediation in international affairs derives from Princen (1992). He distinguishes between two roles for mediators. First there is the neutral mediator, who acts as a facilitator in the conflict resolution. The primary role of the facilitator is to act as a messenger, recognizing the shared interests and the bargaining space. In essence, the solution reflects the common interests of the conflicting parties, and the mediator does not change or affect these interests through his or her own action. The mediator simply provides the channel for negotiations and thereby helps to remove possible psychological barriers to a peace deal, as it is easier to start negotiations through a third party rather than directly contacting the opponent. The other role for a mediator is power political. The mediator is an interested party, and shapes the achieved resolution to the conflict by his or her own power resources, using promises and threats to affect the interest structure of the conflicting parties. The outcome therefore reflects the interests of the mediator as much as those of the conflict parties. Other, newer, studies of mediation (Bercovitch and Gartner, 2009) may suggest a third type of a mediator between the two, based on prominence of procedural strategies, but the principal dichotomy between facilitative and power political mediators remains the same.

When looking at the literature on the EU as an international actor, we can discern three different alternatives. First, there is the view that the EU is, or at least is developing into, a traditional self-interested great power with military resources. Second, there is the idea of the EU as a trade power, whose economic might is its primary interest and vehicle of power in international affairs. Third, there is the idea of the EU as a normative power, whose power rests on persuasion and ability to shape discourses (Manners, 2002). The primary interest of the EU as a normative power is to promote universal norms, such as human rights norms.

If these two typological theories are combined, we can arrive at three possible roles of the EU as a mediator and, therefore, also at three different possible explanations of the success of the EU as a mediator in the Russo-Georgian war. First, the EU can be seen as a facilitator that was successful in mediating the cease-fire to the war because of its perceived impartiality and neutrality. Second, the EU can be seen as an interested party that was successful because it used its economic and, to a lesser extent, its military resources in mediating the conflict. We put the military power and economic power dimensions together here, because it was clear from the outset that the military power of the EU had limited, if any, significance. Third, the EU can be seen as a normative power that was successful in the mediation because of its ability to shape the normative understandings of the conflicting parties, or at least to get them to accept a normatively motivated solution (Parmentier, 2009).

Obviously, the effectiveness of different mediation strategies depends on the context. Bercovitch and Gartner (2009) argue that, on the basis of empirical conflict statistics, it seems that power political strategies work best in high-intensity disputes, whereas a pure facilitative strategy is the least effective. In asymmetric conflicts the role of the mediator is important if it can convince the stronger party to abstain from further escalation of the conflict, and at the same time the weaker party understands that it will have to compromise to a greater degree later if it does not agree to the settlement now. We realize that our sketch, as well as the typological theories upon which the sketch is based, is rather rudimentary. It is seldom, if ever, possible to discern pure types. The roles can nevertheless be seen as ideal-types that make it possible to consider the weight and role of different explanations.

The Russo-Georgian war

As is always the case with armed conflicts and other disputes, there is no objective account of the events of the Russo-Georgian war of 2008. A number of reliable scholarly works on the course of the conflict exist, however (Allison, 2008; Antonenko, 2008; Asmus, 2010; Cheterian, 2009; Chronology, 2008; Fischer, 2008). What we know for a fact, at the moment, is that the Georgian military launched a military operation over the border of the breakaway territory of South Ossetia on the eve of the opening ceremony of the Olympic Games in Beijing on August 7. The Georgian offensive devastated the South Ossetian capital of Tskhinvali, where a number of Russian peacekeepers and hundreds of civilians were killed or wounded in the attacks.

Russia responded with military force immediately on the next day, August 8. It launched its offensive through the Roki Tunnel from North Ossetia, dispelled the Georgian troops from South Ossetia, and advanced over the South Ossetian border towards the Georgian capital of Tbilisi. Russian forces bombed and then occupied the Georgian city of Gori and, having opened a second front from Abkhazia, they took control of the port town of Poti. On August 10 Georgian troops were given the order to retreat from South Ossetia. The Russians stopped their invasion around Gori, 60 kilometres from Tbilisi, and announced that they did not intend to advance on Tbilisi. Meanwhile, in South Ossetia, paramilitary units harassed the Georgian minority population, which fled to areas controlled by the Georgian government.

The UN Security Council met right after the outbreak of hostilities. In the meeting, on August 9, both the Georgian and the Russian envoys accused one another of starting a war that could have grave consequences and would endanger the peace of the whole Caucasus. On August 10 the UNSC convened for the third time in reaction to the ever-escalating crisis, but no solution was found, due to Russia's resistance to a joint UNSC resolution.

The EU reacted to the crisis under French presidency. Foreign Minister Bernard Kouchner flew to Tbilisi together with the OSCE chairman, Finland's Foreign Minister Alexander Stubb, late on August 9. On the way, and the following morning, they drafted a tentative cease-fire proposal on three key issues: cessation of hostilities, recognition of Georgia's territorial integrity, and rapid reestablishment of the status quo ante. Having discussed the plan with Foreign Minister Ekaterine Tkeshelashvili, they presented the proposal to President Mikhail Saakashvili, who accepted it. After having visited the town of Gori at the request of their hosts, Kouchner and Stubb flew to Moscow in order to negotiate a cease-fire with the Russians. However, the French President Nicholas Sarkozy also decided to come to Moscow to negotiate the cease-fire personally. He explained to Kouchner that he did not want his hands to be tied by a paper negotiated in Tbilisi without his input and with someone the Russians hated. He brought with him a new peace plan that was based on the Kouchner–Stubb proposal but had been prepared in Paris (Asmus, 2010, pp. 195–6).

Sarkozy presented his plan to President Dmitri Medvedev on August 12. Sarkozy and Medvedev finally drafted the six principles of the peace plan together on the basis of the French proposal. They included, first, the nonuse of force; second, cessation of hostilities; third, free access to humanitarian aid; fourth, withdrawal of Georgian forces to their normal bases; and, fifth, withdrawal of Russian military to the lines prior to the start of hostilities. The fifth clause included the much-disputed Russian claim for "additional security measures" pending international mechanisms. The final clause called for international discussions on achieving lasting security in Abkhazia and South Ossetia. The reference to respecting the territorial integrity of Georgia was left out of the final peace plan, because the French team regarded stopping the war as a priority. Medvedev accepted the plan the same day, with obvious backing from Prime Minister Vladimir Putin, who also participated in the negotiations.

On August 13 Saakashvili secured Georgia's agreement to the peace plan of President Sarkozy. Saakashvili was not completely happy with the plan; he requested in particular the removal of the sixth clause referring to talks on the future status of South Ossetia and Abkhazia, and President Medvedev agreed to this. Saakashvili signed the modified agreement on August 15 during the visit of US Foreign Secretary Condoleezza Rice. Rice saw her role as convincing the Georgians to agree to a cease-fire that was flawed but necessary, but this had to be done in terms that were not demeaning to the Georgians (Asmus, 2010, p. 209). Medvedev accepted the document on August 16, but Russia did not start troop withdrawals immediately. These steps towards peace won the unanimous support of all EU member states.

A key session of the UNSC was held on August 19. The Russian ambassador rejected the draft resolution presented by France because it insisted on respecting Georgia's territorial integrity and its internationally acknowledged borders. The Russian ambassador claimed that the French draft "separated individual elements of the six-point 'Moscow Peace Plan' and reinterpreted them for propaganda purposes" (UN Security Council, 2008). As Russia was accused of failing to honor the cease-fire plan, it circulated its own UN Security Council Resolution. It reiterated Moscow's view that the peace plan allowed Russia to implement "additional security measures" before leaving Georgia.

The French EU Presidency strictly condemned Russia's de jure recognition of the independence of Abkhazia and South Ossetia on August 26. In the view of the EU, Russia had not respected the agreed six-point agreement, nor had it begun to withdraw its troops in a timely manner. Some member states called for immediate countermeasures. The EU convened an emergency summit on September 1 in Avignon. At the meeting, the EU member states decided to freeze the negotiations on a new cooperation agreement with Russia. There was, however, no agreement on imposing additional sanctions on Russia. The EU was also not willing to send armed EU peacekeepers to Georgia. Instead, the possibility of establishing an autonomous civilian monitoring mission in Georgia was discussed. The EU summit decisions were seen as favorable by Russia. Russian Prime Minister Putin commented on the EU's summit by saying that "Thank God, common sense prevailed. We do not see any extreme conclusions or proposals, and this is very good. We have a foundation to continue dialogue with our European partners" (RIA Novosti, 2008).

Following talks between Sarkozy, EU High Representative Solana, the EU Commission Head José Manuel Barroso, and Russian representatives, Russia agreed on September 8 to withdraw its troops from Georgian territory surrounding South Ossetia and Abkhazia. The rest of the pullout would happen once an international monitoring mission was deployed. The Council of the European Union acted swiftly. It decided on September 15 to establish an autonomous civilian European Union Monitoring Mission (EUMM) of 200 European monitors in Georgia, which was deployed on October 1. Despite Georgian wishes, and because of Russian resistance, the mission did not include any US observers. The EU Council also nominated a Special Representative for the Crisis in Georgia, Pierre Morel, in addition to the existing Special Representative to South Caucasus, Peter Semneby. Russia respected the September 8 agreement and pulled out its military step by step. On October 8 the EUMM could witness that "Russia seems to have completed most of withdrawal" (The European Union Monitoring Mission, 2008).

Relations between the EU and Russia were normalized at the EU–Russia Summit held on November 14 in Nice. The EU saw no further reason to freeze the start of the negotiations for the new strategic partnership agreement, since Russia had "for the most part" respected the instruction to withdraw its forces from Georgia. Russia had not, however, withdrawn its recognition of the breakaway republics, and it still maintained a small troop presence in Georgia; for this reason,

Lithuania criticized the decision to normalize relations. Otherwise, the summit did not produce any major successes, but both sides described the atmosphere of the negotiations as positive. Rather than Georgia, the meeting focused on the global financial crisis and its effects on both the EU and Russia. The EU reiterated that it was willing to support Russia's membership in the WTO.

In December 2008 the EU decided to set up an independent international fact-finding mission that would probe into the causes and course of the Georgian conflict. During the Avignon meeting in September a group of countries, supported by the French presidency, had already called for such an investigating body. The commission head was Swiss diplomat, and former UN special envoy to Georgia, Heidi Tagliavini, and the group consisted of legal and military experts from EU countries.

The EUMM was the most important tool of EU conflict management in the field. It could not prevent small incidents, but overall stabilization and normalization were on the increase. However, the EUMM was not able to utilize its mandate fully, as Russia was not willing to grant the EU monitors access to South Ossetia and Abkhazia. The South Ossetians and Abkhazians, as well as Russia, opposed the EU presence on their territories, since the EU mandate – according to their interpretation – covered only Georgian territory.

In summer 2009, the EUMM remained the only international observer group in Georgia and its breakaway republics. The mandate of the OSCE Mission to Georgia, which had operated in Georgia for over 15 years, was not extended at the end of 2008 due to Russia's opposition. The United Nations Observer Mission in Georgia (UNOMIG), which had been in Georgia from 1993, also came to an end in June 2009. In both cases, the EU invested a great deal of diplomatic energy in its effort to get Russia's approval on extension of the mandates, but was ultimately unable to move Russia on the issue.

At the time of writing (spring 2010) the peace negotiations in Geneva have not produced any major breakthrough. In fact, after a year's negotiations, little actual progress can be witnessed. Positive results have been achieved with regard to the return of internally displaced persons and providing for their security by incident prevention mechanisms and continuous cooperation between the secessionist and Georgian authorities (Co-Chairs of the Geneva Discussions, 2009). Moreover, the fact that the war has not recurred, contrary to much speculation during the summer of 2009, indicates some kind of success of the negotiations.

The EU's role as a mediator

The EU has security, economic, and normative interests in the Caucasus region. With regard to security, general stability was the key goal. The recognition of the South Caucasus as a possible "problem area" for the Union had already been acknowledged as part of the EU security strategy in 2003. According to the strategy, "we should now take a stronger and more active interest in the problems of the Southern Caucasus, which will in due course also be a neighboring region" (European Council, 2003). Since 2003, the European Council had also decided to establish a Special Envoy in the South Caucasus. The EU had tried to help in resolving the "frozen" conflicts of Abkhazia and South Ossetia. As late as June 2008, Solana had travelled to Georgia in order to strengthen the role of the EU in the mediation efforts. The EU's economic interests in the Caucasus region concentrate on the diversification of the EU's energy supplies. Gogolashvili (2009, p. 102) has suggested that the EU's need to export energy ultimately led the EU to include the Caucasus states in the European Neighborhood Policy (ENP). "European" pipeline projects are already underway in the region (Nabucco, Baku-Ceyhan, etc.). Finally, the EU also has normative interests in the region, mostly concerning democracy and human rights promotion. In particular, Georgia's Rose Revolution in 2003 was seen as a demonstration of the expansion of European values and normative ideas. The EU had also sponsored a rule of law mission (THEMIS) as well as a border support mission (EUSR BST) in Georgia.

When open war between Georgia and Russia started in August 2008, the EU was thus already present in the region in a number of ways. In the eyes of the conflict parties the EU enjoyed a reasonable degree of impartiality, at least when compared with other possible actors, such as the US, NATO, the UN or the OSCE. The Georgians viewed the EU positively, although not all recommendations stemming from Brussels of the EU were seen as necessary (Gogolashvili, 2009). On security questions, the EU and the Europeans were seen as too soft. For example, Georgians did not quite trust the Germans in their attempts to mediate in the frozen conflicts, and thought that they were too naïve about Russian interests (Asmus, 2010, p. 156). Russia, in turn, was extremely sensitive towards the US and NATO presence in Georgia. Russia was also skeptical about the UN and the OSCE, and did not prolong the mandates of the observing missions of these organizations in Georgia. By contrast, it allowed the EUMM to operate in the country. As Russian foreign minister Sergei Lavrov (2008) commented, "we are glad that the settlement of the Caucasus crisis has provided a serious subject for our cooperation with the European Union in regional affairs." Lavrov considered it good that "a European solution to the problem" was found.

During the crisis and the subsequent negotiations, the EU introduced an array of actions that reflected the model of an impartial mediator. It refrained from putting blame on either of the parties for the outbreak of the war. The cease-fire was achieved because it was in the interests of both parties – as the Russians said, they had achieved their objectives and did not want to continue the invasion to Tbilisi – and not because the EU had somehow changed or influenced the interest structure or the normative ideas of the parties. The principles that the EU drafted demanded a return to the status quo ante. The EUMM was there to observe and build confidence, not to impose a peace agenda on the parties (Martin, 2010). During the Geneva negotiations, the EU supported the establishment of the incident prevention and response mechanisms that would permit meetings weekly, and even more often if necessary, between international security monitors and local security officials in the areas of tension. Moreover, a special hotline was created, and the parties agreed that regular joint visits should be conducted in the areas to defuse tensions.

Another good example of action based on impartiality was the EU-sponsored fact-finding mission. The report, which was published in October 2009, examined and discussed the roots and causes for the outbreak of the conflict. The fact that the mission head was a Swiss diplomat underlined the image of impartiality. The mission was respected as being neutral by the Russians and the Georgian opposition, but not so much by the Georgian government. The key message of the report was that the Georgian side had initiated the conflict, but that Russia was not an innocent victim (Independent International Fact-Finding Mission, 2009). "Impartial" actions do not, of course, always have neutral effects. During the fact-finding mission it became increasingly clear that it was Georgia that had actually started the hostilities, by bombarding Tskhinvali. This uncomfortable fact, which is still denied by the Georgian government, may have contributed to the deterioration of the atmosphere at the Geneva negotiations in the form of new accusations. The EUMM may actually have had the unintentional effect of strengthening Russia's claim over the independence of South Ossetia, because it has not been able to monitor in South Ossetia or to enforce peace between the parties. Moreover, the effective implementation of the mechanisms introduced in the Geneva negotiations remains an open question, as it is, in the end, dependent on the "good will" of the conflict parties.

The EU acted only to a very limited extent as an interested power political party in the conflict. It tried to influence Russia through freezing negotiations on their relationship after the termination of the Partnership and Cooperation Agreement, but everyone was aware that this was only a symbolic act, not a real pressure that would bring any results. The EU did not want to introduce economic sanctions or other heavier sticks in order to force Russia to withdraw its troops more quickly or to rescind its recognition of the independence of Abkhazia and South Ossetia. The fact that the EU did not resort to any "hard power" measures was, of course, welcomed by the Russians. Neither did the EU use its economic leverage to influence Georgia or the breakaway republics. It granted an aid package that amounted up to €500 million, but this was unconditional, with no political strings. The EU's aims were "rebuilding confidence in the Georgian economy, boosting investment in critical infrastructure including energy and providing shelter, food, and other basic services to the internally displaced" (Ferrero-Waldner, 2008).

The EU's normative influence was most visible in its demand for protecting the rights of the internally displaced, especially women and children. The normative aim of promoting Georgian's territorial integrity has been high on the agenda, but so far the Russians have been unwilling to buy into that norm. The EU itself persuaded the Georgians to accept the presence of Abkhazian and South Ossetian delegations in the peace talks, which would suggest that the EU used its normative power against its normative goals. Its normative power failed in many cases when dealing with Russia, most notably in attempting to prevent the recognition of the breakaway republics and to obtain Russian approval for the extension of the OSCE and UN monitoring missions.

Conclusions

This is not the first attempt to assess the role of the EU in the context of the Russo-Georgian war of 2008. One authoritative assessment by the House of Lords arrives at the following conclusion to its report:

> The EU's response to the conflict in Georgia was rapid and reasonably successful. It persuaded the two parties to accept a ceasefire, and with some delay brought about the withdrawal of Russian troops from all Georgian territory outside South Ossetia and Abkhazia and brought

the parties together for talks in Geneva. This success owed much to the effectiveness of a strong Presidency with whom the Russians were prepared to negotiate. The EU was the obvious and perhaps only credible body to act as intermediary in the conflict, and acted with unaccustomed confidence and authority. (Government Response to the House of Lords' European Committee, 2009)

On the basis of our study we agree with this conclusion in principle. However, we would like to add a few qualifications and discuss the explanations for success through the three different mediator roles that we sketch for the EU.

The role of France in mediating the conflict was prominent, to such an extent that many observers have talked more about the French than the EU role in the conflict, since Solana and the EU institutions did not have a visible presence in the acute phase of the crisis. France's leadership was important, not only because France was a great power, but also because it was seen as being more impartial than many other EU member states: France, for example, had not supported the admission of Georgia into the Membership Action Plan programme at the Bucharest NATO summit in April 2008. As one *Newsweek* article (McNicoll, 2008) put it: "France's historic experience with great power politics and its extensive, well-oiled diplomatic machine undoubtedly lent Sarkozy that extra degree of credibility when negotiating with Moscow." Still, the question remains whether a smaller but equally impartial and active chair would also have been able to act as a broker if it had enjoyed a similar status of impartiality. It is too easy to reach the conclusion that, because France acted successfully as a broker, nobody else could have acted successfully as a broker. For example, in 1999 it was the President of Finland, Martti Ahtisaari, who was brokering the peace to the Kosovo war on behalf of the EU. Moreover, the more relevant question, at least after the coming into force of the Lisbon treaty, is whether the EU foreign minister could play a similar role. What seems clear, however, was that Sarkozy enjoyed the respect of the Russian side, and during the September meeting he was able to use effectively the threat of walking out of the negotiations if the Russians did not adhere to the previous agreements.

The EU and France were able to take the role of the mediator because both the US and the OSCE wanted the EU to play that role. The US, of course, had more military and diplomatic leverage than the EU, and the OSCE was already present in the field, but both the US and the OSCE preferred to support the EU in the conflict. The conflict settlement would have been more difficult, or at least more complicated, if there had been institutional competition in this regard. The Georgian government obviously would have preferred NATO or the US over the EU, but did not have much choice. Anyway, they saw the EU as a better actor than the OSCE or the UN, which were considered weak because of Russia's involvement in the organizations. Most importantly, however, Russia preferred the EU over NATO or the US, which Moscow was accusing of orchestrating the conflict. For Russia, it was a moral victory that the US was left out of the process. Russia had become generally critical of the OSCE, and the EU, led by France, better suited Russian interests.

As far as our theoretical sketch of three different mediating roles is concerned, the success of the EU in mediating between Russia and Georgia was most visible in its role as an impartial facilitator (Frichova Grono, 2010). This is because the EU's actions did not force the conflicting parties into any actions against their direct interests, but tried, rather, to overcome psychological barriers and come up with at least the smallest common denominator, determined by the EU in a pragmatic way (such as the benefit of the nonuse of force). Furthermore, the implementation of the agreements was based on the "good will" of the parties.

If we consider the success of the EU as a principal mediator, using its economic or military leverage to advance its own interests, we can detect only a very minimal role. For example, the ability to send a civilian monitoring mission was hardly dependent on progress within the ESDP. The EU refrained from economic sanctions and used its economic aid in a "structural" or "transformative" rather than a direct manner. These measures did not have any tangible impact on the core issue of the conflict, related to political identity. Therefore it may be said that the EU lacked a comprehensive conflict management strategy (Whitman and Wolff, 2010).

Finally, the EU's role as a mediator did not rely much on its normative power. A normative role was visible, perhaps, in the emphasis on protecting the civilian population, but the EU also had to accept principles that contradicted its understandings of norms. Yet, with regard to the norm of territorial integrity, which has been a high priority for the EU, the EU has been successful only in so far as it has been able to prevent a wider international recognition of the independence of the breakaway republics – but even there a more decisive role was probably played by China, which refused to recognize the republics. Yet, for the sake of pragmatism and stability, the EU has had to accept the de facto independence of Abkhazia and South Ossetia, as well as persuading Georgia to accept Abkhazia and South Ossetia at the negotiation table in Geneva. Moreover, the EUMM was not granted access to the secessionist regions, which can also be counted as a failure of the EU to achieve its normative objectives. There is, indeed, a certain contradiction between the roles of the EU, which has tried simultaneously to be both a neutral facilitator and a normative power. Precisely because the EU has some fundamental ideas and beliefs about key concepts such as state sovereignty and the interpretation of the international law, it is hard for the EU to maintain both its impartiality and its normative objectives if the aims collide in the eyes of the conflict parties, as happened in the aftermath of the crisis. Yet the EU needs to come up with a strategy by which both of these objectives can be sustained.

Such a strategy would require, first, a solution to the EU's impartiality/ normative power paradox, which currently pits the EU's actions against its own principles. Second, the EUMM is doing a good job on the ground by trying to persuade the parties to the conflict to abide by common rules and norms under EU supervision. Yet a more profound strategy should contain realistic, acceptable, and implementable ideas on how to affect the secessionist regions in their pursuit of independence. One of the biggest problems relates to the fact that the EU, as an international actor, is irrevocably involved in the Caucasus without effectively being able to tackle the regional aspect of the crisis, precisely because it has not, so far, been able to pursue its dual role without causing serious internal political contradictions. This is because the EU needs to cooperate simultaneously with both Russia and other Caucasus states: pleasing one is likely to alienate the other. Finding a balance is extremely difficult. In the long term, however, some kind of equilibrium on a general level is more likely than not to materialize, as the EU's track record with Russia has proven that energy policies, for instance, usually weigh more than human rights if the EU has to make a choice. However, it is much harder for the EU as a mediator to find a win–win situation to the current crisis which would also be acceptable to the EU.

The EU has not been able to come up with credible sticks or effective carrots in its relations with Russia since the introduction of the concept of political conditionality in the framework of the EU–Russia PCA agreement (Haukkala, 2010; Kratochvil, 2008). This is probably one reason why some observers are rather skeptical in their assessment of the EU's efforts as far as the Caucasus crisis in the long run is concerned (see, e.g., Merlingen and Ostrauskaite, 2009; Tocci, 2008; Whitman and Wolff, 2010). The academic discussion of the EU as a "normative power" and the EU's self-understanding as a "force for good" aims at combining normative standpoints, not impartiality, with effectiveness in international crises (Manners, 2002; Parmentier, 2009). Yet, in the eyes of the conflict parties, the normativity of the EU may undermine its perceived impartiality. As a mediator, the EU has a hard time living up to its promises, whether or not they are normative in nature. Therefore it appears that the linchpin of the EU's success as a mediator in future crises in the eastern neighborhood is not necessarily the introduction of powerful sticks or strong normative standpoints, which would most likely undermine the EU's role as an impartial facilitator. From the Russian point of view, a sufficiently independent, but not threatening, posture proved to be the key factor that made it possible in the first place for the EU to assume the role of a mediator in the Georgian case.

References

Allison, Roy (2008) "Russia Resurgent? Moscow's Campaign to Coerce Georgia to Peace", *International Affairs*, vol. 84, no. 6, pp. 1145–71.

Antonenko, Oksana (2008) "A War with No Winners", *Survival*, vol. 50, no. 5, pp. 24–36.

Asmus, Ronald D. (2010) *A Little War That Shook the World: Georgia, Russia and the Future of the West*, Houndmills: Palgrave Macmillan.

Baldwin, David (2000) "Success and Failure in Foreign Policy", *Annual Review of Political Science*, vol. 3, pp. 167–82.

Bercovitch, Jacob and Scott Sigmund Gartner (2009) *International Conflict Mediation: New Approaches and Findings*, Abingdon: Routledge.

Cheterian, Vicken (2009) "The August 2008 War in Georgia: from Ethnic Conflict to Border Wars", *Central Asian Survey*, vol. 28, no. 2, pp. 155–70.

Chronology (2008) "A chronology of the crisis", *Strategic Comments*, vol. 14, no. 7, pp. 1–2.

Co-Chairs of the Geneva Discussions (2009) Press Communique, May 19. http://www.consilium.europa.eu (accessed May 23, 2009).

European Council (2003) "A Secure Europe in a Better World", European Security Strategy, Brussels, December 12. http://www.consilium.europa.eu/ (accessed June 28, 2010).

European Council (2008) "Report on the Implementation of the European Security Strategy. Providing Security in a Changing World", Brussels, December 11. http://www.consilium.europa.eu/ (accessed June 28, 2010).

European Union Monitoring Mission (2008) "EUMM Witnesses the Withdrawal of Russian Troops", EUMM Press Release, October 8. http://www.eumm.eu (accessed June 2, 2010).

Ferrero-Waldner, Benita (2008) "Donors conference for Georgia: time to walk or talk", Speech/08/549, Brussels, October 22. http://europa.eu/rapid/pressReleaseAction.do?reference=SPEECH/08/549&format=HTML&aged=08&language=ENG&guiLanguae=en (accessed June 28, 2010).

Fischer, Sabine (2008) "Russia-Georgia Conflict in South Ossetia: Context and Implications for U.S. Interests", *Caucasus Analytical Digest*, no. 1, December. http://www.res.ethz.ch/analysis/cad/details.cfm?id=9438 (accessed June 28, 2010).

Frichova Grono, Magdalena (2010) "Georgia's Conflicts: What Role for the EU As Mediator?", Initiative for Peacebuilding Mediation Cluster, *International Alert*, March 2010. http://initiativeforpeacebuilding.eu/pdf/Georgia_March2010. pdf (accessed August 9, 2010).

Gogolashvili, Kakha (2009) "The EU and Georgia: The Choice is in the Context", *Europe in Dialogue* 1/2009, pp. 90–106.

Government Response to the House of Lords' European Committee (2009) *Government Response to the House of Lords' European Committee Report on the European Union and Russia following the Crisis in Georgia.* http://www. parliament.uk (accessed May 15, 2009).

Haukkala, Hiski (2010) *The EU-Russia Strategic Partnership. The Limits of Post-Sovereignty in International Relations*, Abingdon: Routledge.

Independent International Fact-Finding Mission on the Conflict in Georgia (2009) *Report.* Vols I–III. Available at: http://www.ceiig.ch (accessed October 10, 2009).

Jørgensen, Knud Erik (1998) "The European Union's Performance in World Politics: How Should We Measure Success?", in Zielonka, Jan (ed.), *Paradoxes of European Foreign Policy*, The Hague: Kluwer Law International, pp. 89–xx.

Jouyet, Jean-Pierre and Sophie Coignard (2009) *Une presidence de crises. Les six mois qui ont bousculé l'Europe*, Paris: Albin Michel.

Kratochvil, Peter (2008) "The Discursive Resistance to EU-Enticement: The Russian Elite and (the Lack of) Europeanization", *Europe-Asia Studies*, vol. 60, no. 3, pp. 397–422.

Lavrov, Sergei (2008) Speech by Russian foreign Minister Sergei Lavrov, "The Responsibility of Russia in world politics", International Conference of the Bergedorf Forum, Moscow, October 25.

McNicoll, Tracy (2008) "Sarko Tackles the Bear", *Newsweek* International Edition, September 28.Manners, Ian (2002) "Normative Power Europe: A Contradiction in Terms?", *Journal of Common Market Studies*, vol. 40, no. 2, pp. 235–58.

Martin, Mary (2010) "Crossing Boundaries. The European Union Monitoring Mission to Georgia", in Martin, Mary and Mary Kaldor (eds), *The European Union and Human Security. External Interventions and Missions*, Abingdon: Routledge, pp. 128–44.

Merlingen, Michael and Ostrauskaite, Rosa (2009) "EU Peacebuilding in Georgia: Limits and Achievements", *CLEER Working papers*, no. 6.

Parmentier, Florent (2009) "Normative Power, EU Preferences and Russia. Lessons from the Russian Georgian War", *European Political Economy Review*, no. 9, pp. 49–61.

Princen, Thomas (1992) *Intermediaries in International Conflict*, Princeton: Princeton University Press.

RIA Novosti (2008) September 2. http://en.rian.ru/world/20080902/116488911. html (accessed June 28, 2010).

Solana, Javier (2008) "Discours du Haut Représentant de l'Union européenne pour la Politique étrangère et de sécurité commune", The Annual Conference of the European Union Institute of Security Studies, Paris, October 30.

Tocci, Natalie (2008) "The EU and Conflict Resolution in Turkey and Georgia: Hindering EU Potential Through the Political Management of Contractual Relations", *Journal of Common Market Studies*, vol. 46, no. 4, pp. 875–97.

UN Security Council (2008) SC/9429. http://www.un.org/News/Press/docs/2008/ sc9429.doc.htm (accessed June 28, 2010).

Whitman, Richard G. and Wolff, Stefan (2010) "The EU as a Conflict Manager? The Case of Georgia and its Implications", *International Affairs*, vol. 86, no. 1, pp. 87–107.

7
Russia's New "Monroe Doctrine"

Mette Skak

To us, August 8 is what 9/11 was to the U.S.

Medvedev, 2008

Like the Terminator, Russia is back – back as a major actor in world affairs and as a major headache for security policy decision makers in the Western world. In words, this point was driven home by then Russian President Vladimir Putin in his speech at the Wehrkunde meeting in Munich, February 2007. He argued by pointing to the rise of the BRICs – Brazil, Russia, India, and China – that collectively the four potential economic powerhouses are positioned to overtake the old G7 powers, including the United States, around 2040 (Putin, 2007; Wilson and Purushothaman, 2003). In deeds, the point was emphasized by Russia's five-day war against Georgia in August 2008, which brought Russia's relationship with the Western world down to the frosty level of the Cold War.

The catalyst for war cited by Russian authorities was Georgia's attack on Russian peacekeepers in the rebel region of South Ossetia inside Georgia. The unofficial, but equally important, casus belli was the Georgian President Mikheil Saakashvili's rush to join NATO and the enthusiastic backing he received from the Bush administration because of this. This is evident from Russia's vigorous public protests throughout 2008 over the prospect of a so-called MAP – a Membership Action Plan for joining NATO – being extended to Georgia. Similarly, Russia issued thinly veiled threats against Ukraine if it should draw closer to NATO. In April 2008, on the occasion of the NATO summit in Bucharest that had been expected to decide on a MAP for both post-Soviet states, Russia's Foreign Minister openly warned that "Russia will do everything it can to prevent the admission of Ukraine and Georgia into NATO"

(Sergei Lavrov, quoted in Kramer, 2008, p. 9). Therefore, it makes sense to view Russia's war in Georgia as a proxy war against NATO in general and the United States in particular.

This does not mean that Russia alone was to blame for the war; on the contrary, as officially concluded by an investigation launched by the European Union, Saakashvili has a proven record of nationalistic fervor and seems to have been carried away by the apparent international solidarity surrounding him. But it was chilling to follow how quickly Russian and Western commentary lost all sense of proportion, such as when Russian President Dmitri Medvedev spoke about Russia's 9/11 (cf. above). Dmitri Rogozin, Russia's ambassador to NATO, dubbed Saakashvili the Gavrilo Princip of our times – the man who presumably unleashed World War I (*Reuters*, August 26, 2008). Conversely, US neoconservatives such as Robert Kagan likened Russia's conduct to that of Nazi Germany in the Sudetenland in Czechoslovakia in 1938, a turning point that began Hitler's unstoppable aggression. Long after the cease-fire, even moderate Russian analysts continued to draw ominous analogies implying that Russia's relationship with the Western world might still trigger war if the parties did not engage wholeheartedly in deescalation.

True, the world economic crisis reduces Russia's room for maneuver, whereas the Obama administration in the United States displays both skill and flexibility in its approach to Russia. In particular, by deciding simply to abandon the missile defence project in Europe in September 2009, President Obama did much to reset the button, to borrow Vice President Joe Biden's phrase. But even this remarkable step leaves notorious stumbling blocks to a harmonious East–West relationship untouched. As I shall argue below, these stumbling blocks surfaced soon after Russia succeeded the Soviet Union, and they have regularly resurfaced ever since. I am referring to a particular syndrome within Russian strategic culture, namely Russia's resorting to neo-imperialism and military interventionism towards its post-Soviet neighbors. I shall refer to this syndrome as Russia's New Monroe doctrine, because it turns Russia's formally independent, but weak, neighborhood into an exclusive Russian sphere of influence – just as the original doctrine of US President James Monroe, issued in 1823, turned the whole of the Americas into an exclusive US sphere of influence.

Russia's relations with its post-Soviet neighbors lie outside the immediate bilateral US–Russian relationship and might seem a secondary issue to address. But the end of the Cold War, the commitment of both NATO and the EU to the principle of undivided security, and

Russia's own marketing of itself as having an enlightened European identity (Putin, 2009) makes it impossible not to consider Russia's policy towards its post-Soviet neighbors as "high politics." If my analysis proves valid, it follows that the way to reset the button concerning the triangular relationship between Russia, its vulnerable post-Soviet neighbors, and the West may be through an official shelving of the original Monroe doctrine by the US, a corollary to which I shall return in the conclusion.

First, however, I shall briefly introduce the approach of strategic culture as a way to unwrap the enigma of Russian foreign and security policy. Among other things, I want to stress the dialectics between the more static impulses of strategic culture and the more dynamic forces of globalization, including the transmission of norms. Second, I shall document the resurfacing of interventionism in words – through explicit references to the Monroe doctrine – and deeds in the early post-Cold War Russian foreign policy discourse. Third, I shall point to examples of more enlightened, liberal impulses in Russia's behavior to demonstrate that Russia is more sophisticated than that.

On the approach of strategic culture

Arguably, the approach of strategic culture was one of the earliest theoretical inventions within the political science discipline of international relations. It all began with Nathan Leites' (1951) seminal work on the Soviet Politburo, which sought to map the ideational dimension of foreign and security policy-making in the USSR and other communist states. In other words, the premise behind strategic culture studies is that states are not "like units," as presumed within the approach of neorealism developed much later by Kenneth N. Waltz (1979). States, or rather their decision makers, are seen as being shaped in their outlook by factors such as geography, actual historical experience, notably concerning issues of war and peace on the home front and abroad, and the particular ideological socialization of a given group of foreign and security policy decision makers. In all these respects the revolutionary Marxist Soviet superpower clearly differed from its US counterpart. This insight inspired later contributions on Soviet strategic culture by Jack Snyder.

Strategic culture, thus, refers to the ideational dimension of foreign and security policy. It is about political culture on the level of the political elites, and concerns their views on the use of force and their perception of their country's strategic vulnerabilities and options, or perhaps even its destiny (cf. Gray, 1986). Already these phrases underscore that we are not dealing with the rational choice approach of neorealism, according to which only material capabilities and actual great power polarity within the international system count as variables. On the contrary, strategic culture deals with the immaterial side of foreign and security policy, and allows for the possibility of seemingly irrational behavior.

Strategic culture studies are open to the inclusion of geography as a key variable behind security policy outcomes.[1] Accordingly, David R. Jones (1990, p. 35) posits three levels of inputs into a country's strategic culture:

- *a macro-environmental level* consisting of geography, ethno-cultural characteristics, and history;
- *a meso-level* consisting of current social, economic, and political structures of a society (to which one might add the state-sanctioned ideology if relevant); and
- *a micro-level* of military institutions and characteristics of civil–military relations (to which one might add, in the case of Russia, other equally powerful institutions in foreign and security policy-making, such as the secret services).

Some readers may be provoked by the first bullet point, suspecting that strategic culture brings us back to the static theories of national archetypes. This is not necessarily the case, as I shall argue in detail below. But let us pause for a while and accept geography as destiny and a key variable when explaining the behavior of Russia in world affairs. How about evidence and specific arguments emanating from this? Here I should like to draw upon a fine work on contemporary Russia's existential drama as a political and territorial unit in our universe of competitive market economies by Allen C. Lynch (2005).

Lynch argues that, because of Russia's severe climate and the country's vast size, with no natural, defensible borders, Russia is doomed to pay higher costs for both production (extraction) and security than, say, China, Britain, or the United States. Russia is much more barren even than Canada, being akin to Mongolia or Greenland in population density and climate. Lynch views this as the structural reason for the rise of the uniquely harsh patrimonial state in Czarist Russia and for the reappearance of the strong Russian state and state capitalism under Putin. Already this explains some of the patterns at the meso-level – for instance, Putin's ideology hailing paternalism, state strength, and

Russian great power status (Putin, 1999), the latter implying autonomy. One remarkable source that follows up on Lynch is Stratfor, a private intelligence corporation (Bhalla *et al.*, 2009).

The Stratfor analysts characterize Russia as "among the world's most strategically vulnerable states." They stress the irony in the fact that, in trying to attain security by creating strategic buffers, Russia creates new chronic security problems in the form of new populations hostile to Moscow's rule. To this they add Russia's demographic time bomb as something that makes Russia struggle in vain for lasting greatpower-hood: "it is a declining power in the long run" (Bhalla *et al.*, 2009). Viewed from this perspective, Moscow's punitive action against NATO's intrusion into Georgia in 2008 was just a desperate attempt "to buy Russia more space – and with that space, more time for survival" (Bhalla *et al.*, 2009). This may sound very deterministic. Indeed, scholars agree that strategic culture is a factor of path dependency and resistance to change.

Under certain circumstances, however, strategic culture itself may change. One such causal factor is external shock – for instance, surprise attacks such as 9/11 or Pearl Harbor, or military defeat such as Germany's *Stunde Null* in 1945. Generally speaking, trial and error serves as a mechanism for change, as demonstrated by the disastrous Soviet experiment in building an alternative economic and political order. The Soviet fiasco was what brought the self-proclaimed Leninist Mikhail S. Gorbachev to reform Soviet society and strategic culture. Gorbachev actually succeeded in breaking the spell of Soviet hypermili-tarism[2] through his New Political Thinking. During his time in power the Soviet defense budget went down to a much lower level of GDP, where it has stayed ever since (Ermarth, 2006). The Gorbachev example illustrates another possible factor of change: the coming into power of new generations not committed to the ideology and decisions of earlier times, in this case Gorbachev representing post-Stalininism. This underscores the importance of meso- and micro-level strategic culture analysis of current developments in the country under scrutiny.

Probably the most direct factors of change are impulses coming from abroad. At any rate, what drove the curiosity of the founding fathers of Soviet Studies, such as Leites, was the utterly closed, totalitarian nature of communist political systems. Similarly, the extreme closure of North Korea is what allows this entity to keep its bizarre strategic culture. Conversely, the more open a political system, the more dynamic a strategic culture. It follows that strategic culture cannot be studied in a purely national macro-historical perspective, as is argued by Alastair Iain Johnston (1995). Analysts must allow for possible impulses from abroad due to the contemporary pressure from globalization and the actual opening of postcommunist political systems, as in Russia. The Kremlin is much less open toward democratic norms than one might wish, but no one should underestimate the impact of the Soviet fiasco upon Russian decision makers (cf. Putin, 1999).

To sum up, while strategic culture may be a phenomenon observed primarily at the state level of analysis, the analyst studying the dynamics of strategic culture would be well advised to allow for causal factors operating at the global systemic level of international relations. As maintained by constructivist scholars, one must be sensitive towards such influences as norm transmission, such as the possible embrace by the Kremlin of today's European norms of human rights, the rule of law, and undivided security (Finnemore and Sikkink, 1998). The point is not that liberal norms are the only game in town, because this is obviously not the case. The point is that, due to the empowerment of civil societies through new information technologies, self-proclaimed rising powers such as Russia have to care about their overall legitimacy. This makes the recovery of the Russian state much less of a one-way street than most people think (Hurrell, 2006; Zakaria, 2008, p. 39 f.).

One last remark about the method of studying strategic culture: the field is known for the Gray vs Johnston conflict about whether to include behavior in the concept of strategic culture or to focus exclusively on decision makers' perceptions. Johnston (1995) recommends the latter, as there may be no 1:1 relationship between behavior and perceptions. What I want to establish below, however, is that in the case of post-communist Russia there is very much a 1:1 relationship between words and deeds – that is, between verbal expressions of strategic culture and behavior towards the "near abroad." Naturally, there may be elements of bluff, spin, and negotiating tactics when Russian decision and opinion makers utter their views, but the outside world would be well advised not to dismiss them as mere rhetoric.

Russia's new "Monroe doctrine"

One analyst traces the Russian Monroe doctrine back to April 1992, when Yuri Skokov, head of the Russian Security Council, issued a Programme for National Security of Russia. Skokov challenged the US for predominance all over the world. Not only was Skokov ousted from his post, but by 1993 a virtual Monroe doctrine had materialized, following which

> [...] Russia maintains that it now has a right to intervene militarily in regions of conflict in the FSU (Former Soviet Union), especially when its national interests are threatened. Correspondingly, countries to the south such as Iran and Turkey are unwelcome on the territories of the FSU, as is any type of NATO involvement which would seek to draw the newly independent states into Western Europe's sphere of influence. (Holoboff, 1994, p. 155)

As for a more explicit Monroe doctrine of the early 1990s, I should like to invoke a contribution by one semi-hawkish member of then Russian President Boris Yeltsin's Presidential Council, Andranik Migranian, written in his capacity as an official expert on the Commonwealth of Independent States (i.e. the "near abroad") for the Russian Duma:

> In several articles in *Rossiiskaia Gazeta* I formulated the key idea inspiring all leading politicians right from the President to Foreign Minister Kozyrev. It is about the former Soviet Union's geopolitical space as Russia's vital sphere of interest. In order not to leave anyone in doubt, I drew a parallel to the 'Monroe doctrine'. In a way I sought to formulate a Russian 'Monroe doctrine' applicable upon the situation that has arisen after the dissolution of the Soviet Union. (Migranian, 1994)

He added that the idea had already been embraced by the Head of the Foreign Affairs' Committee of the Duma, Evgeny Ambartsumov, in 1992. Ambartsumov happens to be the man whom most analysts, including himself, associate with Russia's "Monroe doctrine" (Ambartsumov, 1993). Another key foreign policy opinion maker tending in the direction of jingoism towards the "near abroad" in 1992 was Sergei Karaganov. Actually, one may pinpoint the deliberate derailing of Kozyrev's moderate foreign policy as a process that began on March 28, 1992 (Skak, 1996, pp. 137–191).

Migranian's Monroe doctrine deliberations caused a stir in *Nezavisimaia Gazeta*; yet they proved quite accurate as a clue to what motivated Russia's security policy behavior throughout the post-Soviet era. Soon Presidential Directive No. 940 was issued on the "Strategic course of Russia and the member-states of the Commonwealth of Independent States" (CIS) which identified the development of CIS as reflecting Russia's vital interests (*Strategicheskii kurs ...*, 1995). As for the operational pursuit of Russia's national security through peace-keeping in the CIS, the document's article 14 added that "when cooperating with third countries and international organizations in this field [i.e. peace-keeping] the target is to reach their understanding of the fact that this region is above all a Russian zone of interests" (ibid.).

As pointed out by Elaine M. Holoboff (1994) and other analysts, its "peacekeeping" activities were exactly what Russia used as a vehicle for its neo-imperialism towards the "near abroad." In the early post-Soviet years, Russia engaged in military intervention in a partisan manner in several conflicts, starting with its deployment of 700 paratroopers to South Ossetia in July 1992. Simultaneously, Russia let its 14th Army, stationed in the breakaway republic of Transniestria in Moldova – an army that had been party to the brief but bloody civil war between Moldovan and Transniestrian forces – continue to act as a "peacekeeping force" in this very conflict. In December 1992, when Russia intervened in support of the secessionist republic of Abkhazia in Georgia and came under fire, Russian military officials ominously warned that "Russian helicopters land on the territory of Russian military units, which is the territory of the Russian Federation" (quoted from Holoboff, 1994, p. 159, fn. 12). Russia also intervened in support of a communist, and hence secular, government in Tajikistan.

As for the strategic benefits reaped by Russia through these early "peacekeeping" interventions, Holoboff points out that the deployment to South Ossetia legitimized a continued Russian military presence in an area that it considers to be the front line against instability and resurgent Islamic fundamentalism. This also applies to Tajikistan, where there were already concerns in the early 1990s that instability would spread domino-style across Central Asia into Russia itself (Holoboff, 1994, p. 165). This geopolitical reasoning is echoed in recent analyses by Stratfor, the private intelligence source cited earlier, which stress the vital importance of establishing buffer zones for a country like Russia that has no natural defensive option (*The Geopolitics of Russia*, 2008). Similarly, Kramer (2008) argues that the CIS is really a paramount concern for Russia's leaders – a concern looming larger than relations with the West, China, and India. He mentions counterterrorism and Russia's wish to expand intelligence and internal security cooperation with its CIS partners as defensive motivations. According to Stratfor, the bulk of Russia's intelligence activity is targeted at the CIS, not the United States as such.

Perhaps the most vivid illustration of the operational significance of the Russian Monroe doctrine was Russia's reaction to the spread of "color revolutions" in the CIS, beginning with the Rose Revolution in Georgia in late 2003 and culminating in Ukraine's Orange Revolution of 2004–5. Putin refused to see them as anything other than veiled foreign intrusions into Russia's sphere of influence, and reacted by announcing a new Russian model of "sovereign democracy" aimed at keeping foreign political influence away from Russia through a repressive law on NGOs (Skak, 2006; 2007). Revealingly, Putin did not question Russia's own interference in elections in Ukraine, or any other Russian intervention in the internal affairs of CIS countries, such as Russia's use of its gas weapon (Nygren, 2007; 2008).

Putin has not made references to the Monroe doctrine in the explicit manner of Migranian and Ambartsumov, but his earlier cited speech in Munich conveyed a message to NATO along those lines:

> I think it is obvious that NATO expansion does not have any relation with the modernisation of the alliance itself or with ensuring security in Europe. On the contrary, it represents a serious provocation that reduces the level of mutual trust. And we have the right to ask: against whom is this expansion intended? (Putin, 2007)

Putin also lashed out against OSCE, an organization that monitors human rights and elections and seeks to further conflict resolution, for example through its mission in Moldova:

> People are trying to transform the OSCE into a vulgar instrument designed to promote the foreign policy interests of one or a group of countries. [...] Decision-making procedures and the involvement of so-called non-governmental organisations are tailored for this task. (ibid.)

Concerning my argument about the roughly 1:1 relationship between words and deeds within Russian strategic culture, analysts portray Putin's CIS policy as one of less talk, more action – reverse Potemkinization, to use the term invented by Bobo Lo:

> whereas the Yeltsin administration was apt to describe the former Soviet Union as Russia's major foreign policy priority while in practice assigning it second class status, Putin has adopted a less declamatory approach, but one which in reality is far more serious about

exercising Russian influence in the periphery, treating the latter as a *de facto* sphere of influence. (Lo, 2003, p. 16)[3]

On top of all this came President Medvedev's own embrace of the Russian "Monroe doctrine" on August 31, 2008 in the wake of the Georgian war as the fourth and fifth principles among his five principles of Russian foreign policy:

> Fourthly, protecting the lives and dignity of our citizens, wherever they may be, is an unquestionable priority for our country. Our foreign policy decisions will be based on this need. We will also protect the interests of our business community abroad. It should be clear to all that we will respond to any aggressive acts committed against us.
>
> Fifthly, as is the case with other countries there are regions in which Russia has 'privileged interests'. These regions are home to countries with which we share special historical relations and are bound together as friends and good neighbours. We will pay particular attention to our work in these regions and build friendly ties with these countries, our close neighbours. (quoted from Kapila, 2008)

The fourth principle has a direct bearing upon Russia's CIS policy because of the large Russian diaspora living there, as well as in the Baltic states, as a legacy from the USSR and beyond. It mirrors the US principle of reserving for the United States the right to defend its citizens wherever they may be. This may be a noble humanitarian principle, but in the case of Russia there are clear elements of abuse, such as when Russia generously distributed Russian passports to South Ossetians prior to the outbreak of war in 2008.

The fifth principle was interpreted precisely as a new Russian "Monroe doctrine," except for the fact that it was anything but new, as I have demonstrated. Given the context of actual, if brief, warfare in Georgia, one cannot argue the innocence of Medvedev's wording "privileged interests," as some have tried to do. True, on one occasion Russia's Foreign Minister denied that the CIS constitutes a sphere of influence, but then went on to declare the CIS an "absolute priority" in Russia's foreign policy, implying a region over which Russia is willing to sacrifice the harmony in Russia's relationship with the West (Lavrov, 2009). He gave another intriguing clue to current Russian strategic culture:

> The chief conclusion which we draw for ourselves about the outcome of 2008 is that Russia basically completed the era of

'concentration'. And the likely conclusion being drawn by all of the world community is that we are having to do with a qualitatively new geopolitical situation [...]. (Lavrov, 2009)

Lavrov's triumphalism is paradoxical, indeed. The year 2008 unleashed the world economic crisis, which included Russia; it saw interstate war with Georgia, allegedly over South Ossetia, a hard test for the Russian Army; and, finally, 2008 was a year of utter diplomatic fiasco, as not even Russia's closest allies among the CIS countries cared to extend full diplomatic recognition to South Ossetia and Abkhazia, nor did China. The explanation for Lavrov's optimism is found in his further remarks about the rise of the G20 and the BRIC powers, all of which are also G20 members. Russia sees itself as a rising power and the United States as a declining power – just as Putin (2007) does.

As pointed out by Paul Goble (2009), Lavrov was deliberately paraphrasing Czarist Russia's shrewd Foreign Minister Aleksandr Gorchakov when declaring Russia to be past its era of "concentration." Upon Russia's defeat in the Crimean War in 1856, Gorchakov became famous for issuing a circular to the foreign powers with the historic phrase "La Russie ne bouge pas, elle se recueille" (in Russian: "Rossia ne serditsia. Rossia sosredotachivaetsia"). This was a Terminator doctrine of sorts: I'll be back! On this account there is continuity between Lavrov and Evgeny Primakov, who served as Russia's Foreign Minister in 1996–8, and declared Gorchakov to be his role model. Gorchakov's and Primakov's tenures were years of limited room for maneuver, whereas Lavrov's has been one of Russia regaining greatpowerhood, of the Terminator coming back.

There is more than a play on catchphrases in my reference to the Terminator movies. Postcommunist Russia was always adamant that it constituted a great power to be reckoned with, even if this was true mainly thanks to its destructive capacity. Although CIS affairs may be the Kremlin's primary concern, everybody agrees that the second most important concern for Russian decision makers remains Russia's visibility in world affairs. Closely linked to this is Russia's incessant campaigning for a multipolar world and its simultaneous courtship of the United States with the aim of cultivating an exclusive US–Russia relationship, as seen in article 18 of Russia's national security strategy (Putin, 2007; *Strategia natsional'noi bezopasnosti…*, 2009). This source posits another remarkable ambition as Russia's strategic goal, namely to be among the top five economies in the world in terms of GDP within a "medium term perspective" (*Strategia natsional'noi bezopas-nosti,* article 53).

So far, the analysis points toward only one conclusion, and a sinister one at that: Russia pursues an assertive anti-Western policy based on the combined strategic culture of its Monroe and Terminator doctrines. It confirms the finding of Andrew Bennett (1999) about the recurrent pattern of Russia's military interventionism against Russia's neighbor-hood. However, this represents only one side of the coin. The other must also be taken into account, although I can only sketch some exceptions to the rule just established.

The Kremlin's upside

It is tempting to view Russia's proximity to Europe as a nuisance, but Russia's self-proclaimed European identity also gives European inter-national organizations and actors leverage over Russia. Putin once expressed himself in the following way when he was giving a press conference together with European Commission President José Manuel Barroso: "If we in Europe made a certain decision regarding Kosovo, we must behave similarly in other parts of the world [...] The rules should be the same for everyone – that is extremely important" (Putin, 2009). What Putin had in mind was independence for South Ossetia and Abkhazia, perhaps Transniestria, but his remark opened a flank concerning Chechnya. At a minimum Putin's self-serving concession testifies to some norm transmission concerning the rights of ethnic and national minorities.

Similarly, it is worth noticing how Russia sought to legitimize its mil-itary intervention in Georgia in August 2008 by invoking buzzwords from humanitarian law, such as the United Nations' principle of states' *Responsibility to Protect* as laid down by the General Assembly in 2005. In an interview with the BBC Lavrov stated: "According to our Constitution there is also responsibility to protect – the term which is very widely used in the UN when people see some trouble in Africa or in any remote part of other regions. But this is not Africa to us, this is next door. This is the area, where Russian citizens live" (quoted from Global Centre for the Responsibility to Protect, 2008). Although the cited source rejects Lavrov's case on the grounds that Russia acted unilaterally, it views it as reflecting the moral force of the responsibil-ity to protect as a new normative framework of global significance. Indeed, Russia's futile diplomatic offensive over the war in Georgia is instructive of the importance of gaining legitimacy, even for assertive rising powers such as Russia.

Furthermore, it is not just a question of Russia paying lip service to whatever norms are in vogue in the international system. Many works on Russia's membership in idealistic norm-making organizations like the Council of Europe describe Russia as just a pain in the neck for the entire organization. However, it was early in Putin's presidency that Russia took on its Council of Europe obligation to bring an end to capital punishment in Russia by enacting a moratorium, which, despite onslaughts by macho parliamentarians in the Duma, remains intact. Well-informed analysts explain that the tough Kremlin people themselves have come to view the abolition of the death penalty as their personal life insurance in their notoriously unpredictable native country. Perhaps for this reason, Putin decided not to lash out against the Council of Europe in his hawkish Munich speech. In any event, Bill Bowring (2007) concludes that Russia is serious about its Council of Europe membership despite Moscow's increasingly tense relationship with Strasbourg.

On the one hand, the Kremlin categorically refuses to accept NATO enlargement, ignoring the fact that the initiative for this came from the applicant post-communist countries themselves, not NATO headquarters in Brussels. On the other hand, there is an obvious convergence of interests between NATO and Russia in the struggle against the Taliban in Afghanistan, making it valid to some extent to claim that NATO takes care of Russia's national security in a more tangible manner than Russia itself could ever do. This appears to be realized by former intelligence bosses such as Nikolai Bordyuzha, currently the head of the Collective Security Treaty Organization, a military alliance among the most pro-Russian CIS members. He once declared that he saw no need for American forces to depart in haste from bases in Central Asia, and approves of the ISAF operation, which Russia now officially supports by having opened its territory to NATO logistics.

At a meeting of Russian foreign policy opinion makers, Lavrov actually challenged the Russian "Monroe doctrine" of Russia's exclusive sphere of influence by acknowledging that the West may also have its own interests in the CIS countries (Arkhangelsky, 2009). What is more, on an earlier occasion Putin showed himself open to direct Western involvement in solving the highly sensitive Chechen issue: "We have received proposals via certain channels for a larger involvement of Germany and the EU to solve the Chechnya problem. We should like to accept them wholly and completely" (Putin, 2004). In other words, one senses that decision makers in Russia do realize that the game of ensuring Russia's national security cannot forever be framed in the jingoistic zero-sum terms of their "Monroe doctrine." Russia may face uniquely high costs of production and security because of its geography, but earnest offers of win–win games of security cooperation, like ISAF concerning Afghanistan, would alleviate this and, thereby, help to discipline the downside of Russian strategic culture.

Conclusion and policy implications

The above analysis shows that the political scientist Barry Buzan (1991) was wrong when he argued that the end of the Cold War ended the "overlay" – that is, the imposition of the security policy agendas of external actors, either the United States or the USSR – upon a region. Russia has proven capable of again imposing overlay, in the shape of its "Monroe doctrine," on its post-Soviet neighborhood. In this way it has reintroduced the military interventionism for which Russia was always notorious, even if this results from defensive impulses (Bhalla *et al.*, 2008; *The Geopolitics of Russia*, 2008). This means that it is futile and downright dangerous for NATO, the EU, and the United States to confront Russia in its own backyard. The West must address the profound geopolitical drama behind Russia's brutal security policy without sacrificing the legitimate security concerns of the victims of this policy in Russia's "near abroad." The challenge is one of breaking the spell of dualism in Russian foreign and security policy: normal interstate conduct towards the "far abroad" vs. jingoism towards the post-Soviet neighborhood.

This may sound like squaring the circle, and perhaps it is. I believe the way to move forward is to take Russia's, admittedly vain, quest for parity with the United States as the point of departure. The time has come for the United States to renounce officially its own, original Monroe doctrine and make clear that in an era of globalization it is anachronistic for great powers to uphold spheres of influence. Some might object that the Monroe doctrine is no longer operational. If so, then it will be all the easier to shelve it officially. Conversely, others might argue that the US cannot just renounce its veto power over Central and Latin American politics; if that is so, then the West must simply accept Russia's exercise of its veto power. Shelving the US Monroe doctrine may not be a panacea in improving relations with Russia, but it will reset the button in the sense of boosting the legitimacy of Western concerns over Russia's conduct towards its near abroad. It will thus apply gentle pressure on the Kremlin to reconsider its unilateralism, and embolden those who do perceive the need for comprehensive multilateral international security cooperation throughout Eurasia: because, as suggested in the penultimate part of the analysis, Russian strategic culture is neither entirely static nor immune to norm transmission.

Notes

1. The insight that geography matters inspired Stephen Walt to relaunch neorealism as a more context-specific balance-of-threat theory.
2. I am deliberately using the term hypermilitarism. The Soviet economy was militarized to a degree which few analysts seem to grasp. Even in peacetime the resources allotted to the non-civilian sector, relatively speaking, surpassed the military buildup of Nazi Germany (until 1943) (Lynch, 2005, p. 58, cf. pp. 52–4). One former GRU (Russian Military Intelligence) agent who now serves as an expert on defense economy in Russia confirms this, insisting that the CIA's estimate of the Soviet defense burden as a percentage of GDP was ridiculously low – around 25 per cent. In reality it was more like 100 per cent ([sic]; Shlykov, 2008).
3. Migranian himself became notorious again for his follow-up to his Monroe doctrine. In January 1997 he co-authored a blueprint for the deliberate destabilization of selected CIS members, including Georgia and Ukraine, with the aim of preventing them from breaking free of Russia's sphere of influence (Fuller, 1997). This had the unintended effect of scaring the non-Russian CIS members away from comprehensive integration schemes, and causing them to adopt a "soft" attitude instead. The timing of his hawkish initiative was curious, as it came at a time when Zhirinovsky was a dead man in Russian politics and Russian decision makers had barely recovered from the deep trauma inflicted by their first war in Chechnya in 1994–6. In short, it is indicative of the depth of Russia's jingoism.

References

Ambartsumov, Evgeny A. (1993) Personal interview, Moscow, December.
Arkhangelsky, Alexander (2009) "What Countries Care About", April 14. http://www.russiaprofile.org/page.php?pageid=Politics&articleid=a1239728230 (accessed July 1, 2010).
Bennett, Andrew (1999) Condemned to Repetition? The Rise, Fall, Reprise of Soviet-Russian Military Interventionism, 1973–1996, Cambridge, Mass.: MIT Press.
Bhalla, Reva, Laureen Goodrich and Peter Zeihan (2009) "Turkey and Russia on the Rise", *Stratfor Geopolitical Intelligence Report*, March 17. http://eng.i-iter.org/content/stratfor-turkey-and-russia-rise-reva-bhalla-lauren-goodrich-and-peter-zeihan (accessed July 1, 2010).
Bowring, Bill (2007). "Russia's Relations with the Council of Europe under Increasing Strain". http://www.eu-russiacentre.org/assets/files/15%20Feb%20Bowring%20article%20EU-RC.pdf (accessed July 1, 2010).

Buzan, Barry (1991) *People, States and Fear. National Security Problem in International Relations*, Upper Saddle River, NJ: Prentice-Hall.

Ermarth, Fritz W. (2006) "Russia's strategic culture: Past, Present, and…in Transition?", paper prepared for Defense Threat Reduction Agency, United States of America, comparative strategic cultures curriculum, October 31 (22 pp.). http://www.fas.org/irp/agency/dod/dtra/russia.pdf (accessed July 1, 2010).

Finnemore, Martha and Kathryn Sikkink (1998) "International norm dynamics and political change", *International Organization*, vol. 52, no. 4, pp. 887–917.

Fuller, Liz (1997) "1997 in Review: The CIS – Half Alive or Half Dead?", *Radio Free Europe/ Radio Liberty*, Prague, December 22.

Global Centre for the Responsibility to Protect (2008) 'The Georgia-Russia Crisis and the Responsibility to Protect: Background Note', New York: August 19. http://globalr2p.org/media/pdf/GeorgiaRussia.pdf (accessed July 1, 2010).

Goble, Paul (2009) "Moscow is Now Set to Move Beyond Gorchakov's Injunction, Lavrov Says", *Azerbaijan International*, January 23. http://azer.com/aiweb/categories/caucasus_crisis/index/cc_articles/goble/goble_2009/goble_0109/goble_0123_gorchakov.html (July 1, 2010).

Gray, Colin (1986) *Nuclear Strategy and National Style*, Lanham, MD: Hamilton Press.

Holoboff, Elaine M. (1994) "Russian views on military intervention: benevolent peacekeeping, Monroe doctrine, or neo-imperialism?", in Lawrence Freedman (ed.), *Military Intervention in European Conflicts*, Oxford: Blackwell, pp. 154–74.

Hurrell, Andrew (2006) "Hegemony, liberalism and global order: what space for would be great powers?", *International Affairs*, vol. 82, no. 1, pp. 1–19.

Johnston, Alastair Iain (1995) "Thinking about Strategic Culture", *International Security*, vol. 19, no. 4, pp. 32–64.

Jones, David R. (1990) "Soviet Strategic Culture", in Carl G. Jacobsen (ed.), *Strategic Power. USA/USSR*, London: St Martin's Press, pp. 35–49.

Kapila, Subhash (2008) "Russia's Monroe Doctrine: Strategic Implications", South Asia Analysis Group, Paper no. 2879, October 13. http://www.southasiaanalysis.org/%5Cpapers29%5Cpaper2879.html (accessed July 1, 2010).

Kramer, Mark (2008) "Russian Policy toward the Commonwealth of Independent States. Recent Trends and Future Prospects", *Problems of Post-Communism*, vol. 55, no. 6, pp. 3–19.

Lavrov, Sergei (2009) Stenogramma vystuplenia i otvetov na voprosy Ministra inostrannykh del Rossii S.V. Lavrova na press-konferentsii, posviashchennoi vneshnepoliticheskim itogam 2008 goda, v MID Rossii, 16 ianvaria 2009 goda. http://www.mid.ru/brp_4.nsf/0/4D65FB04BAC5FB77C325751600475915 (accessed July 1, 2010).

Leites, Nathan (1951) *The Operational Code of the Politiburo*, New York: McGraw-Hill.

Lo, Bobo (2003) "The Securitization of Russian Foreign Policy under Putin", in Gabriel Gorodetsky (ed.), Russia between East and West: Russian Foreign Policy on the Threshold of the Twenty-First Century, London: Frank Cass, pp. 12–27.

Lynch, Allen S. (2005) *How Russia Is Not Ruled. Reflections on Russian Political Development*, Cambridge University Press.

Medvedev, Dimitri (2008) "Medvedev describes Georgia attack as Russia's 9/11", *The Guardian,* September 13. http://www.guardian.co.uk/world/2008/sep/13/russia.georgia (accessed July 1, 2010).

Migranian, Andranik M. (1994) 'Rossia i blizhnee zarubezhe', *Nezavisimaia Gazeta,* January 12.

Nygren, Bertil (2007) The Rebuilding of Greater Russia: Putin's Foreign Policy Toward the CIS Countries, Abingdon, UK: Routledge.

Nygren, Bertil (2008) "Putin's Use of Natural Gas to Reintegrate the CIS Region", *Problems of Post-Communism,* vol. 55, no. 4, July/August, pp. 3–15.

Putin, Vladimir V. (1999) "Rossia na rubezhe tyshchachiletiya", *Rossiiskaia Gazeta,* December 29. http://www.rg.ru/Prilog/vvd/1231/10.htm (accessed July 1, 2010).

Putin, Vladimir V. (2004) "Putin signals Chechnya initiative", BBC News, December 21. http://news.bbc.co.uk/2/hi/europe/4115279.stm (accessed July 1, 2010).

Putin, Vladimir V. (2007) Speech at the 43rd Munich Conference on Security Policy, February 10. http://www.washingtonpost.com/wp-dyn/content/article/2007/02/12/AR2007021200555.html (accessed July 1, 2010).

Putin, Vladimir V. (2009) Prime Minister Vladimir Putin and European Commission President José Manuel Barroso held a joint news conference, February 6. http://www.themoscowtimes.com/news/article/putin-barroso-spar-over-human-rights/374329.html (accessed July 1, 2010).

Reuters, August 26 2008. http://www.guardian.co.uk/world/2008/aug/26/russia.georgia1 (accessed July 1, 3020).

Shlykov, Vitaly V. (2008) Personal interview in Moscow, January.

Skak, Mette (1996) *From Empire to Anarchy. Postcommunist Foreign Policy and International Relations,* London: Hurst & Co.

Skak, Mette (2006) "Ruslands globaliseringsstrategi", *Politica,* vol. 38, no. 3, pp. 264–79.

Skak, Mette (2007) "Ruslands globalisering: hvor dybt stikker den?", *Nordisk Østforum,* vol. 21, no. 4, pp. 435–56.

Strategia natsional'noi bezopasnosti Rossiiskoi Federatsii do 2020 goda. Utverzhden Ukazom Prezidenta Rossiiskoi Federatsii ot 12 maia 2009, No. 537. http://www.scrf.gov.ru/documents/99.html (accessed July 1, 2010).

Strategicheskii kurs Rossii s gosudarstvami-uchastnikami Sdoruzhestva Nezavisimikh Gosudarstv (1995). Utverzhden Ukazom Prezidenta Rossiiskoi Federatsii ot 14 sentiabria 1995 g. No. 940.

Stratfor (2008) *The Geopolitics of Russia: Permanent Struggle,* October 15. http://www.stratfor.com/analysis/20081014_geopolitics_russia_permanent_struggle (accessed July 1, 2010).

Waltz, Kenneth N. (1979) *Theory of International Politics,* NewYork: McGraw-Hill.

Wilson, Dominic and Roopa Purushothaman (2003) Dreaming with BRICs: The Path to 2050, *Global Economics Paper,* no. 99. Goldman Sachs: October 1. http://www2.goldmansachs.com/ideas/brics/book/99-dreaming.pdf (accessed July 1, 2010).

Zakaria, Fareed (2008) *The Post-American World,* New York: W. W. Norton & Company.

8
Russia, Central Asia, and the Caucasus after the Georgia Conflict

Charles E. Ziegler[1]

The Russo-Georgian conflict of August 2008 was the first time since the collapse of communism that Moscow had employed military force outside its borders. The brief, lopsided war had a major impact on Western Europe and the United States, leading to a temporary severing of NATO–Russian ties, and widespread condemnation of Russian aggression in the United States. The impact of the conflict on Russia's key neighbors – the countries of Central Asia and the Caucasus – was measurably greater, since these states constitute a region critical to Moscow's foreign and security policy and are to varying degrees politically and economically dependent on Moscow. The region commands great power interest because of its large oil and gas reserves and the complicated transit routes for delivering these vital commodities. The predominance of weak authoritarian regimes and unresolved territorial conflicts add instability to this volatile mix.

This chapter examines the foreign policy implications of the Russo-Georgian conflict for the Caucasus and Central Asia. What effect did the Russian–Georgian conflict have on the foreign policies of the states of Central Asia and the Caucasus? Is there evidence that these countries have become more supportive of Russia's foreign policy goals (a bandwagoning effect), as many in the West feared, or has the conflict encouraged these states to look toward other major powers (China, the United States, or Europe) to balance an increasingly aggressive Moscow? Are there other possible comparable situations in the Caucasus or Central Asia where a newly confident and more assertive Russia might intervene? That is, was the Georgia conflict a unique case, or is it an example of Moscow's new willingness to use force in a more aggressive approach to southern neighbors?

Russia after the Georgia conflict

Since Vladimir Putin became President in 2000, Russia has strengthened its capabilities and has worked assiduously to reassert its influence in the vital southern tier, an unstable arc stretching from the Caucasus through Central Asia to Afghanistan. Although Putin had initially accepted the presence of American military forces in Central Asia as part of the Afghanistan campaign, by his second term the Russian President was actively lobbying to have American forces leave the region. At the Shanghai Cooperation Organization (SCO) meeting in Astana in 2005 Moscow sponsored a resolution calling for the departure of the Americans, asserting that the situation in Afghanistan had been stabilized and so US forces were no longer needed. The final statement of the SCO communiqué, however, referred only to "foreign forces," a clear indication that the Central Asian states and China were reluctant to single out the United States for censure ("Deklaratsiia", 2005). The Director of the Center of Shanghai Cooperation Organization Studies emphasized that the determination of the SCO members to maintain chief responsibility for regional security did not specifically target the US, but was directed at all countries and international organizations using the infrastructure of, or stationing troops on the soil of, SCO members in connection with antiterrorist actions (Pan, 2006).

From Moscow's perspective NATO's expansion eastward, together with the presence of US and coalition forces in Central Asia, constrained Russia's pretensions to restore lost influence in the Eurasian region. Russia is a revisionist power, at least along its southern and western periphery, where political turmoil and nationalism frustrate Moscow's objectives. The color revolutions in Georgia, Ukraine, and Kyrgyzstan, followed by the discussions of NATO membership for Georgia and Ukraine, constituted more disturbing evidence of American and Western efforts to establish governments friendly to the West and, by logical extension, hostile to Moscow. Putin and the Russian leadership were convinced that NATO's goal was to replicate the Baltic experience in the Caucasus and Central Asia.

In Russia's Foreign Policy Concept of July 2008 Moscow for the first time defined itself as a Eurasian rather than a European power, according to Igor Morgulov, Russian Minister Counselor to China ("Sino-Soviet Ties," 2008). While the concept of Eurasianism is widely debated in Russia, Moscow intends to signal that, although Russian foreign policy will not neglect Europe, Russia will strengthen ties with the CIS countries, East and South Asia (most notably China), and promote the concept of the BRIC (Brazil–Russia–India–China mechanism). This is part of a larger pattern in which Moscow favors developing centers of power outside the US–Atlantic structure, while inserting itself as an active participant, if not leader, in these groupings.[2] In terms of domestic politics, Eurasianism implies a governing style that is more authoritarian and less pluralistic than North American and European democratic forms of governance.[3] Democratic, pluralist societies along Russia's periphery are threatening because they provide entrée to hostile powers, diminish Moscow's influence in what is viewed as a privileged sphere of interest, and could spark grass-roots opposition within the Russian Federation itself.

President Dmitrii Medvedev confirmed the Eurasian direction of the country's foreign policy by making his first official visit abroad in May 2008 to Kazakhstan – a brief stopover, followed by his primary destination, China. Medvedev's choice reflected the fact that ties with Europe and the United States in the later years of the Bush administration were strained, while those with Asia were relatively good. Kazakhstan has been the least problematic of the Commonwealth of Independent States (CIS) countries for Moscow, and China is easily Russia's most important Asian partner, so the choices were logical. By contrast, the bulk of Putin's foreign trips early in his presidency were to Europe rather than Asia.

Russia's 2009 National Security Strategy assigns priority to developing bilateral and multilateral relations with the CIS states, through the Collective Security Treaty Organization and the Eurasian Economic Community, and to strengthening the political potential of the Shanghai Cooperation Organization. The Strategy states that expansion of NATO to Russia's borders and attempts by the Atlantic Alliance to assume global functions are unacceptable (*Strategiya natsional'noi bezopastnosti*, 2009). The document also lists as a fundamental security threat the presence and possible escalation of military conflicts adjacent to Russia's borders and unresolved border disputes with contiguous states. In order to guarantee the security of state borders, high-tech defensive military complexes are envisioned on the borders of Kazakhstan, Ukraine, Georgia, and Azerbaijan, in addition to upgrading facilities in the Arctic zone, the Caspian region, and the Russian Far East (*Strategiya natsional'noi bezopastnosti*, 2009, articles 41 and 42).

Moscow clearly expected that its Eurasian allies would support Russia's interpretation of the Georgian war; in the end, they were disappointed. At the August 2008 Shanghai Cooperation Organization meeting in

Dushanbe, Tajikistan, China and the Central Asian states refused to take sides, urging Russia and Georgia to resolve their differences peacefully through dialogue, while preserving the unity and territorial integrity of states in accord with international law. The Declaration of the Heads of State did not overtly support Russian aims, nor did it single out Tbilisi for condemnation, as Moscow would have preferred:

> The member states of the SCO express their deep concern in connection with the recent tension around the issue of South Ossetia, and call on the relevant parties to resolve existing problems in a peaceful way through dialogue, to make efforts for reconciliation and facilitation of negotiations. The member states of the SCO welcome the approval on 12 August 2008 in Moscow of the six principles of settling the conflict in South Ossetia, and support the active role of Russia in promoting peace and cooperation in the region. (Dushanbe Declaration of Heads of SCO Member States, 2008)

Russia's resort to military force in the Caucasus produced widely varying reactions among the country's putative allies in the Commonwealth of Independent States. Georgia, not surprisingly, announced its withdrawal from the enfeebled organization. Ukraine's leadership split, with President Viktor Yushenko taking a hard line against Moscow and lobbying for NATO membership, while Prime Minister Yulia Timoshenko avoided directly criticizing Russia. Kazakhstan, which was just beginning to invest heavily in Georgia, balked at supporting Russia through the SCO, and in late August 2008 launched a "Road to Europe" plan in connection with that country's 2010 chairmanship of the Organization for Economic Cooperation and Development (Iacobucci, 2008). Azerbaijan recognized Georgia's territorial integrity and welcomed Georgian refugees, but the vulnerability of the country's oil and gas export routes, illustrated by British Petroleum's decision to shut down the Baku–Tbilisi–Ceyhan (BTC) pipeline temporarily following an explosion on Turkish territory, placed Baku in a difficult position vis-à-vis Moscow. For Central Asia's energy-rich states, the conflict highlighted the vulnerability of transit corridors through the Caucasus, calling into question the viability of Europe's Nabucco gas pipeline project. Heightened instability in the Caucasus could encourage Central Asia's energy producers to ship their products through Russia, as Moscow would prefer, or they might bypass Russia altogether in favor of shipping oil and gas directly eastward to China.

Militarily, the conflict was a mixed success for Russia's armed forces, considering that Moscow had begun preparations for a confrontation with Tbilisi as early as May 2008.[4] The Russian military easily defeated the much inferior Georgian forces, but a number of Russian commentators faulted the army for its outdated weapons systems, lacking precision-guided munitions and performing poorly against Georgia's modest air defenses. The Georgia campaign emphasized the need to develop the "Innovation Army" touted by Minister of Defense Anatoly Serdyukov (Herspring, 2008, p. 28). A major effort towards military modernization and the shake-up of the army was initiated in fall 2008, and plans for reform were announced by President Medvedev in March 2009.

Among the improvements listed by Medvedev as scheduled for implementation by 2011 were improving combat readiness of the strategic nuclear forces, developing and procuring advanced armaments and communications equipment, carrying out additional military exercises, and improving military compensation and housing. Primary threats identified by the Russian President were the potential for regional and local conflicts, international terrorism, and the further expansion of NATO. Defense Minister Anatolii Serdyukov elaborated on perceived threats, specifying US and NATO military presence in Russia's border regions, and singled out the North Caucasus Military District as scheduled for equipment modernization ("Full-Fledged Rearmament", 2009; Poroskov, 2009).

One of Moscow's major concerns is to preserve stability in the northern Caucasus. Chechnya is critical to Russian security, as are the other small republics of the North Caucasus; moreover, the North and South Caucasus are closely linked, historically and strategically. The North Caucasus has become a breeding ground for ethnic conflict, terrorism, and separatism. In recent years the region has seen a spate of political killings, kidnappings, suicide bombings, and human rights abuses. Chechnya has been largely stabilized under the harsh rule of the Kremlin's appointee, Ramzan Kadyrov, but the conflict has spilled over into neighboring Ingushetia, Dagestan, and Kabardino-Balkaria, which continue to be rent by social tensions, corruption, and clan intrigues, and could degenerate into ethnic conflict similar to that in Kosovo (Goble, 2009).[5] Moscow's response to instability in the Caucasus has been to employ force to contain all movements for self-determination or autonomy from Moscow (if not from Tbilisi). Military success against Georgia will only reinforce the tendency to use coercion rather than negotiation to preserve order.

Russia's primary goals in the Caucasus include preventing the disintegration of Moscow's control over the North Caucasus, resisting US presence and influence in the South Caucasus while securing Russia's primacy in the region, maximizing control over the oil and gas routes, restoring Russia's role as a cultural model, and preserving the Russian language as the foreign language of choice in the region (Trenin, 2009). The North Caucasus in particular is the one region in Russia where state control is most tenuous, and the situation appears to be deteriorating. From Moscow's perspective, the prospect of a NATO presence directly adjacent to this volatile region, engaging in Western-style democracy promotion efforts, is clearly a threat to stability.

For Russia, with its resource-based foreign policy and neo-mercantilist mentality, controlling the transit routes for oil and gas pipelines from the Caucasus and Central Asia is also vital. The Baku–Tbilisi–Ceyhan (BTC) oil pipeline and the Baku–Tbilisi–Erzurum (BTE) gas pipeline compete with Russian oil and gas, deny Russia valuable transit fees, and enhance Georgia's energy independence. The economic interests of Russia's elites are closely linked to Russia maintaining a close, influential relationship with the countries of Central Asia and the Caucasus, particularly in the energy sector. Russia's energy supplies to the energy-poor nations of the region, its efforts to monopolize the transit routes, and investments by Russian firms in Central Asia and the Caucasus have restored some of the influence lost in the chaotic Yeltsin years, but Moscow seeks greater control over the region.

By strengthening Russia's clout in the Caucasus, the war raised the costs and risks of Western energy projects designed to transport Caspian Sea oil and gas to Europe. Russian officials have been highly critical of the existing BTC and BTE pipelines, as well as the planned Nabucco project, asserting that regional production will not be sufficient to fill all the planned pipelines. The war with Georgia has raised cautionary flags among Central Asian suppliers and Western investors alike. This serves Moscow's interests, and those of the Russian energy oligarchs, who have worked diligently to close off western routes for Central Asian hydrocarbons. Central Asia's energy exporters – Kazakhstan, Uzbekistan, and Turkmenistan – are unwilling to commit definitively to Nabucco, although all three have agreed to Russian plans to increase the capacity of the Central Asian-Center pipeline (Reuters, 2009).

Russia's actions in Georgia may prove to be a major setback for Western democracy promotion efforts in the CIS. The current Russian leadership, and particularly Vladimir Putin, viewed US and West European support for nongovernmental organizations and opposition parties as attempts to impose Western-style democracy on Russia and its neighbors. To the delight of many in Moscow, in the aftermath of the August war Georgia's civil society launched a wave of protests against

Saakashvili's reckless leadership, calling for him to be ousted. While the Georgian opposition was not pro-Moscow, at least the Kremlin had the satisfaction of knowing that the war eroded support for the Georgian president, whom Putin personally detests (Levy, 2009). A reverse color revolution in Georgia would strengthen the Kremlin's position in the Caucasus and remove a major irritant.

From this perspective, the Georgia operation was an ideal opportunity to turn the tables on the West. As Putin had pointed out on a number of occasions, if Kosovo's independence was legitimate (to the West, if not to Moscow), then why should not Abkhazia and South Ossetia be granted the same right to self-determination? The evidence is persuasive that the people of these territories do not wish to remain part of Georgia. For Moscow, Western protests against Russia's diplomatic recognition of the break-away provinces were simply more evidence of "double standards" – condemning Russia for political failings while preserving friendly relations with odious, but useful, authoritarian regimes. Of course, this line of reasoning ignores the application of a similar double standard to Chechen demands for independence from Russia.

The war has had major implications for the various "frozen conflicts" – the territorial disputes left unresolved after the breakup of the Soviet Union. Moscow is not interested in resolving these frozen conflicts, despite statements to the contrary. As in Georgia, unresolved disputes in Nagorno-Karabakh, Transdniestria, and elsewhere (one might include western Ukraine, northern Kazakhstan, Andijon, and the Uzbekistan–Kyrgyzstan disputes) give Moscow a good deal of leverage over its neighbors. Tellingly, at the April 2008 NATO summit Putin reputedly threatened George W. Bush that Moscow would follow the Kosovo precedent by recognizing Abkhazia and South Ossetia if Georgia were granted a Membership Action Plan. Putin also informed his American counterpart that "Ukraine is not even a state," and that if Ukraine were to be accepted for membership in NATO Russia might "tear away" eastern Ukraine and the Crimea, and Ukraine would simply cease to exist (Allenova *et al.*, 2008). Since the Georgian conflict was played out under a Putin–Medvedev dual power arrangement, such threats may be considered more than the empty rhetoric of a former president.

Central Asia

As relatively small, weak states, the Central Asians have generally sought to maintain good ties with their former colonial power, to

whom they are bound by economic and cultural ties, while developing good relations with the other major powers – the United States,
China, the EU, India, Iran, and Turkey. Turkmenistan under strong-
man Saparmurat Niyazov was the coolest towards Moscow, though the
country's neutralist (read isolationist) policy, neo-totalitarian cult of
personality, and closed society constrained its international options.
The other Central Asian states followed "multi-vectored" foreign policies of maintaining good relations with all countries, with the larger
two (Kazakhstan and Uzbekistan) exercising the greatest leverage internationally. Kazakhstan, with its large oil and gas reserves and under
the skillful leadership of President Nursultan Nazarbaev, has managed to enjoy good relations with the great powers and its neighbors.
Tajikistan has cooperated with Washington in the Afghan campaign,
and the US provides assistance to counter narcotics trafficking and
terrorism, but the presence of some 20,000 Russian troops helped keep
that country firmly in Moscow's orbit. Kyrgyzstan under Askar Akayev
was for years closely aligned with the West, and received considerable
civil society assistance, until the 2005 "Tulip Revolution" and ensuing chaos encouraged Akayev's successor, Kurmanbek Bakiyev, to draw
closer to Moscow.

In Central Asia the foreign policy issues with the greatest potential for
international conflict are unresolved territorial disputes and water rights
issues, particularly those between Uzbekistan and its eastern neighbors. While these issues heighten regional tensions, the probability of
armed conflict among states is low. By contrast, domestic challenges –
religious extremism, ethnic tensions, clan rivalries, popular disaffection
with corrupt and ineffective governance, organized crime, and drug
trafficking – pose far greater problems for Central Asia's leaders. The
concept of balancing is useful in this context, particularly external balancing (since no Central Asian state has sufficient capabilities for internal balancing), but it ignores the more immediate and acute internal
threats. Central Asian strategies are better described by Steven David's
(1991) concept of "omnibalancing," in which weak Third World elites
align with states to balance external and internal threats, ensuring their
hold on power. In this scenario, external threats that might jeopardize
state survival are secondary to internal challenges to leaders' political
survival.

The Shanghai Cooperation Organization provides a forum for Central
Asian states that facilitates this strategy of omnibalancing. For Central
Asian member-states the SCO balances off the big three (Russia, China,
and the US) while enlisting the support of Russia and China against

domestic threats such as terrorism, religious extremism, separatism, and grass-roots opposition (potential color revolutions). China, the organization's most influential member, and Russia are both wary of outside influences (such as the US and NATO) that might transform the political landscape of the region, though they acknowledge the West's role in containing the Taliban. Beijing's growing weight in the SCO and in Central Asia more broadly provides the Central Asians with uncritical support for their dictatorships, and subtle but effective leverage against Moscow's effort to reestablish influence in the region. Preserving the status quo is one goal that the Central Asians and the Chinese share, and this limits Russia's revisionist aspirations. At the SCO summit meeting in September 2008 Moscow pressed China and Central Asia to support its recognition of Abkhazia and South Ossetia, but the other members demurred. The final communiqué did not openly support the Russian position, but rather urged both parties to the conflict to solve their differences in a peaceful way, using dialogue rather than force ("Session of the Council of Heads of State of the SCO", 2008). Russia's Georgia campaign undermined a key collective good of the SCO – preservation of the regional status quo – threatening the interests of Central Asia's leaders as well as those of the Chinese.

In 2008–9 the greatest threat to Central Asia's stability was the global financial crisis and its impact on the region. The economic growth engine of Central Asia, Kazakhstan, was severely impacted by the decline in oil prices; its GDP growth rate dropped from 8.7 per cent in 2007 to just 2.7 per cent in 2008. As real estate and construction sectors faltered, thousands of Kyrgyz and Uzbek guest workers lost their jobs and remittances dried up, heightening the potential for social instability. At their June 2009 SCO summit meeting in Yekaterinburg member states focused on developing trade, investment, and transportation corridors, in addition to strengthening cooperation on security. Chinese President Hu Jintao (2009) pledged $10 billion in credits to help the Central Asian members cope with the crisis; earlier in the year Moscow had promised $7.5 billion in assistance.

China has gradually increased its presence in Central Asia over the past decade, through the multilateral Shanghai Cooperation Organization, by enhancing bilateral political ties, and by rapidly expanding trade relations. Hundreds of thousands of Chinese now live and work in Central Asia. Chinese interest in the Caucasus is more modest, but even there Azerbaijan's hydrocarbon reserves command attention. China shares Moscow's interest in regional political stability, but the two countries are competing for access to the region's energy riches (Ziegler,

2010). While Beijing refrained from officially criticizing China's "strategic partner," Russia, for using force outside its borders, the violation of Georgia's sovereignty, and particularly Moscow's recognition of separatist regions, was a disturbing precedent, given Beijing's determination to quash separatist movements in Taiwan, Xinjiang, and Tibet.[6]

The Central Asian members of the SCO were also troubled by Russia's support for the Abkhaz and South Ossetian separatist movements. Especially disturbing was the reported Russian practice of handing out passports to residents of the two regions; Moscow largely justified its actions against Georgia as defending Russian "compatriots" abroad. The term "compatriots" (*sootechestvenniki*) refers not only to Russian ethnics (*Russkii*), but also to Russified former residents of the USSR who might direct their allegiances first to Russia (Zevelev, 2008; Ziegler, 2006). In Central Asia this includes a large number of ethnic Russians (about five million in Kazakhstan and over one million in Uzbekistan), and others who may not feel comfortable with the indigenizing policies of the Central Asian governments (similar to those of the Ukrainians and Belarusians).

Kazakhstan is the one Central Asian country where the possibility of an ethnic Russian separatist movement exists that could generate support from nationalists inside the Russian Federation. Kazakhstan's northern border, like all the borders of Central Asia, is artificial. Russian settlements in northern Kazakhstan date back several hundred years, and much of Kazakhstan's Russian population (Russians make up nearly one-third of the total) is concentrated in the north; they dominate the cities of Ust-Kamenogorsk, Pavlodar, and Petropavlovsk. In the early 1990s Russian nationalists, among them Aleksandr Solzhenitsyn and Vladimir Zhirinovsky, called for these "historically Russian lands" to be returned to Russia, but the issue gradually subsided.[7] Occasionally, Russian Cossack organizations agitate for separation, and some 300,000 Russian citizens are in Kazakhstan on residential permits, but there is little evidence that Moscow has pursued a strategy of handing out passports as it did in Abkhazia and South Ossetia.

In terms of foreign policy, relations with Russia are a priority for Astana, but Kazakhstan also has a tradition of good relations with Georgia, and Kazakh companies have planned substantial investments in Georgia, as Kazakh President Nursultan Nazarbayev pointed out during his meeting with Dmitrii Medvedev at the SCO summit in Dushanbe (President of Russia website, 2008). Economically Russia is far more important – Russia is Kazakhstan's largest trading partner, with $19.9 billion total turnover in 2008 ("Vladimir Putin Visits Kazakhstan," 2009). Landlocked Kazakhstan has a limited number of transportation routes for the oil that constitutes the bulk of its foreign earnings, and about 80 per cent of its oil exports go through Russia. By contrast, according to the Georgian Ministry of Foreign Affairs, Kazakh–Georgian trade in 2006 was just under $41 million, and, while investments totaling nearly $2 billion had been planned, as of late 2007 Kazakh investment in Georgia had reached only about $225 million ("Relations between Georgia and the Republic of Kazakhstan," 2008). In the wake of the Georgia war, the Kazakh government, citing instability in the Caucasus, pulled out of a grain terminal project in Poti, and KazTransGas dropped plans to reconstruct an oil refinery near the port city of Batumi (Sharip, 2008). Given the pressures of the financial crisis, Russian assistance easily outweighed potential economic cooperation with Georgia.

At the same time Astana promised to maintain close strategic relations with the United States, and in September Kazakhstan hosted NATO for the Steppe Eagle 2008 exercises near Almaty. Kazakhstan also hosted the June 2009 forum of the Euro-Atlantic Partnership Council forum, where NATO Secretary General Jaap de Hoop Scheffer elaborated the goal of deepening NATO's cooperation with its partners in Central Asia to address terrorism, narcotics trafficking, organized crime, and nuclear proliferation (Lillis, 2009). Much of Kazakhstan's continued Western orientation was driven by its impending 2010 chairmanship of OSCE, described by President Nazarbayev as a "national strategic project" expected to enhance the country's image. But Astana did not strengthen its Western contacts at the expense of Russia. The two countries (together with Belarus) concluded a customs union in 2009, and Kazakhstan consistently supported Russian efforts in the CIS and CSTO forums, including the proposed creation of a rapid response force in Osh, a development strongly opposed by Uzbekistan.

Kyrgyzstan's initial reaction to the Russo-Georgian conflict seemed to reflect its weaker position. In February 2009 President Kurmanbek Bakiyev announced, following a meeting with Russian President Medvedev, that his country would terminate the base agreement for the United States and NATO coalition forces to use the Manas airfield in support of the Afghanistan campaign. After meeting with Medvedev in the Kremlin, Bakiyev claimed the Kyrgyz side had anticipated that NATO forces would stay for one to two years at most, not eight (although the original agreement did not specify any time limit). Bakiyev asserted that American compensation for the base was insufficient, even though Russia paid only $22.7 million for the use of its airbase at Kant from 2003 to 2008, while the US was providing Kyrgyzstan with about $130–150 million per year from 2005 to 2008. Bakiyev also complained about Washington's disregard for Kyrgyz sovereignty following the killing of a truck driver by an American guard ("Kyrgyzstan", 2009).

Towards the end of 2008 Moscow had promised the Kyrgyz government it would ramp up its spending for refurbishing the CSTO base at Kant to $30 million per year in 2009 and 2010 (Marat, 2008). Kyrgyzstan's Russian partners proved to be even more generous – the agreement announced at the Collective Security Treaty Organization meeting in Moscow in February 2009 provided for $2.3 billion in aid, loans, and investment funds for joint hydroelectric projects, an enormous sum for this poor country of five million. The aid also came at an opportune time, since the financial crisis impacted remittances sent home by Kyrgyz who had been working in Russia and Kazakhstan (this also affected Uzbeks, Tajiks, and Azeris). Russian and Kyrgyz authorities subsequently reached an agreement extending the lease terms of the Kant bases to forty-nine years, with an automatic twenty-five-year renewal provision (McDermott, 2009).

But Bakiyev also kept his options open. Negotiations between Washington and Bishkek on Manas continued through the first half of 2009, and in June the Kyrgyz government agreed to renew the lease, with the provision that the facility would now be designated a "transit center." However, there was no change in functions, although Bishkek asserted that the facility would be used only to resupply non-military goods for Afghanistan operations. Bakiyev's calculations were purely monetary – to extract the maximum rent possible from its bases, while minimizing his dependence on any one state – and of course to retain his hold on power in the July 2009 elections (which he conveniently won). The Americans increased the annual rent paid for Manas from $17.4 million to $60 million, and designated another $117 million to upgrade the airport's facilities (Marat, 2009; Tynan, 2009b). While some Russian commentators grumbled about this "setback" for Moscow, there were indications that SCO members, concerned about the Taliban's resurgence, were rethinking their opposition to America's presence in the region.[8] Through this skillful balancing act Bakiyev gained additional financial support, and was able to demonstrate his international standing prior to the elections.

Uzbekistan's ties with Russia deteriorated in the months following the Georgia conflict, although Tashkent maintained a show of cooperating with Moscow. President Islam Karimov suspended his country's membership in the Eurasian Economic Community (EurAsEC), and withdrew from participation in the SCO's secondary organizations. Karimov declined to attend the July 2009 informal CIS "racing summit" in Moscow and opposed Russian plans to finance construction of Kyrgyzstan's Kambarata hydroelectric plant.[9] More disturbing for Tashkent, Russia and Kyrgyzstan began planning the reconstruction of an abandoned Russian military base in Osh, in the disputed and volatile Ferghana valley, to counter regional terrorism. The base is a central component of an agreement establishing a Russian-sponsored Collective Operational Reaction Force under the aegis of the CSTO, which Uzbekistan and Belarus refused to sign. A Russian military presence in southern Kyrgyzstan will constrain Tashkent's ability to influence events in the Ferghana valley, and the Uzbek government has complained that the move will likely promote radicalism and militarism.[10]

While relations with Moscow have been tense, Uzbekistan has moved gradually to restore closer ties with Europe and the United States. General David Petraeus, head of US Central Command, was welcomed in February 2009 in Tashkent, where he lobbied the Uzbek government for facilities to sustain the operation in Afghanistan. South Korea President Lee Myung-bak also played a major role in convincing Karimov to allow the US to use the Navoi airport, where Korean Air is undertaking a major renovation of the facilities. Portrayed as a strictly financial arrangement, this was a diplomatic coup for Washington – a deal with Uzbekistan obviates much of the success of Russia's efforts to trump the American military presence in Kyrgyzstan (Tynan, 2009a). President Karimov's fundamental security concerns are internal – fear of religious fundamentalism, domestic opposition, and the country's abysmal economic performance – all of which jeopardize his tight hold on power. By encouraging the major powers to compete for Uzbekistan's resources and its geostrategic location, Karimov strengthens his control over the country.

The 2008–9 economic crisis affected all the Central Asian states, but Uzbekistan, Tajikistan, and Kyrgyzstan have been most seriously impacted by decline in remittances, and the return of unemployed guest workers to their home countries. According to the IMF, Tajik remittances in 2008 from workers abroad were $2.5 billion, half the nation's GDP. It is estimated that some three million Uzbeks, mostly males, have been working abroad in construction and other low-paying jobs, mostly in Russia and Kazakhstan (Harding, 2009).[11] The US is increasing civil and military aid to Kyrgyzstan and Tajikistan in fiscal year 2010 as part of the administration's strategy in Afghanistan, to promote stability and help them avoid becoming failed states, but the amounts are not enough to address the deep poverty of these countries (Kucera, 2009).

Prospects for social instability in Central Asia will increase as more migrants return home to stagnant economies and ineffective governments. Under these circumstances, the region's authoritarian leaders will be more likely to follow Moscow's heavy-handed, repressive tactics to ensure stability and preserve their personal rule than Washington's recommendations for strengthening human rights and civil society.

The Caucasus

Prior to the August 2008 conflict, each of the three states of the southern Caucasus pursued a distinct path in its foreign policy orientations. Georgia, at least after the Rose Revolution of 2003, was clearly pro-Western and anti-Russian, and Moscow responded in kind, with boycotts of Georgian products, military incursions into Georgian airspace, and harassment and deportations of ethnic Georgians living in Russia. By contrast, and somewhat ironically given the strong Armenian lobby in Washington, relations between Russia and Armenia have been close and are likely to remain so. A geographically isolated Yerevan needs Russian support for its claims to Nagorno-Karabakh, and views Moscow as its most effective ally against Azerbaijan and Turkey. Armenia is closely linked to Russia economically, with Russian firms controlling much of the country's energy sector.[12] In addition, Russia has close security ties to Armenia, stationing some 5,000 soldiers at the 102nd Military Base at Gyumri. Dependence on Moscow has aligned Armenia's foreign policy with Russian priorities – unlike Georgia, for example, Armenia has officially rejected the idea of NATO membership. Azerbaijan, with its large oil reserves, has implemented a more balanced policy, cooperating closely with the United States and Europe in developing energy routes that bypass Russia, while preserving cordial ties with Moscow (although Baku obviously resents Russian military assistance to its enemy, Armenia).

The Russia–Georgia war undermined Mikheil Saakashvili's position domestically and internationally. Initial reporting by the Western media portrayed Russia as the aggressor, but when it became apparent that Georgia had initiated the conflict (albeit in response to Russian provocations) Western support became more tempered. Moscow adroitly seized on French President Nicholas Sarkozy's offer to mediate the conflict, thereby marginalizing Washington's role. Within Georgia the recklessness of Saakashvili's adventure led to repeated demonstrations calling for him to be ousted, and strengthened Georgian opposition. The possibility of protests leading to Saakashvili being ousted recalled the 2000 opposition movement that eventually forced Slobodan Milosevic from power in Serbia, and was welcomed by Moscow (Trenin, 2009).

The United States had trained and equipped the Georgian army since 2002, initially providing up to 150 American specialists to work with Georgian troops in the war against terrorism. Later, the Bush administration helped Georgia train and equip several light infantry battalions to deal with terrorists in the Pankisi Gorge. Washington's goal was to stabilize the Georgian government and consolidate its fledgling democracy, assist Tbilisi in containing militants operating on its territory, and secure the energy corridor – the American-sponsored BTC oil pipeline and the BTE gas pipeline. However, Saakashvili took advantage of the country's improved military to attempt to regain the secessionist territories of Abkhazia and South Ossetia, a decision that may undermine Georgia's chances for NATO membership.

In the last days of the Bush administration the United States and Georgia negotiated a framework agreement for a strategic partnership; reportedly, the Obama team was briefed on these developments. When the Obama administration moved quickly to repair relations with Russia, the Saakashvili government was assured that the United States would maintain the strategic partnership, and that US support for Georgia would not be sacrificed for better ties with Russia. The Obama administration proposed $242 million in assistance to Georgia for FY 2010, and Vice President Joe Biden met with Saakashvili in February 2009 in Munich, where he rejected the concept of spheres of influence and defended the right of countries to belong to international alliances of their choice. Vice-chairman of the Joint Chiefs of Staff General James Cartwright reiterated the Obama administration's commitment to the charter of strategic partnership and to providing training and other assistance to the Georgian military ("Saakashvili Hails US-Georgian Military Cooperation," 2009). President Obama himself declared his support for Georgia's sovereignty, territorial integrity, and independence to President Medvedev and Prime Minister Putin during the July 2009 summit in Moscow (Wallander, 2009). Georgian officials hailed these proclamations of US support for Georgia's sovereignty and territorial integrity as consistent with the Bush administration's strong support, but the Obama administration's position is more nuanced.

Azerbaijan, by contrast, has maintained a fairly balanced posture between Russia and the West, although it has developed close energy ties with the US and Europe. Because of Congressional restrictions related to Nagorno-Karabakh (Section 907 of the Freedom Support Act of 1992), US assistance to Azerbaijan prior to 2002 was severely constrained. Following the terrorist attacks of 9/11 the Bush administration convinced Congress that military cooperation with Azerbaijan was needed in the war on terror, and the Senate approved a waiver. From

2002 through 2006 the US provided over $27 million in foreign assist-
ance, with about $14 million in military sales over the same period
("Azerbaijan", 2007). Moscow perceived this as an American attempt to
reduce Russian influence in the Caucasus, and perhaps pave the way for
Azerbaijan and Armenia to seek NATO membership (de Haas, 2007).

Azerbaijan was especially concerned about the effect of the Russo-
Georgian war on the "frozen conflict" of Nagorno-Karabakh. According
to Azerbaijan specialist Anar Valiyev, Azeri public opinion appeared to
support Georgia's efforts to reincorporate its secessionist territories, but
the government in Baku realized that a potentially disastrous confrontation with Moscow could cause it to forfeit its claim to the territory
permanently. Moscow has been the strongest defender of Armenia's
claim to Nagorno-Karabakh, which puts it at odds with Baku's position.
Simply put, Russia's decisive victory intimidated Azeri officials, who
decided to adopt a more cautious approach favoring economic methods
rather than military instruments (in other words, using the country's
oil wealth to buy off Armenia). The conflict also eroded support among
Azeris for NATO membership, according to surveys conducted by the
Caucasus Resource Research Center ("Azerbaijan", 2009).

Officials in Azerbaijan were concerned about preserving recent gains
in the economy and energy spheres; the greatest immediate threat
was the possibility that oil exports through the Baku–Tbilisi–Ceyhan
pipeline might be interrupted. British Petroleum, chief shareholder in
the one million barrel per day pipeline, did briefly suspend deliveries
due to an explosion inside Turkey in early August 2008, attributed by
Turkish officials to Kurdish separatists. Although Georgia claimed that
Russia twice tried to bomb the pipeline, Russia denied the charges, and
BP reported that no attempts had been made on their facilities within
Georgia (O'Byrne, 2008a). The war highlighted the vulnerability of the
Caucasian corridor for oil and gas pipelines, but apparently has not
proved a serious deterrent – in late August 2008 BP announced that
it was expanding the capacity of the BTC pipeline by twenty per cent,
while crude oil production at the Azeri–Chirag–Guneshli fields was to
be ramped up (O'Byrne, 2008b).

Moscow's diplomatic recognition of Abkhazia and South Ossetia
facilitated the Russian neo-mercantilist strategy of monopolizing control over energy resources and transit routes in the Caucasus by giving
Russian companies access to offshore hydrocarbons. In May 2009, state
oil company Rosneft signed a five-year agreement with the government of Abkhazia to explore for oil and gas in the breakaway republic's
territorial waters of the Black Sea. Abkhaz officials have speculated

that oil reserves on the shelf off Abkhazia's Black Sea coast might hold between 350 and 500 million tons. As might be expected, the Georgian government vigorously protested this action as a violation of its sovereignty (Watkins, 2009).

Moscow sought to use its new presence and clout in the Caucasus to promote a solution to the Nagorno-Karabakh dispute, inviting the Armenian and Azeri presidents Serzhe Sargsyan and Ilham Aliyev to Moscow for a November 2008 summit meeting. Medvedev wanted to appear statesmanlike and genuinely interested in playing a constructive role in the region, to show that Moscow could handle problems in its sphere of influence.[13] The talks produced nothing more than a declaration that the two sides would continue to work toward a settlement through the OSCE Minsk Group co-chaired by France, the United States, and Russia (Abbasov, 2008). Additional talks between Aliyev and Sargsyan were held over the following months, but as of late 2009 the Minsk Group's efforts proved futile, and there was little evidence that an agreement on Nagorno-Karabakh would be reached soon. This is not surprising, since the persistence of regional "frozen conflicts" gives Moscow substantial leverage over the protagonists.

The volatile politics of the Caucasus became even more complicated in 2009 when Turkey and Armenia revealed their ongoing negotiations on normalizing relations. Reopening the border with Turkey (closed in 1993) would help ease Armenia's isolation, and could facilitate movement on Nagorno-Karabakh. Traditional enemies Turkey and Russia are enjoying their best relations in years, based in large part on their common disillusionment with US global dominance (Hill and Taspinar, 2006). Turkish–Armenian reconciliation would enhance Ankara's standing in both the Caucasus and Central Asia, possibly at Russia's expense, and demonstrating a constructive role in the Caucasus might improve Turkey's chances of EU membership. Azerbaijan's reaction to a possible Turkish–Armenian rapprochement was to shift closer towards Moscow. In June 2009 Gazprom and the State Oil Company of Azerbaijan (SOCAR) concluded an agreement for Azerbaijan to supply southern Russia with 500 million cubic meters of gas annually, starting in 2010, at market prices. In addition, Azerbaijan reportedly acknowledged Gazprom as a "priority buyer" for Stage 2 of the Shah Deniz gas field, a critical source without which the EU-supported Nabucco would not be viable (Antonova, 2009). Some Azeris have speculated that in this context a move toward NATO membership might provide greater benefits than courting Moscow. But any reconciliation between Turkey and Armenia, and a solution

to the Nagorno-Karabakh issue, will proceed slowly given the deep historic antagonisms between the two.

Russia's actions in the Caucasus will undoubtedly weaken GUAM, the pro-Western organization consisting of Georgia, Ukraine, Azerbaijan, and Moldova. Supported by the United States as an organization resisting Moscow's influence in the Caucasus, GUAM (with Uzbekistan as a member) was largely moribund from its creation in 1997, but was reinvigorated at its May 2006 Kyiv meeting, and renamed the Organization for Democracy and Economic Development – GUAM. Energy and transportation issues were central in the discussions, including the operation of Baku–Tbilisi–Ceyhan for Azerbaijan, and the suspension of Russian gas deliveries in early 2006 for Ukraine. Frozen conflicts are also critical issues for the members, since three of the four (Georgia, Moldova, and Armenia) find themselves subject to Russian manipulation and pressure over their respective disputes, while the fourth (Ukraine) is vulnerable to Russian influence over Crimea and the eastern, ethnically Russian part of the country, which could become another Transdniestria ("GUAM Gets New Life", 2006).

Following the Russian–Georgian conflict the Georgians used the GUAM forum to condemn Russian "aggression," and a US–GUAM ministerial meeting in September 2008 stated that "the international community shall intensify efforts on the settlement of the protracted conflicts in the GUAM area on the basis of sovereignty, territorial integrity and inviolability of internationally recognized borders of GUAM Member States, as well as other basic principles of international law" ("GUAM – United States Joint Statement", 2008).

For Moscow, GUAM, particularly the Ukraine–Georgia–Moldova troika, is viewed as an "axis of evil" designed to force Russia out of the Caucasus, end its support for Transdniestria, and establish energy corridors bypassing Russia ("Axis of Evil", 2005). Although following the war Georgia anticipated a strengthening of GUAM and a weakening of the CIS (from which it withdrew following the conflict), the opposite appears more likely.

For Armenia, the outcome of the Georgian–Russian conflict reinforces the conviction that Russia is the key to its security. While Moscow may not prove useful in securing a resolution to the Nagorno-Karabakh dispute that is to Yerevan's liking, Moscow's support is still vital in restraining Azerbaijan and Turkey. Georgia's decision shortly after the war to close its airspace to transport planes supplying the Russian military base at Gyumri has forced Russia to use Azeri and Iranian corridors, putting Baku in a difficult position. To complicate matters further, while Armenia's President Serzhe Sargsyan has rejected the possibility of NATO membership, in September–October 2008 Armenia hosted military exercises led by NATO (Danielyan, 2008). The outcome of the war, however, appears to have convinced the Armenian leadership that Moscow is the preferred partner, a development that also suggests a strengthening of Armenia's participation in the CSTO.[14]

Conclusion

This brief survey of developments in Central Asia and the Caucasus following the Russia–Georgia war suggests that, while the southern tier states have been impacted in various ways, there has been no significant move to jump on the Moscow bandwagon. Instead, the policy of "omnibalancing" that most of the states have followed in recent years (with the notable exception of Georgia) has continued. In this regional context, balancing refers only to external balancing – cooperating with a third state against an adversary. Internal balancing – building up defensive capabilities in order to deter threats – is clearly not feasible for the small Caucasus and Central Asian states. Ties to the European states, the US, and NATO have not been abandoned – in many respects, in fact, it has been business as usual. Some of Moscow's apparent gains, such as the closing of the Manas air base in Kyrgyzstan, were ephemeral. Similarly, decisions on routing oil and gas pipelines have still not been decided definitively in Moscow's favor.

Bandwagoning is usually defined as weaker states choosing to side with the stronger state or coalition, as a response to either threat or opportunity (Schweller, 1994; Walt, 1987). For the Central Asian states, domestic challenges present more immediate threats than do foreign enemies, so these states tend to engage in omnibalancing. While domestic pressures are significant, external threats present greater problems for leaders in the Caucasus, leading them to choose external balancing or bandwagoning, rather than omnibalancing.[15] The Central Asian and Caucasus states may perceive both threats and opportunities emanating from Russia, but in this highly volatile security environment it is difficult to accurately identify the stronger power or coalition with which to align. The United States is weaker than during the "unipolar moment" of the 1990s, and its long-term commitment to the region is questionable, but America is still far more powerful than Russia in many dimensions. China has great potential, and is rapidly making inroads in Central Asia, if not the Caucasus, but Beijing must confront serious internal problems that will constrain its international rise.

Russia is temporarily resurgent, largely due to high oil and gas prices and Putin's aggressive policies, but its economic fragility, demographic limitations, and political uncertainties do not bode well over the long term. Leaders in Central Asia and the Caucasus understand the limitations of Moscow's power. The solution for these small states is to hedge their bets, cooperating with all the major states and the competing blocs, while avoiding alienating any single actor. In this sense, the Russo-Georgian war did not clearly benefit or harm other countries in the region, other than the direct participants. The one country in the region that has not followed this balancing strategy in recent years is Georgia, which bandwagoned with the US and NATO. Georgia's negative example will in all probability reinforce the other states' tendencies toward omnibalancing rather than bandwagoning.

This study does suggest that Georgia was a unique case, at least within the Central Asia–Caucasus region. Although there are situations (Nagorno-Karabakh and northern Kazakhstan) that could lead to future clashes, these cases are sufficiently different from the Georgia–Russia dispute that we may reject conflict scenarios, at least in the near future. Of course, having succeeded in its objectives by the use of force, Moscow may be tempted to repeat its assertive strategy elsewhere. The truly comparable cases where Russia may employ force in the future are not in Central Asia or the Caucasus, but rather in Moldova's separatist Transdniestra, and Ukraine's Russified Crimea and eastern region. Significantly, these are states that have chosen to bandwagon with the West.

Notes

1. The author would like to thank Ingmar Oldberg and Anar Valiyev for their helpful comments on an earlier version of this manuscript.
2. Other examples of Moscow promoting non-Western organizations to balance US power include the Collective Security Treaty Organization and its efforts to establish an OPEC-style natural gas cartel.
3. For an excellent discussion of the variants of Eurasianism in Russian discourse, see Marlene Laruelle (2009).
4. Russian military analyst Pavel Felgenhauer (2008) reported that in May 2008 Moscow began deploying railroad troops to repair track in Abkhazia. Given road conditions in the former Soviet Union, Russian armor can only be moved by rail.
5. Ingushetia witnessed some of the worst violence – the republic's president was seriously wounded in a bomb attack in June 2009, and a suicide bombing in Narzan in August of the same year killed more than twenty people.
6. Separatism is one of Beijing's oft-repeated "three evils," the other two being terrorism and extremism.
7. There have been some Russian Cossack nationalist movements active in Kazakhstan, and in 1999 twenty-two Russians were arrested in Ust-Kamenogorsk for trying to overthrow the provincial government and establish a Russian Altai republic. See Ziegler (2006, p. 115).

8. In addition to efforts by the Obama administration, Afghan President Harmid Karzai also lobbied Bakiyev to renew the lease during the June 2009 SCO summit. The fact that Bakiyev made his announcement a week after the Yekaterinburg SCO summit implies that Moscow at least tacitly approved the agreement. See Mikhailov (2009). The argument for Moscow's approval is reinforced by the fact that the US and Russia agreed in spring 2009 to the transit of military materiel through Russia to Afghanistan.
9. Kyrgyz and Tajik rivers are the source of most of Uzbekistan's fresh water. Russia also provided financing to modernize the Sangtuda 1 hydroelectric station in Tajikistan.
10. Reportedly, Moscow did not consult Tashkent on the Osh base, which will be located near Uzbekistan's border. See McDermott (2009).
11. The present author was repeatedly told during a June 2008 visit to Uzbekistan that the number was closer to six million.
12. Russian investment in Armenia stood at $1.8 billion as of mid-2009, and state nuclear energy giant Rosatom was seeking a $5 billion contract to rebuild the Metsamor nuclear power station.
13. One of President Medvedev's five principles of foreign policy identifies regions in which Russia has "privileged interests," countries with which Russia shares special historical ties and with which they are bound together (RIA Novosti, 2008).
14. President Sargsyan stated that the lesson of the Georgian war was that for Armenia to become a member of NATO would create dangerous new lines of separation in the Caucasus. He also indicated that, while attractive, Armenia's policy over the past ten years of balancing among Russia, the United States, and NATO was "very dangerous," implying that his country would in the future lean toward Russia (NATO website, 2008).
15. Steven David's (1991, p. 236) theory of omnibalancing is premised on the reasonable assumption that Third World states suffer from weak institutions and low legitimacy, conditions which hold for both the Caucasus and Central Asia.

References

Abbasov, Shahin (2008) "Azerbaijan: Reaction in Baku Muted to Moscow Declaration on Nagorno-Karabakh", Eurasianet.org, November 3. http://www.eurasianet.org/departments/insight/articles/eav110308.shtml (accessed June 26, 2010).

Allenova, Olga, Elena Geda and Vladimir Novikov (2008) "Blok NATO razoshelsya na blokpakety", *Kommersant*, April 7. http://www.kommersant.ru/doc.aspx?DocsID=877224 (accessed June 26, 2010).

Antonova, Maria (2009) "Gazprom gets Priority for Azeri Gas", *The Moscow Times*, June 30.

"Axis of Evil" (2005) *Kommersant*, March 3. http://www.kommersant.com/page.asp?id=-5141 (accessed June 26, 2010).

"Azerbaijan" (2007) Center for Defense Information. http://www.cdi.org/pdfs/azerbaijan.pdf (accessed June 26, 2010).

"Azerbaijan" (2009) "Azerbaijan: Russian 2008 Blitz against Georgia Eroded Ardor for NATO and EU in Baku – Expert", Eurasianet.org. http://www.eurasianet.org/departments/insightb/articles/eav040909a.shtml (accessed June 26, 2010).

Danielyan, Emil (2008) "Georgian Transit Ban Hinders Russian Military Presence in Armenia", Eurasianet.org, October 10. http://www.eurasianet.org/departments/insight/articles/eav101008a.shtml (accessed June 26, 2010).

David, Steven R. (1991) "Explaining Third World Alignment", *World Politics*, vol. 43, no. 2 (January), pp. 233–56.

de Haas, Marcel (2007) "Current Geostrategy in the South Caucasus", Eurasianet.org, January 7. http://www.eurasianet.org/departments/insight/articles/pp010707.shtml (accessed June 26, 2010).

"Deklaratsiia glav gosudarstv-chlenov Shankhaiskoi organizatsii sotrudnichestva", July 5, 2005. http://www.sectsco.org/RU/show.asp?id=98 (accessed June 26, 2010).

Dushanbe Declaration of Heads of SCO Member States (2008). http://en.sco2009.ru/docs/documents/dus_declaration.html (accessed June 26, 2010).

Felgenhauer, Pavel (2008) "Medvedev's Soft-spoken Hard-line Statements", *Eurasia Daily Monitor*, vol. 5, issue 112 (June 12). http://georgiandaily.com/index.php?option=com_content&task=view&id=3067&Itemid=130 (accessed June 26, 2010).

"Full-Fledged Rearmament of Russian Armed Forces to Begin 2011" (2009) ITAR-TASS (March 27).

"Georgia: 2008 Investment Climate Statement", US Department of State. http://www.state.gov/e/eeb/ifd/2008/100871.htm (accessed June 26 2010).

Goble, Paul (2009) "Could Kabardino-Balkaria Become the Kosovo of the Caucasus?" TheMoscowTimes.com (May 19). http://www.themoscowtimes.com/columns/1328/article/could-kabardino-balkaria-become-the-kosovo-of-the-caucasus/377251.html (accessed June 26, 2010).

"GUAM Gets New Life, New Identity" (2006) Eurasianet.org, May 24. http://www.eurasianet.org/departments/business/articles/eav052406.shtml (accessed June 26, 2010).

"GUAM – United States Joint Statement" (2008) September 23. http://guam-organization.org/node/507 (accessed June 26, 2010).

Harding, Luke (2009) "Soviet Relics Feel the Pain as Russian Crisis Deepens", *The Guardian*, April 12. http://www.guardian.co.uk/world/2009/apr/12/russia-tajikistan-recession-guest-workers (accessed June 26, 2010).

Herspring, Dale (2008) "Russian Military Reform and Anatoly Serdyukov", *Problems of Post-Communism*, vol. 55, no. 6 (November/December).

Hill, Fiona and Omer Taspinar (2006) "Turkey and Russia: Axis of the Excluded?" *Survival*, vol. 48, no. 1 (Spring), pp. 81–92.

Hu Jintao (2009) Speech published by the Xinhua news agency, June 16. http://news.xinhuanet.com/english/2009–06/17/content_11553352.htm (accessed June 26. 2010).

Iacobucci, Andrew (2008) "Kazakhstan: Astana Promotes Plan for Expanded Ties with Europe", Eurasianet.org, October 23. http://www.eurasianet.org/departments/insightb/articles/eav102308.shtml (accessed June 26. 2010).

Kucera, Joshua (2009) "Central Asia: Washington Boosts Aid to Region to Bolster Afghan War Effort", Eurasianet.org, May 12. http://www.eurasianet.org/departments/insight/articles/eav051209a.shtml (accessed June 26, 2010).

"Kyrgyzstan: Reshenie po Manasu ozvucheno posledsviia neizvestny" (2009) Ferghana.ru February 4. http://www.ferghana.ru/article.php?id=6053 (accessed June 26, 2010).

Laruelle, Marlene (2009) *Russian Nationalism and the National Reassertion of Russia*, London: Routledge.

Levy, Clifford J. (2009) "The Georgian and Putin: A Hate Story", *The New York Times*, April 19.

Lillis, Joanna (2009) "Kazakhstan: Geopolitical Rivalry Flares at NATO Forum in Astana", Eurasianet.org, June 25. http://www.eurasianet.org/departments/insightb/articles/eav062509.shtml (accessed June 26, 2010).

McDermott, Roger (2009) "CSTO in Crisis as Moscow Secures Second Military Base in Kyrgyzstan", *Eurasian Daily Monitor*, vol. 6, issue 149 (August 4). http://www.jamestown.org/single/?no_cache=1&tx_ttnews%5Btt_news%5D=35357 (accessed June 26, 2010).

Marat, Erica (2008) "Russia Drums up Support for its Airbase in Kyrgyzstan", *Eurasia Daily Monitor*, vol. 5, issue 236 (December 11). http://www.jamestown.org/single/?no_cache=1&tx_ttnews%5Btt_news%5D=34253 (accessed June 16, 2010).

Marat, Erica (2009) "Bakiyev Wins New Geopolitical Game over Manas Base", *Central Asia-Caucasus Analyst* (July 1). http://www.cacianalyst.org/?q=node/5137 (accessed June 26, 2010).

Mikhailov, Grigorii (2009) "I vse-taki oni ostaiutsya? Bishkek mozhet peremostret' reshenie o vyvode bazy 'Manas'", *Nezavisimaya gazeta* (June 8). http://www.ng.ru/gazeta/2009–06-08/ (accessed June 26, 2010).

Morgulov, Igor (2008) "Sino-Soviet Ties Set to Strengthen", *China Daily*, July 20. http://www.chinadaily.com.cn/china/2008–07/30/content_6888112.htm (accessed June 26, 2010).

NATO website (2008) 10 November. http://www.natoinfo.am/eng/?sub=news_sargsyan_nato (accessed June 26, 2010).

O'Byrne, David (2008a) "Turkey says Terrorists behind BTC Blast", *Platts Oilgram Price Report* (August 15).

O'Byrne, David (2008b) "BP Sticks with BTC Expansion Plan", *Platts Oilgram News* (August 25).

Pan Guang (2006) "Astana Summit: Unfolding a New Stage in the Pragmatic Development of the Shanghai Cooperation Organization". http://www.coscos.org.cn/20060123.htm (accessed June 26, 2010). (The Center of Shanghai Cooperation Organization Studies (COSCOS) is affiliated with the Shanghai Academy of Social Science.)

Poroskov, Nikolai (2009) "Nastuplenie na krizis: Reformu armii otlkadyvat' ne budut." *Vremya online*, http://www.vremya.ru/2009/44/4/225112.html (accessed August 7, 2010).

President of Russia website (2008) August 28. http://www.kremlin.ru/eng/text/speeches/2008/08/28/2031_type82914_205851.shtml

"Relations between Georgia and the Republic of Kazakhstan" (2008) Ministry of Foreign Affairs of Georgia. http://www.mfa.gov.ge/index.php?lang_id=ENG&sec_id=375 (accessed June 26, 2010).

Reuters (2009). Report of May 13. http://uk.reuters.com/article/idUKTRE54C4BY20090513 (accessed June 26, 2010).

178   *Charles E. Ziegler*

"Saakashvili Hails US-Georgian Military Cooperation" (2009) Rustavi-2 TV (translated in BBC Monitoring Trans-Caucasus Unit, March 30).
Schweller, Randall L. (1994) "Bandwagoning for Profit: Bringing the Revisionist State Back In", *International Security*, vol. 19, no. 1, pp. 72–107.
"Session of the Council of Heads of State of the SCO" (2008) August 26–7. eng.kremlin.ru/events/details/2008/08/27_205865.shtml (accessed June 26, 2010).
Sharip, Farkhad (2008) "Are Kazakhstan's Economic Bonds with Georgia the Price of Stronger Ties with Russia?", *Eurasia Daily Monitor*, vol. 5, issue 190 (October 3).
Strategiya natsional'noi bezopastnosti Rossiiskoi Federatsii do 2020 goda (2009) May. http://www.scrf.gov.ru/documents/99.html , articles 13, 15, 17 (accessed June 26, 2010).
Trenin, Dmitri (2009) "Russia in the Caucasus: Reversing the Tide", *Brown Journal of World Affairs*, vol. 15, issue II (Spring/Summer), pp. 143–55.
Tynan, Deidre (2009a) "Uzbekistan: Karimov gives Washington the Air Base it needs for Afghan Operations", Eurasianet.org (May 11). http://www.eurasianet.org/departments/insightb/articles/eav051109a.shtml (accessed June 26, 2010).
Tynan, Deidre (2009b) "Kyrgyzstan: US Armed Forces to remain at Air Base for Afghan Resupply Operations", Eurasianet.org (June 23). http://www.eurasianet.org/departments/insightb/articles/eav062309b.shtml (accessed June 26, 2010).
"Vladimir Putin Visits Kazakhstan" (2009) KazakhstanLive.com (International Information Center of the Republic of Kazakhstan), May 20. http://www.kazakhstanlive.com/2.aspx?ProdID=066ba980–4e25–4650-bb20-c92be54e420c&CatID=9f9f8034–6dd6–4f7e-adcf-0f6a7c0406d9&sr=100&page=1 (accessed June 26, 2010).
Wallander, Celeste (2009) Testimony of Deputy Assistant Secretary of Defense for Russia, Ukraine and Eurasia Policy, to the House Foreign Affairs Subcommittee on Europe, 28 July. http://www.internationalrelations.house.gov/111/wal072809.pdf (accessed June 26, 2010).
Walt, Stephen (1987) *The Origins of Alliances*, Ithaca: Cornell University Press.
Watkins, Eric (2009) "Georgia Objects to Rosneft Agreement with Abkhazia", *Oil and Gas Journal* (May 29); "Georgia: Russia to Start Prospecting for Oil in Abkhazia", Eurasianet.org (May 27). http://www.eurasianet.org/departments/news/articles/eav052709.shtml (accessed June 26, 2010).
Zevelev, Igor (2008) "Russia's Policy toward Compatriots in the Former Soviet Union", *Russia in Global Affairs*, no. 1 (January–March 2008). http://eng.globalaffairs.ru/numbers/22/1174.html (accessed June 26, 2010).
Ziegler, Charles E. (2006) "The Russian Diaspora in Central Asia: Russian Compatriots and Moscow's Foreign Policy", *Demokratizatsiya*, vol. 14, no. 1 (Winter), pp. 103–26.
Ziegler, Charles E. (2010) "Russia and China in Central Asia", in James Bellacqua (ed.), *Sino-Russian Relations in the Early 21st Century* (Lexington: University Press of Kentucky).

Part III
Russia, Europe, and Beyond

9
Medvedev's "Fourteen Points": Russia's Proposal for a New European Security Architecture

Nikita Lomagin

> "Security" means the "ability of states and societies to maintain their independent identity and their functional integrity."
>
> Buzan, 1991

There are few things in Russia's foreign policy today that occupy as much attention worldwide as Medvedev's 2008 call for a new European security architecture and his further "fourteen points" proposal for a European Security treaty. Throughout 2009 a large number of government officials and politicians, analysts, and experts from Russia, Europe, the US, and other countries played an active part in the numerous discussions held on the Russian initiative in numerous intergovernmental and nongovernmental forums. On the basis of the results of those discussions, a draft European Security Treaty has been prepared and passed on by President Medvedev to the leaders of the Euro-Atlantic States and the executive heads of the relevant international organizations operating in our common space, such as NATO, the European Union, the Collective Security Treaty Organization (CSTO), the Commonwealth of Independent States (CIS), and the Organization of Security Cooperation in Europe (OSCE). In his message President Medvedev emphasized that Russia is open to any proposals on the subject matter of its initiative, and is counting on a positive response from its partners. Russia's perception of security fits the classical definition by Barry Buzan cited above. Indeed, the primary goal of the Russian state is to be able to maintain its independent identity and its functional integrity.

Although Medvedev's call for a new European security architecture was interpreted, especially in the US, as a ploy to pry Europe from its strategic alignment with the United States, this program is perhaps one of the most important initiatives in the international arena by Moscow since the break-up of the Soviet Union in 1991. As Jeffrey Mankoff observed, "In the early 1990s, the hope was that Russia itself would eventually make its way into NATO. In the early twenty-first century, that prospect looks exceedingly remote: Russia's authoritarian political system disqualifies it, and few Europeans or Americans would seriously contemplate extending NATO's Article 5 collective security guarantee all the way to the Russo-Chinese frontier ... For a time, Moscow hoped to use the OSCE as an alternative, only to sour on the idea when the OSCE began openly criticizing the conduct of Russian elections" (Mankoff, 2009, p. 308).

Thus, the Kremlin has long since given up on joining NATO or forging a substantive partnership with the European Union in the area of security or even defense. Russia views NATO as a Cold War remnant and the EU as little more than a common market with some crisis management capabilities, even after ratification of the Lisbon Treaty. As a result, the Russian leadership is doing its best to rally bilateral support for its initiative among major European powers such as France, Germany, Italy, and Spain, and some traditionally loyal states, such as Finland and Greece. Of course, it realizes that the greatest and most pressing challenge is to convince Washington to take the Russian proposal seriously and, thus, to define a road map in order to set out a credible process towards a new pan-Eurasian security settlement.

How should one read the Russian initiative? Is it a merely a reflection of Russia's traditional identity as one of the Great Powers that wants to be visible and, thus, actively participate in agenda setting in the security area? Does Medvedev's plan have any substance or is it just empty rhetoric? Are Russia's calls for new European security architecture really about avoiding the decision on whether to tie the country's fate to the West or to rising centers of power in Asia? To what extent is the idea of building a 21st-century pan-European security community realistic, since East and West continue to diverge, as they have done since 2003 if not before?

Contrary to a widely shared view in the West that "those who speak for Russia have made plain what they oppose but not what they propose instead" (Legvold, 2009), Medvedev's proposal seems to have both real substance and all the symbolic features of the major foreign policy initiative of his presidency so far. This paper addresses three interrelated issues. First, why did he introduce the new security doctrine, and into which theoretical framework does it fit? Second, given the current and likely future security challenges confronting Russia and Eurasia in general, how can a politically acceptable security framework replace the old one inherited from the Cold War era? Finally, given the skepticism on the part of the US and NATO leadership regarding Russia's proposal, how might the major objectives of Medvedev's security plan be achieved?

The theoretical framework of the causes of the long peace in Europe and Eurasia, which means, inter alia, security for Russia, is well established in the literature. Two of the most popular theories of peace – economic liberalism and peace-loving democracies – are not relevant to the issue at hand (Mearsheimer, 1999, p. 128). A third theory of peace, obsolescence of war, proposes that modern conventional warfare had become so deadly by the 20th century that it was no longer possible to think of war as a sensible means to achieve national goals. This theory does not ascribe the absence of war to nuclear weapons, but instead points to the horrors of modern conventional war (Mueller, 1989). However, many recent cases have shown that it is possible to score a quick and decisive victory in a conventional war and avoid the devastation that usually attends a protracted conventional war (Mearsheimer, 1999, p. 129). Thus, the main wisdom from a realist perspective insists that the only option left is reliance on nuclear weapons, for nuclear war cannot be won, since neither side can escape devastation by the other, regardless of the outcome on the battlefield. Hence, it would be logical to expect that nuclear deterrence should remain the backbone of any future security architecture in the region.

Indeed, nuclear weapons occupy an exceptional role in Russia's contemporary military doctrine. At the same time, a nuclear arsenal is not the only instrument to guarantee national security. Its role might change if a new security community were to emerge in the area bordering Russia on the west and the east. The term "security community" was coined by Karl Deutsch. According to Deutsch, it was the security communities that had eliminated "war and the expectation of war within their boundaries" (Deutsch, 1969). A security community was defined as "a group of people which has become 'integrated' in the sense that there is real assurance that the members of the community will not fight each other physically, but will settle their disputes in some other way" (Deutsch, 1969, p. 5). In his research Deutsch concluded that there were three conditions essential for the success of a pluralistic security community, namely "compatibility of major values relevant to political decision-making," "the capacity of the participating political units or governments to respond to each other's needs, messages and actions quickly, adequately, and without resort to violence," and the "mutual predictability of behaviour" (Deutsch, 1969, pp. 66–7). In Deutsch's work emphasis was placed on communication between political units: increased transactions between them brought increases in mutual dependence. For a community to be created, this high level of transactions must be accompanied by mutual responsiveness, so that the demands each side makes on the other can receive adequate and sympathetic treatment. This would not only preclude the need for aggressive action to achieve ends but would also build up a feeling of trust.

The concept of a security community corresponds with regime theory – a theory within international relations derived from the liberal institutional tradition that argues that international institutions, or regimes, affect the behavior of states (or other international actors). It assumes that cooperation is possible in the anarchic system of states. While realism predicts that conflict should be the norm in international relations, regime theorists say that there is cooperation despite anarchy. Often they cite cooperation in trade, human rights, and collective security, among other issues. The most commonly cited definition of regimes comes from Oran R. Young (Young, 1980) and Stephen Krasner. Krasner defines regimes as "institutions possessing norms, decision rules, and procedures which facilitate a convergence of expectations" (Krasner, 1983). Regimes are social structures, and, as with other social institutions, regimes may be more or less formally articulated– in our case Medvedev proposed to develop a legally binding European Security treaty – and may or not be accompanied by explicit organizational structure.

From the "Berlin Doctrine" to a draft treaty of European Security

Politics is a very symbolic business. It is not surprising that President Dmitrii Medvedev delivered a major foreign policy speech on June 5, 2008 in Berlin, the city that used to symbolize the East–West divide. Medvedev's speech in Berlin on his first trip to the West as President set the tone for renewed reflections on an expanded Euro-Atlantic Community that would include Russia not on Western but instead on shared terms.

The fall of the Berlin Wall was perceived in Russia as a huge leap towards the unification of Europe. Many dividing lines have been removed since then – above all, relations between East and West have been liberated from the constraints of the ideological confrontation. At the same time, pan-European military–political collaboration has yet to make the qualitative leap and create a strong and cohesive partnership, in other words a "common pan-European home" stretching from Vancouver to Vladivostok, in order to meet effectively the new challenges and threats.

The underlying idea of President Medvedev's "Berlin Doctrine" was to formalize in international law the principle of indivisible security as a legal obligation, pursuant to which no nation or international organization operating in the Euro-Atlantic region is entitled to strengthen its own security at the expense of the security of other nations or organizations. The initiative had a unifying character and was designed to harness the potential of states and international organizations to create a truly indivisible space of equal security for all the states of the Euro-Atlantic region within a framework of common "rules of the game" and mechanisms for their application.

Medvedev's "Berlin Doctrine" contained several basic principles for building such a pan-European Security architecture. First, every Euro-Atlantic state should have a voice; second, all relevant international organizations – the European Union, NATO, OSCE, CSTO, CIS – should be included; third, the treaty should be based on new rules binding on all; and, fourth, it should deal with a wide range of trans-regional security threats in the wider Eurasian space. Medvedev proposed a new kind of cooperation in the field of hard security, to upgrade the current system of Euro-Atlantic security into a long-lasting system based on legally binding reciprocal and common commitments.

Later the same year, President Medvedev repeatedly called upon his European and Atlantic counterparts to put in place a Treaty on European Security. In his address to the World Policy Conference in Evian on November 8, 2008 President Medvedev stated that his idea was to convene a pan-European security conference with the participation not only of individual states, but also of international organizations active in Eurasia. The Russian representatives have insisted, in the true spirit of modern democracy, that a conference such as they have been advocating should be held with open, not closed, doors.

Helsinki was chosen by Medvedev as yet another symbolic place to specify Medvedev's views on Europe's future security architecture. In the early 1970s Helsinki was the home city for a three-stage Conference for Security and Co-operation in Europe (CSCE) and for the so-called "Helsinki process" that resulted in the CSCE Helsinki Final Act, which was signed by the thirty-five participating nations on August 1, 1975.

Thus, it is not surprising that in his speech at the University of Helsinki on April 20, 2009 President Medvedev referred to "the spirit of Helsinki" – that is, openness, a spirit of collaboration, new attitudes, and mutual respect, all of which became the key for resolving international problems at that point. Medvedev called for a future treaty of European security as a kind of "Helsinki Plus" treaty: a confirmation, continuation, and effective implementation of the principles and instruments born out of the Helsinki process, but adapted to the end of ideological confrontation and the emergence of new subjects of international law in the 21st century. The proposals were based on the view that, although the world has changed, European security is still far from perfect.

In words of the Russian president, "certain political forces are still obsessed by the need to expand what they see as obligatory military-political alliances, which by the way often act to the detriment of European security. The rules of international law are applied selectively, based on so-called political expediency, and sometimes simply ignored…. There are quite a few examples of this in contemporary Europe: the military operation in the Balkans, the recognition of Kosovo, the Caucasus crisis resulting from the attack on South Ossetia last year, and the crisis in talks on the Treaty on Conventional Armed Forces in Europe. These examples could be multiplied indefinitely" (Medvedev, 2009). In general, across the post-Soviet space and elsewhere in Eurasia, territorial borders are notoriously unstable. Moreover, unless a new security umbrella is put in place, violence could erupt in the other "frozen conflicts" (Pabst, 2009).

Indeed, the Georgian crisis revealed once more the inadequate prevailing security arrangements in the wider European and Eurasian space. None of the existing organizations is capable of adjudicating transnational, interstate territorial disputes or resolving the fate of regions that seek autonomy. What Europe and Eurasia require is a different security architecture that can minimize the ubiquitous risk of conflict contagion and provide long-term political settlements. The dominant security organizations in Eurasia are all ill adapted to this imperative. NATO in particular lacks a coherent conceptual basis. Originally designed to provide collective defense guarantees in exchange for limited national sovereignty, the North Atlantic Treaty Organization has been transformed into an attacking alliance, waging "humanitarian warfare" in the Balkans and converting Afghanistan to democracy by force. The NATO–Russia Council is nothing more than a talking shop designed to pacify Moscow and to provide a semblance of Euro-Atlantic cooperation. Eastward expansion has already proven to be divisive and destabilizing, as seen in Georgia and the Ukraine. Obviously, many in the West call for a return to a situation in which military action cannot be undertaken by anyone without there being a wide consensus and without it being based on serious justifications. As Eric Hobsbawm has said, "The world cannot function if someone can just say, 'I am strong enough to do what I want, and therefore I will do it'" (Hobsbawn, 2003, p. 22). Thus, a new approach to the architecture of European security is needed.

Medvedev suggested that such solutions could be developed through multifaceted cooperation among the Russian Federation, the European Union, and the United States of America. The idea is "to develop a large-scale legally binding European treaty on security, which is based on the equality and mutual respect of all the signatories." For this reason, Russia has invited all states and organizations operating on the European continent to work together to come up with coherent, up-to-date, and, most importantly, effective rules of the game. Medvedev has called for a summit to be held with all Euro-Atlantic states and international organizations. "In that way we could identify the best platform for further negotiations and agree on an agenda," he concluded.

Medvedev's fourteen points

On November 29, 2009 the Kremlin published a draft of a European Security Treaty. Medvedev's program, at least in a number of its points, resembles the program drawn up by Woodrow Wilson, who had enunciated peace aims in his famous "Fourteen Points." Contrary to popular belief, Wilson's program was concerned less with lofty ideals of humanitarianism than with quite specific proposals to achieve national and international justice by making states more perfect nation-states. As Davis Thomson has noted, "The first five points, indeed, outlined general principles of peacemaking. But none of these proved practicable or acceptable after 1918."[1] Still, the above-mentioned programs have at least two things in common in terms of tone and content. First, both documents advocate multilateralism in the security area and adherence to law. Second, they are quite idealistic and maybe even naïve in terms of the tools needed for their implementation. But, if Wilson from the very beginning put international public opinion above all else as a key instrument to influence decision makers around the world,[2] Medvedev has yet to explore such an option.

The Russian proposal is based upon almost all existing norms of international security law set forth in the Charter of the United Nations, Declaration on Principles of International Law concerning Friendly Relations and Cooperation among States (1970), and the Helsinki Final Act of the Conference for Security and Cooperation in Europe (1975), as well as provisions of the Manila Declaration on the Peaceful Settlement of International Disputes (1982) and the Charter for European Security (1999).

The essence of the Russian program can be reduced to the following six points: first, parties should cooperate on the basis of the principles of indivisible, equal, and undiminished security; second, a Party to the Treaty shall not undertake, participate in, or support any actions or activities significantly detrimental to the security of any other party or parties to the treaty; third, a party to the treaty which is a member of military alliances, coalitions, or organizations shall seek to ensure that such alliances, coalitions or organizations observe principles set forth in the Charter of the United Nations, the Declaration of Principles of International Law concerning Friendly Relations and Cooperation among States in accordance with the Charter of the United Nations, the Helsinki Final Act, the Charter for European Security and other documents adopted by the Organization for Security and Cooperation in Europe; fourth, a party to the treaty shall not allow the use of its territory and shall not use the territory of any other party with the purpose of preparing or carrying out an armed attack against any other party or parties to the treaty or any other actions affecting significantly the security of any other party or parties to the treaty; fifth, a clear mechanism is established to address issues related to the substance of this treaty, and to settle differences or disputes that might arise between the parties in connection with its interpretation or application. Finally, the treaty is to be open for signature by all states of the Euro-Atlantic and Eurasian space from Vancouver to Vladivostok as well as by the following international organizations: the European Union, the Organization for Security and Cooperation in Europe, the Collective Security Treaty Organization, the North Atlantic Treaty Organization and the Community of Independent States and is subject to ratification by the signatory states and to approval or adoption by the signatory international organizations.

Herein lies the obvious "added value" of a new treaty compared with the provisions previously adopted in the highest-level documents within the CSCE/OSCE and the NATO–Russia Council. Russia sees the treaty as a reaffirmation of the principles guiding security relations among states – first of all, respect for the sovereignty, territorial integrity, and independence of states and the inadmissibility of the use of force or the threat of its use in international affairs (Grushko, 2009). The entire Medvedev program might be summed up as very idealistic: one state's aspiration for greater security must stop at exactly the point where the next state might feel insecure. The Russians have invoked one of the basic Christian principles: do unto others as you would have others do unto you.

Although the simplest explanation for Medvedev's initiative might be found in pure bureacratic games by Russia's Security Council and Ministry of Foreign Affairs (MFA), both of which had to produce foreign policy and security papers for the new president, the initiative under consideration appears to be more than just routine paperwork. First of all, the security architecture in Europe had become an issue of central importance for Russia long before Medvedev moved to the Kremlin. During its whole post-Soviet history, Russia has felt quite uncomfortable as an outsider in the process of building a new security order of which the US-led NATO was a central element.[3] As early as the spring of 1996, Russia's minister of foreign affairs, Yevegeny Primakov, compared adjusting to the prospect of NATO enlargement to "sleeping with a porcupine – the best we can do is reduce its size and keep its quills from making us too miserable." As Strobe Talbot has recalled, at that time Russia suggested three conditions that, if accepted by NATO, might make enlargement palatable to Russia: a prohibition against stationing nuclear weaponry on the territory of new members; a requirement for joint decision making between Russia and NATO on any issue of European security, particularly where use of military force was involved; and codification of these and other restrictions on NATO and rights of Russia in a legally binding treaty (Talbot, 2002, p. 218). None of the conditions was fulfilled.

More than a decade later the new military doctrine of Russia (2010) clearly states that the "existing international security architecture including its legal mechanism does not provide equal security for all states." Moreover, NATO's ambitions to become a global actor and to expand its military infrastructure eastwards are mentioned at the top of the list of Russia's main external military threats (*Military Doctrine of the Russian Federation*, 2010).

Second, there is widespread belief, not only in Russia but also in the West, that the current European security architecture is far from ideal. The Ministers of Foreign Affairs of the OSCE Participating States stated in their Athens Ministerial Declaration that only a new "Greater Europe," with a global vision and shared goals, will be able to ensure enduring stability on the continent, contribute globally to international peace and security, and be competitive in that evolving global context. The Declaration continues:

> To achieve this goal, much remains to be accomplished. We continue to be seriously concerned that the principles of the Helsinki Final Act and OSCE commitments are not fully respected and implemented; that the use of force has not ceased to be considered as an option in settling disputes; that the danger of conflicts between states has not been eliminated and armed conflicts have occurred even in the last decades; that tensions still exist and many conflicts remain unresolved; that stalemates in conventional arms control, resolution of disagreements in this field, resumption of the full implementation of the CFE Treaty regime and restoration of its viability requires urgent concerted action by its State Parties....

The OSCE Chairman-in-Office, Greek Prime Minister and Foreign Minister George Papandreou, concluded that the OSCE's work was not complete, and that "Dividing lines also remain in our minds. Distrust, prejudices and misperceptions can only but divide. We have to eliminate them. And the best way to do so is to engage in an open, frank and bona fide dialogue. We have to understand each other; to understand the perspectives, concerns and specificities, but also understand how much we have in common" ("Conclusions of the OSCE Ministerial Council in Athens", 2009).

The NATO Secretary-General also acknowledged that in an age of globalized insecurity existing security mechanisms need serious adjustments because "static, heavy metal armies are not going to impress terrorists, pirates or computer hackers...Security today is about active engagement..." (Rasmussen, 2010). Following the same logic, leading security experts advocate the creation of a global security web in order to meet new security challenges. For instance, Zbigniew Brzezinski argues that "the paradox of our time is that the world, increasingly connected and economically interdependent for the first time in its entire history, is experiencing intensifying popular unrest made all the more menacing by the growing accessibility of weapons of mass destruction – not just to states but also, potentially, to extremist religious and political movements. Yet there is no effective global security mechanism for coping with the growing threat of violent political chaos stemming from humanity's recent political awakening" (Brzezinski, 2009).

The economic recession that has dominated both national politics and international relations for almost two years makes a pan-Eurasian security settlement more important than at any point since the end of the Cold War. The whole range of old and new security challenges calls for a strong and growing mutual interest in security cooperation between the leading countries in Eurasia. A new framework is all the more necessary since the prevailing security and defense organizations in East and West, such as NATO or the Shanghai Cooperation Organization (SCO), cannot cope with the emerging global constellation of overlapping spheres of influence where the rival, transnational interests of "great powers" collide and their client states clash. This constellation portends more insecurity and conflict across the Eurasian space, especially in parts of Eastern Europe, the Balkans, the Caucasus, and the Caspian, as well as Central Asia. Even skeptics believe that the basic idea of building a security system that embraces Russia more comprehensively than existing institutions such as the NATO–Russia Council is one to which the US and Europe should pay more attention (Brzezinski, 2009, p. 308). Third, the moment of suggesting a new initiative by the Kremlin was quite appropriate, given the relative decline of hard and soft power of Western states as a result of the war in Iraq and the global economic meltdown. As Adrian Pabst recently stated:

> Since the disaster of Iraq, Guantánamo and Abu Ghraib – the U.S.A. (and her allies) have lost credibility and the moral authority to claim global leadership. Support for Mikheil Saakashvili's reckless aggression and his corrupt regime revealed once more Western double standards and the Atlanticist disregard for genuine democracy and justice. Similarly, the economic crisis spelled the end of the neoliberal "Washington consensus" and confirmed the failure of the Western-dominated international architecture to regulate global finance or to reduce worldwide poverty and inequality...Thus, the "Atlantic unipole"...has already ceased to shape and direct global geo-politics and geo-economics. (Pabst, 2009)

Moreover, it seems that the prime concerns of governments in the NATO states in these post-crisis years will be with domestic economic instability and (in the case of the United States) with meeting challenges in the Middle East – Iran, Afghanistan, and Iraq – where resources of other powers (first of all, China and Russia) and regional organizations (SCO and Collective Security Treaty Organization) will be in demand.

On the one hand, the relative revival of Russia provides a chance for Russia and Russian-led regional institutions to be heard. Indeed, certain developments in post-Soviet space, such as the strengthening of the Collective Security Treaty Organization and its recognition by the UN General Assembly,[4] emergence of a customs union among Russia, Belarus and Kazakhstan, and general growth of Russia's soft power in the region embodied, inter alia, in an influx to Russia's main cities of dozens of thousands of migrants from Central Asia – all this symbolized a revival of Russia as the core within the CIS.

Fourth, the willingness of Russia's president to advocate a legally binding treaty stems not only from the bitter experience of his predecessors,[5] but also from his background as a lawyer who prefers formal agreements to mere verbal agreements. According to Russia's Minister of Foreign Affairs, Sergei Lavrov, "Dmitry Medvedev's proposal for a new security pact sets a litmus test for the honesty of the West versus Moscow ... The treaty was necessary to implement declarations made in the 1990s that 'we are all friends, security is indivisible and nobody's security can be enhanced at the cost of others'" (Lavrov, 2010b).

Fifth, a survey of world opinion on general principles of world order conducted by the Council on Foreign Relations in November 2009 revealed some signs of potential support for Medvedev's security program ("World Opinion on General Principles", 2009). In particular, international polling indicates a strong consensus that world order should be based on a multilateral system led by the United Nations or a group of regional powers, rather than a system based on hegemony or bipolarity. Large majorities in countries around the world reject a hegemonic role for the United States, but do want the United States to participate in multilateral efforts to address international issues. Also, large majorities around the world have endorsed having a stronger United Nations. Support for working through the United Nations is somewhat tempered, especially among smaller countries, when poll questions highlight the prospect of subordinating national policies to collective decision-making processes.

In international polling large majorities around the world favor the United Nations having the right to authorize the use of military force for a wide range of contingencies. The approval of the UN Security Council plays a powerful – and in many cases a necessary – role in conferring legitimacy on the use of military force. Among Europeans and Americans, the North Atlantic Treaty Organization (NATO) does

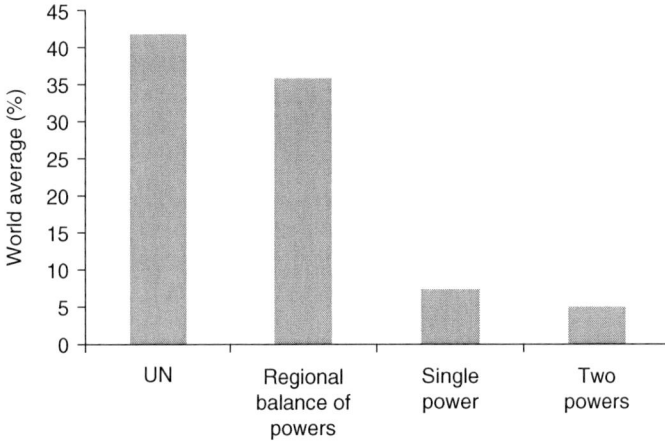

Figure 9.1 What is the best framework for achieving peace and stability?

Source: From the International Institutions and Global Governance program, "World Opinion on General Principles of World Order", a CFR.org Backgrounder, copyright © 2009 by the Council on Foreign Relations, Inc. Reprinted with permission. http://www.cfr.org/publication/20017 (accessed April 7, 2010).

provide some legitimacy, but by much smaller margins than the United Nations. Moreover, there will eventually be the challenge of Russia's willingness to take into account its rising Eastern neighbor China in a new system of Euro-Atlantic security. Indeed, the "Chinese factor" as Moscow's security concern has not been raised publicly by the Russians, although it cannot be ignored much longer, if only for the fact that, as a result of global economic crises, there has been a further shift of power in favor of Beijing, which sooner or later might try to project its power onto not only Africa and Latin America, but also its neighbors. Therefore, Russia's plan to engage a growing China in a Euro-Atlantic security architecture may become the second most important effect of Medvedev's initiative. It means that "all affected parties," including the Shanghai Cooperation Organization, in which China plays a key role, will participate.

Implementation phase

The Russian draft European security treaty was posted on the president's website on November 29, 2009. The biggest diplomatic initiative involves not only Russia's top diplomats, who are working very actively in all international forums in order to promote Medvedev's plan, but also Russia's closest allies from the Security Cooperation Treaty Organisation (SCTO). Kazakhstan, which now holds the chairmanship in the OSCE, has made Russia's plan one of its main priorities. The OSCE is the world's largest regional security organization. Its fifty-six members include the United States and Russia.[6]

The Security Cooperation Treaty Organization firmly supported Kazakhstan's activities as the leader of the OSCE. On March 25, 2010 ministers of foreign affairs of the SCTO countries issued a special statement about the urgent need to strengthen the OSCE as a platform for holding equal political dialogue among all OSCE member states and increasing the contribution of the Organization in the strengthening of European security. The SCTO foreign ministers also supported the idea of an OSCE summit later this year (Statement by Ministers of Foreign Affairs of the CSTO member States, 2010).

After meeting with European Union officials in late January 2010, the Kazakh foreign minister Kanat Saudabayev asserted that European leaders may be ready to discuss Russia's new security plan for the continent at an international summit meeting, perhaps this year. The last OSCE summit took place in 1999. The agenda for a new meeting has not been identified, but Russian proposals for a security treaty, which Western critics see as an attempt to undermine NATO, "could potentially be one of the subjects," Mr Saundabayev said (cited in Castle, 2010).

With no clear position among the European Union's twenty-seven nations, the bloc responded cautiously to Russia's proposal. Lutz Güllner, spokesman for the Union's foreign policy chief Catherine Ashton, stated that the Kazakhs had suggested discussing security at a summit meeting. Asked why another summit was necessary, Mr Saundabayev highlighted Afghanistan, the global economic crises, and the fact that "important changes took place in the architecture of European security." A top Kazakh diplomat met at the end of January with Ms Ashton; the European Union president, Herman van Rompuy; the President of the European Commission, José Manuel Barroso; and Miguel Ángel Moratinos, foreign minister of Spain, which holds the rotating presidency of the union. According to Kazakh sources, "Mrs. Ashton has promised to look into that matter but underlined that the final decision lies with the OSCE" (cited in Castle, 2010).

German Chancellor Angela Merkel believes that Russian President Dmitry Medvedev's European security initiative should be discussed in the OSCE framework. She has said that the discussion of the Russian proposal "will be invigorated" in the near future (Merkel, 2010). In practical terms, Merkel suggested the possibility of trilateral discussions about European security among Germany, France, and Russia. This idea met with full support in Moscow (Nesterenko, 2010). In general, in the European Union "there is a genuine understanding of the urgency for having a summit" (Castle, 2010).

In this regard European perceptions of security might vary from the American view. While Europe and North America share a number of societal beliefs, and while they are still cooperating in a military sense within the NATO alliance, their societies are drifting apart. Social democracy is not taking root in the United States. Moreover, within Europe there is already widespread unease or clear opposition against NATO military actions outside Europe, or its expansion into areas that were never in Europe's sphere of influence. "This is particularly so in the countries of Western, Northern and Southern Europe. These are already more advanced into new thinking about European and international relations, having experienced the benefits of peace based on reconciliation and economic growth far longer than those have who joined the EU only recently and who often look more in the rear-mirror of history than to future opportunities. But the reluctant support among Europeans will be waning rapidly as soon as they understand that the new Russia is no threat for them as the Soviet Union was" (Schepers, 2009).

However, Medvedev's initiative has received a lukewarm reaction from Washington and NATO headquarters. In late February 2010, US Secretary of State Hillary Clinton rejected Russia's call for a new European security treaty, saying that Europe's security would be strengthened by a closer cooperation between Russia and NATO (Clinton, 2010). NATO Secretary General Anders Fogh Rasmussen said in December 2009 that NATO was ready to discuss Medvedev's ideas, but there was no need for a new security treaty. The NATO chief added that there are enough documents ensuring Euro-Atlantic security, and that conflicts happen because some countries do not comply with the principles enshrined in these documents (Merkel, 2010). It is clear that President Medvedev's intention is to change the terms of the debate on the future of security in Europe away from NATO towards a new body that includes Russia as a founding member. As such, his proposal is unacceptable to many EU countries and also to the United States.

The most difficult step in the rapprochement between the two competing positions is the recognition by Europe of Russia's security fears. They have historic roots and, while Europeans may perceive them as unfounded, given their belief in their own new worldviews, they are real enough for Russians. There is a proven method from the Cold War days to reduce these fears. Between NATO and Russia, there should be as many "Finlands" as possible, starting with Belarus and Ukraine. These countries are free to determine their own political and economic models, but they should remain neutral and not join any military alliance.[7]

Of course, Medvedev's proposal for a treaty will not be sufficient to shape a new security architecture. Much must be done to underpin a new pan-European security regime with a new pattern of cooperation, common, or at least harmonized, security agendas, and better interaction among all security organizations and factors acting in the area from Vancouver to Vladivostok. The Russian Ministry of Foreign Affairs has outlined five areas crucial for progress in building a new security architecture.

The first requirement is to relaunch serious, goal-oriented discussions on the role of arms control and confidence-building measures, especially in the domain of conventional forces in Europe. The Conventional Armed Forces in Europe (CFE) Treaty, signed in November 1990, set equal limits on the numbers of tanks, armored combat vehicles (ACVs), heavy artillery, combat aircraft, and attack helicopters that NATO and the former Warsaw Pact could deploy between the Atlantic Ocean and the Ural Mountains. With the breakup of the Warsaw Pact and the dissolution of the Soviet Union after the Cold War, the CFE Treaty states overhauled the treaty after three years of negotiations. The Adapted CFE Treaty was concluded and signed at the Organization for Security and Co-operation in Europe (OSCE) summit in Istanbul in November 1999. Under the agreements, several NATO members pledged not to increase their territorial ceilings of treaty-limited equipment (TLE), and Russia agreed to reduce its TLE in Georgia and withdraw its military presence from Moldova. Only Belarus, Kazakhstan, Russia, and Ukraine have ratified the adapted treaty. The United States and NATO allies have conditioned their ratification of the Adapted CFE Treaty on Russia's fulfilling its Final Act pledges. In July 2007 Russia suspended implementation of the Adapted CFE Treaty until the others ratify it.

Russia believes that an arms control dialogue is the best way "to get more security with less means, and...to overcome remaining suspicions in relation to military intentions, planning and force generation." As Russia's deputy minister of foreign affairs suggested, "The beauty of arms control is in its ability to translate political intensions into understandable language of numbers, limits, locations, information and verification regimes. And we should not be talking only about technicalities how to bring in motion Adapted-CFE regime, but should think creatively about the very relevance of arms control instruments in evolving security environment and necessary steps to increase their viability. NATO declares to be transparent about its military activity. We welcome this intention. But we are also looking forward to get from our NRC partners their vision of concrete parameters of 'substantial combat forces' – one of the key provisions of the Founding Act, signed in Paris in 1997" (Grushko, 2009).

Second, better cooperation among all security organizations and actors in the Euro-Atlantic area is also needed. An important contribution here could be the implementation in good faith of the NATO– Russia Council (NRC) Work Program for 2010 and of the document "Taking the NRC forward." Another important contribution – with the EU – would be to start negotiations on an agreement on cooperation in crisis management. The positive experience of Russian participation in the EU mission in Chad / Central African Republic provided political impetus to the process of establishing a legal and operational framework for joint actions of the EU and Russia in crisis situations. And we should not forget about the need to create a joint EU–Russia institutional body that will allow joint decisions to be made and implemented in the security sphere, with responsibility shared between the parties.

Third, the elaboration of common approaches to global threats to the security of our citizens, societies, and states is required. Within the NRC, Russia is willing to launch a process of common threat assessment in the security spheres relevant to the NRC. A similar process is ready to start in the framework of "Corfu."

Fourth, there is a need for a clear common set of guiding rules to be uniformly applied to settle all crisis situations, including the frozen conflicts. Russia has circulated within OSCE its proposals aimed at establishing uniform approaches to the prevention and peaceful resolution of conflicts, which should be based on the inadmissibility of the use of force, negotiations, and voluntary agreements between the parties to the conflicts without outside imposition of unilateral solutions. Russia is ready to work on these issues within the context of the "Corfu Process," as well as in the framework of the OSCE documents, such as Vienna Document 1999 Chapter on Risk Reduction.

And, fifth, the possibility of establishing a common security agenda is becoming more and more realistic. NATO readiness to engage Russia in the process of defining a new strategic concept is a very positive sign. It is in the common interest of Russia and NATO to avoid mutually competing and interfering security agendas, especially in the areas where Russia and NATO face common challenges, be it drug trafficking or organized crime, money laundering, energy and cyber-security, climate change, and so on. Russian Foreign Minister Sergei Lavrov made it clear that all Russia's initiatives, whether in the sphere of politico-military security or in the sphere of creating a new legal framework for energy cooperation, are "united by a desire to forge teamwork in dealing with specific problems. They do not presuppose unilateral action but imply a uniting of efforts and the use of multilateral forms of addressing contemporary issues in any area. Of course, our goals in promoting these initiatives are very clear. We have no hidden agendas. We want stability around our borders, and strive to provide the most favorable external conditions in order to tackle the vital tasks of modernizing our economy and transferring it on to an innovative track" (Lavrov, 2010b).

Comprehensive security remains Russia's main objective. But the commitment to comprehensive security should not be used as a pretext not to advance on hard security. Since the adoption of the Helsinki Final Act in 1975 many things have changed in Europe. All European states – with the sole exception of Belarus – have become full-fledged members of the Council of Europe, which through its legally binding instruments (the Court, monitoring mechanisms) is bringing us together in the broader range of issues that we describe as soft security (Grushko, 2009).

Meanwhile, the current uncertain situation in the security area encourages Russia to take an active role, because, as Lavrov believes, one "who does not care about national interests, is doomed to lose. That is why Russia supports building of Collective rapid reaction forces within CSTO. We have to admit that nobody will take care about our security...though the doors for honest and equal relationship and joint projects should be open" (Lavrov, 2010c).

Conclusion

It appears that the key issue is not about keeping the status quo in terms of the security architecture in Eurasia, but, rather, what a new security mechanism should look like – should it be a NATO-centric structure, which means turning the North Atlantic Treaty Organization into a forum for consultation on worldwide security issues,[8] including all rising powers, such as China, India, and Pakistan, or should it be a new institutional framework based upon a legally binding treaty guaranteeing equality and indivisibility of security of all states?

Medvedev's "Fourteen Point" program certainly represents continuity with Russia's security policy advanced about fifteen years ago. It represents one of the first "positive" Russian foreign policy initiatives since the collapse of the USSR. The initiative has both real substance and all the symbolic features to be expected of the major foreign policy initiative of Medvedev's presidency so far. The program's main added value is twofold: it aims at the construction of a new security regime in Europe on new principles of the indivisibility of international security and the inclusiveness of all interested actors; one of the main objectives of Medvedev's security plan is not only to upgrade the already existing (and ineffective) system but also to expand it into the Asia-Pacific region, in order to have a common security space from Vancouver to Vladivostok. Obviously, building such an architecture would preserve Russia's security interests both in the West and in the East. It would also pave the way for integrating a rising China and other countries of Asia into a dense network of European security institutions (Borodavkin, 2010).

Notes

1. The remaining nine points covered all the main territorial changes that seemed to be required for a stable settlement in Europe, and they were quite specific. President Wilson elaborated and extended the more general principles of peacemaking in a number of further speeches between February and September 1918, but these specific points were never modified. The lofty idealism infused into Allied peace aims by Wilson was to be a heavy liability in the years to come. See Thomson (1966, pp. 571–2).
2. Woodrow Wilson believed that the new world order must be based not on "covenants of selfishness and compromise" between governments, but on "the thought of the plain people who enjoy no privilege and have very simple and unsophisticated standards of right and wrong ... [and] might be sustained by the organized opinion of mankind" (quoted in Carr, 1945, p. 34).
3. For a detailed account of the Russian leadership's perception of security architecture and NATO expansion, see, for instance, Mankoff (2009, pp. 165–75). It is worth mentioning that many in the West as well opposed NATO expansion from the start, chief among them the late US statesman George Kennan, creator of the "containment" doctrine. He called expansion "the most fateful error of American policy in the entire post-Cold-War era." Kennan predicted that it would "inflame the existing nationalistic, anti-Western and militaristic tendencies in Russian opinion, restore the atmosphere of the cold war to East-West relations" (Kennan, 1997). The historian John Lewis Gaddis (1998, p. 145) was equally critical: "Some principles of strategy are so basic that when stated they sound like platitudes: treat former enemies magnanimously; do not take on unnecessary new ones; keep the big picture in view; balance ends and means; avoid emotion and isolation

in making decisions; be willing to acknowledge error. ... NATO enlargement, I believe, manages to violate every one of the strategic principles just mentioned." For further criticism of NATO expansion see also Reiter (2001) and Russett and Stam (1998).

4. Although CSTO received the status of an observer at the UN General Assembly in 2004, it did not sign a special treaty on cooperation with the United Nations until March 2010. The Treaty was supported by the General Assembly by consensus. The Russian text of the Declaration between the UN and CSTO was signed in Moscow on March 18, 2010 (see "Sovmestnaia deklaratsiia", 2010).

5. There is a widely held belief in Russia, based upon accounts by Mikhail Gorbachev, Evgenii Primakov, and other Russian key politicians, that the US leadership has broken its commitment not to expand NATO as a precondition for German reunification. Contrary to this, former Secretary of State James Baker rejected Russian suggestions that the West had broken a promise made in 1990 not to expand NATO into eastern Europe. Baker, who oversaw US foreign policy as communism collapsed in the Soviet Union and its satellite states, said he had "only floated the idea" during talks with Soviet leader Mikhail Gorbachev. "This was a negotiating position briefly considered by the U.S. in regard to East Germany only in talks about German unification and then promptly discarded" (Kim, 2009).

6. Believing that the OSCE has become a human rights agency, Russia has suggested that in this area, where the Council of Europe, the OSCE, and the EU are very often operating on parallel tracks, better division of labor is needed in order to achieve the most efficient use of the comparative advantages of the above-mentioned organizations.

7. The term "Finlandization" derives its name from Finland's 1948 agreement with the Soviet Union, under which Helsinki agreed not to join alliances challenging Moscow or to serve as a base for any country challenging Soviet interests. In return, the Kremlin agreed to uphold Finnish autonomy and respect Finland's democratic system. In 1988 the Danish political scientist Hans Mouritzen proposed a general theory of Finlandization known as "adaptive politics." Mouritzen stressed the fundamental difference between a Finlandized regime and a client, or "puppet," state, explaining that the former makes some concessions to a larger neighbor in order to guarantee important elements of its independence – voluntary choices that the latter could never make (Gilley, 2010).

8. According to the NATO Secretary General, "the Alliance should become the hub of security partnerships."

References

Borodavkin, A.N. (2010) "Asia-Pacific Region and National Security of the Russian Federation", Statement by the Russian Deputy Minister of Foreign Affairs, A.N. Borodavkin, at a Conference of the Federation Council of Russia, March 18.

Brzezinski, Zbigniew (2009) "An Agenda for NATO. Toward a Global Security Web", *Foreign Affairs*, September/October.

Buzan, Barry (1991) People, States, and Fear: An Agenda for International Security Studies in the Post-Cold War Era, London: Longmans.

Carr, E.H. (1945) The Twenty Years' Crisis, 1919–1939: An Introduction to the Study of International Relations, 2nd edn, London: Macmillan.

Castle, Stephen (2010) "Kazakhstan Uses Its Voice as Leader of O.S.C.E", *The New York Times*, January 28. http://query.nytimes.com/gst/fullpage.html?res=9B02 EFDD173CF93BA15752C0A9669D8B63 (accessed June 30, 2010).

Clinton, Hillary (2010) "Clinton's Remarks on the Future of European Security", January. http://www.cfr.org/publication/21364/clintons_remarks_on_the_future_of_european_security_january_2010.html?breadcrumb=%2Fregion% 2F323%2Feurope (accessed June 30, 2010).

"Conclusions of the OSCE Ministerial Council in Athens – Declaration Charts the Way Ahead for Dialogue on European Security" (2009) Athens, December 2. http://www.mfa.gr/www.mfa.gr/Articles/en-US/03122009_ALK1329.htm (accessed June 30, 2010).

CSTO-UN Treaty (2010).http://www.panarmenian.net/eng/world/news/45672/ (accessed June 30, 2010).

Deutsch, Karl (1969) Political Community and the North Atlantic Area: International Organization in the Light of Historical Experience, Princeton: Princeton University Press.

Gaddis, John Lewis (1998) "History, Grand Strategy, and NATO Enlargement", *Survival*, vol. 40, no. 1 (Spring).

Gilley, Bruce (2010) "Not So Dire Straits. How the Finlandization of Taiwan Benefits U.S. Security", I. January/February. http://www.foreignaffairs.com/ articles/65901/bruce-gilley/not-so-dire-straits (accessed June 30, 2010).

Grushko, Alexander (2009) "Proposals from the Russian President Dmitry Medvedev on the New European Security Treaty: Origins and Prospects". Statement by Mr Alexander Grushko, Deputy Minister for Foreign Affairs of the Russian Federation, at International Conference "Towards a New European Security Architecture?" London, December 9. http://www.iiss. org/programmes/russia-and-eurasia/events/conferences/conferences-2009/ towards-a-new-european-security-architecture/keynote-address-alexander-grushko/ (accessed June 30, 2010).

Hobsbawn, Eric (2003) The New Century. In conversation with Antonio Polito, London: Abacus.

Kennan, George F. (1997) "A Fateful Error", *New York Times*, February 5, p. A19.

Kim, Lucian (2009) "Baker Says Gorbachev Got No Promises on NATO Expansion to East", March 19. http://www.bloomberg.com/apps/ news?pid=newsarchive&sid=aN0Q_J9CA6GU (accessed June 30, 2010).

Krasner, Stephen D. (ed.) (1983) *International Regimes*, Ithaca, NY: Cornell University Press.

Lavrov, Sergei (2010a) "Lavrov Sees Pact as Litmus Test", *The St Petersburg Times*, no. 1542, p. 3, Tuesday, January 26.

Lavrov, Sergei (2010b) "Minister of Foreign Affairs Sergey Lavrov's Congratulations on the Occasion of Diplomatic Worker's Day", February 9. http://www.mid.ru/brp_4.nsf/e78a48070f128a7b43256999005bcbb3/35bbc4 323c3f63dcc32576c6004b53e2?OpenDocument (accessed June 30, 2010).

Lavrov, Sergei (2010c) "New Initiatives in the Year of Russia's Chairmanship in the CIS", Transcript of a Statement by Russia's Minister of Foreign

Affairs Sergei Lavrov at the International Economic Forum of CIS Member States, Moscow, March 5. http://www.mid.ru/brp_4.nsf/ e78a48070f128a7b43256999005bcbb3/e6df2b7f97cbe009c32576e0002aa5c0 ?OpenDocument (accessed June 30, 2010).

Legvold, Robert (2009) "The Russia File. How to Move Toward a Strategic Partnership", *Foreign Affairs*, July/August 2009.

Mankoff, Jeffrey (2009) *Russian Foreign Policy: the Return of Great Power Politics*, New York: Rowman & Littlefield Publishers, A Council on Foreign Relations Book.

Mearsheimer, John (1999 "Back to the Future. Instability in Europe after the Cold War", in Gideon Rose and James F. Hoge, Jr, *Foreign Affairs Agenda: New Shape of World Politics*, New York: Foreign Affairs Press.

Medvedev, Dimitrii (2009) "Speech at Helsinki University and Answers to Questions from Audience", President of Russia Official Web Portal. http://eng. kremlin.ru/text/speeches/2009/04/20/1919_type82912type82914type84779_ 215323.shtml (accessed April 5, 2010).

Merkel, Angela (2010) "Russia's European Security Initiative Should Get Fair Hearing – Merkel", March 8. http://en.rian.ru/russia/20100308/158129142. html (accessed June 30, 2010).

Military Doctrine of the Russian Federation (2010) February 5. http://www.sras. org/military_doctrine_russian_federation_2010 (accessed June 30, 2010).

Mueller, John E. (1989) *Retreat from Doomsday: The Obsolescence of Major War*, New York: Basic Books.

Nesterenko, A. (2010) "Briefing by A. Nesterenko, the official Representative Russia's MFA", March 11. http://www.mid.ru/brp_4.nsf/171aab5ddf3ec3c2 c32575d7004629c8/0e6ae0269f76efa5c32576e4004e8301?OpenDocument (accessed June 30, 2010).

Pabst, Adrian (2009) "The Berlin Doctrine", *Russia in Global Affairs*, no. 1 (January–March).

Rasmussen, Anders Fogh (2010) "Speech at the 46th Munich Security Conference", February 7. http://www.securityconference.de/Program.425+M 5dc18ed7f2e.0.html?&L=1 (accessed June 30, 2010).

Reiter, Dan (2001) "Why NATO Enlargement Does Not Spread Democracy", *International Security*, vol. 25, no. 4, pp. 41–67.

Russett, Bruce and Allan C. Stam (1998) "Courting Disaster: An Expanded NATO vs. Russia and China", *Political Science Quarterly*, vol. 113, no. 3 (Fall), pp. 361–82.

Schepers, Stefan (2009) "The Logic of European History", *Russia in Global Affairs*, no. 1 (January–March). http://eng.globalaffairs.ru/numbers/26/1263.html (accessed June 30, 2010).

"Sovmestnaia deklaratsiia o sotrudnichestve mezhdu Sekretariatami Organizatsii Ob"edinnennnykh Natsii I Organizatsii Dogovora o Kollektivnoi Bezopasnotsi" (2010). http://www.mid.ru/brp_4.nsf/0/2BFA3FD9CD78EA5FC 32576EF0047445C (accessed July 4, 2010).

"Statement by Ministers of Foreign Affairs of the CSTO Member States in Regard with Chairmanship of Kazakhstan in the OSCO" (2010) March 25. http:// www.mid.ru/brp_4.nsf/0/70FA04E0F62B2FD9C32576F2003ADB1A (accessed June 30, 2010).

Talbot, Strobe (2002) *The Russia Hand: A Memoir of Presidential Diplomacy*, New York: Random House.

Thomas, David (1966) *Europe Since Napoleon*, London: Penguin Books, pp. 571–2.

"World Opinion on General Principles of World Order" (2009) The Council on Foreign Relations, November 19. http://www.cfr.org/publication/20017

Young, Oran R. (1980) "International Regimes: Problems of Concept Formation", *World Politics*, vol. 32, pp. 331–56.

10
From the "New World Order" to "Resetting Relations": Two Decades of US–Russian Relations

Roger E. Kanet

The standard message in the mainstream US media is that Russia under Vladimir Putin and Dimitri Medvedev has defected from its earlier commitments to creating a liberal democracy and a true market economy and to joining the European/Western community of nations. Rather, Putin and those around him are presented as latter-day pupils of Russian and Soviet authoritarianism and imperialism, committed, first, to recreating the empire that collapsed in 1991 with the implosion of the Soviet Union.[1] Periodic Russian economic pressure on Ukraine, the so-called cyber-war against Estonia in spring 2007, and the invasion of Georgia in August 2008 are presented as evidence of Russia's commitment to reverse the geopolitical changes that occurred in post-Cold War Europe and to reestablish its regional dominance and its position as a global power. There is much that is attractive – and accurate – in such a simple and straightforward explanation for the deterioration of Russian relations with the United States and with Europe and for Russia's much more assertive dealings with neighboring states than those that characterized Moscow's policy under President Yeltsin. Russia has reemerged as something of a bully in its relationships with its near neighbors and appears intent on supporting virtually any political leadership intent on challenging US global dominance – such as those in Venezuela, Cuba, and Iran.

On the other hand, such an explanation virtually ignores Russian efforts in the 1990s to join the Western community – albeit on terms of equality, not as a second-class member – and the systematic rebuff that

Moscow received throughout the entire first decade of the existence of the Russian Federation. Among US-based analysts, Stephen F. Cohen (2000) and Andrei Tsygankov (2010) have been part of the handful who have challenged the standard interpretation and presented a more nuanced assessment of what went wrong in the Russian relationship with the West.[2]

When President George H.W. Bush finally recognized that the Soviet leadership had abandoned its commitment to global confrontation with the capitalist West in favor of joining the global economic and political system dominated by the West, he began speaking of a "new world order" in which military confrontation had been abolished and differences between states and peoples would be resolved through peaceful negotiation (Bush, 1990). The enthusiastic expectations of the early 1990s about the emergence of a "new world order," the development and likely consolidation of democracy across the former Soviet Union, and the successful integration of Russia into the Western community of democratic states, have been dispelled by a combination of Western, especially US, triumphalism and the realities of Russian political culture and the resulting semi-authoritarian political system that has emerged in Russia.

Soon after the Soviet collapse Washington diverted its attention away from developments in Russia, as it reveled in the "victorious" outcome of the Cold War and focused on benefiting from the fruits of that victory, as well as being faced with a whole series of unexpected challenges to stability in the Balkans, Africa, and elsewhere. Many analysts (Cohen, 2000; Trenin, 2007) have correctly noted that throughout the 1990s Russian interests were downplayed, or simply ignored, by Washington and Brussels, largely on the assumption that Russia was no longer relevant as a great power and its interests need not be taken into account when the West was making important foreign policy and security decisions. As the United States pushed through its policy preferences in a broad range of areas – the restructuring and expansion of NATO, military intervention in former Yugoslavia, a unilateral and assertive response to the terrorist attacks of September 2001 and the resulting invasion and occupation of Iraq and policy toward the broader Middle East, the emplacement of a missile defense system in Central Europe, attempts to limit or contain Russian influence on the development and distribution of natural gas resources from Central Asia, and so on – Moscow's concerns were simply left out of the policy calculations or, if raised, they were quickly brushed aside as irrelevant or hostile.

Throughout the 1990s Russian leaders often voiced their strong objections to US initiatives, such as when President Yeltsin stormed out of an OSCE meeting on Chechnya in 1999, but generally they were in no position to do anything more than complain, then eventually acquiesce to those initiatives. As a result Russian–US relations visibly deteriorated until they reached the point in early 2001 – just weeks after George W. Bush took over the White House – of mutual diplomatic expulsions and recriminations. Throughout the 1990s the specific issues that increasingly divided Moscow and Washington concerned matters that continue to divide the two countries today. They began with NATO expansion and the more general incorporation of former Soviet dependencies and even constituent republics, from Bulgaria to Estonia, into what Moscow views as a US-dominated political and security sphere, and included NATO intervention in former Yugoslavia, criticism of Russian domestic political developments, and a series of other developments. After a brief attempt to reestablish a collaborative relationship on the basis of equality after the terrorist attacks in the United States of September 2001 and after the turnaround in the Russian economy, President Putin determined that Moscow would always be treated as an outsider by the West, not as a full partner, and that Russia should "go it alone." Moreover, Putin's plans for reasserting central authority across the breadth of Russia did not mesh well with the Western concept of democracy. But "democracy" was reinterpreted as "sovereign democracy," a term that quickly emerged as a theoretical explanation and justification for Russia's independent, even unilateralist, approach to foreign and security policy, as well as for the top-down approach to domestic political control. By the December 2007 parliamentary elections, "sovereign democracy" had become part of the political program of United Russia, Russia's governing party, now headed by President Putin himself.

One major result of the Russian leadership's redefinition of Russia's role in world affairs during the past decade has been Russia's emergence as a revisionist power, committed to rolling back some of its geopolitical losses that occurred after the collapse of the former Soviet Union and to returning Russia to the status of a major world power. This involves, first and foremost, Moscow's reasserting its position as the dominant actor in former Soviet space, in the areas of Russia's "privileged interests," as President Medvedev noted soon after Russia's military intervention in Georgia in August 2008 (Medvedev, 2008a). Closely related to the reassertion of Russian influence in border areas, however, has been the commitment to challenging the global dominance – or attempted dominance – of the United States.[3] Thus, since the US decision to invade Iraq, Moscow has increasingly and loudly criticized virtually all aspects of US policy – foreign and domestic – and has gone out of its way to collaborate, at least rhetorically and symbolically, with states such as Venezuela and Cuba that share Russia's opposition to US unilateralism.[4]

The objective of the present chapter is to track recent Russian relations with the United States – focusing on the period since the US intervention in Iraq in spring 2003 – to support the argument that Russian leaders have pursued a policy of independence, even confrontation if deemed necessary, in their relations with the United States, as well as with Europe, as part of a new assertive approach to achieving policy objectives and protecting Russia's national interests. The following discussion of Russian–US relations is divided into four sections: the first briefly outlines the deteriorating relationship in the final years of Yeltsin's presidency; the second deals with the revival of Russia as a major power under Putin and Medvedev; the next examines in some detail the impact of that revival on Russian relations with the United States; and the fourth and final section outlines possible future scenarios for the relationship.

The end of the Yeltsin era

President Yeltsin appointed Yevgenii Primakov as foreign minister in 1996. He placed more emphasis than his predecessor on Russia's status as a great power, despite its current economic and political problems, and argued that its foreign policy should be based on an "equal partnership" with the United States (Gornostaev, 1998; Primakov, 1996). Primakov justified Russia's policies in pragmatic terms of Russian national interest, not theoretical ties to the democratic West. This meant, for example, a focus on Russia's primacy in security and political developments within the territory of the former Soviet Union – a point that remains central in Russian policy more than a decade later.

The Russians increasingly opposed US-initiated economic sanctions against a number of countries viewed as important potential international partners for Russia. At the time of US and British military air strikes in Iraq in retaliation for repeated Iraqi refusals to cooperate with UN weapons inspectors in late 1998, President Yeltsin spoke of "gross violations of the UN Charter." When the West began to bring pressure on Yugoslavia in 1998 over the issue of Kosovo, the Russians placed Yugoslav territorial integrity far above the issue of human rights and threatened various forms of retaliation if the West bombed Yugoslavia.

The issue that raised the most serious Russian concerns at this time – an issue that remains important a decade later – was NATO's decision to proceed with eastward expansion into former Soviet-controlled Europe.[5] Moscow pursued a major campaign against NATO expansion prior to the Madrid meetings of NATO in July 1997. However, when NATO invited the Czech Republic, Hungary, and Poland to join the alliance, Russia reluctantly accepted the decision, since it had few ways of realistically opposing it. Russia shifted its opposition to NATO expansion from East Central Europe to the Baltic states – but also failed to stop the inclusion of those states seven years later. The push in 2008 by the Bush Administration to extend NATO membership to Georgia and Ukraine was a central factor in triggering the much more aggressive Russian response. The key difference from the earlier period in explaining Moscow's reaction was the much stronger economic and even military position from which it was operating in 2008 and the significant shift in Russia's policy orientation under Putin.

By 2000, when Vladimir Putin took over the presidency, the state of Russia's relations with the United States had reached a post-Cold War low. However, given its weak position because of its economic dependence on the West, Moscow was often forced to back down when faced with US opposition. While the issues that divide Russian–American relations in early 2010 have their roots in political and security developments a decade or more earlier, what has changed is the unwillingness of Moscow to accept a position of weakness or dependence in Russian relations with the West.

Putin, Medvedev and the rebuilding of Russia as a major power

Early in his presidency Vladimir Putin made clear his commitment to establishing Russia's position as the preeminent regional power and as an important international actor. Essential preconditions for the fulfillment of these objectives, as described in the "Foreign Policy Concept" (2000), were the internal political stability and economic viability of Russia. Russia needed to overcome inclinations toward separatism, national and religious extremism, and terrorism. Putin moved forcefully in reasserting central governmental control in Russia. The economy showed strong signs of turning around in 1999–2001. High growth rates continued, and even increased in the following years – not merely in the oil and gas sector, but across broad sectors of the economy. These political and economic gains, however, occurred along with growing disregard for the civil liberties and democratic processes to which Putin's government was nominally committed – developments that were strongly criticized by both Washington and Brussels.

Russia under Putin continued to seek allies who shared his commitment to preventing the United States from assuming a dominant global role that would represent, in the words of the "Foreign Policy Concept," a threat to international security and to Russia's goal of serving as a major center of influence in a multipolar world. Most of the issues on which Russia and the United States had already disagreed in the mid-1990s continued to plague that relationship. Until the terrorist attacks on the United States in September 2001 there was little evidence that these disagreements would disappear soon – in particular since they derived from core elements of the two countries' respective foreign policy commitments. In fact, after a very brief hiatus immediately after 9/11, when the President went out of his way to be cooperative with Washington, those issues reemerged and continue to undermine Russian–US relations in spring 2010.

Putin's success in dealing with the major domestic problems challenging the Russian state meant that Russia increasingly faced Europe and the United States from a position of increased stability and strength. Putin's reassertion of central control over the territory of the Russian Federation – by conquering Chechnya, eliminating the election of provincial governors, suppressing domestic opponents and critics (especially the independent media), and playing on Russian citizens' fears of domestic terrorism, crime, and general chaos – played an important role in strengthening the Russian state, which at times had seemed on the verge of collapsing. Besides rebuilding the foundations of the Russian state, at great cost to political liberty and democracy, as a precondition for Russia's ability to reassert itself as a major power, Putin and his associates benefited greatly from the exponential rise in global demand for gas and oil – at least until the global financial collapse of fall 2008 – and the ensuing revitalization of the Russian economy. This, in turn, contributed to Russia's ability to pursue a much more active and assertive foreign policy, as many analysts have noted.[6] The longer-term impact of the collapse of the global economy since late summer 2008, and the dramatic drop in energy prices, on the Russian economy and on Russia's ability to pursue an assertive foreign policy is yet to be seen.

Thus, Putin was quite successful, and fortunate, during the eight years of his presidency in establishing the economic and political foundations for a strong centralized state as the prerequisite for Russia reasserting itself as a major player in international political and security affairs. While the voices calling for Russia to resume its role as a great, global, power in the 1990s had been strident but not realistic, similar voices have today taken the dominant position in Russian politics, and are based upon realistic expectations of achieving many of their goals. Supporters of this policy include former President Putin himself, who made clear in his statement to the Russian parliament and people that "the collapse of the Soviet Union was the greatest geopolitical catastrophe of the century" (Putin, 2005). This comment was followed early in 2007 by Putin's broad attack on virtually all aspects of US policy, delivered at an international security conference in Munich, which made clear Russia's new assertive and nationalistic approach to foreign policy, beginning with its relations with the United States (Wagstyl, 2007).[7] The rhetoric emanating from Moscow after the military incursion into Georgia confirmed the image of a revisionist state intent upon reestablishing its dominant role, at least along its periphery, and one that simply will no longer deal with the rest of the world on any other terms but its own (Levy, 2008a; Medvedev, 2008c). From Moscow's perspective, however, its policy goals are not revisionist, but are merely intended to reestablish Russia's legitimate position in the aftermath of the West's having taken advantage of Russian decline in the immediate post-Cold War period.

By May 2008, when Putin turned the presidency over to Dmitry Medvedev, Russia had reemerged as a major player in European economic and political affairs and the dominant actor in most of post-Soviet space. The foundation of this new role has been Russia's semi-monopoly over the extraction and distribution of natural gas and oil across much of Eurasia, and the growing direct influence that this semi-monopoly provides over the economies of neighboring states. The gas war between Russia and Ukraine in January 2009 and its implications for European consumers of Russian gas made clear both the importance to Moscow of its control of oil and gas exports in the pursuit of foreign policy objectives and its willingness to use the leverage resulting from that control.[8]

Before turning to a more detailed discussion of specific developments in Russian relations with the United States in the recent past, it is important to note, at least briefly, the relationship between the growing assertiveness in Russian foreign policy and domestic political developments. As Russia's leaders abandoned the halting efforts at democratization that had characterized the first decade of the Russian Federation and increasingly reestablished the institutions and policies of a semi-authoritarian state, they have also seized upon economic growth and a growing sense of Russian nationalism as the foundations on which to build support among broad segments of the population. The economic boom, which resulted in more than doubling the gross domestic product per capita of the Russian population, was an important element in the popularity of former President Putin and in the support for his policies.

Public opinion polls and anecdotal information indicate widespread public support for the return of Russia to great power status; more specifically, Russians overwhelmingly supported the Kremlin's decision to invade Georgia in August 2008 (Barnard, 2008). In relation to this broad sense of nationalism, the Putin–Medvedev leadership has increasingly focused on the dangers to Russia presented by foreign enemies, of which the United States is virtually always listed first. The Foreign Policy Concept (2008) issued by President Medvedev in late July 2008, immediately prior to the intervention in Georgia, represented a break with earlier versions of the Concept, even though in effect it merely codified changes that had already occurred over recent years. First, unlike the Concept issued at the beginning of the Putin presidency, it focuses on external, rather than internal, challenges to Russian security – with US global dominance at the very top of the list. In line with the extensive discussion of "sovereign democracy" in Russia, the Concept stipulates that global competition is acquiring a civilizational dimension, which suggests competition between different value systems and development models within the framework of universal democratic and market economy principles. The new FPC maintains that the reaction of the historic West to the prospect of losing its monopoly in global processes finds its expression, in particular, in the continued political and psychological policy of "containing Russia" ("Foreign Policy Concept", 2008). The document emphasizes Russia's independence and sovereignty as the foundation on which all Moscow's relations with the outside world must be built.

A resurgent nationalism, integrated with an almost paranoid concern for security,[9] underlies Moscow's current approach to the outside world. But Western policy has contributed to that concern. As both Vladimir Putin and Dmitri Medvedev have repeated on numerous occasions, Russia is a major power whose interests have simply been ignored by the West, especially a would-be hegemonic Washington. With the return of Russia's power base – in particular in economic terms – Russia simply will not stand by and permit those interests to be pushed aside. It will not permit itself either to become a dependent supporter of US policy initiatives or to be shunted aside into the "dustbin of history."

Russia and the United States since 9/11

In the immediate aftermath of the terrorist attacks on New York and Washington, President Putin offered Russian support to the United States in its initial response to the attacks. This initiative opened a brief period in which relations between the United States and Russia were generally more cordial than they had been for a number of years. The divisions between the two countries were overshadowed by the obvious areas of collaboration – especially in combating terrorist threats. Russia supported the US military intervention against al-Qaeda and the Taliban in Afghanistan, in part by facilitating US access to air bases in Central Asia that proved to be important in the US pursuit of military operations in Afghanistan. However, by the summer and fall of 2002, as the Bush Administration pushed for military intervention and regime change in Iraq, the relationship rapidly unraveled. In fact, the Russian Federation, along with key US allies France and Germany, comprised the core opposition to US demands for direct military intervention against Saddam Hussein's Iraq. It is from this point that we can track the deterioration of relations between Moscow and Washington, which by early 2009, at the time of the transfer of presidential power to Barack Obama, had reached the level of confrontation on a variety of issues of central concern to the foreign policy of both countries. These issues concerned, first and foremost, the relative standing and role of the two countries in the international system. More specifically, however, they concerned Russia's lack of input in key global discussions about future security, the West's political, security, and economic encroachment in areas viewed in Moscow as Russia's sphere of influence, and the West's position on a whole series of important international developments. In the following pages, we will discuss briefly a number of these issues that divide Moscow and Washington and the likelihood of their resolution in the near future.

US unilateralism and the Russian response

Among the most central and consistent themes in Russian foreign policy in recent years has been the call for the reestablishment of a multipolar international political system in which all major powers, including especially Russia, have an equal voice. This theme has been central to most of the major speeches of Russian leaders over the past decade, even prior to the resurgence of Russia as a major international player. The 2000 version of *The Russian Foreign Policy Concept*, for example, made the point throughout that Russia was committed to a multipolar approach to international security and that "(t)he strategy of unilateral actions can destabilize the international situation, provoke tensions and the arms race, aggravate interstate contradictions, national and religious strife."[10] In his strongly critical attack on the United States and NATO, presented at an international security conference in Munich in 2007, President Putin (2007) noted: "The United States has overstepped its borders in all spheres – economic, political and humanitarian – and has imposed itself on other states. ... One-sided illegitimate action hasn't solved a single problem and has become a generator of many human tragedies, a source of tension." Moscow's criticism did not let up under President Medvedev, as was evident from his criticism of the United States for encouraging Georgia's "barbaric aggression" against South Ossetia in August 2008 and for using the ensuing Russia–Georgia war as an excuse to expand NATO further (Medvedev, 2008b).

This source of division between the United States and the Russian Federation has been at the root of many of the other areas of disagreement for more than a decade and is one that will be difficult to resolve. It concerns the very way in which the leaderships of the two countries view themselves and their dealings with the rest of the world. Despite the change in administration in Washington and the abandonment of the most egregious elements of a unilateralist and assertive US nationalist foreign policy, US decision makers will continue to view the United States as an "exceptional" state, one destined to provide global leadership, as they have for more than two centuries.[11]

Such an approach to dealing with Russia will continue to cause problems, for in very many respects the Russians have a similar view of themselves as unique masters of their own destiny, completely independent actors, and a legitimate global power. This is the message that Putin, Medvedev, and other Russian leaders have been so insistent in conveying in recent years. "Sovereign democracy," as the theoretical underpinning of the Russian political system, calls for Russian unilateralism in foreign and security policy, in so far as that is possible.

Moscow and the US–EU challenge to Russia's sphere of influence

Quite a number of the conflicts between Russia and the West result from what Russia views as a deliberate attempt by the West to undermine Russia's legitimate interests and the attempt to limit and contain

Russia's revival as a great power. This reaction relates to the dramatic shift in the status of the territory between the Russian Federation and Western Europe, all of which was at one time part of a Soviet-dominated "empire" – either internal or external – and most of which is now integrated into Western economic, political, and security institutions. NATO and EU expansion eastward has been viewed in Moscow as the result of purposeful Western programs aimed at expanding the West's geopolitical dominance in Europe and directly undermining Russia's role and its long-term security. The Russians ignore the fact that the initiative for inclusion came from the Central European peoples themselves – in part because of forty years of Soviet domination in the region – and that the West was, in fact, responding to these initiatives. Of course, this also fits well with EU and US objectives of expanding Western institutions throughout the region.

Ever since the most recent expansions of NATO and EU membership, relations between Russia and those organizations have deteriorated significantly. In part, this stems from the much more assertive efforts of Moscow to reestablish its influence in the broader Central and East European region. On the other hand, the entrance of postcommunist members into the EU has added a significant level of complexity to EU–Russian relations, as new members such as Poland and the Baltic states demanded that the organization take a stand on a variety of issues that have challenged Russian policy (DeBardeleben, 2009). Poland, for example, stymied efforts to renegotiate a new EU–Russian Partnership and Cooperation Agreement for more than a year in response to Moscow's embargo of the importation of Polish meat products, which the Poles viewed as politically motivated (Lobjakas, 2007).[12]

Some of the new members of the European Union have been strongly critical of bilateral deals negotiated with Russia by other EU members to build new gas pipelines from Russia to Europe that will bypass their territory. Once again Poland has been the most vocal in its criticisms of the implications of such a pipeline, both for its own interests and for the future development of a common EU energy policy. Among the new challenges to the Russian–EU relationship, however, perhaps the most visible have related to the active role that Poland, Lithuania, and other postcommunist states played in supporting political reform in Ukraine, Georgia, and even Belarus – political reform that has generally been interpreted by Moscow as a challenge to its interests.[13] During and after the Orange Revolution in Ukraine in late 2004, the Polish government was among its most active advocates and supporters in Europe (Kuzio, 2004). Postcommunist EU member states also backed developments in

Georgia associated with the Rose Revolution of 2003, which brought a Western-oriented government to power in Tbilisi (Whitmore, 2008).

We have focused on the impact of EU expansion into what the Russians view as their legitimate sphere of interest and influence. Although this development obviously does not impinge directly on the Russian–American relationship, it has clear implications. First, there is the fact that all the new member states of the EU have also joined NATO since 1998. Moreover, as a group they have generally supported US foreign and security policy – for example, in the run-up to the Iraq War, and in contributing military support to the US-led operations in Iraq and Afghanistan. The position of these countries in backing the United States is quite understandable, given the history of the second half of the twentieth century and the concern that some of their governments have about the impact of the revival of a strong Russia for their future security.[14] It is important to recall that, in addition to US and European attempts to take advantage of Russia's weakness during the 1990s to push eastward to contain the revival of Russian influence – which is the predominant Russian interpretation – the countries of the region also vigorously pursued membership in both NATO and the EU as part of their escape from Russia and "return to Europe." The most recent illustration of Russia's reactions to what are viewed as challenges to Russian honor, or Western incursions into legitimate Russian spheres of influence, has been in relation to the so-called cyber-war conducted against Estonia in 2007,[15] the mounting pressures against Georgia that culminated in military intervention in August 2008 and the ensuing diplomatic recognition of the breakaway regions of South Ossetia and Abkhazia, and the gas war with Ukraine in January 2009. All these developments were more complex than this simple listing implies. But the element that ties them together is the attempt by an increasingly assertive Russia to make clear to its near neighbors that on issues on which Moscow has a strong position it is willing to use the capabilities at its command – capabilities that have increased over the past decade – in order to accomplish its goals. Whether the matter concerns what the Russians view as dishonor to the heroes of the Great Patriotic War and an interpretation of the "liberation" from Nazi domination seen as demeaning to Russia, as in the case of Estonia, or the growing friction between Georgia and Russia ever since the shift in Tbilisi to a government committed to closer ties with, even integration into, Western institutions, the leaders in Moscow will no longer simply watch Western influence increase. In the case of both Ukraine and Georgia, the added factor of Washington's pushing for admission of the two states into NATO in spring 2008 no doubt played an important role in the Russian decision to forestall such a development.

From Moscow's perspective, US actions in Central Asia, in conjunction with the Russian-backed expansion of military involvement after 9/11 as part of the war on terror, also raised concerns about US meddling in an area of special Russian interest. Yet the expulsion of the Americans from Uzbekistan in 2005 and the ensuing solidification of Russian relations with most of the countries of the region have weakened the United States as a competitor for influence in Central Asia.[16] However, from Moscow's perspective, the issue of the US role in undermining Russian influence in neighboring states and facilitating, even encouraging, their entrance into Western institutions, especially NATO, remains a serious impediment to improved Russian–US relations.

Russian charges of a US military threat

Distinct from, but closely related to, the matter of US and Western challenges to Russia's sphere of influence is the Russian charge that the United States and NATO represent a serious threat to Russian security because NATO's placement of forces in countries immediately along Russia's borders undermines the level of mutual trust and, thus, requires Russia to respond in like fashion. The Bush Administration's decision to go ahead with the development and placement of the first stage of an anti-missile defense system in the Czech Republic and Poland, and the decisions of the two Central European countries to finalize the agreements despite Russian opposition, provide clear evidence of the serious divisions in Russian relations with the United States, but also of the nature of Moscow's relations with its former client states. Washington has simply not taken seriously Russian leaders' regular assertions that they view the placement of an anti-missile system, even one as modest in size as that currently planned, as a challenge to their own long-term security. Nor have the Russians accepted Washington's arguments that the system is meant solely and exclusively as possible protection against rogue states – read Iran – that might develop nuclear weapons. On the other hand, the speed with which the Poles and Czechs finally ratified the agreements with the United States in August 2008 – after long domestic debates – made it clear that the Russian military intervention in Georgia, and renewed concerns about the long-term nature of their relations with Russia, played a major role in their decisions.[17] No doubt President Medvedev's announcement in his address to the Russian Parliament on November 5, 2008 reinforced concerns throughout Central Europe, as he announced the likely deployment of Russian missiles in the Kaliningrad Region along the Polish border and the expansion of capabilities for electronic warfare against NATO in the area (Medvedev, 2008c). Soon after the new Obama administration made overtures toward improving bilateral relations, including modification of the proposed missile defense system, the Russians reversed their position on this issue (MacAskill and Traynor, 2009; "Russia Ready", 2009).

Thus, the issues of NATO expansion and the absorption of additional former Soviet republics, as well as the introduction of US anti-missile defenses into Central Europe, appear to be non-starters in terms of their impact on the possibility of a normalization of Russian relations with the United States. Only a complete change in the way that the Russians view these issues, or a US decision that the cost involved in continuing to pursue them is too high, is likely to remove them as serious hindrances to improved relations. There is now good evidence that the Obama administration is not committed either to developing a missile defense shield or to further NATO expansion.

Russian gas and oil exports and US efforts at economic containment

As early as the mid-1990s, as part of an overall approach toward Russia that had much in common with a strategy of containment, the United States began to advocate the development of oil and gas pipelines to Western Europe that would skirt Russian territory and, thus, reduce the potential of Russia's gaining further leverage over either Central Asian exporters or the Western purchasers of energy (Ebel and Menon, 2000; Ziegler, 2005). During the past decade, as Moscow began to use the supply of gas and oil to neighboring states as an explicit foreign policy tool,[18] Washington became even more concerned about Western energy dependence on Russia and renewed its role in encouraging the development of alternative routes for the delivery of energy, especially natural gas, from the new fields in Central Asia to the West. The Russians, understandably, have viewed this US initiative – especially in conjunction with the expansion of NATO eastwards – as a continuation of a policy of containment.

US efforts since the 1990s to contain Russian influence over the delivery of energy to Europe have failed to accomplish their objectives; Russia has effectively outmaneuvered the United States in its relations with the oil- and gas-producing countries of Central Asia. Although several pipelines have been completed that avoid Russian territory, Moscow has been successful in reestablishing solid political and economic relations with the authoritarian regimes of Central Asia. They have signed new agreements with Kazakhstan and Uzbekistan that will result in expanded supplies of gas and oil destined for European consumers through the existing and planned pipeline network that crosses Russian territory (Hahn, 2007; Kramer, 2007). At the time of the Russian intervention in Georgia, Moscow signed new agreements with Central Asian producers for the expansion of their gas exports through Russia, rather than via southern pipelines favored by the United States (Bhadrakumar, 2008). This is all part of a Russian effort to increase control over the flow of oil and gas to Europe as a prelude to being in a position to influence, indirectly at least, the political orientation of key European governments on issues such as the status of secessionist regions of Moldova and Georgia, Russian policy in Chechnya, and so on.

Russia and its important Western partners – especially Germany and Italy – have also put in place plans for the future distribution of oil and gas to Europe that will greatly reduce the possible interference of current transit states such as Ukraine and Belarus by avoiding those transit states altogether. The so-called gas war between Russia and Ukraine in January 2009 provides probably the best evidence, from a Russian perspective, that it has to reduce this dependence. The planned Nord Stream pipeline under the Baltic Sea directly from Russia to the coast of Germany, as well as the more recently announced South Stream pipeline that will run under the Black Sea from Russia directly to Bulgaria and on to Italy, will expand Russia's domination over the gas markets of Europe, while reducing the possibility of countries such as Ukraine, Belarus, or Poland disrupting those flows. Overall, Russia has positioned itself effectively to control the production and distribution of energy across almost the entirety of former Soviet space and, thus, to Europe as well, as part of former President Putin's commitment to reestablish Russia as a major global actor. The dependence on external sources for virtually all the gas and oil needs of some countries in the European Union, and their willingness to make bilateral deals with Russia outside the context of a common EU policy (notably Germany), has greatly aided Russia in its attempt to employ energy as a foreign policy tool. It has also contributed to the divisions within the European Union and between the United States and key EU member states on the issue of the future of EU energy policy. However, the impact of the January 2009 Russian–Ukrainian gas war has, at least for the time being, influenced European states to reconsider the implications of their dependence on Russia for energy ("EU Urged to Reconsider Strategic Energy Goals", 2009).

Other outstanding disagreements

In addition to the issues discussed here, a long list of other policy disagreements divided Moscow and Washington as the new Obama

Administration took over control of US foreign policy. These included a number of outstanding territorial issues such as Russia's refusal to recognize the Western-supported independent state of Kosovo, in contrast to its recognition – in part, in retaliation – of the independence of the Georgian breakaway republics of South Ossetia and Abkhazia and subsequent de facto incorporation of the two into the Russian Federation. In both these cases the United States and Russia have taken opposing positions. But this issue, as we have already noted earlier, is part of a much broader concern over Russian and US policy toward those states in Eastern Europe that have declared their intention to join NATO and the European Union. The status of both Russian–Georgian and Russian–Ukrainian relations and the impact of their conflicts on Moscow's policy toward Washington remain near the top of the list of priorities – although the change of government in Ukraine in early 2010 has already resulted in an improvement in Ukrainian–Russian relations (Harding, 2010).

Just as important, however, is the divergence between Moscow's and Washington's assessments to date on carrying out the "war on terror." Although the issue of US policy in Iraq no longer dominates bilateral relations as it did immediately prior to and after the US invasion of Iraq, the two countries continue to differ seriously on this subject. The matter of Russian treatment of the former breakaway republic of Chechnya has also been an issue of some importance, since the United States – as well as the European Union – has periodically condemned the Russians for their brutal treatment of both insurgents and the population at large. But the manner in which the United States has conducted its "war on terror" without real input or consultation with other states, including especially Russia, has contributed to the friction between the two states.

Over the past several years, the Russians have also pursued a very visible policy of establishing closer ties with states openly critical, even hostile, to the United States and to US interests. This includes the expansion of economic ties with Cuba and Venezuela, accompanied by showy collaborative military exercises (Blank, 2010; Levy, 2008c; Schwirtz, 2009), and vetoes of Western efforts in the United Nations to expand pressures on the murderous regime in Zimbabwe and to bring a halt to the ethnic cleansing in Sudan.

Finally, Moscow has begun to "show the flag" far from Russian territory, as illustrated by its collaborative military operations with the Venezuelans and the recent flexing of its military muscles with the resumption after more than fifteen years of naval and air patrols off the northern coasts of Scandinavia and the planting of the Russian flag at the bottom of the Arctic ("Intelligence Brief", 2007). These activities, along with the regular, very critical attacks on the United States and on US policy, appear to have two purposes: first, to reaffirm the position that Russia is an independent and important world actor that can and will pursue its own interests, and, second, to build – or rebuild – a set of relationships with states that share Russia's opposition to Washington's policies and will support it in various international venues.

Toward the future

Where is this relationship likely to go in the near future? Analysts agree that for both countries an improvement is important, if they are going to be able to deal with issues of importance to their national interests. First and foremost, the issues of international terrorism and the challenges from militant Islam are matters of concern to both governments, and cooperation in dealing with them remains important. In fact, despite the serious deterioration in relations during the Bush administration and the heightened hostile rhetoric, collaboration in this area, in particular concerning military operations against the Taliban and al-Qaeda in Afghanistan, continued. The solution of other matters of mutual interest to Moscow and Washington, such as the possible development of nuclear weapons by Iran, an important issue on which the two countries have not agreed, are likely possible only with an improvement in bilateral relations and a less confrontational approach than we have witnessed in recent years. In some respects, Russian–US relations in recent years have followed a path illustrated best by the cycle of escalation described as a "security dilemma." After each decision by one side or the other to pursue a particular policy – whether the US decision to begin building a protective missile shield, or the Russian decision to "solve" its problems with Georgia by military intervention – the level of mutual hostility rose and led to a retaliatory action on the part of the other side.

Although most of the issues that divide the two sides are matters viewed as serious and central to interpretations of national interest and, thus, not easy to resolve, the election of a new US president committed to implementing a new approach to relations with the rest of the world has provided an opportunity for a new start in Russian–US relations. In fact, after closed discussions on January 26, 2009, the Russian ambassador to NATO implied that Russia and NATO were in the process of regularizing relations suspended in the wake of the Russia–Georgia war of summer 2008 (Baker, 2008; Mass, 2009). This information, in addition to the announcement that Russia will not deploy Iskander missiles targeted on US facilities in Poland and/or the Czech Republic, and considered within the context of a possible new orientation in US foreign policy under President Obama, raises hopes of a possible improvement in relations between the two countries.

One issue in the Russian–US relationship that had to be handled almost immediately concerned arms control, a matter largely ignored during the entire Bush administration. For example, the Bush Administration decided to let the START treaty of 1994, which monitored and limited a variety of nuclear weapons, simply expire in 2009 rather than negotiate a renewal or an extension of the agreement (Boese, 2008). In fact, President Obama has made the reduction of the nuclear threat a centerpiece of his security policy, and the Russian Federation and the United States signed a new arms control treaty on April 8, 2010 (Baker and Bilefsky, 2010).

The new tone of cooperation in American foreign policy has already helped to improve the environment for Russian–US interactions.[19] Moreover, there exists a substantial area of overlapping interest between the Russian Federation and the United States relating to other aspects of arms control, international terrorism, weapons of mass destruction, and now the global economic slowdown. However, there is one set of issues on which US and broader Western compromise would appear to be impossible without abandoning their principles. Russia cannot be permitted to veto the continuation of the development of close ties between former Soviet republics and clients with the West. The rush to membership in the EU and NATO that began with the collapse of the external and internal Soviet empires two decades ago was not orchestrated in Washington or Brussels – even though it was welcomed there – but rather in the countries that had just escaped half a century, or more, of Soviet domination.

Whether Moscow's newfound assertiveness in its relations with its near neighbors will undercut prospects for improved relations will depend almost entirely on Moscow's flexibility in dealing with these countries as sovereign equals and not as a part of a revitalized "Greater Russia." What is clear is that areas of mutual interest exist between Moscow and Washington where both sides could benefit by renewed cooperation, that the new administration in Washington seems willing to back off from some of its predecessor's policy initiatives deemed most unacceptable in Moscow, and that the leadership in Moscow seems willing to test a return to a less assertive approach to the Russian–US relationship.

Notes

The following chapter draws upon Kanet (2010).

1. One finds a rather extreme version of this picture in Lucas (2008).
2. See also the work of Dmitri Trenin (2007) on Russian relations with Europe and the United States, which points to the impact of Western actions and inactions, as well as to those of the Russian Federation, on the deterioration of the relationship. Moreover, P. Terrence Hopmann (2010), the *doyen* of American students of the Organization for Security and Cooperation in Europe, has tracked the relationship of Russia and the Western members of OSCE in the 1990s and the systematic way in which virtually every Russian proposal was rebuffed until, even before Putin emerged as the new Russian leader in 2000, OSCE and Russian integration into Western institutions had lost their attractiveness in Moscow.
3. Former President Putin's (2007) opposition to US dominance was expressed forcefully in his speech at a security conference held in Munich in early 2007.
4. For a discussion of recent Russian criticisms of the United States and the West in general, see Shlapentokh (2008).
5. In a nationally televised interview in August 2008, President Medvedev stated: "We do not need illusions of partnership. When we are being surrounded by bases on all sides, and a growing number of states are being drawn into the North Atlantic bloc and we are being told, 'Don't worry, everything is all right,' naturally we do not like it" (cited in Levy, 2008b). At the time of the first decision to expand NATO membership eastward, George F. Kennan (1997), architect of the US containment policy forty years earlier, warned that to expand NATO "would be the most fateful error of American policy in the entire post-cold war era" and "may be expected to inflame the nationalistic, anti-Western and militaristic tendencies in Russian opinion; to have an adverse effect on the development of Russian democracy; to restore the atmosphere of the cold war to East-West relations; and to impel Russian foreign policy decidedly not to (US) liking."
6. However, as some analysts have argued, the revived role of Russia as a regional and global political actor is based extensively on oil and gas production and exports, despite recent improvements in other aspects of the Russian economy. See, for example, Hancock (2007).
7. What most Western commentators and analysts missed in Putin's remarks was his assertion that Russia was willing to work with the United States as an equal in areas related to the continued reduction of nuclear weapons and other arms control measures (Putin, 2007).
8. It is important to note that, in the Ukrainian–Russian confrontation over gas supplies, as in the Georgian–Russian military conflict in summer 2008 over South Ossetia, Russia was not the only party at fault. The leaders of both Ukraine and Georgia contributed significantly to the confrontations. On European reactions to the policies of these countries, see Taylor (2009) and Petrovič (2009).
9. It is important to recognize that the US decision to pursue a policy of de facto containment of Russia, beginning as early as the mid-1990s, as noted earlier in this chapter, has reinforced Moscow's concerns for security and

for its future role in areas adjacent to Russian territory and viewed as crucial to Russia's long-term interests.

10. The 2008 version of *The Foreign Policy Concept* (2008) echoes these points: "The unilateral action strategy leads to destabilization of international situation, provokes tensions and arms race, exacerbates interstate differences, stirs up ethnic and religious strife, endangers security of other States and fuels tensions in international relations."

11. There is an extensive literature dealing with this topic, some of which is cited in Kanet (2008). The foreign and security policy team surrounding President Obama shares this perspective of its predecessors, although not its view of the appropriate means to be used to achieve it. Writing on this topic for a Russian audience, Andrei P. Tsygankov (2008) has summarized the arguments concerning "American Exceptionalism."

12. Similar Lithuanian objections to resuming negotiations were finally overcome in November 2008.

13. President Medvedev (2008c) pointedly noted: "We really proved – including to those who sponsored the current regime in Georgia – that we are able to protect our citizens." First, and primarily, he was referring to the United States, but also Poland and other postcommunist states that had supported the Saakashvili government. In like vein, Prime Minister Putin also presented the Russian intervention in Georgia as a response to Cold War-style provocations by the United States (cited in Levy, 2008b).

14. National debates about joining NATO made it clear that, for virtually all those countries requesting membership, concerns about Russia and their own future security played an important role (Mattox and Rachwald, 2001).

15. In 2007, after the Estonian government decided to move a Soviet war memorial from the center of Tallinn to its international military cemetery, Russians in both Estonia and the Russian Federation mounted attacks on the Estonian government and its embassy in Moscow. This was followed by the cutting off of Russian oil and coal deliveries, and a massive cyber-attack that virtually closed down the information technology sector of this former Soviet republic ("A Cyber-Riot", 2007; Dempsey, 2007).

16. The uncertainty in early 2009 concerning the renewal of permission for the US use of an airbase in Kyrgyzstan, including Russia's large new loan and the US financial counterproposals, evidenced the ongoing competition for influence in the region (Barry and Schwirtz, 2009).

17. The final Polish and Czech decisions to sign agreements for the placement of radar and anti-missile systems in their countries occurred soon after the Russian intervention in Georgia and were, no doubt, influenced by concerns about Russia's more assertive role in the region. See Kulish (2008).

18. The most comprehensive treatment of Russia's political use of energy supplies to neighboring states, as part of a policy in which economic tools have complemented more traditional military capabilities, can be found in Nygren (2007).

19. In the early weeks of his presidency, Barack Obama sent a letter to his Russian counterparts suggesting that he would not proceed with the deployment of a new missile defense system in Europe if the Russians would help by bringing pressure on Iran to stop the development of nuclear weapons (Baker, 2008).

References

Baker, Peter (2008) "Obama Offered Deal to Russian Secret Letter", *The New York Times*, March 2, 2009. http://www.nytimes.com/2009/03/03/washington/03prexy.html (accessed June 27, 2010).

Baker, Peter and Dan Bilefsky (2010) "Russia and U.S. Sign Nuclear Arms Reduction Pact", *The New York Times*, April 8. http://www.nytimes.com/2010/04/09/world/europe/09prexy.html (accessed June 27, 2010).

Barnard, Anne (2008) "Russians Confident That Nation is Back", *The New York Times*, August 15. "Russians Confident That Nation is Back" (accessed June 27, 2010).

Barry, Ellen and Michael Schwirtz (2009) "Kyrgyzstan Says it will Close US Base", *New York Times*, February 3. http://www.nytimes.com/2009/02/04/world/europe/04kyrgyz.html?partner=rss&emc=rss (accessed April 28, 2009).

Bhadrakumar, M.K. (2008) "Russia Takes Control of Turkmen (World?) Gas", *Asia Times*, July 30. http://www.atimes.com/atimes/Central_Asia/JG30Ag01.html (accessed June 27, 2010).

Blank, Stephen J. (2010) "Russia and Latin America: Motives and Consequences", paper presented to Challenges to Security in the Hemisphere Task Force, April 13. https://www6.miami.edu/hemispheric-policy/Blank_miamirussia_04–13-10.pdf (accessed June 27, 2010).

Boese, Wade (2008) "START Decision Put Off to 2009", Arms Control Association, December. http://www.armscontrol.org/act/2008_12/START (accessed February 2, 2009).

Bush, George H.W. (1990) "Toward a New World Order", a transcript of former President George Herbert Walker Bush's address to a joint session of Congress and the nation, September 11. National Archives. http://www.sweetliberty.org/issues/war/bushsr.htm (accessed June 27, 2010).

Cohen, Stephen F. (2000) *Failed Crusade: America and the Tragedy of Post-Communist Europe*, New York: W.W. Norton.

"A Cyber-Riot" (2007) *The Economist*, May 12, p. 55.

DeBardeleben, Joan (2009) "The Impact of EU Enlargement on the EU-Russian Relationship", in Roger E. Kanet (ed.), *A Resurgent Russia and the European Union*, Dordrecht: Republic of Letters Publishing, pp. 93–112.

Dempsey, Judy (2007) "EU and NATO Seek to Quell Russia-Estonia Spat", *International Herald Tribune*, May 3. http://www.iht.com/articles/2007/05/03/news/union.php (accessed June 27, 2010).

Ebel, Robert and Rajan Menon (eds) (2000) *Energy and Conflict in Central Asia and the Caucasus*, Lanham, MD/New York: Rowman & Littlefield Publishers.

"EU Urged to Reconsider Strategic Energy Goals" (2009) EurActiv.com, January 22. http://www.euractiv.com/en/energy/eu-urged-reconsider-strategic-energy-goals/article-178733 (accessed February 2, 2009).

The Foreign Policy Concept of the Russian Federation (2000) Approved by the President of the Russian Federation V. Putin, June 28. http://www.fas.org/nuke/guide/russia/doctrine/econcept.htm (accessed June 27, 2010).

"The Foreign Policy Concept of the Russian Federation: 31.07.2008" (2008) *MaximsNews, News Network for the United Nations and the International*

Community. http://www.maximsnews.com/news20080731russiaforeignpoli-cyconcept10807311601.htm (accessed June 27, 2010).

Gornostaev, Dmitrii (1998) "Novoe v staroi kontseptsii Primakova", *Nezavisimaia gazeta*, March 17. http://www.ng.ru/archive/ (accessed June 27, 2010).

Hahn, Melissa (2007) "Moscow Achieves Success with Kazakh Oil Deal", *Power and Interest News Report*, May 29.

Hancock, Kathleen J. (2007) "Russia: Great Power Image versus Economic Reality", *Asian Perspective*, vol. 31, no. 4, pp. 71–98.

Harding, Luke (2010) "Viktor Yanukovych Promises Ukraine will Embrace Russia", *Guardian.co.uk*, March 5. http://www.guardian.co.uk/world/2010/mar/05/ukraine-russia-relations-viktor-yanukovych (accessed June 27, 2010).

Hopmann, P. Terrence (2010) "Intergovernmental Organisations and Non-State Actors, Russia and Eurasia: The OSCE", in Maria Raquel Freire and Roger E. Kanet (eds), *Key Players and Regional Dynamics in Eurasia: The Return of the "Great Game"*, Houndmills, UK: Palgrave Macmillan, pp. 238–70.

"Intelligence Brief: Russia Reasserts Power with Thermobaric Weapons and Bomber Runs" (2007) *Power and Interest News Report*, November 8.

Kanet, Roger E. (2008) "A New U.S. Approach to Europe? The Transatlantic Relationship after Bush", *International Politics*, vol. 45, no. 3, 348–63.

Kanet, Roger E. (2010) "From Cooperation to Confrontation: Russia and the United States since 9/11", in Bertil Nygren, Bo Huldt, Patrik Ahlgren, Pekka Sivonen, and Susanna Huldt (eds), *Russia on our Minds. Russian Security Policy and Northern Europe, Strategic Yearbook 2008–2009*, Stockholm: National Defence College, pp. 61–88.

Kennan, George F. (1997) "NATO Expansion Would Be a Fateful Blunder", *The New York Times*, February 5. http://www.nytimes.com/1997/02/28/opinion/28iht-edlet.t_53.html?pagewanted=1?pagewanted=1 (accessed June 27, 2010).

Kramer, Andrew E. (2007) "Central Asia on Front Line in Energy Battle", *The New York Times*, December 20, pp. C1, C6.

Kramer, Andrew E. (2007) "Central Asia on Front Line in Energy" (accessed June 27, 2010).

Kulish, Nicholas (2008) "Georgian Crisis Brings Attitude Change to a Flush Poland", *The New York Times*, August 21. http://www.nytimes.com/2008/08/21/world/europe/21poland.html (accessed June 27, 2010).

Kuzio, Taras (2004) "Poland Plays Strategic Role in Ukraine's 'Orange Revolution' ", *Eurasia Daily Monitor*, The Jamestown Foundation, December 9. http://www.jamestown.org/single/?no_cache=1&tx_ttnews%5Btt_news%5D=27278 (accessed January 31, 2009).

Levy, Clifford J. (2008a) "Russia Adopts Blustery Tone Set by Envoy", *The New York Times*, August 27. http://www.nytimes.com/2008/08/28/world/europe/28moscow.html (accessed June 27, 2010).

Levy, Clifford J. (2008b) "Putin Suggests U.S. Provocation in Georgia Clash", *The New York Times*, August 29. http://www.nytimes.com/2008/08/29/world/europe/29putin.html?ref=europe (accessed June 27, 2010).

Levy, Clifford J. (2008c) "Russia and Venezuela Confirm Joint Military Exercises", *The New York Times*, September 8; "Russia and Venezuela Boost Ties", *BBC News*, September 26, 2008. http://news.bbc.co.uk/2/hi/europe/7636989.stm (accessed February 2).

Lobjakas, Ahto (2007) "EU Suspects Political Motives in Russia-Poland Meat Row", *Radio Free Europe Radio Liberty*, May 22. http://www.rferl.org/content/Article/1076640.html (accessed January 31, 2009).

Lucas, Edward (2008) *The New Cold War: Putin's Russia and the Threat to the West*, Houndmills, UK: Palgrave Macmillan.

MacAskill, Ewen and Ian Traynor (2009) "US scraps Plans for Missile Defence Shield in Central Europe", *Guardian.co.uk*, September 17. http://www.guardian.co.uk/world/2009/sep/17/missile-defence-shield-poland-obama (accessed June 27, 2010).

Mass, Warren (2009) "The Expanding War in Afghanistan", *New American*, January 28; "Russia Welcomes NATO's Willingness to resume Cooperation", *RIA Novosti*, March 5. http://en.rian.ru/world/20090305/120443337.html (accessed March 13, 2008).

Mattox, Gale A. and Arthur R. Rachwald (eds) (2001) *Enlarging NATO: The National Debates*, Boulder, CO: Lynne Rienner Publishers.

Medvedev, Dmitry (2008a) "Medvedev Sets Out Five Foreign Policy Principles in TV Interview", *Vesti TV*, 31 August *BBC Monitoring*, translated in *Johnson's Russia List*, JRL 2008–163, September 2, 2008.

Medvedev, Dmitry (2008b) "Medvedev Speech at the National Unity Day Reception", www.Kremlin.ru.

Medvedev, Dmitry (2008c) See, also, President Medvedev's State of the Nation address in November 2008. "Russian President Medvedev's First Annual Address to Parliament", *Rossiya TV*, November 5, 2008, translated in *Johnson's Russia List*, JRL 2008-#292, November 6, 2008.

Nygren, Bertil (2007) *The Rebuilding of Greater Russia: Putin's Foreign Policy Toward the CIW Countries*, Abingdon, UK: Routledge.

Petrovič, Heronim (2009) "Farce ums Gas: Russland, die Ukraine und die EU-Energiepolitik", *Osteuropa*, vol. 59, no. 1, pp. 19–35.

Primakov, Evgenyi (1996) "Rossiia ishchet novoe mesto v mire" (interview with E. Primakov), *Izvestiia*, March 6; see, also,

Putin, Vladimir (2005) President's speech to the Federal Assembly, April. BBC Monitoring. "Putin Focuses on Domestic Policy in State-of-Nation Address to Russian Parliament". Source: *RTR Russia TV*, Moscow, in Russian, 0800 GMT April 25, 2005; translated in *Johnson's Russia*, JRL 2005-#9130, April 25, 2005.

Putin, Vladimir (2007) See "Putin's Prepared Remarks at 43rd Munich Conference on Security Policy", delivered February 10. http://www.washingtonpost.com/wp-dyn/content/article/2007/02/12/AR2007021200555.html (accessed March 2, 2009).

"Russia Ready not to aim Iskander Missile Systems against USA" (2009) *Pravda.ru*, January 28. http://english.pravda.ru/russia/politics/28–01–2009/107026-russia_iskander_usa-0 (accessed February 2, 2009).

Schwirtz, Michael (2009) "Russia and Cuba Take Steps to Revive a Bond", *The New York Times*, January 31. http://www.nytimes.com/2009/01/31/world/europe/31castro.html (accessed June 27, 2010).

Shlapentokh, Vladimir (2008) "Behind the Five-Day War: The Ideological Backing of Putin's Regime", *Johnson's Russia List*, JRL 2008–195, October 23, 2008.

Taylor, Paul (2009) "Europeans Souring on Ukraine, Georgia", Reuters, January 14; reprinted in *Johnson's Russia List*, JRL 2009-#11, January 16, 2009.

Trenin, Dmitri V. (2007) *Getting Russia Right*, Washington; Carnegie Endowment.

Tsygankov, Andrei P. (2008) "Otnosheniia SShA s Rossiei v sovremennoi amerikanskoi politologii", *Mezhdunarodnye Protsessy*, vol. 6, no. 3. http://www.intertrends.ru/eighteenth/005.htm (accessed March 12, 2009).

Tsygankov, Andrei (2010) *Russia's Foreign Policy: Change and Continuity and National Identity*, Lanham, New York: Rowman and Littlefield Publishers, 2nd edn.

Wagstyl, Stefan (2007) "The Year Russia Flexed Its Diplomatic Muscle", *Financial Times*, December 17; reprinted in *Johnson's Russia List*, JRL 2007-#257, December 17.

Whitmore, Brian (2008) "Will Brussels Get Tough with Moscow?", *RadioFreeEurope/RadioLiberty*, July 13. http://www.rferl.org/articleprintview/1183415.html (accessed June 27, 2010).

Ziegler, Charles E. (2005) "Energy in the Caspian Basin and Central Asia",in Roger E. Kanet (ed.), *The New Security Environment. The Impact on Russia, Central and Eastern Europe*, Aldershot, UK/Burlington, VT: Ashgate Publishing, pp. 210–18.

11
Russia, NATO Enlargement, and "Regions of Privileged Interests"

John Berryman

Introduction

In the aftermath of the Georgian war, and five days after Moscow's unilateral recognition of the independence of the breakaway regions of South Ossetia and Abkhazia, on August 31, 2008 Russian President Dmitri Medvedev set out Russia's five foreign policy principles of the new world order. The last principle emphasized that, as for other great powers, "there are regions in which Russia has privileged interests" (President of Russia, 2008).

In line with long-established US policy, Moscow's claim was dismissed by both the outgoing Bush administration and the new Democratic administration. In his famous speech to the Munich Security Conference in February 2009, in which he sought to "press the reset button" to improve US–Russian relations, the new US Vice-President Joseph Biden rejected Russia's claims to a sphere of influence in the post-Soviet space and underlined the principle of international law that "sovereign states have a right to make their own decisions and choose their own alliances" (Biden, 2009). In his keynote speech to the New Economics School in Moscow in July 2009, US President Barack Obama likewise rejected "the 19th century view that we are destined to vie for spheres of influence and that great powers must forge competing blocs to balance one another" (Obama, 2009). In October 2009 Alexander Vershbow, the new US Assistant Secretary of Defense for International Security Affairs, and previously US Ambassador to Moscow, reaffirmed Obama's comments and demanded that "Russia's leaders *must accept* [italics added] that an enlarged NATO is not a threat to Russia" (Vershbow, 2009).

Vershbow's insistence that the alliance, by definition a grouping of states against an external challenge, did not represent some sort of hedge against Russian ambitions failed to convince. In February 2010 Russia's new Military Doctrine identified NATO's attempt to extend its military infrastructure eastward to Russia's borders and add new members as key national security concerns, and Medvedev restated his opposition to the "endless expansion" of NATO (McDermott, 2010; Reuters, 2010b). Alexei Bogaturov, Deputy Director of the Russian Academy of Sciences Institute of International Security Problems, emphasized: "Russia does not want to return to the policy of confrontation with the west but it also cannot concur with the systematic attempts of the US-NATO tandem to break through to a situation of absolute power supremacy over Russia" (Bogaturov, 2009).

This chapter examines Russia's efforts over almost two decades to maintain its influence in its "regions of privileged interests" in the face of NATO's post-Cold War eastward enlargement, and explores the "hard power" implications of the August 2008 Russia–Georgia War for NATO and Russia. Russia's response to the eastward enlargement of the "soft power" institution of the European Union (EU) and its European Neighborhood Policy (ENP) and Eastern Partnership (EaP) are examined elsewhere in this volume (see Chapter 12 by DeBardeleben in this volume and DeBardeleben, 2009).

Russia and NATO enlargement

With the termination in 1989 of the Soviet sphere of influence in Eastern Europe and the subsequent implosion of the USSR in 1991, fifteen Newly Independent States (NIS) emerged. The collapse of the Soviet empire transformed the balance of power in Eurasia. As Alexei Arbatov observed, "Falling apart, the Soviet empire lost its far and near bridgeheads, semi-colonies and full colonies, and even its core...started to break up into smaller pieces. In this sense, the Soviet Union went the way of the world's other empires" (Arbatov, 1993, p. 23).

However, looking back to the collapse of the Russian Empire in 1917, observers feared that, after a period of consolidation, like the Bolsheviks in 1920–1, Russia might embark on a "neo-imperialist" *reconquista* to reintegrate Transcaucasia and Ukraine (Cornell, 2007, pp. 17–23). This course of action was rejected. Although Russian military forces were actively deployed to stabilize regional conflicts in Moldova, Georgia, and Tajikistan, Moscow recognized that it was economically and militarily incapable of reconstructing an empire by means of a reintegration of the NIS within a "single military–strategic space." Instead, Yeltsin pursued "an enlightened post-imperial integrationist course" within the framework of the Commonwealth of Independent States (CIS). Perceiving itself to be a multinational state that had eschewed empire at home and abroad, like any great power Russia nonetheless felt that its historical links and interests in the post-Soviet space demanded assertive policies to preclude the extension of potentially hostile outside influence into its neighborhood (Lynch, 2000).

Apart from the constraints that Russia's much reduced position imposed on its relations with the NIS, for Moscow the wider international repercussions of the Soviet collapse were equally unwelcome. Russia was viewed in the West as a defeated nation, and earlier oral assurances to Gorbachev that, with the reunification of Germany in NATO, any further eastward enlargement of the alliance would be ruled out were dismissed. While the Clinton administration employed the rhetoric of "cooperative security," Moscow's diplomatic efforts to shape a post-Cold War pan-European security system, based on enlarged powers for the Conference on Security and Cooperation (CSCE), which included Russia as a full partner, were rebuffed. Although Gorbachev, and subsequently Russia, had withdrawn over one million troops and associated personnel from Central Europe and the Baltic states, and although much of Russia's western frontier now lay east of the new states of Belarus and Ukraine (approximating the position which the Russian Empire last enjoyed in the 17th century), Russia's still formidable military capability engendered deep insecurities within the region. Moscow was, therefore, advised by US Deputy Secretary of State, Strobe Talbott, to reject its "sphere of influence" policy and abandon its objections to NATO enlargement. In 1999 the Czech Republic, Hungary, and Poland entered the alliance (Berryman, 2009, pp. 167–9; Kober, 2008, p. 2). The hard-line Washington analyst, Peter Rodman, concluded: "The only potential great-power security problem in Central Europe is the lengthening shadow of Russian strength, and NATO has the job of counter-balancing it. Russia is a force of nature: all this is inevitable" (Lieven, 2007, p. 25). The first stage of NATO's exuberant post-Cold War enlargement was complete.

Immediately following Yeltsin's dramatic resignation on New Year's Eve 1999, Acting President Vladimir Putin made clear his determination to reverse Russia's trajectory of decline and humiliation, and avert the prospect of the disintegration of the Russian Federation (RF) (Putin, 1999). However, recognizing Russia's weak international position, in his first term President Putin initially pursued the "politics of the possible" and sought to avoid picking fights Russia could only lose – be it over the establishment of American bases in Central Asia, Washington's unilateral abrogation of the Anti-Ballistic Missile Treaty, or the decision of the 2002 NATO Prague Summit to proceed to the second stage of NATO's enlargement. In 2003, as the US invaded Iraq, Russia evacuated its forces from Bosnia and Kosovo, thus effectively ceding the western Balkans to the western sphere of influence. In 2004 the former Soviet Republics of Estonia, Latvia, and Lithuania, together with Romania, Bulgaria, Slovenia, and the Slovak Republic, entered NATO, pushing NATO's border 1,100 km (620 miles) to the east. In the same year, ten Central European states, plus Malta and Cyprus, were invited to join the EU. Only after 2004, in his second term as President, did Putin find himself able to take full advantage of the fivefold rise in oil and gas prices and begin the task of reestablishing Russia as a regional great power. At the centre of this new struggle for geopolitical advantage (which had now displaced the ideological contestation of the Cold War) was Putin's determination to resist what he saw to be the destabilizing challenge of US-inspired "color revolutions," road-tested in Georgia 2003–4 and Ukraine 2004–5, and to block any prospect of a third stage of NATO's eastward enlargement (Berryman, 2005; Kobrinskaya, 2005; Trenin, 2009, pp. 9–12).

In the debate over what some termed the "New Cold War" between a resurgent Russia and the West, NATO hawks and commentators with a Central European or Baltic focus continued to view Russia as a revisionist neo-imperial power, and urged the Kremlin to accept the "virtual inevitability" of NATO's further eastward enlargement (Brzezinski, 1997; Brzezinski and Sullivan, 1997; Bugajski, 2003–4; 2004; 2007; Karabeshkin and Spechler, 2007, pp. 350–2; Lucas, 2008).

Realist and constructivist scholars, by contrast, saw Putin's combative foreign policy to be "in the classic 19th-century European mold...[seeking]...to reassert Russia's traditional role as a great power and re-establish its dominant position in the former Soviet sphere" (Blackwill, 2008, p. 77; see also Gvosdev, 2007; Kotkin, 2008; Sakwa, 2008; Simes, 2007). Andrei Tsygankov and Dmitri Trenin argued that, in seeking to become a normal great power, Russia displayed no imperial desire to challenge the formal sovereignty of the NIS, but preferred to use "soft power" to assert its claims to be a regional hegemon. They pointed to the way Putin revitalized bilateral diplomatic and economic relations within the CIS, brusquely ended Soviet-era subsidies of oil and gas supplies to the NIS, and established new institutions of economic integration such as the Eurasian Economic Community and the Single Economic Space. Thanks to an enormous rise of seasonal migration into Russia's booming economy, the remittances provided a vital contribution to the economies of Tajikistan, Kyrgyzstan, Azerbaijan, Georgia, Armenia, and Moldova. Fostering the spread of Russia's culture, media, and language, the cultural predominance of Russia in Eurasia was becoming comparable to that of the US in the Americas (Trenin, 2008a; Tsygankov, 2005; 2006). It was argued that, as a modernizing multinational state, Russia was seeking to become "the regional hegemon, not the imperial overlord, of the southern tier" (Suny, 2007, p. 68).

Addressing the broader question of Russia's place in Europe, the American scholar, Charles Kupchan, noted that the incorporation of defeated France into the post-1815 Concert of Europe and the incorporation of defeated Germany into the post-World War II development of the European project and NATO enabled these powers to reemerge as cooperative rather than humiliated and resentful powers. By contrast, Kupchan pointed to the construction by Washington of an Atlantic order that still effectively treated Russia as an outsider. Anticipating President Medvedev's later European Security Initiative, Kupchan urged that a Euro-Atlantic security architecture be constructed that would incorporate NATO, the EU, and Russia (Kupchan, 1999; 2002; Kupchan and Kupchan, 1991). Henry Kissinger and George Shultz likewise recognized Russia to be an insecure new polity, seeking, "sometimes clumsily...acceptance as equals in a new international system rather than as losers of a cold war to whom terms could be dictated" (Kissinger and Shultz, 2008).

After World War II the US had identified Western Europe and the Asia Pacific as areas vital to US security interests, adding to this in the 1980s the Persian Gulf region of the Middle East. Many Russian observers (and some critical western commentators) now maintained that the US was playing a new post-Cold War "Great Game" in Eurasia, seeking to establish its influence in the Black Sea, Caspian Sea, and Central Asian regions, encircling Russia with a ring of US and NATO military bases with a view to securing access to strategic energy resources. Moreover, under the banner of establishing a democratic peace in Europe, the US was also seeking to consolidate its military and political leadership of the region through the expansion of NATO (Ivashov, 2007; Jackson, 2002; Karaganov, 2007; Leontiev, 2008; Migranyan, 1994; Pushkov, 2007; see also Cohen, 2006; Layne, 2006; Lieven, 2007). Alexei Bogaturov argued: "Any U.S. foreign policy document confirms that Washington includes the whole world in the sphere of its interests. The Americans have the conviction that no other country may have military or political interests in the western hemisphere, North America, and even in the Middle East...and they view Moscow's and Beijing's attempts to set up zones of exclusive interests as encroachments on their interests" (Bogaturov, 2005, p. 3).

Overlooking the fact that the Central European and Baltic states had themselves opted to join the alliance, Russia's best-known commentator on international relations, Sergei Karaganov, complained that the first two waves of NATO enlargement were "nothing more than the extension of its zone of influence and in the most sensitive military and political spheres ... coupled with a repeated refusal to recognize Russia's right to have its own zone of influence" (Karaganov, 2009b) He repeatedly asked Western experts, "Do you not understand that [a] large country with a great history will revive and will never agree to NATO expansion to its historical territories?" (Karaganov, 2009a). The opportunity for Russia to act arose in 2008.

The April 2008 NATO Bucharest "enlargement summit" offered immediate NATO membership to Croatia and Albania, and agreed that, in principle, Georgia and Ukraine would eventually become members of NATO. Nonetheless, in spite of the rash personal support of President Bush, Membership Action Plans (MAPs) were not offered to Ukraine and Georgia. In view of Ukraine's close 300-year historic, ethnic, cultural, and economic association with Russia, not to speak of its 1,576-km (979-mile) border with Russia, it was belatedly recognized by some NATO member states that, quite apart from the lack of public support within Ukraine for NATO membership, to offer NATO's Article V security guarantee to the forty-six million people of Ukraine in the face of Moscow's fierce opposition would pose unacceptable risks. Despite the higher level of support for NATO membership within Georgia (excluding the secessionist regions of South Ossetia and Abkhazia), some NATO member states felt that, in view of the unresolved conflicts between Tbilisi and these regions, Georgia also could not yet be accepted into NATO (Berryman, 2009, pp. 174–81).

The August 2008 Russia–Georgia war

Like most wars, the roots of the August Russia–Georgia War are tangled. In particular, Russia's war aims have attracted attention. For Ronald Asmus, one of the American officials responsible for the design and implementation of NATO's eastward enlargement, though the disagreements between Russia and Georgia over South Ossetia and Abkhazia were real ones, the August 2008 war was not fought over the future status of these two regions, but was, rather, the consequence of Georgia's desire to align itself with the West and Russia's determination to block such a development (Asmus, 2010a). The August conflict was a war over NATO enlargement – in effect a proxy war between Russia and the US (Charlemagne, 2009). Georgia, one of Russia's weakest neighbors, was effectively made an example by Moscow *pour encourager les autres* (Rondeli, 2010).

Andrei Illarionov, a former economic adviser to Putin and now a fierce critic of the Kremlin, argues that from 1991, determined to maintain its dominance in the South Caucasus, Russia sought to destabilize independent Georgia by manipulating its disputes with Abkhazia and South Ossetia. The deterioration in relations between Russia and Georgia following the "Rose Revolution" of 2003–4 saw the mass distribution of Russian passports to the population of the two regions, and, following Western recognition of Kosovo's declaration of independence in February 2008, Putin set in hand preparations for Russia's recognition of the independence of the two regions. In this view, the issue of Georgia's possible membership of NATO simply intensified Russia's pressure on Georgia, but did not cause it (Illarionov, 2009). Others have suggested that Moscow only abandoned its efforts to stay neutral in the disputes between Tbilisi and the two regions after what it saw to be Saakashvili's attempt to secure South Ossetia by force in August 2004 (Migranyan, 2004). Sergei Markedonov, Director of the Department of Interethnic Relations at the Institute of Political and Military Analysis, Moscow, and a respected Russian authority on the Caucasus, argues that Saakashvili's approach was to ensure that Georgia's responsibility for the inter-ethnic conflicts in the two regions was laid at Russia's door. The Georgia–Abkhazia and Georgia–Ossetia conflicts, therefore, effectively turned into Russian–Georgian conflicts. In Markedonov's view, Russia's swift response to the attack on South Ossetia by Georgian forces in August 2008 was governed by a concern that, should Russia stand aside, forces in the North Caucasus might seek to emulate Georgia's actions (in, for example, the conflict over North Ossetia's Prigorodny district) (Markedonov, 2007; 2008).

Wherever the historical truth may lie, against a backdrop of rising Russia–Georgia tensions initially focused on Abkhazia, on July 15, 2008 a major Russian military exercise, Kavkaz-2008, was mounted by the North Caucasus Military District (MD)[1]around Georgia's borders. It involved more than 8,000 troops, including ground forces, airborne troops, and units of the Russian Black Sea Fleet based in Sebastopol. Following the conclusion of the exercise on August 2, many of the troops were maintained on a state of alert, suggesting that Moscow was looking to draw a line in the sand to underline its determination to maintain its *droit de regard* in the region (Blandy, 2009; Cornell, 2008).[2]

Even if it can be argued that Saakashvili was deliberately provoked by Moscow and inadequately restrained by Washington, both the EU Tagliavini report on the war and Saakashvili's Georgian critics suggest that his rash authorization of an ill-prepared Georgian assault on Tskhinvali on August 7, 2008 precipitated a war he was bound to lose. Rather than securing control of South Ossetia by force, in a five-day war Georgia lost 20 per cent of its territory (*The Economist*, 2009; Lukyanov, 2009b).

Pavel Felgengauer, one of Russia's best-informed military analysts, has claimed that Russian war plans envisaged that the conflict with Georgia might, terrifyingly, escalate to involve the US and NATO (Felgengauer, 2009, p. 162). In the event, with America's military already overstretched by its commitments in Iraq and Afghanistan, there could be no thought of a US–NATO military response to Moscow's swift despatch of military forces across its borders, the first such occasion since the 1979 Soviet intervention in Afghanistan. Notwithstanding the temporary suspension of the NATO–Russia Council and calls for a "coalition against Russia's aggression" by a procession of Western leaders who flew into Tbilisi and Kiev, in the absence of any concerted Western action the August war represented a reverse for NATO, a sidelining of the EU and OSCE, and an unambiguous humiliation for the Bush administration, which had invested so much in Saakashvili's project to restore the territorial integrity of Georgia. As an American analyst quipped, "Indignation is not policy" (cited in Berryman, 2009, pp. 182–3; Blank, 2009; Cooley and Mitchell, 2009).

The Russia–Georgia war and European security

Implications of the war for NATO

Henry Kissinger had remarked of Britain's unexpected military response to the Argentinian occupation of Las Malvinas in 1982, "No great power retreats for ever" (Almond, 2008). Reflecting on the August 2008 war, Richard Betts observed: "None but the most ethnocentric idealists should have been surprised when Moscow had the temerity to start acting like a great power again" (Betts, 2009, p. 36). Moscow's decisive employment of "hard power" to defend its interests did not, therefore, so much change as expose the shift in the balance of power in Eurasia (Friedman, 2008).

The impact of the war on NATO's enlargement was decisive. Although the western Balkan states of Bosnia-Herzegovina, Montenegro and Macedonia are still on track to join NATO, and in principle the door remains open to membership of NATO by Georgia and Ukraine, the war effectively halted NATO's eastward enlargement – an objective that had eluded Moscow for almost two decades. Although joint training exercises with the US and NATO continue, for Georgia NATO membership is off the agenda, and Tbilisi has been advised to pursue the longer-term objective of membership of the EU (Reuters, 2010c; Rifkin, 2009, pp. 94–5). During his official visit to Moscow in March 2010, the newly-elected President of Ukraine, Viktor Yanukovych, indicated that there was no question of Ukraine joining NATO (although Ukraine may likewise seek to move closer to the EU) and that Russia's Black Sea Fleet will be permitted to use the historic Crimean port of Sebastopol beyond the current expiry of its lease in 2017 (Harding, 2010).

Apart from its impact on NATO enlargement, the "guns of August" came as a profound shock to the new NATO member states of Poland and the Baltic states. At the time of their entry into the alliance in 1999 and 2004, to reassure Moscow, no contingency plans to provide military assistance to these new member states were developed, nor were land drills held on their territory. Radek Sikorski, shortly to become Poland's Foreign Minister, complained in the spring of 2007: "Our American colleagues say not to worry, that NATO will protect us, but rhetorical assurances are too easy ... Poland is haunted by the memory of fighting Hitler alone in 1939 while our allies stood by. Never again will we allow ourselves to be egged on by paper guarantees not backed by practical means of delivery" (Sikorski, 2007). Concerned that NATO's quest for new expeditionary out-of-area capabilities for deployment in Afghanistan had allowed the alliance to lose sight of its core Article V territorial defence obligations, in the aftermath of the war Poland and the Baltic states now demanded changes in NATO planning and deployments to provide a greater measure of strategic reassurance (Berryman, 2009, pp. 169, 171, 183).

Despite the less than enthusiastic response of some of NATO's member states (notably Germany and Italy), contingency plans were developed, and in March 2010 joint exercises by US, French, Polish, and Lithuanian aircraft were conducted over Lithuania. In June 2010 a joint ten-day amphibious exercise by up to 500 US marines and Estonian forces approximately 100 km from the Russian border in northern Estonia is likely to generate a sharp reaction from Moscow, while in the autumn a joint military exercise in Latvia will involve 2,000 troops from Latvia,

Lithuania, Estonia, and the US. Although small, it will be the largest such exercise in the area since the three Baltic states joined NATO in 2004 (*The Economist*, 2010b; Ganin, 2010). Additionally, a *Patriot* missile battery will be deployed in Poland close to the border with Russia's exclave of Kaliningrad (Reuters, 2010a).

Since President Medvedev's European Security Initiative has, to date, attracted little support, suggestions of NATO membership for Russia have once more been floated (Emerson, 2010). They have attracted little support in Western capitals. Moreover, pursuing its course as an independent great power, for the moment Russia displays no interest in joining what it perceives to be an anti-Russian NATO. As Dmitri Rogozin, Russia's nationalist envoy to NATO, has boasted, "Great powers do not join coalitions, they create coalitions. Russia considers itself a great power" (Pop, 2009). For the present, therefore, Russia remains outside Europe's primary security organization, and the Kremlin's hopes of constructing a "Europe without dividing lines," fulfilling Gorbachev's vision of a "Common European Home," have yet to be realized (Lukyanov, 2009a).

Implications of the war for Russia

To rectify deficiencies in its C4ISR (command, control, communications, computers, intelligence, surveillance, and reconnaissance) systems exposed by the war, in 2009 Russia purchased Israeli-made spy drones – the first official Russian procurement of Western weapons systems since 1945 (Felgengauer, 2009, p. 168). Moscow has also agreed to a contract with Paris to purchase a 21,300-ton *Mistral*-class amphibious assault vessel and jointly build three more under license in Russian shipyards. Admiral Vladimir Vysotsky, Head of the Russian Navy, claimed that with such ships his forces could have accomplished their mission in the Black Sea in 2008 in forty minutes instead of twenty-six hours (*The Economist*, 2010a). If the contract is fulfilled, it will represent the biggest-ever sale of military hardware to Russia by a NATO country. Since the availability of such warships will undoubtedly improve Russia's capacity to project its hard power within the Black Sea and Baltic Sea regions, the deal has understandably raised concerns within Georgia, the US, and France's Baltic and Black Sea NATO allies (AP, 2010; Davies, 2010).

The international consequences of Moscow's recognition of the independence of South Ossetia and Abkhazia look uncertain. Recognized by only Russia, Nicaragua, Venezuela, and the Pacific island of Nauru, they have joined the ranks of the partially recognized statelets such as Kosovo, the Turkish Republic of North Cyprus, and Taiwan. While international talks on the future of South Ossetia and Abkhazia proceed at Geneva, the OSCE mission and UNOMIG have been withdrawn. Much as Kosovo remains effectively an EU protectorate, South Ossetia and Abkhazia look likely to remain Russian protectorates for some time to come. Russian bases capable of housing 4,000 military personnel have been completed at Dzhavy and Tskinvali in South Ossetia, and a base in Abkhazia will accommodate at least 3,000 Russian troops and border guards. The Soviet-era Bombora air and military base outside the Abkhaz port of Gudauta is also to be upgraded, and the naval facilities at the Abkhaz port of Ochamchire are being developed (Blandy, 2009; Bloomberg, 2010; Mitchell, 2009; *The Moscow Times*, 2010).

What of the wider international implications of the war for Russia and its neighbors? It is claimed that the war and Russia's identification of its "regions of privileged interests" signaled that the South Caucasus and the rest of the CIS remained part of Russia's sphere of influence, in which the rights of sovereign nations to run their affairs would be subordinated to Russian control (Cornell, 2008, pp. 313). Closer examination suggests that this claim is somewhat exaggerated.

First, much to Moscow's acute embarrassment, none of the CIS member states, including Russia's closest allies in the Collective Security Treaty Organization (CSTO), supported Moscow's hurried recognition of the independence of South Ossetia and Abkhazia. It has been suggested that their decisions reflected neither disapproval of the Russian action nor any sympathy for Georgia and its leadership, but a determination to demonstrate that they were "not Russia's clients but sovereign states" (Trenin, 2009, p. 14). Moreover, since several of the former Soviet republics have large ethnic Russian minorities and possess Russian territories, any such recognition of the regions could additionally have threatened their own sovereignty (Aslund, 2009).

Second, despite Putin's and Medvedev's hatred of Saakashvili, no attempt was made to effect regime change and subordinate sovereign Georgia to Russian control.

Third, in response to the suggestion that Russia has failed to shed its imperial instincts, Dmitri Trenin argues that "Russia does not want to restore the Soviet Union or the tsarist empire. It wants, however, to create a region in which its interests would have precedence over those of any other country"... "the Kremlin calls the CIS its sphere of interests to avoid the discrediting description of spheres of influence. This phrase is not merely a play on words, but a much looser, less exclusive concept. To illustrate, Moscow wants to be surrounded by a string of Finlands, not a bunch of Warsaw Pact states" (Trenin, 2008b, pp. 119–20).

Although membership of NATO has been under discreet consideration in Helsinki for some time, with a 1,300-km (623-mile) border with the RF, the EU member state of Finland has historically enjoyed excellent relations with Russia, and the Finnish Prime Minister, Matti Vanhanen, has stated that the main lesson of the war is the need for closer ties with Russia (Giles and Eskola, 2009; *The Moscow Times*, 2009). It may be that, in the "breathing space" created by the August 2008 war, a new "Finlandization" (membership of the EU but not NATO) may be a way forward for Ukraine and Georgia, both of which, like Finland, have significant borders with Russia (Asmus, 2010b).

There remains the more general question of the "double standard" implicit in Washington's demand that sovereign states within Russia's neighborhood should have the unconstrained freedom to choose their own alliances. As most realist scholars accept, in the rough world of international politics all great powers seek to exercise dominant influence in their own neighborhoods and are interested in denying access to potential rivals. A variety of instruments may be employed – be it buffer zones, spheres of influence, spheres of interest, or, where deemed unavoidable, armed intervention. As Charles Kupchan has remarked, "the United States would hardly sit by idly if Russia formed an alliance with Mexico and Canada and started building military installations along the U.S. border" (Kupchan, 2002, p. 14).

However, as the comments of Biden, Obama, and Vershbow suggest, there is no sign whatsoever that the Obama administration will abandon this propensity to lecture Moscow. Sergei Markedonov and others will therefore likely maintain their view that Russia is doing nothing more than reasserting its great power prerogatives in its neighborhood in a fashion not dissimilar to the US role in Latin America, the Israeli role in the Middle East, Australia's in Oceania, and France's in its former colonies in Africa (Markedenov, 2009. On China's spheres of influence see Munro, 1994). With the persistence of such deeply entrenched differences in the strategic perspectives and mind-sets of Moscow and Washington, it seems likely that Russian–US differences over the former Soviet borderlands will continue severely restricting the "reset" in US–Russian relations.

Notes

1. The territory of the Russian Federation is divided into six military–administrative units based on the military districts established in the Soviet

period; these include four districts in European Russia (Moscow, Leningrad, North-Caucasian, and Volga-Ural) ("Russian Military Districts", 2009).
2. It was, in the Soviet parlance, "not accidental" that this author was in Sebastopol in August 2008.

References

Almond, Mark (2008) "Plucky little Georgia? No, the cold war reading won't wash", *The Guardian*, August 8.

AP (2010) "Georgia Puzzled by France's Proposed Mistral Sale", *The Moscow Times*, March 4. http://www.themoscowtimes.com/news/article/georgia-puzzled-by-frances-proposed-mistral-sale/400872.html (accessed June 30, 2010).

Arbatov, Aleksei (1993) "Empire or great power?", *New Times*, no. 1, May 20, pp. 22–4.

Aslund, Anders (2009) "The Leader of the CIS is Lonely and Weak", *The Moscow Times*, October 28. http://www.themoscowtimes.com/opinion/article/the-leader-of-the-cis-is-lonely-and-weak/388309.html (accessed June 30, 2010).

Asmus, Ronald (2010a) *A Little War That Changed the World: Georgia, Russia and the Future of the West*, Basingstoke: Palgrave Macmillan.

Asmus, Ronald (2010b) "Finlandization of Georgia and Ukraine", *The Moscow Times*, March 3. http://www.themoscowtimes.com/opinion/article/finlandization-of-georgia-and-ukraine/400808.html (accessed June 30, 2010).

Berryman, John (2005) "Putin's International Security Priorities", in Roger E. Kanet (ed.), *The New Security Environment: Russia, Central and Eastern Europe*, Aldershot: Ashgate, pp. 31–52.

Berryman, John (2009) "Russia, NATO Enlargement, and the New 'Lands in Between'", in Roger E. Kanet (ed.), *A Resurgent Russia and the West: The European Union, NATO and Beyond*, Dordrecht, The Netherlands: Republic of Letters Publishing, pp. 163–88.

Betts, Richard K (2009) "The Three Faces of NATO", *The National Interest*, no. 100, March/April, pp. 31–8.

Biden, Joseph (2009) Remarks by Vice President Biden at the 45th Munich Security Conference, February 7, 2009. http://www.whitehouse.gov/the_press_office/RemarksbyVicePresidentBidenat45thMunichConferenceonSecurityPolicy/ (accessed June 30, 2010).

Blackwill, Robert D. (2008) "The Three Rs: Rivalry, Russia, and 'Ran'", *The National Interest*, no. 93, January/February, pp. 68–73.

Blandy, Charles W. (2009) *Provocation, Deception, Entrapment: The Russo-Georgian Five Day War*, March, Caucasus Series 09/01. Shrivenham: Advanced Research and Assessment Branch, Defence Academy of the United Kingdom. http://www.da.mod.uk/colleges/arag/document-listings/caucasus/09(02)CWB.pdf/view (accessed June 30, 2010).

Blank, Stephen (2009) "From Neglect to Duress: The West and the Georgian Crisis before the 2008 War", in Svante E. Cornell and S. Frederick Starr (eds), *The Guns of August 2008: Russia's War in Georgia*, Armonk, New York and London: M. E. Sharpe, pp. 104–21.

Bloomberg (2010) "Bases Go Up in Rebel Regions", *The Moscow Times*, February 26. http://www.themoscowtimes.com/news/article/bases-go-up-in-rebel-regions/400459.html (accessed June 30, 2010).

Bogaturov, Alexei (2005) "The Sources of American Conduct", *Russia in Global Affairs*, no. 1, January–March. http://eng.globalaffairs.ru/printver/821.html (accessed June 30, 2010).

Bogaturov, Alexei (2009) "Khochesh otkrytoi sistemy – stroy zakrytyi blok? [You want an open system – to build a closed block?]", *Nezavisimaya Gazeta*, June 15. http://www.ng.ru/courier/2009–06–15/9_block.html (accessed June 30, 2010).

Brzezinski, Zbigniew (1997) *The Grand Chessboard: American Primacy and its Geostrategic Imperatives*, New York: Basic Books.

Brzezinski, Zbigniew and Paige Sullivan (eds) (1997) *Russia and the Commonwealth of Independent States: Documents, Data, and Analysis*, Armonk, New York and London: M. E. Sharpe.

Bugajski, Janusz (2003–4) "Russia's New Europe", *The National Interest*, Winter, pp. 84–91.

Bugajski, Janusz (2004) *Cold Peace: Russia's New Imperialism*, Washington, DC: Praeger for the Centre for Strategic and International Studies.

Bugajski, Janusz (2007) *The Eastern Dimension of America's Allies*, October. Carlisle, PA: Strategic Studies Institute, US Army War College. http://www.strategicstudiesinstitute.army.mil/pubs/display.cfm?PubID=813 (accessed June 30, 2010).

Charlemagne (2009) "A new balance in Europe", *The Economist*, November 21, p. 52.

Cohen, Stephen F. (2006) "The New American Cold War", *The Nation*, July 10.

Cooley, Alexander and Lincoln A. Mitchell (2009) "No Way to Treat Our Friends: Re-casting Recent U.S.-Georgian Relations", *The Washington Quarterly*, vol. 32, no. 1, January, pp. 27–41.

Cornell, Svante E. (2007) *Georgia After the Rose Revolution: Geopolitical Predicament and Implications for U.S. Policy*, February. Carlisle, PA: Strategic Studies Institute, US Army War College. http://www.strategicstudiesinstitute.army.mil/pubs/display.cfm?pubID=757 (accessed June 30, 2010).

Cornell, Svante E. (2008) "War in Georgia, Jitters All Round", *Current History*, vol. 107, no. 711, October, pp. 307–14.

Davies, Lizzy (2010) "Sarkozy angers allies with ship sales to Russia", *The Guardian*, March 2.

DeBardeleben, Joan (2009) "The Impact of EU Enlargement on the EU-Russia Relationship", in Roger E. Kanet (ed.), *A Resurgent Russia and the West: The European Union, NATO and Beyond*, Dordrecht, The Netherlands: Republic of Letters Publishing, pp. 93–112.

The Economist (2009) "The blame game", October 3, pp. 48–9.

The Economist (2010a) "The cruel sea", February 13, p. 40.

The Economist (2010b) "The next salvo", 20 February, p. 40.

Emerson, Michael (2010) "Russia in Europe and the West", *CEPS European Neighbourhood Watch*, Issue no. 58, March 31. http://www.ceps.eu/panel6 (accessed June 30, 2010).

Felgengauer, Pavel (2009) "After August 7: The Escalation of the Russia-Georgia War", in Svante E. Cornell and S. Frederick Starr (eds), *The Guns of August*

2008: Russia's War in Georgia, Armonk, New York and London: M. E. Sharpe, pp. 162–80.

Friedman, George (2008) "The Russo-Georgian War and the Balance of Power", August 12. http://www.stratfor.com/print/121845 (accessed June 30, 2010).

Ganin, Konstantin (2010) "U Rossii reshili poigrat na manyovrakh: NATO nachinayet seriyu voyennykh uchenyi ryadom s eyo granitsami [They've Decided to have Manoeuvres on Russia's Doorstep: NATO Begins a Series of Military Exercises Near Its Borders]", *Kommersant*, March 4. http://www.kommersant.ru/doc.aspx?DocsID=1331423 (accessed June 30, 2010).

Giles, Keir and Susanna Eskola (2009) *Waking the Neighbour- Finland, NATO and Russia*, Special Series 09/14, November. Shrivenham: Advanced Research and Assessment Branch, Defence Academy of the United Kingdom. http://www.finlandnato.org/public/download.aspx?ID=49566&GUID=%7B7CB8A086-C30A-4246-8355-411A3BDE2FE7%7D (accessed June 30, 2010).

Gvosdev, Nikolas (2007) "Parting with Illusions: Developing a Realistic Approach to Relations with Russia", *Policy Analysis*, no. 611, February 29. http://www.cato.org/pub_display.php?pub_id=9229 (accessed June 30, 2010).

Harding, Luke (2010) "Ukraine leader promises better ties with Russia", *The Guardian*, March 6.

Illarionov, Andrei (2009) "The Russian Leadership's Preparation for War, 1999–2008", in Svante E. Cornell and S. Frederick Starr (eds), *The Guns of August 2008: Russia's War in Georgia*, Armonk, New York and London: M. E. Sharpe, pp. 49–84.

Ivashov, Colonel-General Leonid G. (2007) "Russia's Geopolitical Horizons", *International Affairs* (Moscow), vol. 53, no. 4, pp. 74–81.

Jackson, William D. (2002) "Encircled Again: Russia's Military Assesses Threats in the Post-Soviet World", *Political Science Quarterly*, vol. 117, no. 3, Autumn, pp. 373–400.

Karabeshkin, Leonid and Dina R. Spechler (2007) "EU and NATO Enlargement: Russia's Expectations, Responses and Options for the Future", *European Security*, vol. 16, nos. 3–4, September–December, pp. 307–28.

Karaganov, Sergei (2007) "A new epoch of confrontation", *Russia in Global Affairs*, no. 4, December. http://eng.globalaffairs.ru/printver/1148.html (accessed June 30, 2010).

Karaganov, Sergei (2009a) "The Magic Numbers of 2009", *Russia in Global Affairs*, no. 2, April–June. http://eng.globalaffairs.ru/printver/1279.html (accessed June 30, 2010).

Karaganov, Sergei (2009b) "Russia will save the west", *The Moscow Times*, December 29. http://www.themoscowtimes.com/opinion/article/russia-will-save-the-west/396905.html (accessed June 30, 2010).

Kissinger, Henry A. and George P. Shultz (2008) "Building on Common Ground With Russia", *The International Herald Tribune*, October 1.

Kober, Stanley (2008) "Cracks in the Foundations: NATO's New Troubles", *Policy Analysis*, no. 608, January 15, pp. 1–15. http://www.cato.org/pub_display.php?pub_id=8875 (accessed June 30, 2010).

Kobrinskaya, Irina (2005) "The CIS in Russian Foreign Policy: Causes and Effect", in Hazel Smith (ed.), *Russia and Its Foreign Policy: Influence, Interests and Issues*, Saarijarvi: Kikimora Publications for the Aleksanteri Institute, pp. 75–92.

Kotkin, Stephen (2008) "Myths of the new cold war", *Prospect*, Issue 145, April.

Kupchan, Charles (1999) "Turning Adversity into Advantage: Russia in NATO", in Mathias Jopp and Hanna Ojanen (eds), *European Security Integration: Implications for Non-Alignment and Alliance*, Helsinki: Ulkopoliitinen instituuti & Institut fur Europaische Politik and WEU Institute for Security Studies, pp. 215–35.

Kupchan, Charles (2002) *The End of the American Era: U.S. Foreign Policy and the Geopolitics of the Twenty-First Century*, New York: Alfred A. Knopf, pp. 255–74.

Kupchan, Charles and Clifford Kupchan (1991) "Concerts, Collective Security, and the Future of Europe", *International Security*, vol. 16, no. 1, Summer, pp. 114–61.

Layne, Christopher (2006) *The Peace of Illusions: American Grand Strategy from 1940 to the Present*, Ithaca and London: Cornell University Press.

Leontiev, Mikhail (2008) *Bolshaya Igra* [The Great Game], Moskva: Izdatelstvo.

Lieven, Anatol (2007) "The Mutual Responsibility and Irresponsibility of the West and Russia', *International Affairs* (Moscow), vol. 53, no. 4, pp. 21–33.

Lucas, Edward (2008) *The New Cold War: How the Kremlin Menaces both Russia and the West*, London: Bloomsbury.

Lukyanov, Fyodor (2009a) "Rethinking Security in 'Greater Europe' ", *Russia in Global Affairs*, no. 3, July–September. http://eng.globalaffairs.ru/ numbers/28/1298.html (accessed June 30, 2010).

Lukyanov, Fyodor (2009b) "Russia's Georgia Problem One Year On", *Russia in Global Affairs*, no. 4, October–December. http://eng.globalaffairs.ru/ engsmi/0/1307.html (accessed June 30, 2010).

Lynch, Dov (2000) *Russian Peacekeeping Strategies in the CIS: The Cases of Moldova, Georgia and Tajikistan*, Basingstoke: Macmillan, in association with the Royal Institute of International Affairs.

McDermott, Roger (2010) "New Russian Military Doctrine Opposes NATO Enlargement", *Eurasia Daily Monitor*, vol. 7, issue 27, February 9. http://www.jamestown.org/single/?no_cache=1&tx_ttnews%5Btt_ news%5D=36023&tx_ttnews%5BpackPid%50=7&cHash=4835e7096f (accessed June 30, 2010).

Markedonov, Sergei (2007) "The Paradoxes of Russia's Georgia Policy", *Russia in Global Affairs*, no. 2, April–June. http://eng.globalaffairs.ru/printver/1116. html (accessed June 30, 2010).

Markedonov, Sergei (2008) "Regional Conflicts Reloaded?", *Russia in Global Affairs*, no. 4, October–December. http://www.eng.globalaffairs.ru/ printver/1247.html (accessed June 30, 2010).

Markedonov, Sergei (2009) "Squabbles over the post-Soviet space", *Open Democracy*, April 20. http://www.opendemocracy.net/print/47744 (accessed June 30, 2010).

Migranyan, Andranik (1994) "Unequal partnership", *The New York Times*, June 23.

Migranyan, Andranik (2004) "Saakashvili dobivayetssya nezavisimosti Abkhazii i Yuzhnoy Osetii [Saakashvili is trying to secure independence for Abkhazia and South Ossetia]", *Izvestiya*, September 17. http://www.izvestia. ru/comment/article405381/ (accessed June 30, 2010).

Mitchell, Lincoln A. (2009) "Holding pattern: Russia-Georgia relations remain tense", *Jane's Intelligence Review*, vol. 21, no. 10, October, pp. 26–9.

The Moscow Times (2009) "Finland Sees Lesson in Russia-Georgia War", October 12. http://www.themoscowtimes.com/news/article/finland-sees-lesson-in-russia-georgia-war/387206.html (accessed June 30, 2010).

The Moscow Times (2010) "Russia Signs Deal to Build Military Base in Abkhazia", February 18. http://www.themoscowtimes.com/news/article/russia-signs-deal-to-build-military-base-in-abkhazia/400019.html (accessed June 30, 2010).

Munro, Ross H. (1994) "China's Waxing Spheres of Influence", *Orbis*, vol. 38, no. 4, Fall, pp. 585–606.

Obama, Barak (2009) Remarks by the President at the New Economic School Graduation, Moscow, July 7, 2009. http://www.whitehouse.gov/the_press_office/Remarks-By-The-President-At-The-New-Economic-School-Graduation (accessed June 30, 2010).

Pop, Valentin (2009) "Russia does not rule out future NATO membership", *EU Observer*, April 1. http://euobserver.com/9/27890?print=1 (accessed June 30, 2010).

President of Russia (2008) Interview given by President Dmitry Medvedev to Television Channels Channel One, Rossia, NTV. http://www.un.int/russia/new/MainRoot/docs/warfare/statement310808en.htm (accessed June 30, 2010).

Pushkov, Alexei (2007) "Missed Connections", *The National Interest*, no. 89, May–June, pp. 74–81.

Putin, Vladimir Vladimirovich (1999) "Rossiya na rubezhe tysiacheletii [Russia at the turn of the millennium]", *Nezavisimaya Gazeta*, December 30. http://www.ng.ru/politics/1999-12-30/4_millenium.html (accessed June 30, 2010).

Reuters (2010a) "Military Denies Plans to Boost Baltic Fleet over Patriot Deployment", *The Moscow Times*, January 22. http://www.themoscowtimes.com/print/article/military-denies-plans-to-boost-baltic-fleet-over-patriot-deployment/397960.html (accessed June 30, 2010).

Reuters (2010b) "Medvedev Objects to 'Endless' NATO Expansion", *The Moscow Times*, February 26. http://www.themoscowtimes.com/news/article/medvedev-objects-to-endless-nato-expansion/400438.html (accessed June 30, 2010).

Reuters (2010c) "US Warship Conducts Joint Training with Georgia", *The Moscow Times*, March 3. http://www.themoscowtimes.com/news/article/us-warship-conducts-joint-training-with-georgia/400788.html (accessed June 30, 2010).

Rifkin, Malcolm (2009) "The right path for Georgia", in Adam Hug (ed.), *Spotlight on Georgia*, London: The Foreign Policy Centre, pp. 92–8. http://fpc.org.uk/fsblob/1079.pdf (accessed June 30, 2010).

Rondeli, Alexander (2010) "The return of realpolitik: a view from Georgia", *Open Democracy*, February 18. http://www.opendemocracy.net/print/50360

"Russian Military Districts" (2009) http://www.globalsecurity.org/military/world/russia/mo-md.htm (accessed June 30, 2010).

Sakwa, Richard (2008) "New Cold War or twenty years crisis? Russia and international politics", *International Affairs*, vol. 84, no. 2, March, pp. 241–67.

Sikorski, Radek (2007) "Don't Take Poland for Granted", *The Washington Post*, March 21.

Simes, Dmitri (2007) "Losing Russia", *Foreign Affairs*, vol. 86, no. 6, November/December, pp. 36–52.

Suny, Ronald (2007) "Living in the Hood: Russia, Empire, and Old and New Neighbours", in Robert Legvold (ed.), *Russian Foreign Policy in the Twenty-First Century and the Shadow of the Past*, New York: Columbia University Press, pp. 35–76.

Trenin, Dmitri (2008a) "Pragmatic power: Russia's assertive foreign power", *Jane's Intelligence Review*, vol. 20, no. 1, January, pp. 32–35.

Trenin, Dmitri (2008b) "A Less Ideological America", *The Washington Quarterly*, vol. 31, no. 4, Autumn, pp. 117–23.

Trenin, Dmitri (2009) "Russia's Spheres of Interest, not Influence", *The Washington Quarterly*, vol. 32, no. 4, October, pp. 3–22.

Tsygankov, Andrei P. (2005) "Vladimir Putin's vision of Russia as a normal great power", *Post-Soviet Affairs*, vol. 21, no. 2, pp. 132–58.

Tsygankov, Andrei P. (2006) "If Not by Tanks, then by Banks? The Role of Soft Power in Putin's Foreign Policy", *Europe-Asia Studies*, vol. 58, no. 7, November, pp. 1079–99.

Vershbow, Alexander (2009) "Crafting the new Strategic Concept: Ambitions, Resources and Partnerships for a 21st century Alliance", October 22. http://nato.usmission.gov/Texts/Vershbow10222009.asp (accessed June 30, 2010).

12
Revising the EU's European Neighborhood Policy: The Eastern Partnership and Russia

Joan DeBardeleben

As is well known, the European Union (EU) initially intended to include Russia in its European Neighborhood Policy (ENP). Russia's rejection of this approach and insistence on a more equal "strategic partnership" set the EU's eastern policy on a two-track mode.[1] In other words, through the ENP one set of policies and priorities was established for non-member countries constituting the western (i.e., non-Central Asian) Soviet successor states, along with countries in the Mediterranean region and North Africa. In parallel, the EU continued to develop its relationship with Russia based on the Partnership and Cooperation Agreement (PCA), which went into effect in December 1997, augmented by the Four Common Spaces (Economic Space, Space of Freedom, Security and Justice, Space of External Security, Space of Research and Education) and the associated Roadmaps (see Commission, 2010). Since its initiation in 2004 ENP has undergone some revisions, particularly based on an assessment in late 2006, but most recently with the launch of the Eastern Partnership (EaP) policy in May 2009, directed at six of the European ENP countries (Azerbaijan, Armenia, Belarus, Georgia, Moldova, and Ukraine). At the same time, in the face of fits, delays, and starts, the EU–Russia relationship has continued on a different track, now at the stage of negotiating a new EU–Russia agreement to replace the 1997 PCA.

This chapter explores the implications of this two-track policy, particularly as it impacts the EU–Russian relationship. The thesis put forward is that Russia's initial rejection of ENP (which was in part a function of the way the policy was formulated) has set in place an unintended trajectory that is likely to have longer-term impacts on the nature of

EU–Russian relations. One might conceive of this as a form of "path dependence" or as a form of institutional bias that makes certain outcomes more likely than others. The upshot of the analysis is to see the formation of the two-track trajectory as both reflecting preexisting tensions in the EU–Russian relationship and also setting a direction that has the potential to "freeze" this trajectory into the institutional and normative framework of the EU's external policy.

Placing all the European non-EU Soviet successor states in one basket (along with a group of non-European countries), ENP had several features that made it difficult for Russia to accede to when it was initiated after the May 2004 enlargement of the EU, suggesting that the EU may have misunderstood the Russian agenda in proposing its inclusion in the policy. First, the initiative was formulated unilaterally by the EU, so that Russia was an object of the policy rather than coauthor of a joint strategy to stabilize the EU's new eastern frontier. This contrasts with another earlier initiative intended to deal with regional issues, the Northern Dimension, which, although initiated by the Nordic states (in particular Finland), included Russia from an early stage as an equal partner. Second, the bilateral nature of the policy did not suggest a "regional" approach that Russia would help to shape in the future. Third, Russia was unhappy about being put in the same category as countries clearly having less power and status in the region.

An alternative approach, the creation of a regional and multilateral framework for the stabilization and development of non-EU Eastern Europe, drafted in consultation with Russia and other countries, was apparently not seriously considered or was rejected by the EU, and likely would have been unacceptable to several new member states on the front line of the EU–Russian border (Poland and the Baltic states). For one thing, such an approach could be read as making countries such as Ukraine and Moldova the object of the joint machinations of the major EU countries and Russia, which would be the dominant actors in such a process. In addition, it could be viewed as sacrificing the sovereign rights of these and other post-Soviet countries to chart their own (hopefully democratic and market-oriented) political destinies. Second, once the ENP had been announced, it would have been difficult to retract or reframe it in the face of the Russian rejection. At the outset of the ENP both the Russian and EU positions looked reasonable, reflecting differing understandings of their own interests and of their normative priorities.

Three factors have helped to cement the two-track character of the EU's eastern policy over time. The first includes institutional and political realities affecting EU policy-making, particularly the addition of the Central and East European countries as new member states, which added strong advocates for the two-track approach, in the interests of closer EU relations with Ukraine, Moldova, and Belarus. A second factor relates to internal problems of the ENP itself, which are discussed below. Finally, exacerbated tensions between the EU and Russia over a variety of issues, including energy transit through Ukraine, the Georgian conflict, and continuing concerns about human rights violations in Russia, made a rethinking of the bifurcated approach unlikely. The result has been movement toward perception on the Russian side of a "zero-sum" game between the EU and Russia in the area of Russia's near abroad, and an unstated viewpoint within the EU that the Russian factor can be "factored out" as a primary consideration in formulating policies towards the EU's other eastern neighbors. In other words, the two-track policy seems increasingly to imply segmentation between the EU's ENP eastern policy and its Russian policy. This mind frame, in turn, makes certain policy decisions in both spheres more likely than others, setting in place a self-reinforcing dynamic.

Belarus represents an ambiguous case in this two-track approach. Initially identified by the EU as being, in principle, covered by the ENP, Belarus was, de facto, not eligible for participation in ENP programs because of EU objections to human rights and authoritarian political practices. On the contrary, economic sanctions and restrictions on the travel of Belarusian leaders to the EU were introduced; EU support has been directed primarily at promoting civil society and democratic forces in Belarus. Announcement of Belarus' inclusion in the Eastern Partnership in early 2009 and the EU's lifting of sanctions evoked particular objections from Russia. Since Belarus' inclusion would contradict many of the principles underlying the ENP (discussed below), the decision likely appeared to Russia to be political – an unabashed effort on the part of the EU to extend its influence into Russia's sphere of influence.

Contrasting approaches: the ENP and the EU-Russia strategic partnership

A fundamental starting point for this analysis is to delineate the similarities and distinctions between the way in which the EU relates to neighbors through the vehicle of the ENP and the way that the

EU–Russian strategic partnership has developed since 2004. Some key points of similarity and distinction are the following:

(a) The issue of possible future EU membership. Neither the ENP nor the strategic partnership with Russia foresees future EU membership. Yet ENP parties (Ukraine and Moldova particularly) aspire to eventual EU membership, whereas Russia does not. Furthermore, some EU member states (such as Poland and Romania) support eventual membership status for some ENP countries (Ukraine and Moldova in particular), whereas there are no EU member states advocating Russian membership in the EU.

(b) The role of conditionality. ENP explicitly includes the notion of conditionality, whereas the strategic partnership with Russia sidesteps the issue. Russia explicitly rejects conditionality, whereas the EU is ambiguous as to whether it has abandoned conditionality in its relationship with Russia.

(c) The issue of symmetry of power. ENP, while explicitly positing joint ownership of the policy with the target countries, in fact involves a clearly asymmetrical power relationship, since the EU defines the framework for partnerships and provides funding to ENP countries to realize the implementation of appropriate policies and standards. The EU–Russia relationship is based on an assumption of equality of power, reinforced by Europe's energy dependence on Russia. While Russia is prepared to accept convergence on some matters, the terms of the partnership are a matter of negotiation.

(d) The differing role of norms and interests. The ENP explicitly seeks to "Europeanize" the Eastern partner countries to values promoted by the EU. In its relations with the EU, Russia emphasizes the primary importance of interests, a position broadly accepted by the Russian population (DeBardeleben, 2008).

ENP in many of its features represents an extension of enlargement policy, but without the enlargement prospect. This contradiction is, as Casier (2008) and others have pointed out, the source of many paradoxes and dilemmas of ENP, a point we return to later. As Pélerin argues, "the choice of the tools, instruments, and methods of the ENP has been largely inspired by the experience of the 2004 enlargement" (2008, p. 59).[2] The principles applied to ENP – such as the importance of conditionality, the asymmetry of power, and the Europeanization dynamic – were also key aspects of the accession that led up to the May

2004 and January 2007 enlargements. Furthermore, as Pélerin points out, the role of the Commission in the ENP resembles greatly its role in enlargement, particularly "the Commission is the main interlocutor of the applicant states." Likewise, ENP "grants the Commission the most active role in the implementation of this policy on the EU side" (Pélerin, 2008, p. 59), which, he explains, is based on the political, legal, and institutional environment in which the policy emerged, as well as the Commission's successful experience in shepherding the just-completed 2004 enlargement to completion (Delcour and Tulmets, 2009).

In contrast, the strategic relationship with Russia could not follow this dynamic, primarily because Russia objected to the principles. The EU, therefore, has had to work out a new modus vivendi in its policy towards Russia, being unable to seek effective guidance from experience and hindered by differing interests of the member states. While the EU has other strategic partnership agreements with third countries (e.g., with Brazil, Canada, China, India, Japan, Mexico, South Africa, and the US), none are similar to the relationship with Russia. Russia is the only strategic partner that borders EU member states, with the historic and intense mix of conflict, forced association, and, at times, cooperation in the relationship. Thus, the concept of strategic partnership provides the EU with little guidance in formulating the principles of interaction with Russia. Furthermore, in the 1990s, before Russia's renewed international and regional self-assertion under Vladimir Putin's leadership, many of the principles contained in the ENP were de facto applied by the EU to Russia under the guise of its assistance programs, such as TACIS. Specifically, the relationship in the 1990s was asymmetrical, involving the attempted exercise of conditionality by the EU, as well as an effort to Europeanize Russia and export European norms to it. The shift to a "strategic partnership" model has required a wholesale rethinking of the foundations and groundwork for the relationship.

With its rejection of the ENP, Russia demanded a turning point, setting the stage for the EU's two-track eastern policy. While the ENP track is fairly well articulated and has developed through a fully defined institutional and legal structure (with associated financing, vehicles, documents, and forms of interaction with partners), the relationship with Russia has a less clear trajectory, particularly given the numerous irritants that have the potential to stall progress. The perceived authoritarian shift in Russia has put a sharp edge on debates within the EU as to whether normative issues should be abandoned entirely in defining the strategic partnership.

Problems with the European neighborhood policy

While the foundations of the ENP were fairly clearly articulated in 2004 and the main instruments of implementation (Action Plans, Country Reports) have unfolded with most partners, the policy appeared to have some inadequacies in its initial period of operation, particularly in relation to the eastern neighbors. An evaluation of the policy in 2006 led to some corrective actions. The fundamental difficulties, some acknowledged explicitly in EU documents and in other cases identified by expert observers, were several.

Most importantly, the structure of incentives has not been adequate to stimulate action to bring domestic change in the partner countries in line with EU objectives (Wolchuk, 2009, p. 190). According to the widely cited model developed by Schimmelfennig and Sedelmeier (2004), in order to achieve compliance with EU conditionality requirements, rewards must be credible and adequately rapid, and exceed the costs of domestic adoption. Because there is no promise or clear prospect of EU membership, yet the structure of ENP is quite similar to previous enlargement policy (as noted above), the rewards have not been sufficient to stimulate real reform. The inadequacy of incentives spans several policy fields. In economic terms the problem is specifically identified by the European Commission in a December 2006 document "On Strengthening the European Neighborhood Policy" (Commission, 2006): "an important part of the incentives of the ENP – for instance in terms of market access and integration and other economic benefits – will only bear fruit later. This creates a real difficulty for partner countries in building the necessary domestic support for reform." On the other hand, Casier sees this situation as generating a "dilemma of enlargement," which might ultimately lead to a further enlargement process if partner countries actually were to comply with conditions set out by the EU. Given the current resistance within the EU to further enlargement (with the possible exception of Croatia and Iceland), in the short to medium term this translates into a frustrating situation for partner countries (Motyl, 2009).

A second and related issue concerns the principle of conditionality. In the outcomes of proceedings of the Council of the European Union in June 2007, this concern is directly acknowledged: "A number of partners have been reluctant to establish ENP Action Plans precisely because of the conditionality aspects that these entail" (Council, 2007, p. 4). However, the Council document does not elaborate on the nature of the reluctance to accept conditionality, which seems to involve a reaction to the implied superiority and arrogance of the EU in imposing its standards, in what is nominally a relationship of partners. Despite this difficulty, the EU has been reluctant to abandon the principle in the context of the ENP, as we will see below.

A third related problem is what Casier refers to as the "Schengen paradox," namely that greater freedom of mobility inside the EU seems to necessitate a stronger security barrier on the EU's external borders (2008, p. 21), thereby reinforcing an image of "Fortress Europe" and making Europeanization seem like a one-way street. This dilemma has very tangible ramifications, with political overtones, since it can affect public perceptions quite directly. As the 2006 Commission document notes, "The length and cost of procedures for short-term visas ... is a highly 'visible' disincentive to partner countries, and an obstacle to many of the ENP's underlying objectives" (Commission, 2006, pp. 3–4). In its Communication on the Eastern Partnership in 2008, the Commission reiterated that it had received a clear message about the importance of the issue: "Partners emphasize that mobility is a key litmus test for engagement with the EU ... ." (Commission, 2008b).

Finally, the EU has been unsuccessful in making a credible contribution to the resolution of key regional conflicts (e.g., in relation to Armenia and Azerbaijan, or Transnistria), which many see as a prerequisite for progress in other areas in the affected countries (Commission, 2006).

A problem rarely if ever mentioned in internal EU documents assessing the ENP is the Russian dimension, except in relation to regional conflicts. Since several of the countries involved in the ENP have either ambivalent or conflictual relations with Russia that directly affect the domestic political context, this omission seems significant. For example, Ukraine's difficulties in transforming domestic practices in line with EU guidelines cannot be abstracted from the country's conflicted geopolitical position between the Russia and the EU and associated internal regional polarization. At the very least, the lack of an EU membership perspective combined with the reality of Russian influence likely holds back implementation of broad-scale Europeanizing reforms. Yet, in discussions of ENP weaknesses, this dynamic is not openly acknowledged. Likewise, the close relationship between Belarus and Russia is also not an explicit point of discussion in considering the prospect for Belarusian inclusion in the ENP. The necessity of involving Russia in the resolution of regional problems in Moldova and Georgia is acknowledged, but not in the context of the ENP.

This is not to say that Russia is ignored in the formulation of the EU's eastern policy. In addition to the PCA, Russia is, for example, eligible for funding under the European Neighbourhood & Partnership Instrument (ENPI) ("European Neighbourhood & Partnership Instrument", 2007) and is included in new initiatives involving some ENP countries, such as the "Black Sea Synergy" (Commission, 2006). Nonetheless, the larger pattern is one of segmentation of the ENP from the EU's Russia policy.

The operation of the ENP and adjustments to it

Action plans with partner countries were concluded in most cases in the period between 2004 and 2006 on the following schedule, based on prior country reports that assessed the situation of each partner in a range of areas: Moldova and Ukraine (February 2005); Armenia, Azerbaijan, Georgia (November 2006); no Action Plan with Belarus. Action Plans provide country-specific objectives, covering a wide array of areas such as improvement of democratic governance, observance of human rights and rule of law, conflict resolution in tension zones, economic/legal measures to bring convergence with EU regulations, environmental protection and social security, border management and security, and measures relating to economic development and energy cooperation. Fulfillment of these Action Plans, as well as the general progress of the ENP, undergoes periodic review. Most recently, in May 2010, the European Commission issued a series of detailed progress reports to the European Parliament and the Council on particular countries covered by the ENP.[3]

As noted, a broader assessment of the ENP that took place in 2006 led to recommendations for some adjustments to the policy, responding to the weaknesses mentioned above. The first involved an effort to improve incentives for partner countries to encourage realization of objectives and goals set out in Action Plans. A first set of incentives relate to "deep trade and economic integration," which would include attention to non-tariff barriers, regulatory convergence, and "products of the most importance to [ENP partners]" (Commission 2006, p. 3). The result would be a "new generation of 'deep and comprehensive free trade agreements (FTAs)' with all ENP partners, like the one that the EU intends to negotiate with Ukraine" (Commission 2006, p. 3; 2008b, p. 2). The negotiations with Ukraine commenced in February 2008, just prior to Ukraine's admission to the World Trade Organization (WTO) in May of that year, so that Ukraine provides a model for other ENP countries. A new Governance Facility was also added to provide a reward for the best performers, introducing an implicit competition between ENP countries (General Affairs, 2007). Improved incentives were also to be offered by increased efforts to remove obstacles to mobility of persons through visa facilitation and border management, which is associated with an additional objective, increased people-to-people contacts (Commission 2006, pp. 5–8). These improved incentives do not, however, involve backing away from conditionality, but rather reframing it as "positive conditionality."

In addition to the incentives issue, structural adjustments were proposed. One involved adding a "thematic dimension" to the ENP (in addition to the country-based foundation of the program). A second involved augmenting the bilateral focus of the ENP with horizontal linkages between ENP partners and multilateral vehicles. A Presidency Progress Report issued by the General Affairs and External Relations Council noted that "a strong focus on cross-cutting sectoral themes" would provide "a multilateral complement to its main bilateral tracks with individual countries." Fields where this would apply include governance and rule of law, justice and security issues, economic cooperation, transport, energy and environment, and border and migration management (General Affairs, 2007). Most of these ideas were taken over into the Eastern Partnership policy, although the definition of multilateral fields was somewhat different.

How was Russia treated in considering these adjustments to the ENP? Little mention was made of Russia in these discussions, except in relation to conflict zones. A "non-paper" ("Expanding on the Proposals", n.d.) explaining the Commission's points in its December 2006 Communication on "Strengthening the ENP," includes a brief final section on "Engaging the Russian Federation." The section notes considerable overlaps and potential synergies between concerns of the ENP and the Road Maps developed with Russia in the EU–Russia strategic partnership. While acknowledging that involvement of the Russian Federation could occur, "as warranted by the issues at stake" in various "informal formats of the EU's policy dialogue with ENP neighbors" (presumably relating to cross-thematic horizontal linkages), the approach is highly cautious:

> However, given its decision not to participate in the ENP, political objections to Russia's involvement in these informal formats may be raised, and Russia itself may also not be amenable. Accordingly, any such involvement would need to be carefully considered; only occurring where there are clear and common EU/ENP interests and no objections from the parties concerned. ("Expanding on the Proposals", n.d., p. 30)

The inclusion of Russia in more formally structured initiatives, particularly those that affect regional security and environment, is anticipated, most notably in the newly created Black Sea Synergy Initiative (Commission, 2007). As pointed out in the Presidency Progress Report of 2007, the exclusion of non-ENP countries from this initiative would undermine the effectiveness of the proposal (General Affairs, 2007). Formed on a somewhat similar basis to the Northern Dimension, and in light of Romanian and Bulgarian accession to the EU, the idea is not to create new institutions to compete with existing ones such as the Black Sea Economic Council, but rather to generate a framework to facilitate cooperation using existing vehicles. Security concerns seem to be at the forefront, although a wide range of potential areas of cooperation is mentioned in the context of the Synergy, including involvement of civil society, environment, and migration issues. Little information is available about Russian participation in or reactions to the initiatives, but it can be anticipated, as Arkady Moshes suggests, that Russia is concerned about its status as "object" of the policy rather than being involved from the beginning in its conception:

> Moscow seems to be concerned about the developments it has witnessed in the region. In February 2008 it criticized the final document of the "Black Sea Synergy" meeting in Kyiv. Although all other EU and Black Sea Economic Cooperation states supported the report, Russia disliked it apparently because the document called for increased EU involvement. The media reaction to the regional energy summit in Kyiv in May 2008 was openly agitated. (Moshes, 2008).

The Eastern partnership: the next stage in the EU's two-track approach?

On the initiative of Poland and Sweden, a new direction in the ENP, relating specifically to the eastern Soviet successor states, was launched between the EU and the six participating partners (Azerbaijan, Armenia, Belarus, Georgia, Moldova, and Ukraine) at the Prague summit on May 6, 2009 ("Joint Declaration", 2009). Integrating some elements of the 2006 evaluation of the ENP, the Eastern Partnership also reflects the significant influence of the May 2004 enlargement on the EU's external policy (Dangerfield, 2009, pp. 1742, 1751). Poland in particular had made it a foreign policy priority to support the efforts of Ukraine to pursue both EU and NATO membership; another important Polish priority was to support democratic development in Belarus. Cianciara (2008, p. 3) concludes that "Polish diplomats believe that, if EU consents to the

[Eastern Partnership] project, it may attach more importance to Eastern neighbors and as a consequence the chances for the future membership of Ukraine and Moldova will significantly increase." Other motives for the initiative may have been to assure a higher priority for Eastern Europe vis-à-vis the French presidency's emphasis on a Mediterranean strategy, as well as to specifically address problems facing Eastern countries in a distinct policy framework. Tensions with Russia related to gas transit pipelines through Ukraine (both in January 2009 and earlier) and the Georgia crisis may have made some member states more receptive to the Polish–Swedish initiative (Averre, 2009, p. 1,694; Peters *et al.*, 2009, p. 6).

The European Union embraced the Eastern Partnership idea fairly quickly. Initial hesitations were resolved in favor of Belarus' inclusion. Previous EU policy towards Belarus was not seen as having been effective in bringing change to the country; at the same time the Belarusian elite gave signals of a greater readiness to engage the EU. Exercising the hoped-for diplomatic tact, Alexander Lukashenko sent a deputy rather than attending the Prague summit himself, thereby heading off a potentially rocky start to the launch of the project if protestors had reacted to the president's presence.

Several key elements distinguish the Eastern Partnership from the earlier thrust of the ENP, in addition to the greater inclusion of Belarus (Peters *et al.*, 2009). Gänzle (2009, p. 1723) suggests that the policy "does not present a fundamental shift in terms of the EU's approach," but that "it has significantly altered the boundaries of EU governance in Europe." While some of these elements pick up on the recommended adjustments in the 2006 assessments of the ENP, the Eastern Partnership takes them further and makes them more explicit. First is the emphasis on horizontal connections between the Eastern partners (facilitated by the EU) and a distinctive multilateral aspect of the policy. Through these vehicles it is expected that partners will be able better to share experience and information, and disseminate best practices. Seminars, meetings, and working sessions will facilitate transnational communication and cooperation. These will include meetings of heads of states on a biannual basis, annual meetings of Ministers of Foreign Affairs as well as ministerial conferences in particular sectors, bringing together senior officials working on particular common themes, and "panels to support the work of the thematic platforms in specific areas" (Commission, 2008b). The thematic platforms are: "democracy, good governance and stability;" "economic integration and convergence with EU policies," with the possible goal of building a "Neighborhood Economic Community;"

"energy security;" and "contacts between people." Increased funding is also provided. In short, the hoped-for result is not only closer economic and political relationships between the partner countries and the EU, but also the creation of a tightly knit set of associations between the partner countries themselves. While the possibility of third party involvement (including Russian) is specifically mentioned in guidelines for multilateral projects, this is not a central feature of the program. In some cases (e.g., energy security) Russian involvement might seem to be critical to success; in other areas it might well remain peripheral. The successful inclusion of Russia in particular projects would apparently depend on particular negotiations at the time.

A second theme in the Eastern Partnership is the goal of bringing the EaP partners into a much closer relationship with the EU in ways that are visible to average citizens. A new vehicle, the Association Agreement (replacing the earlier Partnership and Cooperation Agreements), signals this intent. Specific initiatives that might raise visibility include the goal of "establishing a deep and comprehensive free trade area" with each country and, even more importantly, "Mobility and Security Pacts," which could involve a progression of steps including visa facilitation, waiving of visa fees, and dialogues on visa-free travel (Commission, 2008a). Some first steps have already been achieved in this area with Ukraine and Moldova. These measures, in order to address what Casier has labeled the Schengen dilemma, would be combined with better cooperation in border management.

Third, while downplaying its visibility, the Eastern Partnership retains the notion of conditionality: "The level of ambition of the EU's relationship with the Eastern partners will take account of the extent to which these values are reflected in national practices and policy implementation," the values being "mutual commitments to the rule of law, good governance, respect for human rights, respect for and protection of minorities, and the principles of the market economy and sustainable development" (Commission, 2008b, p. 3). Despite the continuing role of conditionality, the European Partnership initiative was warmly received by the prospective partner countries, and seen as a particularly important achievement for Poland, applauded by a wide range of member states, including the Baltic States. More recently, the lack of a membership prospect has again elicited some reservations in Ukraine, and Averre (2009, p. 1,695) raises the possibility that the Eastern Partnership may generate new expectations that will not be fulfilled.

The Russian reaction was, not unexpectedly, much more negative; the issue of Belarus' involvement raised particular concern (Stewart,

2009). The prevailing perception of the policy is expressed rather neutrally by an article in *Kommersant* as being "directed at strengthening the position of Brussels in the post-Soviet space" (Gabuev, 2008). In relation to Belarus in particular, the establishment of closer relations with the EU is frequently interpreted as leading to a reduced inclination on the part of Belarus to move forward with integration processes with Moscow ("Razgovor", 2009). While the official Belarusian position emphasizes the need for the country to pursue good relations with both the EU and Russia,[4] commentators in Russia have also observed that the delay in the release of a second tranche of Russian credit to Belarus in early 2009 may have encouraged Minsk's positive response to the EU initiative (Khodasevich, 2009). Some Russian observers speculate that the Eastern Partnership might even mark a turning point in Belarus' relationship with the West; more generally, Moscow may fear that Belarus could be moved onto the other track of the EU's dual policy to the East. While warning against exaggerating the importance of the Eastern Partnership, one commentator observes that "it is fully possible that just this initiative will, in the long run, be the basis for fundamental integration of Belarus into a unified Europe" (Klochikhin, 2009). The invitation of Lukashenko to the EU's Prague summit, despite continuing objections to Belarusian human rights policies, reinforces an interpretation of the EU's policy as based on geopolitical interests rather than normative commitments espoused by the EU. From the Belarusian side, on the other hand, interest in the initiative is probably primarily economic, so subsequent developments suggest that the EU's efforts to leverage political reforms may face a difficult road ("Belarus", 2009, p. 6).

More broadly, the Eastern Partnership may reinforce a general sense in Moscow that Russia is being edged out of its own legitimate sphere of influence. As Moshes notes,

> it is not difficult to understand why Russia would be far from welcoming forums in which it is not a participant of discussions but an object. There is an emerging (albeit weak) circle of solidarity that excludes Russia and blurs boundaries between EU members and non-members. At the same time, it symbolically points to differences between "Wider Europe", understood as "ENP Europe," and Russia. (Moshes, 2008)

In short, the Eastern Partnership has the potential to cement further the two-track nature of the EU's eastern policy. Whereas the ENP's initial bilateral approach meant that "all roads lead to Brussels," the multilateral nature of the Eastern Partnership could reinforce a net-worked EaP area that includes Russia only as an ad hoc "add-on" in particular cases.

Conclusion

The implications of Russia's self-assertion in rejecting the ENP in 2004 may be long-lasting and profound. While EU spokespersons can easily explain Russia's exclusion from the Eastern Partnership as being based on Russia's own preferences, the dual-track trajectory equally reflects the manner in which the EU initially framed the ENP. As the ENP has developed, the Eastern Partnership "amendment" to the ENP reflects the influence and interests of new member states intent on weaning Russia from its imperial tradition and tutoring East European neigh-bors in norms of democratization and market economics that will make them more stable neighbors and, possibly, ready for eventual EU candidate status.[5]

  The Eastern Partnership has the potential to establish mechanisms that will deepen the ties and links between the Eastern partners in a way that will widen the policy and practice gap with Russia. A Working Paper of the Commission (Commission, 2008c) suggests that these new mechanisms may include many of the vehicles used within the EU itself to encourage member states to work cooperatively toward real-ization of common objectives in areas that are within member state (rather than Community) jurisdiction (for example, through the Open Method of Coordination). Such measures encourage mutual learning and the socialization of policy elites to desired practices and norms. Some of the watchwords in the Commission document (2008c) are "exchange of experience," "exchanges of best practices," "dedicated workshops," "peer reviews," "training and networking," "multilateral cooperation," "twinning projects," "multilateral dialogues," "assess-ment of options," and "thematic workshops." These vehicles encourage a capacity for mutual learning,[6] for evaluation of outcomes, for seek-ing new paths of improved policy performance, and, possibly, for the creation of epistemic communities between EaP partners themselves as well as with EU member states. Poland quite explicitly sees itself as a tutor and guide for countries such as Ukraine and Belarus as they embark on Europeanization. The deep, cross-cutting, multifaceted hori-zontal mechanisms foreseen in the Eastern Partnership distinguish it from the largely bilateral nature of previous ENP approaches. Whether these mechanisms will be successful in speeding up convergence with EU practices and norms, and with socializing elites, bureaucrats, and a broader circle from the active public in EaP countries is a question for the future. However, Wolchuk (2009, p. 202) argues that in Ukraine it is "the emergence of a pro-reform, pro-European enclave within the state apparatus" that has already been the clearest effect of the ENP's Action Plan; the EaP multilateral initiatives could extend and expand this type of dynamic. Ironically, if this deep socialization and learning process does not occur in the Eastern partner countries, the policy will have failed in its objectives, whereas, if it succeeds, the approach may well widen the cultural and policy gap with Russia, while possibly pushing the EU toward further enlargements.

Whether the "path dependence" of this dual-track trajectory can be adjusted to include mechanisms that will include Russia within this newly expanding space of European interaction appears to depend primarily on the outcome of discussions between the EU and Russia. However, it also depends on an assertive and concerted effort on the part of the EU to build linkages to Russia within the framework of the Eastern Partnership. As noted, some vehicles designed for use in the Eastern Partnership are open to Russia, but incentives for Russia to engage and a willingness of EaP partners to accept that engagement, while important (Meister and May, 2009, p. 3), may pose challenges. Since the EU–Russian relationship is defined as bilateral and "strategic" (evoking the language of mutual interests rather than mutual learning), the "fit" with EaP mechanisms, which are multilateral and "normative," may be difficult. Vehicles to obviate or resolve these contradictions would be important markers of an effort to mitigate the polarity in the EU's eastern policy. Ongoing initiatives that link Russia with EU states, such as various cross-border projects, including five new ones approved in November 2009 (two involving EU new member states, Estonia, Latvia, Lithuania, or Poland) ("European Neighborhood Policy in Action", 2009), are positive steps; but these projects most often do not include both EaP partner countries and Russia. The introduction of shared budgets and a common management structure in such projects reflects an intention to promote a sense of "shared ownership" and mutual responsibility, notions congruent with the logic of the Eastern Partnership. Haukkala (2009) suggests that over time "Russia might be persuaded to abandon the current zero-sum logic and embrace the win-win logic propagated by the Union itself." However, this progression may be unlikely if Russia is excluded from the planning stages of regional initiatives and only invited on board later.

Another possibility is that the two tracks of the EU's eastern policy could follow parallel routes, at least in particular thematic areas, making possible "bridges" between the tracks. A particularly difficult issue involves energy, where Russia, the EU, and the EaP countries all have their own vital interests and goals at stake (Van der Meulen, 2009), making the EaP platform less likely to provide an appropriate venue for their resolution, even though two of the new EaP "flagship initiatives"[7] are in this area. Following Forsberg and Seppo (2009), in an area where vital interests are at stake, normative appeals are likely to be less effective than a well-thought-out strategy using a combination of incentives and resources.

Overall, the normative gap that has emerged between Russia and the West, and particularly the skepticism in some new member states, has reduced the trust that may be vital for inclusion of Russia in the space for dialogue and interaction that the EaP is trying to create. Much will depend on domestic developments in Russia, particularly whether these will feed liberalization and economic modernization, or whether they will nurture defensive nationalistic tendencies. EU efforts to encourage liberalization and modernization in Russia will no doubt continue, reflected in the launch of a Partnership for Modernization at the EU–Russia Summit in Rostov-on Don on May 31 – June 1, 2010 ("Joint Statement on the Partnership", 2010). However, the outcome will also depend on the internal developments within the EU, and whether strong voices will emerge to support a priority on constructing wider two-way paths between the two tracks of the EU's eastern policy.

Notes

I am grateful to the Social Sciences and Humanities Research Council of Canada for a Standard Research Grant to support this research, and to Susan Stewart and Stefan Gänzle for comments on an earlier draft of this chapter.

1. Referring to the work of H. Timmermann and C. Hillion, S. Gänzle (2009, p. 1724) points out that in the l990s the EU also applied a dual track approach, "separating the Central and Eastern European countries (including the Baltic states) from the Newly Independent States."
2. This point notwithstanding, EU documents frequently reiterate that ENP is "distinct from the process and policy of EU enlargement." See, for example, General Affairs and External Relations Council (2007).
3. Links to these are available for individual countries on the EU website: http://ec.europa.eu/world/enp/documents_en.htm#3 (accessed July 2, 2010).
4. See the comment by Sergei Martynev, the head of the Ministry of Foreign Affairs of Belarus, in Shpakov (2009).

5. On the impact of EU enlargement on EU–Russian relations more generally, see DeBardeleben (2009).
6. I am grateful to Jonathan Zeitlin for stimulating my thoughts along these lines based on an answer to a question following his discussion of the Open Method of Coordination in a lecture at the Mannheim Center for Social Research, June 9, 2009.
7. See the website of the European Commission, External Relations, http://ec.europa.eu/external_relations/eastern/initiatives/index_en.htm (accessed February 4, 2010).

References

Averre, Derek (2009) "Competing Rationalities: Russia, the EU, and the 'Shared Neighbourhood'", *Europe-Asia Studies* vol. 61, no. 10, first published November 3, 2009 (iFirst).

"Belarus: President seeks to define conditions of dialogue with the EU" (2009) *East Week*, no. 32, September 23, Centre for Eastern Studies, Warsaw. http://www.osw.waw.pl/en/publikacje/eastweek/2009-09-23/belarus-president-seeks-define-conditions-dialogue-eu (accessed July 2, 2010).

Casier, Tom (2008) "The New Neighbours of the European Union: The Compelling Logic of Enlargement", in Joan DeBardeleben (ed.), *The Boundaries of EU Enlargement: Finding a Place for Neighbours*, Basingstoke, Houndsmill: Palgrave Macmillan, pp. 19–32.

Cianciara, Agnieszka K. (2008) "Eastern Partnership – opening a new chapter of Polish Eastern policy and the European Neighbourhood Policy?", *Analyses and Opinions*, no. 4 (June), Institute of Public Affairs, Warsaw.

Commission of the European Communities (2006) "Communication from the Commission to the Council and the European Parliament, 'On Strengthening the European Neighbourhood Policy'", COM(2006) 726 final, December 4. http://ec.europa.eu/world/enp/pdf/com06_726_en.pdf (accessed July 4, 2010).

Commission of the European Communities (2007) "Communication from the Commission to the Council and the European Parliament, 'Black Sea Synergy – A New Regional Cooperation Initiative'", COM(2007) 160 final, April 11. http://ec.europa.eu/world/enp/pdf/com07_160_en.pdf (accessed July 2, 2010).

Commission of the European Communities (2008a) "Communication from the Commission to the Council and the European Parliament: Eastern Partnership", COM(2008) 823 final, December 3. http://eurlex.europa.eu/LexUriServ/LexUriServ.do?uri=COM:2008:0823:FIN:EN:PDF (accessed July 2, 2010).

Commission of the European Communities (2008b) "Communication from the Commission to the Council and the European Parliament 'Implementation of the European Neighbourhood Policy in 2007'", COM(2008) 164, April 3. http://ec.europa.eu/world/enp/pdf/progress2008/com08_164_en.pdf (accessed July 4, 2010).

Commission of the European Communities (2008c) "Commission Staff Working Document accompanying the 'Communication from the

Commission to the Council and the European Parliament Eastern Partnership'", SEC (2008) 2974/3. http://ec.europa.eu/external_relations/eastern/docs/sec08_2974_en.pdf (accessed July 2, 2010).

Commission of the European Communities (2010) "EU-Russia Common Space, Progress Report 2009", March. http://ec.europa.eu/external_relations/russia/docs/commonspaces_prog_report_2009_en.pdf (accessed July 2, 2010).

Council of the European Union (2007) "Outcome of Proceedings: Strengthening the European Neighbourhood Policy – Council Conclusions", 11016/07, Brussels, June 19. http://register.consilium.europa.eu/pdf/en/07/st11/st11016.en07.pdf (accessed July 2, 2010).

Dangerfield, Martin (2009) "The Contribution of the Visegrad Group to the European Union's 'Eastern' Policy: Rhetoric or Reality?", *Europe-Asia Studies*, vol. 61, no. 10, first published November 3, 2009 (iFirst).

DeBardeleben, Joan (2008) "Public Attitudes toward EU-Russian Relations: Knowledge, Values, and Interests", in Joan DeBardeleben (ed.), *The Boundaries of EU Enlargement: Finding a Place for Neighbours*, Houndmills, Basingstoke: Palgrave Macmillan, pp. 70–91.

DeBardeleben, Joan (2009) "The Impact of EU Enlargement on the EU-Russian Relationship", in Roger E. Kanet (ed.), *A Resurgent Russia and the West: The European Union, NATO, and Beyond*, Dordrecht, Netherlands: Republic of Letters Publishing, pp. 93–112.

Delcour, Laure and Elsa Tulmets (2009) "Pioneer Europe? The ENP as a Test Case for the EU's Foreign Policy", *European Foreign Affairs Review*, vol. 14, pp. 501–23.

"European Neighbourhood & Partnership Instrument: Cross-Border Cooperation Strategy Paper 2007–2013, Indicative Programme 2007–2010" (2007). http://ec.europa.eu/world/enp/pdf/country/enpi_cross-border_cooperation_strategy_paper_en.pdf (accessed July 2, 2010).

"European Neighbourhood Policy in Action: launch of cross-border co-operation programmes with Russia" (2009) Europa press releases Rapid, Brussels, November 18. http://europa.eu/rapid/pressReleasesAction.do?reference=IP/09/1727&format=HTML&aged=0&language=EN&guiLanguage=en (accessed July 2, 2010).

"Expanding on the Proposals contained in the Communication to the European Parliament and the Council on 'Strengthening the ENP' – COM (2006) 726 final of 4 December 2006: ENP Thematic Dimension" (n.d.) non-paper, http://ec.europa.eu/world/enp/pdf/non-paper_thematic-dimension_en.pdf (accessed July 3, 2010).

Forsberg, Tuomas and Antti Seppo (2009) "Power without Influence? The EU and Trade Disputes with Russia", *Europe-Asia Studies*, vol. 61, no. 10, pp. 1805–23.

Gabuev, Aleksandr (2008) "Evrosoiuz obustraivaetsia na postsovetskom prostanstve", no. 228, December 13. http://www.kommersant.ru/doc.aspx?fromsearch=cef6f242–9eb7–4210–9db9–8c6360706029&docsid=1093940 (accessed July 2. 2010).

Gänzle, Stefan (2009) "EU Governance and the European Neighbourhood Policy: A Framework for Analysis", *Europe-Asia Studies*, vol. 61, no. 10, first published November 3, 2009 (iFirst).

General Affairs and External Relations Council (GAERC) (2007) "Strengthening the European Neighbourhood Policy: Presidency Progress Report", June 18–19,

264   *Joan DeBardeleben*

updated July 25, 2008, http://www.euractiv.com/en/enlargement/european-neighbourhood-policy-enp-archived/article-129625 (accessed July 2, 2010).

Haukkala, Hiski (2009) "From Zero-Sum to Win-Win? The Russian Challenge to the EU's Eastern Neighbourhood Policies", *European Policy Analysis,* issue 12, November, Swedish Institute for European Policy Studies. www.sieps.se/en/publications/european-policy-analysis/from-zero-sum-to-win-win-the-russian-challenge-to-the-eus-eastern-neighbourhood-policies-200912e.html (accessed July 2, 2010).

"Joint Declaration of the Prague Eastern Partnership" (2009) Prague, May 7. www.consilium.europa.eu/uedocs/cms_Data/docs/pressdata/en/er/107589.pdf (accessed July 2, 2010).

"Joint Statement on the Partnership for Modernization: EU-Russia Summit, 31 May- 1 June 2010" (2010), Rostov-on-Don, June 1. http://www.consilium.europa.eu/uedocs/cms_Data/docs/pressdata/en/er/114747.pdf (accessed July 3, 2010).

Khodasevich, Anton (2009) "Minsk znaet, kyda det' rossiskie millianardy", *Nezavisimaia gazeta,* March 2.

Klochikhin, Evgenii (2009) "Belorussie zainteresovalas' evropeiskoi al'ternativou", *Nezavisimaia gazeta,* no. 72, p. 4, April 9.

Meister, Stefan and Marie-Lena May (2009) "Die Östliche Partnerschaft der EU – ein Kooperationsangebot mit Missverständnissen", *DGAPstandpunkt,* Deutsche Gesellschaft für Auswärtige Politik e.V., September, no. 7. http://www.dgap.org/publikationen/view/1dea1eef3a99908a1ee11de8f87331da46d128b128b.html (accessed July 2, 2010).

Moshes, Arkady (2008) "Slowly But Surely? The European Neighborhood Policy as a New Framework for Transatlantic Integration", *PONARS Eurasia Policy Memo,* no. 13. http://ceres.georgetown.edu/esp/ponarsmemos/page/55898.html (accessed July 2, 2010).

Motyl, Alexander J. (2009) "Ukraine Between Russia and the European Union: An Analysis of the Present Situation", Cicero foundation Great Debate Paper, no. 09/6, October. http://www.cicerofoundation.org/lectures/Alexander_J_Motyl_Ukraine.pdf (accessed July 2, 2010).

Pélerin, Jérémie (2008) "The ENP in Interinstitutional Competition: An Instrument of Leadership for the Commission", in Dieter Mahncke and Sigelinde Gstöhl (eds), *Europe's near Abroad: Promises and Prospects of the EU's Neighborhood Policy.* Brussels: P.I.E. Peter Lang, College of Europe Series, no. 4, pp. 47–65.

Peters, Ketie, Jan Rood and Grzegorz Gromadzki (2009) "The Eastern Partnership: Towards a New Era of Cooperation between the EU and its Eastern Neighbours?", Revised Overview Paper, EU Policies Seminar Series, Clingendael European Studies Program, The Hague, December 2009. http://www.policypointers.org/Page/View/10479 (accessed July 2, 2010).

"Razgovor s pozitsii tret'ei sily" (2009) *Kommersant,* no. 18, February 3. http://www.kommersant.ru/doc.aspx?fromsearch=078a070d-9e52–49d0–8fc0-cdfbc042ef1e&docsid=1112387 (accessed July 2, 2010).

Schimmelfennig, Frank and Ulrich Sedelmeier (2004) "Government by Conditionality: EU Rule Transfer to the Candidate Countries of Central and Eastern Europe", *Journal of European Public Policy,* vol. 11, no. 4, pp. 661–79.

Shpakov, Iurii (2009) "Vozmozhnost' otoiti ot Rossii", *Vremia novostei*, no. 25, February 13. http://www.vremya.ru/print/223029.html (accessed July 2, 2010).

Stewart, Susan (2009) "Russland und die Östliche Partnerschaft: Harsche Kritik, punktuelles Kooperationsinteresse", *SWP-Aktuell* 2009A/21, April Stiftung Wissenschaft und Politik. http://www.swp-berlin.org/produkte/swp_aktuell_detail.php?id=10617 (accessed July 2, 2010).

Stratenschulte, Eckart D. (2007) *Europas Politik nach Osten: Grundlagen – Erwartungen*, Strategien, Hamburg: Merus Verlag.

Van Der Meulen, Evert Faber (2009) "Gas Supply and EU-Russia Relations", *Europe-Asia Studies*, vol. 61, no. 5, pp. 833–56.

Wolchuk, Kataryna (2009) "Implementation without Coordination: The Impact of EU Conditionality on Ukraine under the European Neighbourhood Policy", *Europe-Asia Studies*, vol. 61, no. 22, pp. 187–211.

13
The EU–Russia Energy Relationship: European, Russian, Common Interests?

Susanne Nies

Introduction

One quarter of the European Union's gas supply stems from Russia, oil supply plays an important role too, and Russia has become the third largest trading partner of the EU, with energy predominating. Debates in the media and academia thus focus very much on the question of whether Russia, humiliated according to many during the 1990s, "back" now as an "energy power," uses or might use the "energy weapon" against the EU. In addition, it goes without saying that the 2004 and 2007 EU accession of former Soviet bloc states has increased sensitivity and shed light on their existing overdependence on Russian energy sources. Should the EU be alarmed and diversify away from Russia? Conflicts between Russia and other former Soviet republics are manifold and continuing, with energy often being an important catalyst. The Russian–Georgian war in August 2008 was a harsh reminder of the potential renewed Russian imperialism in its former hegemonic sphere. And the Russo-Turkmen "Gas War" in 2009 illustrated the tools Russia was ready to use in order to change the terms of trade.[1]

Conflicts among CIS countries concern specifically the pipeline-dependent gas trade that ties together Russia, Turkmenistan, Ukraine, and the EU. And no satisfying answer has yet been given to the question of whether and how infrastructures created in and for the Soviet past might be adapted to a totally changed geopolitical environment. The fact that politics as a whole and energy – especially gas and electricity interconnection – are interwoven constitutes a major challenge to the analyst. In 2009–10 we witnessed a shift in the terms of trade in gas markets, in that demand dropped sharply throughout 2009 (Pirani (ed.), 2009) because of the financial crisis – a situation that is likely to continue to have an impact for some years, at least (IEA, 2009). An additional supply, of cheap liquefied natural gas (LNG), has arrived on the European markets as a result of US nonconventional gas production (shale gas) and puts additional pressure on the traditional long-term contract system in continental Europe with its oil–gas price links. All these factors enhance a shift from producer to consumer-dominated markets and are likely to weaken Russia's position.[2] One should also not forget the sharp drop – more than a quarter – in consumption of Russian gas in crisis-shaken major consumer countries, such as Ukraine – not to mention Russia itself, whose industrial production contracted by 20 per cent in 2009. In a time of extensive overhaul of energy policies and the changing mix of energy sources to be used, in part because of concerns about climate change and energy efficiency, uncertainty about future demand and supply is tremendous. This, in turn, handicaps investments in infrastructure for the future. Unfortunately, the latter have to be conceived and realized far in advance in order to have the right capacities at hand at the right time and to have time to cope with the lengthy process of authorization and the *nimby* (not-in-my-back-yard) phenomenon of local resistance to new infrastructure. Russia and the EU thus share an interest in decreasing uncertainty, in order to create positive conditions for investments where they are of mutual concern. This chapter assesses the EU–Russia energy relationship, including Russian, European, and potential common interests that will drive those relations. The energy relationship between the EU and Russia is very much a trade relationship concerning oil, and especially gas. Reciprocal investments in the energy sector are as yet limited, because of regulatory uncertainty, but also due to preventive measures such as the "third country clause" that the EU included in its legal position: this clause stipulates that any country or enterprise originating from a third country outside the EU's legal space has to respect certain rules – for instance, the unbundling of transmission and generation – prior to investing in EU infrastructure. This clause, clearly targeting Gazprom, has been called by media the "Gazprom Clause." Moreover, electricity interconnection, although under discussion, is so far nonexistent, for both political and technical reasons.

The discussion begins with a brief overview of past relations and then addresses the following questions:

- how is the EU–Russia energy relationship institutionally organized?
- does Russia use energy as a tool for power politics, and with respect to whom?

- which institutional design is needed to set up a comprehensive and reliable energy relationship between Russia and the EU, including transit countries such as Ukraine?
- what are Russian, as well as European, interests, and where do they diverge or overlap?

Focusing on the EU–Russia energy relationship and leaving aside the bilateral relations between EU member states and Russia necessarily reflects a limited approach. EU external energy policy is only at an early stage of development; it gains prominence with each energy crisis situation, but is put into question by states and markets as soon as desecuritization has taken place. Finally, the bigger a member state, the more it will try to organize relations bilaterally with Russia – for example, Germany, France, Italy; the smaller a state is, the more it will try to rely on the EU's instruments, and force the others to act as a group; this has been especially true of the new member states in the East.

Legacies

Energy relations are long-term relationships: a look back at the *longue durée* of experiences allows us to assess the quality of the relationship and common interests of the past, as well as conflicts. Gas and oil pipelines appeared after World War II and after the evolution away from coal, especially between the 1950s and 1960s (*Novyie Izvestija*, 2009). Their construction followed distinct approaches on either side of the Iron Curtain. These differences continue to this day and make themselves apparent principally through the excessive dependence of new EU member states vis-à-vis Russia. These links thus reflect past relationships. One may be surprised by the existence of "bridges" that pierced the Iron Curtain during the Cold War from Austria and West Germany. This precursory role was criticized, notably by the Americans. West Germany would quickly become the first Western client of the USSR. That Poland was bypassed in these East–West gas pipelines crossing through the Curtain is interesting to keep in mind in the context of the current debate over Nord Stream and the map of European gas pipelines. This also partly explains coal's dominance in this country, atypical for Europe. The introduction concludes with the status quo of a unified Europe since 1989, following the fall of the USSR. The disappearance of this imperial power coincides with the proliferation of independent state actors within Europe, and with the redistribution of the "energy cards" within the former USSR, which created new opportunities but also big risks for the EU and the whole of Europe. Evolving transit countries are a source of crisis, as is the pathology of East–East relations. The status of "transit country" then came to summarize the politicization of energy transit, an issue that had not existed in the past. The example of Western Europe shows that integration and interdependence – a high level of integration into European and international structures – are the best protection against the risk of energy blackmail. It was, however, necessary to establish a code of conduct, a common judicial framework. The fall of the USSR also made room for multiple oil and gas pipeline projects, alternative routes, and the reconstruction of energy industries in Eastern Europe. This type of project proliferation was unheard of during the Cold War.

Sorting out transit countries: German Democratic Republic and Austria

The first energy bridge to cross the Iron Curtain was through Austria, a country that had imported electricity from Eastern countries since 1956 (and from Russia since 1985). But, above all, Vienna imported gas, beginning in 1968, through the *Brotherhood* – Bratstvo – pipeline. Better known and more strategic for the European Community were the agreements made between Bonn and Moscow at the beginning of the 1970s. The German economics minister Karl Schiller and his Soviet counterpart signed an accord linking the Ruhrgas and Gazprom monopolies and Deutsche Bank in the following project: the FRG would receive supplies of 0.5 bcm of gas per year in 1973, and 3 bcm per year beginning in 1978, in exchange for 1.2 million tons of pipes manufactured by Mannesmann, plus a very advantageous loan of 1.2 billion Deutsche Marks to the USSR. This agreement, the first of its kind, was known as the "Gas-for-Pipes" deal (*Erdgasröhrengeschäft*). This accord served other EC member states, which would in turn sign supply agreements with the USSR, in order to connect to German infrastructures. The East–West barter model was simple. The USSR needed Western currency and technology, while Western European countries – West Germany, France, Austria, Italy, and Belgium – looked to diversify their energy supply away from oil and to diminish their reliance on Dutch gas. And, at the same time, the subsidized prices for "brother countries" and the very complex barter trades reinforced interdependence within the Soviet bloc.

The previously unseen rapid development of the gas industry and exploitation of networks was possible only after the first oil crisis in 1973. It was, thus, a true catalyst for the first series of long-distance gas pipelines connecting the East to the West. *Détente* was the political context during the 1970s, and both sides had an interest in East–West commercial exchanges. The USSR was growing more and more dependent on the export of raw materials, which by the end of the 1970s made up 62.3 per cent of their GNP. As already mentioned, this economic and energy rapprochement between the East and the West faced resistance and criticism from the United States, notably during the second series of contract negotiations between the USSR and Ruhrgas.

Legacies of the 1990s: hydrocarbon transport and the consequences of the collapse of the Soviet Union

The dissolution of the USSR and the Soviet bloc had four major consequences directly related to energy:

- new relationships and new energy prices within the former USSR,
- the proliferation of states and transit countries,
- the collapse of production and consumption,
- and the stagnation in the maintenance and restoration of infrastructures

New relationships, new prices within the former USSR

The Central European countries that sought integration into Western structures now had to pay world market prices for gas and oil imported from Russia, or at least negotiate a special reduced price, usually in convertible currency. The increase of consumers – from the former Soviet sphere – now paying world market prices could be considered an economic advantage for Russia, a point that is often overlooked. New transit countries began to benefit from their geography and, in turn, began charging Russia higher transit fees.

The proliferation of states and transit countries

Out of the European part of the USSR seven independent states emerged: Russia, Ukraine, Belarus, the three Baltic States, and Moldova. From then on, all new Russian projects went through transit states, notably Ukraine, on which 90 per cent of Soviet gas exports depended in 1992, and Belarus. Moreover, this traditional gas export route now went through not only two countries – Ukraine and Czechoslovakia – but three: Ukraine, the Czech Republic, and Slovakia with the breakup of Czechoslovakia in 1993. These states acted in their own self-interest, which led Russia to consider establishing direct routes. In fact, only one direct link existed, which had connected the USSR to Finland since 1974. And it was not until 2003 that a second direct link, this time to Turkey – Blue Stream – was constructed. The proliferation of states in Eastern and Central Europe following the disintegration of the Soviet empire created new tensions, conflicts, and pathologies.

The collapse of production and consumption

Following the economic shocks provoked by the disintegration of the Soviet bloc and the often irresponsible experiments in this unprecedented political–economic transition, Russia's gross domestic product (GDP) shrank by 40 per cent, and energy consumption consequently decreased by around a third (OECD, 1997). Commercial exports to former satellites and CIS countries also decreased because of their decline and their decreasing consumption. Oil production, which had made the USSR the world's number one producer, fell by half between 1988 and 1995 – from 600 million tons in 1988 to 350 for the CIS (500 to 300 million tons alone for Russia) (Favennec, 2007, p. 190). The only advantage of the decrease in domestic demand within the ex-USSR during this period was that it allowed the CIS and Russia to maintain their exports of oil, as well as of gas, despite the drop in production. It is clear that today's changing trade patterns remind Russia of its experience in the 1990s.

Stagnation in the maintenance and restoration of infrastructures

The managerial collapse became clearly evident in terms of infrastructures. The period from 1985 to 2000 was marked by deterioration of existing infrastructure and stagnation in implementing new projects and in developing domestic fields. These fields were from then on open to exploitation by foreigners (see, notably, the 1996 law on PSAs (Production Sharing Agreements)). And unfortunately, even in the recent period of high oil and gas prices, investment has not caught up. Today's conditions are clearly detrimental for new investment because low hydrocarbon prices, the global economic crisis, and uncertainty of demand compromise investment.

The institutional dimension of EU–Russia energy relations

The institutional dimension of the EU–Russia energy relationship includes three main elements. All of them are very much improvised, put into question, and currently under revision. To date, the EU and Russia lack legally binding instruments ruling their energy relationship. Negotiations prove to be very difficult in a worsened general geopolitical climate. A constructive strategy with and concerning the common neighborhood area, without necessarily integrating it into one or the other area, is also missing – one of many examples revealing the lack of appropriate ideas and instruments to organize the post-Cold War world.

The three existing elements are:

- the Partnership and Cooperation Agreement of 1994 between the EU and Russia,
- the Energy Charter Treaty and the recent Russian proposal to substitute it, and
- the EU–Russia Energy Dialogue.

Finally, Russian and EU legislation and their impact on one another also deserve attention.[3]

The PCA and its energy dimension

The Partnership and Cooperation Agreement (PCA) ratified in 1997, and entering into force in 1999, was set up to enhance the political dialogue between Russia and the European Union, and was followed by similar agreements with eleven other former Soviet Republics (European Commission, 2010; Partnership and Cooperation Agreements, 2009). The ambition was to promote democracy, trade, and convergence; energy is dealt with in article 65, and indirectly in article 12 referring to the freedom of transit. The agreement covered a ten-year period that expired in 2009, but anticipated automatic extension until a new agreement had been concluded. Negotiations over the follow-up began in July 2008, but were suspended one month later because of the war in Georgia. They resumed in 2009. According to the Russian representative in Brussels, Vladimir Chizov, "there was no hurry, but the only important question is the quality of the final document" (Chizov, 2009). In response to the desires of both participating parties, the second PCA will reinforce the energy dimension in concrete aspects, such as the amount and terms of buying, shipping, and marketing of natural gas, oil, and electricity. Yet volatile diplomatic relations and the lack of trust, as well as opposing concepts of such arrangements as the Energy Charter, continue to handicap the negotiations. In the meantime, the process advances on narrower and more specific fields, such as a nuclear partnership agreement, with negotiations ongoing since December 2009 ("Green light from the Council", 2009).

The Energy Charter Treaty

The PCA contains a clause (article 105) referring to the Energy Charter Treaty, which transfers energy-related questions to this legal framework. Several attempts have been made to find a solution to the lack of an East–West legal framework. At the initiative of the Dutch prime minister in the early 1990s, the Energy Charter was born, conceived of as a framework for dialogue and cooperation on energy between Western and Eastern Europe. The European Energy Charter (1991) became the "Energy Charter Treaty" in 1994 and has spread beyond Europe, with fifty-one members having signed it. The treaty scheme is intended to improve investment security for the producers and supply security for the consumers. Signed by fifty-one members, plus the EU Commission and EURATOM, the Charter Treaty is a legally binding multilateral instrument. Its weaknesses, nevertheless, stem from the fact that producer countries such as Russia and Norway never ratified it, while countries that did ratify it, such as Ukraine, did not respect the rules ("About the Charter", 2010; Seliverstov, 2009). Thus, lacking commitment from two prime producers, the ECT never functioned properly, and impeded progress on energy legislation and normalization.

During the Khabarovsk EU–Russia Summit on May 21–22, 2009 the EU and Russia came up with two proposals that were both rejected. The EU required an early warning mechanism for transit crises as part of the Energy Charter Treaty, obliging producer and transit country to deliver contracted gas, regardless of their bilateral conflict. President Medvedev insisted on the adoption of his mid-April proposal of "a new global Energy Treaty" replacing the ECT (Medvedev, 2009). Three points are important here. First, Medvedev suggested extending the list of energy resources: not only oil and gas, but also nuclear fuel, electric energy, and coal should be covered by the treaty. Second, with respect to members, which today are mostly consumer countries, Moscow desired to see the principal world energy players included, such as the USA, Canada, China, India, and Norway. And finally, he insisted on a clearly defined process of conflict resolution in the case of a transit crisis, which pointed clearly to the Ukrainian example. Although at the beginning of 2010 the EU Commission seemed to be more open to considering the Russian proposal (Savytsky and Dubrovyk, 2010), a principal decision had to be taken concerning the inclusion of the interests of both the consumer and the producer country – an unheard-of thing, since all the existing organizations, OPEC and the rest, focus clearly on either one side or the other. Here, precisely, is the point: defining the rules of the game of interdependence is the most important requirement in EU–Russia energy relations.

EU–Russia energy dialogue

Finally, the EU–Russia energy dialogue adopted in 2000 was set up to compensate for the absence of cooperation within the ECT. Four topics of common interest have been put forward, including security of supply, investment in the Russian energy sector, climate change, and nuclear energy ("EU-Russia Energy Dialogue", 2006).The energy dialogue is, as the name implies, not legally binding, but constitutes a permanent consultative mechanism. The three existing frameworks prove insufficient today: the PCA has not yet been renewed or updated, the energy dialogue is purely consultative, and the ECT is in transition, even more so since the Russian president suggested its complete replacement. This incomplete legal patchwork reflects today's situation.

As for EU and Russian legislation, the two most important developments are:

- for the EU, the adoption of the third package and the Lisbon Treaty, including an energy paragraph (Article 176)
- for Russia, the two federal laws of the Russian Federation of April 2008 amending the foreign investments regime in the strategic sectors of the Russian economy, including energy (Seliverstov, 2009, p. 16)

These measures reflect a high degree of distrust, and constitute additional obstacles to mutual investments. Moreover, bilateral agreements continue, such as the cooperation between ENI and Gazprom or between Siemens and Rosatom, to cite just two recent examples. The EU again seems to remain a weak actor in this field.

Oil and gas East-West

The following section elaborates on the major energy issues tying together Russia and the EU: hydrocarbon supply, especially the regional commodity, gas. As for other energy issues, deliberately omitted here, one should stress that mutual investments in the energy sector have been rather limited due to different regulations, regulatory uncertainty, and preventive measures from both sides. Liberalization of the Russian electricity sector has opened the door to some European investment. On the other hand, some Russian investment has taken place in Southeast European enterprises – for example, in the Serbian Company NIS, as well as shares in the potential future gas hub in Baumgarten/Austria. Consortia between Gazprom and Western Enterprises exist for common infrastructure projects such as Nord Stream or South Stream.[4] East–West electricity interconnection between IPS/UPS (the Russian grid) and UCTE (the European grid), which is on the long-term agenda, has been studied, but will not be realized any time soon (Nies, 2010a).

Focusing our major interest on gas is also justified by the very nature of the Russian enterprise Gazprom, which is a constant concern for European policy-makers. This public enterprise, with the fourth highest level of capitalization in the world, at $350 billion before the financial crisis, represents 8 per cent of the Russian GDP and 20 per cent of Russia's tax revenues, and numbers 400,000 employees. It is present in all economic sectors, from banking to electricity, chemicals, transport, media, nuclear energy, and so on, and is considered as being a state within the state, interwoven with politics, different from a "normal" European enterprise.

Oil

We have witnessed, since the end of the Soviet Union, an adaptation of Russian oil infrastructure to the world markets, in the sense that access to the sea has been created, and a pipeline avoidance strategy has been pursued. Druzhba, the major oil pipeline legacy from Soviet times, was in fact the result of politics, the desire to tie the Soviet empire together. Europe's oil supply is, thus, still tied to two principal pipelines of the Druzhba system, but it largely depends on the world market and supply by oil tanker. While Russia represents an important supplier, an assumption exists that Russia has peaked as a supplier, and the current underinvestment in oil fields and infrastructure worries the EU. Moreover, the Caspian Sea's unclear legal status is slowing down the development of these fields. Currently, there are very few new oil pipeline projects, which is not the case for gas. On the contrary, we are witnessing an increase in oil tanker transport, such as the construction of the Primorsk Oil Port in the Baltic Sea, or the extension of Novorossiysk and exports via the Turkish straights. Primorsk and the Baltic Pipeline System (BPS) create direct access between the producer and consumer, while avoiding former Soviet Union transit countries. This is a strategy that Gazprom and Russia are also pursuing with regard to gas. As for the Turkish straits, facing permanent congestion and at risk from the increasing number of tankers, Russia is taking a more and more active role in negotiations with Ankara, and participating in infrastructure projects, beginning with the signature of some twenty memoranda of understanding in 2009. As for investments for the exploitation of resources, Russia has changed its approach, as the Production Sharing Agreements (PSAs) for Sakhalin and the legislation of the early 2000s demonstrate. In this sense, Sakhalin is a symbol of this major shift in trends, and of the Russian authorities' will to control foreign investment in their country, notably in this industry.

At the center of all debates: gas

Russia, with the largest gas reserves in the world, currently exports reserves mostly from Western Siberia, and is the most important EU supplier. After a decline in economic production and an unprecedented political crisis in the 1990s, Russia seemed to be making a comeback until the financial crisis of 2008–9, since when it has been facing a collapse in demand as well as in prices. In terms of gas production, Russia did not exceed its 1991 levels (650 bcm) until 2006. While Siberian reserves make up more than 90 per cent of Russian exports, Eastern Siberia and the Far East are only beginning to be exploited. In order to remain at the current level of production, the development of new fields is crucial – in Northwestern Siberia, on the Yamal Peninsula, and in the Shtokman fields in the Barents Sea. The potential for Russian exports is largely influenced by its domestic consumption: two-thirds of its gas is consumed domestically, since the country opted for gas instead of coal or nuclear energy during the 1980s (the "gas pause"). Current Russian growth was accompanied by an increase in domestic consumption, further heightened by very poor energy efficiency, a lack of economic incentive to change this, and low domestic prices. To summarize, numerous authors doubt Russia's ability to satisfy the growing EU demand in the medium term (Goetz, 2004, p. 24; Tönjes and Jong, 2007, p. 8). Russia must rely on gas from Central Asia and pursue a strategy that assures deliveries from Turkmenistan, Uzbekistan, and Kazakhstan; Russia has a close relationship with Turkmenistan, and some major errors in pricing. The "OPEC gas project" also fits in with this thinking. This project, presented by Vladimir Putin at the start of 2002, aims to create a "Eurasian alliance of gas producers," grouping the four countries noted above, and intended to counter the EU community's attempts to liberalize the gas market beyond its borders.[5] As for competing consumers of Russian energy, there are currently no gas pipelines going from Russia to the East Liquified Natural Gas (LNG)[6] projects and gas pipelines have been planned to transport gas to Japan, and another pipeline from Kovytka, west of Baikal, would supply China.

However, these projects are currently not advanced, and it is appropriate to question Russia's LNG ambitions in general. The abandonment of an LNG project on February 8, 2008 in the Baltic region is indicative, and raises the question of whether or not this translates into a Russian preference for gas pipelines and the European market. In the meantime, a first LNG terminal has been opened by Russia.

These assessments are at variance with Russia's LNG commitments in the coming years. While certain observers view Total's entrance into the Shtokman consortium as a sign that Russia wishes to benefit from French know-how in the LNG field, others emphasize Russia's enormous delay in this area (Kupchinsky, 2007).

Concerns over direct links

As a legacy of Soviet times, Russia had only one small direct gas pipeline to a consumer country, namely Finland. All other pipelines were transit pipelines to more distant customers. Not until the construction of the underwater gas pipeline to the Turkish market was a second direct pipeline installed. But that decision was based on an overestimation of the market at that time and, even today, the huge expenses for Blue Stream have not been recovered by exports. In the 1990s only two gas pipelines were constructed: Jamal, through Belarus and Poland, which for the first time bypassed Ukraine, and Blue Stream. All others date from before 1990, as Table 1 illustrates. The table also reveals transit state Ukraine's extreme dependence on Russian exports.[7] As already mentioned, Russia's strategy consists of promoting direct links, even if the price is higher than using the existing networks or the construction of parallel gas pipelines, such as Jamal II. This approach is interpreted as one of the consequences of the Russia–Ukraine and Russia–Belarus conflicts in 2006 and 2009, to mention only the most widely reported transit crises that seriously damaged Russia's image as a reliable supplier. As opposed to oil pipelines, extensions and increases in capacity are still possible for Russian gas pipelines. While the EU shares the same concerns about direct links and avoiding "problem countries," it nevertheless finds itself in a dilemma over the solidarity expected of it vis-à-vis new member states and neighbors.

Polemics over new gas infrastructure projects

We have witnessed for some years now in Europe a constant debate over diversification of routes, as well as diversification of supply. If the most advanced of the projects, Nord Stream, is a project of diversification of routes – the already mentioned direct link – as much as South Stream, which is less advanced and the most expensive, alternative to

Table 1 Gas Pipelines Between Russia and Europe via Ukraine, Belarus, and Finland

Pipeline	Route	Transit Countries	Owner / Operator	Length (km)	Capacity (bcm / year)	In service since
Yamal–Europe	Torzok/Yamal (Russia) – Frankfurt (Oder) (Germany)	Belarus, Poland	Gazprom for the Russian parts, Belarus, EuRoPol Gaz (48 per cent Gazprom, 48 per cent PGNiG, 4 per cent Polish Gas-Trading S.A.) for the Polish part	4,187, 2,932 of which is in Russia, 575 in Belarus, 680 in Poland	31 (EIA), 33 (Gazprom, Yafimava and Stern), 33 in Belarus, 20 in Poland (Victor and Victor)	1997 (Belarus–Poland), September 1999 (Russia–Belarus)
Northern Lights / Beltransgaz / Siyaniye Severa	Russia – Ukraine	Belarus	Gazprom for the Russian part, Beltransgaz for the Belarusian part	–	25 (Victor and Victor), 14 in Belarus (Yafimava and Stern)	–
Finland Connector	Russia – Finland	–	–	–	20 (Victor and Victor)	1973, enlarged in 1999
Bratstvo (north)	Russia – Germany	Ukraine, Slovakia, Czech Republic, Austria	Gazprom for the Russian part	–	30 (Victor and Victor)	–
Bratstvo (south) / Trans-Balkan	Russia – Turkey	Ukraine, Moldova, Romania, Bulgaria	Gazprom for the Russian part	–	20 (Victor and Victor)	–
Urengoy	Urengoy (Russia) – Germany/Austria	Ukraine, Slovakia, Czech Republic	Gazprom for the Russian part	5,000	40 (Victor and Victor)	–

Continued

Table 1 Continued

Pipeline	Route	Transit Countries	Owner / Operator	Length (km)	Capacity (bcm / year)	In service since
Progress / Yamburg	Russia – Ukraine	–	Gazprom for the Russian part	–	30 (Victor and Victor)	–
Soyuz / Orenburg	Russia – Ukraine	–	Gazprom for the Russian part	–	30 (Victor and Victor)	–
Soyuz / Orenburg	Russia – Ukraine	–	Gazprom for the Russian part	–	30 (Victor and Victor)	–

Ukrainian transit, Nabucco is a different type of project, and focuses on the diversification of suppliers.

Nord Stream is a gas pipeline project of around 1,200 km offshore, connecting Vyborg in Russia to Greifswald in Germany. It has caused debate and controversy in Europe since 2005 because it bypasses Central European countries and conjures up the nightmares brought on by the possibility of a Russian–German deal to the detriment of neighboring states between them. Agreement on the project was reached in the fall of 2005 between Chancellor Schroeder, today the president of the Nord Stream Administrative Council, and the Russian president Vladimir Putin. In reality, the idea of this project is not new. The proposal was first made in the early 1990s by a Soviet–British joint venture (Sovgazco), which foresaw the UK as a consumption market. British gas demand was indeed in full swing after the liberalization of the electricity industry, with demand at around 55 bcm per year. The idea, however, was finally abandoned because of a lack of confidence in Gazprom and the high costs of the project (Victor and Victor, 2004, p. 32). Nord Stream has successfully finished the feasibility studies and will be constructed soon, potentially starting operation by the middle of the current decade. Until then the Ukrainian transit route will remain the most important, even though it has shrunk from 90 per cent in 1991 to 80 per cent now, and will decline further when Nord Stream becomes operational, to some 60 per cent (Nord Stream first string), or 50 per cent or less when the second string of Nord Stream becomes operational.

South stream and Nabucco

Access to the huge Caspian gas reserves remains an important point on the agenda of both Russia and the EU. While some in the EU advocate the so called "Southern Corridor," complementary with the three others (East (Russia), North (Norway), and South (Algeria)), without transiting Russia, Russia intends, first, to maintain control over western exports

Table 2   Gazprom's Export Routes

Pipeline	Route	Capacity 2006	Capacity 2010	Capacity 2012
Brotherhood/Union (Soviet pipeline grid)	Russia–Ukraine–Central Europe	130 bcm	130 bcm	130 bcm
Polar Lights (Soviet pipeline grid)	Russia–Belarus–Ukraine–Central Europe	25 bcm	25 bcm	25 bcm
Trans-Balkans (Soviet pipeline grid)	Russia–Ukraine–Balkans	20 bcm	20 bcm	20 bcm
Finland connector (Soviet pipeline grid, extended in 1999)	Russia–Finland	20 bcm	20 bcm	20 bcm
Yamal–Europe (in operation since 1999)	Russia–Belarus–Poland–Western Europe	33 bcm	33 bcm	33 bcm
Blue Stream (in operation since 2002)	Russia–Black Sea–Turkey	16 bcm	16 bcm	16 bcm
Nord Stream pipeline (if operational in 2010 and 2012 respectively)	Russia–Baltic Sea–Germany	–	28 bcm	56 bcm
South Stream (if operational in 2010)	Russia–Black Sea–Bulgaria–Austria/Italy	–	–	30 bcm
Total export capacity to	Central and Western Europe	244 bcm	272 bcm	330 bcm

Source: Heinrich (2007, p. 87).

from former Soviet space, and, second, to create new infrastructure meant to limit its dependency on the Ukrainian transit route. Table 2 summarizes existing and planned routes for Russian gas exports in 2006 and projected for 2012.

In 2006, following the Russian–Ukrainian gas conflicts, the EU put Nabucco onto its list of priority projects. This move has been reinforced further by the Ukraine–Russia gas crisis in January 2009 and the decision of the EU to fund Nabucco with 200 million Euros. With a length of 3,300 kilometres, and investments estimated at around seven to eight billion Euros, this pipeline aims to supply Western Europe with gas from Central Asia, the Caspian Sea, and the Middle East, while completely bypassing Russian territory. But, while the aspect of bypassing Russia was emphasized in 2006, when the Russian–Ukrainian crisis was interpreted in Kiev's favor, today it is less talked about among experts. The planned route passes through Turkey, Bulgaria, Romania, and Hungary, and to Baumgarten, Austria, where it finally connects with the European gas network. Nabucco could become the EU's fourth largest supply source, with 30 bcm, if one believes the operators and the EU, but this is seriously brought into question by lack of supply and demand, and the changing terms of trade of the gas market in the light of the financial crisis.

To everyone's surprise, Gazprom made known, in mid-2007, its plans for a project with ENI on the construction of an offshore gas pipeline,[8] South Stream in the Black Sea, in addition to Blue Stream. Recently, in 2009, EDF joined the consortium. This gas pipeline will leave from the Russian Beregovaya compressor station and travel over 900 km to Varna, Bulgaria. Its southern branch will then pass through Greece towards southern Italy, and its northern part will go through Serbia, Hungary, and Slovenia towards northern Italy, with a branch also going to Austria. It could begin service in 2013, and, like Nord Stream, would have the advantage of avoiding Belarus and Ukraine, as well as Turkey. However, apart from Nord Stream, the prospects of the two projects for the Southern Corridors are rather poor in the light of an unfavorable investment climate, although they could potentially lead to an improvement in Russian–Ukrainian relations that might bring with it a stable agreement on gas transport following the recent presidential elections in Ukraine.

Russian, European, common interests?

The discussion up to this point has shed light on the legacies of the EU–Russia energy relationship, on the institutional dimension today, and on the gas market as the core element of energy relations. It was also important to underline the changing environment of the relationship, with the financial crisis and its impact on energy markets, especially consumption and investment, the Lisbon Treaty and new energy legislation. What are the prospects for the future, and where do interests diverge or coincide? This final section of the chapter presents the main assumptions for the future.

Russia's interests

Russia is interested in

- remaining the major player in the important European gas market. This means, more specifically, having reliable and economical transit routes or direct infrastructure (ideally controlling the infrastructure); having access, and ideally control, over cheaper central Asian gas, with Russia remaining the only export route for these countries; and coming to terms with, and containing, other producers, such as Iran.
- having security of demand in the coming decades, in order to engage in investments. The current uncertainty of demand due to climate policies and security of supply concerns in the EU main market for Russia, as well as the financial crisis and a potential change in terms of trade – spot sales instead of long-term contracts, the end of oil–gas price linkage, more LNG, and so on – have increased insecurity of demand from a Russian perspective.
- increased energy efficiency (flaring, transport, etc.). Russia uses energy dependency as a tool for power politics where it pursues these specific energy interests, or other political interests. The use of dependency is selective, and has never concerned the EU as a whole. Conflict occurs especially with the new member states, but also with the other former parts of the Soviet empire (Nygren, 2007; 2008). These conflicts reveal the unfinished transition in the former Eastern bloc, and unsettled terms of trade here. As far as EU member states are concerned, the EU has declared the reinforcement of interconnection, as well as the diversification of the concerned members, to be a priority, and has given legal constraint to solidarity among member states with the Lisbon Treaty.

The EU's interests

The EU is interested in a reliable supply of gas and oil, which means

- settled transit regimes;
- advantageous prices;

- independent access to Central Asian markets without being obliged to use the Russian transit, which, in fact, is not a transit but a monopoly on export;
- diversification in the energy mix, especially of the new member states, in order to avoid supply shocks such as happened during winter 2009;
- energy efficiency in the producer countries also.

Diverging and Common Interests

If Russia's and the EU's interests clearly diverge on the issue of the Central Asian resources – direct access for the EU, via Russian transit from a Russian perspective – there are two main common interests to be identified.

Common interest in security of supply and security of demand

More transparency on policy debates, scenarios, and investment via a reinforced energy dialogue, or within the PCA, could benefit both the consumer and the producer. The huge investment required both upstream and downstream (IEA, 2009) can only be realized through a common effort to achieve transparency, in order to set up favorable investment conditions well in advance. Energy efficiency is a very important dimension here, as well, and technological innovations should be shared as much as investment efforts in the field: experts estimate, to cite only one example, that the gas destroyed in flaring during oil production is equivalent to the quantity of supplies destined for the EU!

Common interest for reliable rules of the game

Legal commitment is required in order to set up a comprehensive and reliable energy relationship between Russia and the EU, as well as with transit countries such as Ukraine. Today's existing framework, despite containing useful elements, has proven to be insufficient, since not all parties are included as members, and parties cannot agree on decisive elements. Russian proposals for amending the Energy Charter should be studied thoroughly, and an improved framework put in place, ratified by producers and consumers.

Ukraine: convergence and divergence of interest

As for the common neighborhood area, and especially Ukraine, with its prime importance as a transit country, it should be a priority, from an economic point of view, for both the EU and Russia to ensure the largest possible transit potential via this country, including the modernization of the infrastructures. Nevertheless, interests might diverge here, in that some parts of the Russian elite, pursuing a revisionist agenda with respect to the post-Cold War status quo, might call Ukrainian sovereignty into question. This would be unacceptable to the EU, which must be careful of any geopolitical change in this country. On the basis of the minimum consensus of reliable transit rules, necessary investment, compliance of Ukraine with reforms, and so forth, a trilateral agenda could be set up among Kyiv, Brussels, and Moscow.

To conclude, the EU and Russia have progressively become interdependent since the 1970s, an interdependence which has brought stability to their relationship, through mutual interest.

Beyond energy issues, Russian commitment to playing a positive role in major international issues is needed: from Afghanistan to the Middle East, from nonproliferation to climate change policies. Improving the quality of exchange and setting up a "win–win situation" of more security demand and supply, for example via the elaboration of common scenarios and more transparency on both sides, could be an important step. Setting up a common Russian–European agency to cover this concern, as the International Energy Agency (IEA) was set up after the oil crisis in order to represent consumer interests, could be useful, even potentially within the framework of the IEA itself.

Conflicts arise over the relationship each side has with the successor countries of the former Soviet Union – Ukraine, Central Asia – and, although divergent perceptions will persist for some time, some form of institutionalized exchange on these will be necessary, ideally in association with the third party countries with which we are concerned here.

Notes

1. On April 8, 2009 Gazprom reduced the volume in the gas pipelines from Turkmenistan to Russia by 90 per cent without warning, with the consequence of blowing up the line in Turkmenistan. For a detailed discussion of this, see Pirani (2009, pp. 27 ff.), who views this and other similar "accidents" as a deliberate part of Russian policy.
2. In long-term contracts with Gazprom, gas prices follow oil prices with a six or nine-month lag. Pirani (2009, p. 6) emphasizes the uncertain future for exports of Russian gas to Europe: they increased steadily from 100 billions of cubic meters (bcm) in the early 1990s to 155–170 bcm per year by 2009, but then dropped sharply.
3. For a presentation and critical assessment, see Seliverstov (2009).
4. For an overview on EU and Russian legislation, see Seliverstov (2009).
5. For the debate over a gas OPEC, see Goetz (2004, pp. 24–5).

6. The process of liquifying natural gas involves cooling it to −161 degrees Celsius, which liquifies it. Then it can be transported by gas container ships, to be regasified at its destination.
7. For the Russian–Ukrainian energy relationship and the conflict in January 2006, see the analyses of Nies (2009) and Pirani (2009).
8. Gazprom and ENI signed Memorandums of Understanding at the end of 2007, in order to proceed with the first feasibility study of the project.

References

"About the Charter" (2010) *Energy Charter.* http://www.encharter.org/index. php?id=7 (accessed June 29, 2010).

Chizov, Vladimir (2009) cited in http://www.easybourse.com/bourse-actualite/ marches/2nd-update-russia-s-medvedev-warns-eu-on-eastern-europe-ties-672670 (accessed June 20. 2010).

"EU-Russia Energy Dialogue" (2006) *EurActiv,* October 22. http://www.euractiv. com/en/energy/eu-russia-energy-dialogue/article-150061 (accessed June 20. 2010).

European Commission (2010) *External Relations.* http://ec.europa.eu/external_ relations/russia/index_en.htm (accessed July 4, 2010).

Favennec, Jean-Pierre (2007) *Géopolitique de l'énergie,* Technip: Paris.

"Gazprom gives up a project to produce LNG in the Baltic region" (2008) *Estweek,* Warsaw, February 13.

Goetz, Roland (2004) "Russlands Erdöl und Erdgas drängen auf den Weltmarkt", *SWP Studie* 34/2004, Berlin.

"Green light from the Council for the Commission to negotiate a broad Nuclear Partnership Agreement with Russia" (2009). http://europa.eu/rapid/ pressReleasesAction.do?reference=IP/09/1990&format=HTML&aged=0&lang uage=EN&guiLanguage=en (accessed June 20. 2010).

Heinrich, Andreas (2007) "Poland as a transit country for Russian natural gas", Koszalyn Institute of Comparative Economic Studies, Koszalin, Poland.

IEA (2009) *World Energy Outlook 2009,* Paris: IEA.

Kupchinsky, Roman (2007) "Russia: Gazprom Looks to a LNG Future", *RFE/RL,* July 16.

Medvedev, Dmitry (2009) "Russia's Medvedev Warns EU On Eastern Europe Ties", *EasyBourse,* May 22. http://www.easybourse.com/bourse/actualite/2nd-update-russia-s-medvedev-warns-eu-on-eastern-europe-ties-672670 (accessed June 20, 2010).

Mitrova, Tatiana (2009) *Analyses of the Future Russian Energy Policy and Gas Sector Development,* Energy Research Institute, Russian Academy of Sciences, May 2009.

Nies, Susanne (2009) *Ukraine, a transit country in deadlock?,* Paris: IFRI.

Nies, Susanne (2010a) *At the speed of light? Electricity interconnection for Europe,* Paris: IFRI.

Nies, Susanne (2010b) *Gas and Oil to Europe. Perspectives on Infrastructure,* 2nd edn, Paris: IFRI.

Nygren, Bertil (2007) *The Rebuilding of Greater Russia: Putin's Foreign Policy Toward the CIS Countries*, Abingdon, UK: Routledge.

Nygren, Bertil (2008) "Putin's Use of Natural Gas To Reintegrate the CIS Region", *Problems of Post-Communism*, LV, no. 4, July–August, pp. 4–17.

OECD (1997) *Economic Surveys: The Russian Federation, 1997*, Paris.

Partnership and Cooperation Agreements (2009). http://europa.eu/legislation_summaries/external_relations/relations_with_third_countries/eastern_europe_and_central_asia/r17002_en.htm (accessed June 29, 2010).

Pirani, Simon (2009) *The Impact of the Economic Crisis on Russian and CIS Gas Markets*, NG 36 Working Papers, Oxford Institute for Energy Studies, Oxford, November.

Pirani, Simon (ed.) (2009) *Russian and CIS Gas Markets and Their Impact on Europe*, Oxford: Oxford University Press.

Savytsky, Oleksii and Alla Dubrovyk (2010) "New rules of the old 'game'", *The Day Weekly Digest*, February 2. http://day.kiev.ua/291411/ (accessed June 29, 2010).

Seliverstov, Sergei (2009) *Energy Security of Russia and the EU: current Legal Problems*, Paris: Note de l'Ifri, April.

Stern, Jonathan (2005) *The Future of Russian Gas and Gazprom*, Oxford: Oxford University Press.

Tönjes, Christoph and Jacques J. de Jong (2007) *Perspectives on Security of Supply in European Natural Gas Markets*, The Hague: Clingendael International Energy Programme. http://www.clingendael.nl/publications/2007/20070800_ciep_misc_toenjes.pdf (accessed July 4, 2010).

Victor, David G. and Nadjeda M. Victor (2004) *The Belarus Connection: Exporting Russian Gas to Germany and Poland*, James A. Baker III Institute for Public Policy, Rice University, working paper 26.

Yafimava, Katja and Jonathan Stern "The 1997 Russia-Belarus Gas Agreement", *Oxford Energy Comment*, Oxford Institute for Energy Studies. http://www.oxfordenergy.org/pdfs/comment_0107–3/pdf (accessed July 4, 2010).

Conclusion

Roger E. Kanet

In the second decade of the 21st century the peoples of the world face a number of serious challenges to their future, as Timothy Garton Ash (2004) has argued so clearly. These challenges include global terrorism stemming from fundamentalist Islamic movements; issues associated with the transition of global power and influence from the West to Asia, particularly to China; global poverty, which lies at the root of much of the migration that is challenging the developed countries; and, finally, global warming and other environmental problems that threaten to degrade the environment on which we depend for our very existence. Ash maintains that these challenges should be viewed not simply as threats to Western civilization as we have come to know it over the past half millennium, but also as opportunities for the countries of Europe and North America to join together to ensure a bright future for themselves and the other peoples of the world.

In many respects Ash's argument can – and, in fact, should – be expanded to include the Russian Federation as an active participant in dealing with global changes that, in large part, will affect Russia as well. Most of these problems impact Russia as much as they concern what Ash terms the "Free World." In some cases – such as those associated with possible nuclear proliferation that would provide terrorist groups with nuclear weaponry – Russia has much to bring to a larger collaborative effort.

What is evident is the fact that Russia is once again a major player in world affairs, even if the bases of the role remain questionable, and that Russia's political elite will not accept treatment of Russia as a junior partner of the sort that Washington and Brussels envisaged in the first decade or so after the demise of the USSR. But the real and long-term interests of Russia, Europe, and the United States overlap significantly and in many respects can only be met effectively through a cooperative approach of the sort outlined by Ash.

However, as the chapters that comprise the present volume make clear, the foundations for that type of cooperation have yet to be developed. Issues of status and a unilateral approach to decision-making in world affairs – especially in Moscow and Washington – continue to divide these countries. Not until the leaderships of Russia, the European Union, and the United States recognize that the issues that divide them are far less important, in the longer term, than those in which they can all benefit from cooperation is the situation described here likely to change.

Reference

Ash, Timothy Garton (2004) *Free World: America, Europe, and the Surprising Future of the West*, New York: Random House.

Index